LEVERAGING AI FOR BUSINESS INNOVATION

Digital Transformation: Accelerating Organizational Intelligence

Print ISSN: 2811-0552
Online ISSN: 2811-0560

Series Editor: Jay Liebowitz *(Rollins College, USA)*

According to a report released by Veritis in 2021 "the global digital transformation market size is anticipated to reach USD 1009.8 billion by 2025 from USD 469.8 billion in 2020. The demand for digital transformation services is expected to rise at a Compound Annual Growth Rate (CAGR) of around 16.5% over the forecast period from 2021 to 2025. The growing adoption of digital technologies, including Artificial Intelligence (AI), cloud computing, big data, the Internet of Things (IoT), and Machine Learning (ML), is driving the growth of the digital transformation market." To be competitive in today's fast-changing marketplace, organizations need to apply the "alphabet" of digital transformation.

The focus of the book series is unique and will cover the various perspectives on organizational digital transformation, namely business & management, technology, legal and ethics, and social aspects.

Published:

Vol. 10 *Leveraging AI for Business Innovation*
edited by Jay Liebowitz and Peter McAlindon

Vol. 9 *Digital Transformation in Healthcare*
edited by Jay Liebowitz

Vol. 8 *Achieving Digital Transformation through Analytics and AI*
edited by Jay Liebowitz

Vol. 7 *Digital Transformation and Society*
edited by Jay Liebowitz

Vol. 6 *Strategic Risk, Intelligence and Digital Transformation*
by Eduardo Rodriguez

Vol. 5 *Digital Transformation for Entrepreneurship*
edited by Susanne Durst and Aive Pevkur

Vol. 4 *Digital Strategies and Organizational Transformation*
edited by G Reza Djavanshir

Vol. 3 *Doing Well and Doing Good: Human-Centered Digital Transformation Leadership*
by Cheryl Flink, Liora Gross and William Pasmore

More information on this series can be found at https://www.worldscientific.com/series/dtaoi

Digital Transformation
Accelerating Organizational Intelligence
– Volume 10

LEVERAGING AI FOR BUSINESS INNOVATION

Edited by

Jay Liebowitz
Peter McAlindon

Rollins College, USA

World Scientific

NEW JERSEY • LONDON • SINGAPORE • BEIJING • SHANGHAI • HONG KONG • TAIPEI • CHENNAI • TOKYO

Published by

World Scientific Publishing Co. Pte. Ltd.

5 Toh Tuck Link, Singapore 596224

USA office: 27 Warren Street, Suite 401-402, Hackensack, NJ 07601

UK office: 57 Shelton Street, Covent Garden, London WC2H 9HE

Library of Congress Cataloging-in-Publication Data
Title: Leveraging AI for business innovation / editors, Jay Liebowitz, Rollins College, USA, Peter McAlindon, Rollins College, USA.
Description: Hackensack, NJ : World Scientific, [2026] | Series: Digital transformation: accelerating organizational intelligence, 2811-0552 ; vol 10 | Includes bibliographical references and index.
Identifiers: LCCN 2025020924 | ISBN 9789819816330 hardcover | ISBN 9789819816347 ebook | ISBN 9789819816354 ebook other
Subjects: LCSH: Technological innovations--Management | Artificial intelligence--Industrial applications
Classification: LCC HD45 .L43684 2025 | DDC 658.5/14--dc23/eng/20250613
LC record available at https://lccn.loc.gov/2025020924

British Library Cataloguing-in-Publication Data
A catalogue record for this book is available from the British Library.

For any available supplementary material, please visit
https://www.worldscientific.com/worldscibooks/10.1142/14397#t=suppl

Desk Editors: Kannan Krishnan/Monali Ghanekar

Typeset by Stallion Press
Email: enquiries@stallionpress.com

To our young grandsons, Zev and Ori, where AI is part of their lives and they may not even know it yet…. (JL)

To the next generation of innovators and entrepreneurs, may your ventures soar on the wings of artificial intelligence as you shape tomorrow's innovations today. (PM)

https://doi.org/10.1142/9789819816347_fmatter

Foreword

The Strategic Importance of Specialized Domain Models (SDMs) in Modern Business Planning

Introduction

Strategic planning has been a cornerstone of organizational success since the late 20th century. Groundbreaking frameworks such as portfolio planning, popularized by the Boston Consulting Group and McKinsey & Company, provided structures that helped businesses allocate resources effectively, formulate competitive strategies, and align organizational objectives. However, these frameworks were developed in an era of bounded rationality, where human cognitive limitations necessitated hierarchical structures and methodical planning processes. The advent of Artificial Intelligence (AI) challenges these traditional paradigms, particularly with the rise of Large Language Models (LLMs) and their specialized counterparts, Specialized Domain Models (SDMs). This essay explores why SDMs represent a critical frontier for business leaders, transforming strategic planning and reinforcing unique competitive advantages.

Differentiating LLMs, SLMs (Small Language Models), and SDMs (Specialized Domain Models)

AI-powered language models fall into various categories, including Large Language Models (LLMs) and Small Language Models (SLMs). LLMs, such as OpenAI's GPT models, are designed for general-purpose applications, leveraging vast datasets to generate insights and perform a wide range of tasks. Small Language Models (also abbreviated as SLMs) are lightweight versions of LLMs, optimized for computational efficiency and less resource-intensive tasks. While these models have utility in specific scenarios, their scope is often limited by their size and generality.

Specialized Domain Models (SDMs), on the other hand, are tailored for specific industries, domains, or organizational needs. These models incorporate domain-specific knowledge, enabling them to deliver insights and solutions that align closely with business objectives. In the context of strategic planning, the Center for AI-EDGE (Executive Decision-Making, Governance and Execution) at Rollins College's Crummer Graduate School of Business focus on *Specialized Domain Models* makes more sense because they do the following:

- **Focus on Business Contexts**: Specialized models can address unique challenges and opportunities within an organization's domain.
- **Enhance Competitive Advantage**: By embedding proprietary knowledge and processes, SDMs help preserve organizational differentiation.
- **Bridge Strategy and Execution**: Unlike general-purpose models, SDMs align closely with strategic goals, facilitating actionable outcomes.

Given these advantages, the emphasis on specialized domain models in business contexts reflects their ability to deliver precision, relevance, and strategic value.

The Legacy of Traditional Strategic Planning

To fully appreciate the evolution of strategic planning, it is crucial to examine the foundational limitations that shaped organizational structures and processes. Key theoretical frameworks—such as Herbert Simon's Bounded Rationality, Peter Drucker's theory of the firm, and Jay Galbraith's organizational structure and processes—highlight the constraints under which firms operate, informing traditional strategic planning practices.

1. **Bounded Rationality**
   Herbert Simon's concept of bounded rationality posits that human decision-making is constrained by limited information, cognitive capacity, and time. Organizations were thus designed to mitigate these limitations

by creating hierarchical structures, delegating decision-making, and standardizing processes. Strategic planning frameworks such as portfolio management were essential in simplifying complexity, breaking down decisions into manageable parts, and ensuring consistency across large organizations. However, these methods inherently assumed that decision-makers operate within significant cognitive and informational limits, leading to inefficiencies and suboptimal outcomes.

2. **Peter Drucker's Theory of the Firm**
   Peter Drucker emphasized that the purpose of a firm is to create value for its customers, which requires clarity in mission and goals. However, he also acknowledged the inherent friction within organizations due to competing priorities, communication barriers, and resource allocation challenges. Strategic planning systems emerged as tools to align diverse functional areas, mitigate conflicts, and ensure that all parts of the organization contributed to the overarching mission. Despite these efforts, the traditional reliance on human managers and hierarchical systems often resulted in silos and misalignment, limiting the firm's ability to adapt to rapid environmental changes.
3. **Jay Galbraith's Organizational Structure and Processes**
   Jay Galbraith's work focused on the interplay between organizational design and the ability to process information effectively. He argued that firms need to balance task specialization with coordination mechanisms to manage complexity. This led to the creation of functional departments, centralized decision-making, and formalized planning processes to address the span of control problem—the limit to how many people or tasks a manager can oversee effectively. Galbraith's insights underscored the trade-offs between efficiency and flexibility, which shaped traditional organizational structures and the role of strategic planning in managing these tensions.

These concepts collectively explain why traditional strategic planning frameworks, such as those outlined by Richard Hamermesh, focus on dividing strategies into levels (business unit, corporate, and institutional) and emphasize the importance of structured processes. Portfolio planning, for instance, provided a way to address bounded rationality by categorizing businesses and simplifying resource allocation. However, these systems were built on the assumption that decision-making and organizational design must work around human cognitive limits and the constraints of hierarchical control.

Implications for Strategic Planning

To understand the evolution of strategic planning, consider the example of General Electric (GE) under the leadership of Jack Welch. GE's implementation of portfolio planning was instrumental in identifying underperforming divisions for divestiture, allowing the company to redirect resources to high-growth areas such as healthcare and energy. This approach not only improved resource allocation but also showcased the limitations of over-reliance on portfolio grids, as some mature divisions later proved more profitable than anticipated.

Richard G. Hamermesh's seminal 1986 Harvard Business Review article, *Making Planning Strategic*, highlights the enduring principles of strategic planning. Key takeaways include the following:

- **Multi-Level Strategy Framework**: Strategy operates at the business unit, corporate, and institutional levels, each requiring tailored approaches.
- **Resource Allocation and Growth**: Portfolio planning effectively identifies opportunities for resource optimization but struggles to foster internal innovation and growth.
- **Leadership and Institutional Goals**: Planning is insufficient without leadership that articulates vision and institutional values.

Despite its merits, traditional strategic planning faced limitations. Mature businesses were often mismanaged as "cash cows," while planning systems grew overly bureaucratic. Moreover, the static nature of portfolio grids often led to missed opportunities in dynamic markets.

Setting the Stage for AI

The emergence of AI, and particularly advanced natural language platforms, challenges these foundational assumptions:

- **Bounded Rationality**: AI vastly expands cognitive capacity by processing large datasets, identifying patterns, and generating insights far beyond human capabilities.
- **Span of Control**: AI agents enable managers to oversee more complex operations with greater precision, reducing the reliance on hierarchical structures.

- **Organizational Design**: The need for rigid functional departments diminishes as AI facilitates cross-functional collaboration and dynamic resource allocation.

These developments suggest that the core limitations driving traditional strategic planning and organizational structures are becoming obsolete. As AI continues to evolve, it will transform not only how firms plan strategically but also how they are structured and operate functionally. The following section explores Hamermesh's contributions to strategic planning and how they align with or diverge from these transformative trends.

The Shift to AI-Enhanced Strategy

To understand the impact of AI-enhanced strategies, consider Stitch Fix, an online personal styling service. Stitch Fix leverages AI to analyze customer preferences and inventory data, creating highly personalized recommendations. By combining AI insights with human stylists' expertise, the company has significantly compressed cycle times for product selection and improved customer satisfaction. This approach demonstrates how generative AI tools, such as LLMs, expand cognitive capabilities to enable faster and more targeted decision-making. Another example is Tesla's use of AI for real-time vehicle diagnostics and autonomous driving development, showcasing how SDMs can address specific industry challenges, enhancing operational efficiency and innovation.

Overcoming Bounded Rationality

The airline industry provides an illustrative case of overcoming bounded rationality with AI. Consider Delta Airlines' deployment of AI-powered tools for predictive maintenance. By analyzing vast amounts of sensor data from aircraft, Delta can anticipate mechanical issues before they occur, reducing delays and increasing safety. This mirrors Toyota's lean manufacturing principles but scales decision-making far beyond human cognitive limits.

Similarly, SDMs enable organizations to process complex datasets and simulate outcomes at scales that were previously unimaginable, overcoming traditional cognitive limitations.

The Role of LLMs and SDMs in Strategy

LLMs are well suited for addressing macro-level strategic challenges. They can perform the following:

- **Analyze Market Transitions**: Identifying emerging opportunities and disruptions in global markets.
- **Generate Competitive Insights**: Synthesizing industry reports, customer feedback, and competitor data.
- **Facilitate Scenario Planning**: Modeling potential outcomes of strategic decisions.

SDMs, in contrast, excel at refining internal processes and preserving organizational uniqueness. Key applications include the following:

- **Protecting Intellectual Property**: The aerospace industry highlights the importance of proprietary SDMs. For example, Lockheed Martin employs specialized AI models to design advanced aircraft components, ensuring that intellectual property remains secure.
- **Optimizing Operational Efficiency**: Tailored models ensure that internal workflows align with strategic objectives, fostering innovation while maintaining efficiency.
- **Enabling Continuous Improvement**: SDMs provide iterative feedback, allowing organizations to refine their strategies and processes dynamically.

Challenges and Considerations

An illustrative example of cultural resistance to AI adoption is Nokia's failure to adapt its business model during the smartphone revolution. Despite being a market leader, Nokia's organizational inertia prevented it from embracing innovation, leading to its decline.

While the potential of SDMs is immense, their adoption poses significant challenges:

- **Cultural Resistance**: Organizations must shift from cost-cutting mindsets to innovation-driven strategies.
- **Ethical Implications**: The integration of AI agents blurs the line between human and machine roles, raising questions about organizational culture and accountability.

- **Absorptive Capacity**: Firms must balance the rapid deployment of AI with the ability of employees and systems to integrate these tools effectively.

Conclusion: The Imperative for SDMs

Organizations can best leverage SDMs and AI, in general, for business innovation by applying seemingly ease-to-use advanced computational technologies to enhance operational efficiency, drive decision-making, and unlock new revenue streams. Companies such as Klarna have already demonstrated the potential of AI by integrating it into their operations, replacing certain human tasks, and enabling AI agents to work collaboratively with human agents. This collaboration has significantly enhanced customer engagement and allowed companies to respond dynamically to evolving market trends.

The question, though, remains whether a human-centered AI approach will prevail or if “strong AI” will emerge as the dominant player in the coming years. To explore this critical question, this book offers worldwide perspectives on how AI will shape the future of business innovation and entrepreneurship.

One thing is certain—there are exciting times ahead as AI continues to redefine how businesses operate and innovate, presenting unparalleled opportunities for those who embrace its transformative potential.

In an era where infinite cognition is at humanity’s fingertips, the strategic focus must evolve. SDMs represent not just a tool for optimization but also a catalyst for redefining business planning and organizational structures. Companies that invest in SDMs will not only enhance their decision-making capabilities but also secure their competitive advantages in a landscape characterized by rapid technological change. Business leaders must prioritize SDM development, recognizing it as a cornerstone of modern strategic planning and a key driver of long-term success.

Anil Menon
Dean, Crummer Graduate School of Business,
Rollins College, Winter Park, Florida, USA
amenon@rollins.edu

https://doi.org/10.1142/9789819816347_fmatter

About the Editors

Jay Liebowitz recently served as the Professor of Business Innovation and Industry Transformation and Founding Director of the AI-EDGE Center in the Crummer Graduate School of Business at Rollins College. He previously served as the inaugural Executive-in-Residence for Public Service at Columbia University's Data Science Institute. He was previously a Visiting Professor at the Stillman School of Business and the MS-Business Analytics Capstone & Co-Program Director (External Relations) at Seton Hall University. He previously served as the Distinguished Chair of Applied Business and Finance at Harrisburg University of Science and Technology. Before HU, he was the Orkand Endowed Chair of Management and Technology in the Graduate School at the University of Maryland University College (UMUC). He served as a Full Professor in the Carey Business School at Johns Hopkins University. He was ranked one of the top 10 knowledge management researchers/practitioners out of 11,000 worldwide and was ranked #2 in KM Strategy worldwide according to the January 2010 *Journal of Knowledge Management*. At Johns Hopkins University, he was the founding Program Director for the Graduate Certificate in Competitive Intelligence and the Capstone Director of the MS-Information and Telecommunications Systems for Business Program, where he engaged over 30 organizations in industry, government, and not-for-profits in capstone projects.

Prior to joining Hopkins, Dr. Liebowitz was the first Knowledge Management Officer at NASA Goddard Space Flight Center. Before NASA, Dr. Liebowitz was the Robert W. Deutsch Distinguished Professor of Information Systems at the University of Maryland-Baltimore County, Professor of Management Science at George Washington University, and Chair of Artificial Intelligence at the U.S. Army War College.

Dr. Liebowitz is the Founding Editor-in-Chief of *Expert Systems With Applications: An International Journal* (published by Elsevier; ranked as a top-tier journal; Thomson Impact Factor from June 2021 is 8.665). He is a Fulbright Scholar, IEEE-USA Federal Communications Commission Executive Fellow, and Computer Educator of the Year (International Association for Computer Information Systems). He has published over 45 books and a myriad of journal articles on knowledge management, analytics, financial literacy, intelligent systems, and IT management. Dr. Liebowitz served as the Editor-in-Chief of Procedia-CS (Elsevier). He is also the Series Book Editor of the *Data Analytics Applications* book series (Taylor & Francis), as well as the Series Book Editor of the new *Digital Transformation: Accelerating Organizational Intelligence* book series (World Scientific Publishing). In October 2011, the International Association for Computer Information Systems named the "Jay Liebowitz Outstanding Student Research Award" for the best student research paper at the IACIS Annual Conference. Dr. Liebowitz was the Fulbright Visiting Research Chair in Business at Queen's University for the Summer 2017 and a Fulbright Specialist at Dalarna University in Sweden in May 2019. He is in the Top 2% of the top scientists in the world, according to a 2019 Stanford Study. As of 2021, he is the Visiting Distinguished Professor at the International School for Social and Business Studies in Slovenia. His recent books are as follows: *Data Analytics and AI* (Taylor & Francis, 2021), *The Business of Pandemics: The COVID-19 Story* (Taylor & Francis, 2021), *A Research Agenda for Knowledge Management and Analytics* (Elgar Publishers, 2021), *Online Learning Analytics* (Taylor & Francis, 2022), *Digital Transformation for the University of the Future* (World Scientific, 2022), *Cryptocurrency Concepts, Technology, and Applications* (Taylor & Francis, April 2023), *Pivoting Government Through Digital Transformation* (Taylor & Francis, 2024), and *Developing the Intuitive Executive: Using Analytics and Intuition for Success* (Taylor & Francis, 2024). His newest book, *Regulating Hate Speech Created by Generative AI*, was published by Taylor & Francis in August 2024. He has lectured and consulted worldwide.

Peter McAlindon is the Entrepreneur in Residence at the Crummer Graduate School of Business at Rollins College as of 2012. He served six years as the Executive Director of the Center for Advanced Entrepreneurship at the Crummer Graduate School of Business, where he pioneered a program with NASA to commercialize NASA intellectual property with MBA student teams and directed the largest venture pitch competition in central Florida. He is also a Co-founder of venVelo, a Florida-based seed capital fund.

His expertise includes start-up ventures, angel capital, human–computer interaction, product design and development, research methods, and statistics. He is the Founder and Chief Executive Officer of Blue Orb Inc., a central Florida-based technology company that develops computer technology for persons with disabilities. He holds seven patents related to computer keyboards and typing methodologies. He's been recognized for innovation, including honors and awards from the DaVinci award committee, Liberty Mutual, top honors for accessible technology at the Consumer Electronics Show in Las Vegas, and has been awarded multiple grants from the National Science Foundation's SBIR program. He has lectured and consulted nationwide and serves on many boards that serve children and young adults with special needs.

A native of Michigan, he graduated with honors from the University of Michigan and holds an MAS in Aeronautical Science from Embry-Riddle Aeronautical University and a Ph.D. in Industrial Engineering from the University of Central Florida with an emphasis in Human Factors and Ergonomics.

https://doi.org/10.1142/9789819816347_fmatter

List of Contributors

Zafer Adiguzel
Sakarya University of Applied Sciences, Turkey; Koc University, Turkey
zaferadiguzel@subu.edu.tr

Steve J. Bickley
School of Economics and Finance, Queensland University of Technology, Australia; Australian Research Council (ARC) Training Centre for Behavioural Insights for Technology Adoption (BITA), Australia; Panalogy Lab Pty Ltd, Brisbane, QLD, Australia
s.bickley@qut.edu.au

Casey Carnes
Crummer Graduate School of Business, Rollins College, Winter Park, Florida, USA
ccarnes@rollins.edu

Kuanchin Chen
Department of Computer Information Systems and Center for Business Analytics, Western Michigan University, Kalamazoo, MI, USA
Kc.chen@wmich.edu

Robert G. Cooper
McMaster University Business School, Canada
robertcooper@cogeco.ca

Michael Eakins
Institute for Simulation and Training, University of Central Florida, Orlando, USA
michael.eakins@ucf.edu

José A. Fernández-Calvo
AI Center, Miami Dade College, Miami, Florida, USA
josefernandezcalvo@gmail.com

Leonie Hallo
The University of Adelaide, Adelaide, South Australia, Australia
Leonie.hallo@adelaide.edu.au

Angela Hamilton
Institute for Simulation and Training, University of Central Florida, Orlando, USA
angela.hamilton@ucf.edu

Max Hooper
Global Blockchain Ventures, Orlando, USA
info@gbv.fund

Isar Meitis
Multiplai, USA
isar@multiplai.ai

Rajiv Menon
Informulate, Orlando, Florida; AIAR, Orlando, Florida
Rajiv.menon@informulate.net

David Metcalf
Institute for Simulation and Training, University of Central Florida, Orlando, USA
David.Metcalf@ucf.edu

Marigo Raftopoulos
Tampere University, Finland
marigo@strategicinnovationlab.com

Terry M. Sanks
Beusse Sanks, PLLC, Orlando, Florida, USA
tsanks@firstiniplaw.com

Yang Song
Techlent Inc., USA
Ysong0424@gmail.com

Devon Veller
Institute for Simulation and Training, University of Central Florida, Orlando, USA
devon.veller@ucf.edu

Andrzej Wodecki
Warsaw University of Technology, Department of Management, Warsaw, Poland
Andrzej.wodecki@pw.edu.pl

Wenkai Zhou
Roy E. Crummer Graduate School of Business, Rollins College, Winter Park, Florida, USA
wzhou@rollins.edu

https://doi.org/10.1142/9789819816347_fmatter

Contents

https://doi.org/10.1142/9789819816347_0001

Chapter 1

AI Tools and Techniques to Increase the Likelihood of Success in Startups

Peter McAlindon

Crummer Graduate School of Business, Rollins College,
Winter Park, Florida, USA

1. Introduction

AI is transforming the startup landscape by changing how companies form, operate, and scale. AI enhances operational efficiency by automating routine tasks, such as data entry, customer service, social media management, project management, and financial reporting (Nishar & Sullivan, 2024; Nielsen, 2023). Early-stage companies are increasingly leveraging artificial intelligence (AI) to enhance their growth and competitiveness (Lee, Kim, & Ivan, 2024). This enables startups to maintain leaner teams, allowing them to focus on core activities while improving efficiency and scalability (Tilo, 2023). As AI becomes an integral part of the startup ecosystem, it democratizes access to capabilities that previously required large teams and substantial resources, enabling companies to automate processes, gain valuable insights, and innovate rapidly. Additionally, AI accelerates product development by facilitating rapid prototyping, user testing, feedback analysis, and predictive analytics for assessing product-market fit. These capabilities help startups bring products to market more quickly and efficiently (Rios-Campos *et al.*, 2024).

AI-powered analytics provide startups with data-driven insights that enhance decision-making. Integrating AI and automation within startups reshapes operations and drives innovation (Anane-Simon & Atiku, 2023; Statista, 2023). Startups can analyze market trends, predict outcomes, optimize pricing strategies, and improve product recommendations, enabling them to make informed choices and gain a competitive edge.

Startups that incorporate AI into their business models gain a competitive advantage (Kollmann *et al.*, 2021). Entrepreneurs can use AI to rapidly generate and test multiple hypotheses about their business model, analyze customer feedback in real time, and make data-driven pivots when necessary. For example, tools such as GPT-4o can help create multiple versions of minimum viable product (MVP) descriptions, while platforms such as Firebase and Mixpanel can provide instant analytics on user behavior and engagement.

Customer experience is another area where AI has a profound impact. Through 24/7 chatbot support and sentiment analysis, startups can better understand customer feedback and enhance interactions. AI also enables personalized experiences across different platforms, ensuring users feel valued (Edelman & Abraham, 2022).

Due to AI's efficiency gains, the funding dynamics in the startup ecosystem are evolving (Jensen, 2024). Some startups may choose to bootstrap rather than seek venture capital, as AI allows them to achieve more with fewer resources. AI can also help create stronger pitches and business plans for those seeking investment by providing in-depth data analysis that showcases growth potential.

2. Why Startups Fail and How AI Can Help Them Succeed

Startups fail for a myriad of complex and often interrelated reasons. According to research from CB Insights (CB Insights, 2019, 2024) and various entrepreneurship scholars and practitioners (Crowne, 2002; Dias & Teixeira, 2017; Eisenmann, 2021; Ries, 2011), the primary causes include lack of market demand, running out of cash, poor team dynamics, getting outcompeted, pricing issues, and ineffective marketing. More fundamentally, many startups fail because they build products or services that don't solve real problems, fail to adapt to changing market conditions, or scale prematurely before establishing product-market fit (CB Insights,

2019; Bruno, McQuarrie & Torgrimson, 1992; Ries, 2011; Blank & Dorf, 2020).

The timing and pace of failure can vary dramatically. Some startups fail quickly due to fundamental flaws in their business model or market approach, while others experience a slower decline due to operational inefficiencies or inability to scale effectively (Eisenmann, 2021; Ries, 2017; Blank & Dorf, 2020). The first 18–24 months are particularly critical, with studies showing that approximately 20% of startups fail in their first year and around 60% fail within their first three years (CB Insights, 2019; Eisenmann, 2021; Walsh & Cunningham, 2016, 2017).

AI can help reduce these failure rates in several critical ways. First, AI-powered market intelligence tools can provide deeper, more accurate insights into market demand and customer needs before significant resources are invested (Weber *et al.*, 2021). Such tools can analyze vast amounts of data from social media, online reviews, and market reports to identify genuine market opportunities and potential pitfalls. For example, natural language processing can analyze customer sentiment across multiple channels to validate product concepts from a minimum viable product (MVP) through full development.

On the operational side, AI can help startups manage their cash flow more effectively through predictive analytics and automated financial modeling. Machine learning algorithms can forecast revenue, identify potential cash flow problems months in advance, and suggest optimization strategies. This addresses one of the most common causes of startup failure—running out of money before achieving sustainability (Eisenmann, 2021).

AI can also help startups compete more effectively by automating routine tasks and enabling small teams to operate with the efficiency of much larger organizations. Through tools such as automated customer service, AI-powered marketing optimization, and intelligent process automation, startups can focus their limited human resources on strategic activities while maintaining high operational standards.

For the critical challenge of product-market fit (Zacharakis *et al.*, 2017), AI can accelerate the learning process through rapid testing and iteration. A/B testing powered by machine learning can quickly identify which features resonate with users, while AI analytics can track and predict user behavior patterns. This allows startups to adapt their products more quickly and effectively to market needs, reducing the risk of building something nobody wants.

Perhaps most importantly, AI can serve as an early warning system for potential problems. By analyzing patterns across various business metrics, AI can identify concerning trends before they become critical issues. This might include detecting decreasing customer engagement, identifying operational inefficiencies, or highlighting potential competitive threats. Such early warnings give startups the opportunity to course-correct before problems become terminal.

However, it's crucial to note that while AI can help mitigate many common causes of startup failure, it isn't a silver bullet. AI tools must be implemented carefully, thoughtfully, and in a sound business strategy. The most successful startups use AI to enhance their core competencies and support their strategic objectives rather than viewing AI implementation itself as a strategy. When properly leveraged, AI can significantly reduce the risk of failure by providing better information, enabling more efficient operations, and allowing faster adaptation to market changes.

One key issue Eisenmann highlighted in his book "Why Startups Fail" is the problem of "bad bedfellows." AI can play a crucial role in helping startups avoid this pitfall by analyzing potential partnerships, employee fits, and investor relationships. Advanced analytics and AI-powered due diligence tools can assess the compatibility of potential stakeholders, while AI recruiting tools evaluate the cultural fit and capabilities of potential team members. As Eisenmann notes, "the causes of failure are always complicated," but leveraging AI can help detect warning signs early, allowing startups to make better-informed decisions (Eisenmann, 2021).

Another significant failure pattern is the "false start," which occurs when startups rush to launch without sufficient preparation. AI can enhance the pre-launch exploration phase that Eisenmann emphasizes by using natural language processing and sentiment analysis tools to analyze customer needs and market demands more thoroughly before launching. This approach directly addresses Eisenmann's warning that "if you skip this upfront research, your first product may miss the mark" (Eisenmann, 2021).

When it comes to managing growth, Eisenmann cautions against premature scaling. AI tools can provide essential support by monitoring key performance indicators in real time, predicting resource needs before they become critical, identifying optimal timing for expansion, and systematically analyzing customer feedback and market responses. These capabilities empower startups to scale responsibly and strategically.

AI can help mitigate excessive focus or tunnel vision by enabling startups to monitor multiple market segments simultaneously, identify emerging opportunities outside of their core focus, track competitor movements and market changes, and analyze diverse customer feedback across different segments (Bygrave & Zacharakis, 2014). This broader perspective can provide critical insights that ensure startups remain agile and responsive to shifting market dynamics.

Understanding when to pivot is a critical skill for entrepreneurs. Analyzing market signals and trending data, monitoring customer engagement metrics, identifying emerging market opportunities, and evaluating the potential success of different pivot options (Blank & Dorf, 2020; Ries, 2011). This data-driven approach can guide strategic shifts when necessary, and AI can help significantly in this regard.

While AI offers unprecedented opportunities for startups, it's crucial to approach its implementation strategically. The integration of AI should create sustainable value without becoming a resource drain or distraction from core business objectives. Startups must carefully consider how AI can best serve their specific needs and goals rather than adopting it indiscriminately (World Economic Forum, 2023; Hann & Watts, 2023).

3. AI Adoption and Growth in Startups

The AI adoption curve in the startup ecosystem follows a clear S-shaped pattern, with the steepest growth occurring in early 2023 (Jones, 2024; Grigul, 2024). This rapid rise in AI tool adoption among startups has been remarkable, transforming how new companies form, operate, and scale (IBM, 2022; Statista, 2021; Wodecki, 2023). The number of startups utilizing AI across various economic sectors is rapidly increasing (Rios-Campos, *et al.*, 2024).

As of August 2024, approximately 70% of startups are paying for at least one AI tool, indicating a move beyond the early adoption phase and into a period of market saturation (Jones, 2024; Wodecki, 2023). The initial growth was driven by the release of OpenAI's low-cost ChatGPT subscription, which sparked widespread interest and adoption.

The curve varies across industries, with SaaS companies leading in AI adoption at nearly 80% (Verified Market Research, 2022). However, the adoption rate is not uniform across all sectors, with some industries showing more cautious approaches due to regulatory constraints or the nature of their operations (Grigul, 2024; Nishar & Sullivan, 2024).

As the curve progresses, we're seeing a shift from general-purpose AI tools to more specialized, industry-specific solutions. The median startup is now paying for two AI products, up from one at the beginning of the year, indicating room for growth in specialized AI tools (Nishar & Sullivan, 2024).

The financial investment in AI is also following an upward curve, with the average monthly AI spend for startups increasing from about $2,000 in early 2023 to $5,000–$6,000 in recent months (Nishar & Sullivan, 2024). This growth is driven by increased usage of AI subscriptions and API access to larger AI models (Soroushian, 2024).

AI presents several key challenges for startups. Startups often face significant barriers when scaling AI tools, especially regarding resource allocation and expertise (Sørensen & Lahr, 2022; Oladigbolu, 2024). Startups must also navigate complex data privacy regulations and ethical considerations, including addressing potential bias in AI models. Finally, there's a risk of over-dependence on AI solutions at the expense of human judgment and creativity (Lerner, 2023; World Economic Forum, 2023). These challenges require careful consideration and balanced approaches to AI implementation.

4. The Role of Human Intuition

Human intuition, shaped by experience, emotional intelligence, and pattern recognition, possesses unique strengths that AI cannot fully replicate. Human intuition often proves superior to AI-driven analysis in complex social situations, such as negotiating with investors, building strategic partnerships, or understanding subtle market shifts (McAlindon, 2024). Entrepreneurs' gut feelings about people, timing, and opportunities frequently stem from a deep, tacit understanding of human psychology and market dynamics that AI systems struggle to quantify. This intuitive grasp of complex social and emotional factors remains a crucial advantage in situations requiring empathy, creativity, and nuanced judgment (McAlindon, 2024).

However, human intuition can be fallible, particularly when dealing with large datasets, complex statistical patterns, or situations where cognitive biases come into play. In these scenarios, AI often outperforms human judgment by objectively processing vast amounts of information and identifying patterns that might escape even the most experienced entrepreneur. For instance, while a founder might have a "feeling" about customer preferences, AI can analyze millions of data points to reveal actual behavior patterns and preferences that contradict intuitive assumptions. Similarly, AI excels at identifying subtle market trends or operational inefficiencies that human observation might miss.

The ideal approach combines the strengths of human intuition and AI capabilities. For example, in product development, AI can provide data-driven insights about user behavior and feature preferences, while human intuition guides the creative process and ensures emotional resonance with users. In marketing, AI can optimize campaign performance metrics, while human intuition shapes the overall brand strategy and creative direction. This complementary relationship allows startups to benefit from the computational power of AI and the nuanced understanding that comes from human experience and behavior.

There are also situations where the effectiveness of intuition versus AI depends on the specific context and available data. Human intuition might provide better guidance than AI models trained on outdated or irrelevant data. Conversely, in stable markets with rich historical data, AI can often make more accurate predictions than human intuition. Understanding when to rely on each is a critical skill for entrepreneurs.

The most successful startups recognize that the question isn't whether intuition or AI is better but how to leverage both effectively. They use AI to enhance and inform intuitive decision-making while maintaining the human judgment necessary for strategic thinking and relationship building. This balanced approach allows startups to benefit from the speed and precision of AI while preserving the creative and emotional intelligence that drives innovation and builds lasting business relationships.

The relationship between intuition and AI isn't static—it evolves as technology and the entrepreneur's experience grow. As AI systems become more sophisticated and entrepreneurs gain more experience with AI tools, the boundary between intuitive and AI-driven decision-making becomes more fluid. The key is developing the wisdom to know when to trust each and how to use them in concert to make better decisions.

Building and running a startup often requires more intuition than AI tools or knowledge alone can provide (Horowitz, 2014). Horowitz emphasizes that there's no formula for dealing with the hardest problems in business—those where conventional wisdom doesn't apply, and leaders must make tough decisions with incomplete information. He covers a wide range of topics, including how to manage one's own psychology as a leader, hire and fire employees, and navigate company culture.

Horowitz provides practical advice on various aspects of running a business, such as the intricacies of laying off employees, the challenges of training and performance management, and the complexities of company politics, none of which has an AI tool equivalent currently available. He emphasizes the importance of hiring for strengths rather than lack of weaknesses and provides guidance on how to set clear expectations and provide effective feedback (Horowitz, 2014). There are a few AI tools to help in this regard, but they still don't compare to one's intuition.

Horowitz emphasizes several crucial aspects of leadership, including the importance of maintaining transparency with employees, building a strong company culture, and making timely decisions even with imperfect information. He particularly stresses the significance of proper training programs for scaling companies and maintaining quality as organizations grow. Throughout his book, Horowitz argues that successful CEOs must focus on three primary elements—taking care of people, products, and profits—and acknowledges that there are often no good answers, not even via AI, only hard choices, that must be made (Horowitz, 2014).

5. Applications of AI

AI can be a powerful force multiplier for startups, enabling small teams to accomplish tasks that previously required significant manpower and financial resources. AI tools in startups have shown great promise for business value creation and decision-making (Perifanis & Kitsios, 2023; Kipwise, 2024). From automating customer service interactions to generating marketing content, analyzing market trends, and optimizing operations, AI tools can help startups operate with the efficiency of much larger organizations (Bennett, 2023; Kamboj, 2024).

These advanced language models can assist startups in various tasks, from drafting business models to generating creative marketing ideas. These capabilities can be particularly valuable during the critical early stages when resources are limited and the pressure to scale quickly is high. The alignment of AI tools with business strategy has been identified as a key enabler of competitive advantage in startups (Kitsios & Kamariotou, 2021). Successful implementation often involves starting with one or two high-impact areas and gradually expanding AI usage as the organization matures. These critical early stages include, generally, the following:

6. Problem Identification and Solution

AI is being leveraged to analyze vast amounts of unstructured data from social media, forums, review sites, and news sources to identify patterns of consumer complaints, frustrations, and unmet needs (Bezhovski *et al.*, 2024). AI applications allow entrepreneurs to quickly analyze large datasets, uncovering emerging market needs and customer frustrations that can serve as the foundation for new business ideas (Barsoux *et al.*, 2022). Natural Language Processing (NLP) algorithms can process millions of conversations and comments to surface recurring pain points and emerging problems across different industries and market segments (Jansen *et al.*, 2023). This helps entrepreneurs identify opportunities that might not be obvious through traditional market research methods. Entrepreneurs are increasingly using AI technologies such as data mining and sentiment analysis to identify market gaps and customer pain points that may otherwise go unnoticed (Gluggioli & Pellegrini, 2023).

Predictive analytics and trend analysis tools are being used to forecast emerging problems before they become widely recognized (Blank, 2023). By analyzing historical data patterns, demographic shifts, and technological developments, AI can help entrepreneurs anticipate future challenges and needs. Some entrepreneurs are using AI to monitor regulatory changes, technological advancements, and social movements to identify new problem spaces that will need solutions in the near future. Students are also using it to evaluate NASA's patent value in a given market. By leveraging AI tools for analyzing customer feedback and market trends, entrepreneurs can identify unmet needs that have the potential for innovation and business success.

AI-powered competitive analysis tools are helping entrepreneurs identify gaps in existing solutions. Several AI tools can analyze competitor products, services, and customer feedback to highlight underserved needs or inadequately addressed problems. Machine learning algorithms can also analyze patent databases and academic research to identify promising areas where new technologies could be applied to solve existing problems in novel ways. Blue Ocean Strategy has as its overall lesson to encourage businesses to move away from fierce competition in saturated markets or "red oceans" and instead seek untapped market spaces or "blue oceans (Kim & Mauborgne, 2015).

AI tools are also being used to validate problem hypotheses by analyzing market size, customer willingness to pay, and implementation feasibility. This helps entrepreneurs focus on problems that not only need solving but also represent viable business opportunities (Barsoux *et al.*, 2022). However, it's important to note that AI remains a tool for discovery and validation. Successful entrepreneurship still requires human judgment to evaluate which problems are worth solving and how to approach them effectively.

7. Minimum Viable Product (MVP)

AI is transforming the MVP development process by enabling startups to create more sophisticated prototypes faster and with fewer resources (Bezhovski *et al.*, 2024). Machine learning models can now generate functional code, design elements, and even entire user interfaces based on basic input parameters or descriptions. This allows startups to rapidly prototype different versions of their product without extensive development resources, significantly reducing the time from concept to testable MVP (Bennett, 2023).

Low-code and no-code AI platforms are particularly revolutionary in MVP development. These platforms enable non-technical founders to create functional applications by leveraging pre-built AI components for common features, such as user authentication, data processing, and basic automation. Startups can quickly assemble these components to create working prototypes that can be tested with real users, gathering valuable feedback before investing in full-scale development.

AI is also being used to optimize MVP testing and iteration. Machine learning algorithms can analyze user interactions, feedback, and behavioral data to identify which features are most valuable and which need improvement (Bezhovski *et al.*, 2021). This data-driven approach helps startups make more informed decisions about what to include in their final product, reducing the risk of building unnecessary features or missing critical functionality. Some startups are using AI to conduct A/B testing automatically, adjusting features and user interfaces in real time based on user behavior (Bennett, 2023).

Generative AI is emerging as a powerful tool for MVP development, particularly in areas such as content creation, design, and user experience. Startups can use these tools to generate placeholder content, create multiple design variations, and even simulate different user scenarios. This allows them to present a more polished MVP to potential users and investors without the traditional resource requirements.

AI tools are accelerating startups' product development cycles. GitHub Copilot, for instance, assists developers with code completion and generation, potentially reducing development time and costs (Kamboj, 2024). Additionally, AI can help with product-market fit predictions and rapid prototyping, enabling startups to launch and iterate on products more quickly (Bennett, 2023).

8. Customer Development and Support

Engage early and often with potential customers to validate assumptions, understand their needs, and improve your business model based on feedback. AI-powered customer support has become a critical differentiator for startups, enabling them to provide 24/7 service without the massive overhead of large support teams. Many startups are deploying sophisticated chatbots and virtual assistants that can handle tier-1 support queries, ranging from basic troubleshooting to account management and frequently asked questions. These systems are increasingly capable of understanding context and natural language, providing more human-like interactions while continuously learning from each conversation.

On the customer development front, startups are using AI to analyze vast amounts of customer data to identify patterns, preferences, and pain points. Machine learning algorithms process customer interactions, social media mentions, support tickets, and usage analytics to create detailed customer personas and journey maps (Sen, 2024). This helps startups identify opportunities for product improvements and new features before customers explicitly request them. Some startups are also using AI-powered sentiment analysis to monitor brand perception and customer satisfaction in real time (Jensen, 2024).

Predictive analytics is another key area where AI is making an impact. Startups are implementing systems that can forecast customer churn by analyzing behavioral patterns and engagement metrics. When these systems detect signs of potential customer dissatisfaction or declining engagement, they can trigger proactive interventions through automated campaigns or alert customer success teams to reach out personally. Some advanced implementations even use AI to personalize these interventions based on the customer's history and preferences (Bennett, 2023).

9. Market Research

AI-powered analytics provide startups with data-driven insights that enhance decision-making. Startups can analyze market trends, predict outcomes, optimize pricing strategies, and improve product recommendations, enabling them to make informed choices and gain a competitive edge. Identify the target market, size, and competition.

AI is revolutionizing market research by enabling startups to gather and analyze vast amounts of data at unprecedented speeds and lower costs. Machine learning algorithms can now process massive amounts of unstructured data from social media, online reviews, forums, news articles, and other digital sources to identify market trends, consumer sentiment, and competitive intelligence. This allows startups to gain real-time insights without relying solely on traditional, time-consuming market research methods.

Natural Language Processing (NLP) is being used to conduct automated sentiment analysis and topic modeling across multiple languages and markets. Startups can quickly understand how their brand or product is perceived in different regions, identify emerging market opportunities, and track competitor movements. AI tools are also being used to analyze visual content, such as social media images and videos, to understand product usage patterns and lifestyle trends that might not be captured in text-based research (Statista, 2023, 2024).

Predictive analytics is helping startups forecast market trends and consumer behavior patterns (Bennett, 2023). By combining historical data with real-time market signals, AI models can identify emerging trends before they become mainstream, giving startups a first-mover advantage. Some startups are using AI to create detailed market simulations, testing different scenarios and strategies before making significant investments in new products or markets.

AI-powered survey tools are transforming traditional market research methods. They use machine learning to optimize questionnaire design, reduce bias, and automatically identify meaningful patterns in responses. These tools can adapt questions in real time based on previous responses, leading to more insightful data collection. Additionally, AI is being used to validate survey responses and identify potential data quality issues, ensuring more reliable research outcomes.

10. Go-to-Market Strategy

AI is revolutionizing how startups develop and execute their go-to-market (GTM) strategies by streamlining processes and providing data-driven insights (Lu, 2024). Through AI-powered analysis, startups can better understand their target market and customer behavior and predict market trends, enabling more informed decision-making in their GTM approach (Paliwal, 2024).

AI helps startups define their target audience more precisely by analyzing vast amounts of customer data and market information. This analysis helps identify customer segments, their pain points, and preferences, allowing startups to craft more targeted value propositions and marketing messages (Lu, 2024). The technology also assists in competitive analysis by monitoring competitor activities, pricing strategies, and market positioning, helping startups differentiate themselves effectively (Coleman, 2024).

In terms of execution, AI platforms help automate and optimize various aspects of the GTM strategy, from content creation to sales enablement (Copy.ai, 2024). For example, AI can generate personalized marketing materials, automate customer communications, and provide real-time insights for sales teams. This automation allows startups to operate more efficiently with leaner teams while maintaining consistent messaging across all channels (Copy.ai, 2024).

Furthermore, AI enhances GTM strategies by enabling startups to test and refine their approach continuously. Through data analysis and predictive modeling, startups can assess the effectiveness of different marketing channels, optimize pricing strategies, and identify the most promising market opportunities (Lu, 2024; Thompson, 2024). This data-driven approach helps startups allocate resources more effectively and adapt their GTM strategies based on real-time market feedback and performance metrics.

11. Monetization Strategy

AI significantly aids startups in developing and refining their monetization strategies through various capabilities. It conducts real-time market analysis to assess competitor pricing and market dynamics, enabling startups to identify optimal price points via predictive modeling and test various pricing scenarios. This analysis helps uncover new revenue opportunities by recognizing market patterns.

Another critical area where AI excels is customer segmentation. It analyzes customer behaviors, preferences, and spending patterns, allowing startups to predict customer lifetime value and target high-value segments. This insight leads to personalized pricing and tailored offerings for different customer groups, enhancing engagement and loyalty.

AI also optimizes revenue models, such as subscriptions and freemium options, forecasting the potential revenue for each. AI enhances overall revenue generation by assessing optimal subscription tiers and identifying the right moments for upselling and cross-selling. Additionally, dynamic pricing capabilities allow startups to adjust prices based on demand and competition, helping mitigate churn with personalized discounts and optimize pricing strategies for different regions.

Furthermore, AI supports customer retention by predicting churn risks and suggesting targeted strategies for engagement and loyalty. It also optimizes payment processing by detecting fraud, recommending suitable payment methods, and predicting potential transaction failures, improving overall transaction success.

Finally, AI facilitates testing and refining monetization approaches through A/B testing, measuring the impact of pricing changes, and evaluating promotional effectiveness. Thus, it offers data-driven recommendations for continuous improvement. By leveraging these AI capabilities, startups can create effective and adaptive monetization strategies that enhance revenue streams.

12. Funding

The global funding for AI startups has surged dramatically, especially in the U.S., where companies raised billions, underlining the profitability potential of AI technologies (Kenyon, 2021). AI startups such as UiPath, Databricks, and Grammarly have demonstrated significant growth by showcasing AI's practical impact in automation, analytics, and communication, leading to multi-million-dollar funding rounds (Singh, 2024; Jensen, 2024).

One significant application is in developing data-driven investor pitches. AI-powered tools such as PitchBob and Gamma.app are helping startups create compelling pitch decks by analyzing vast amounts of data to illustrate potential growth and returns. These tools can generate sleek, easy-to-read presentations that resonate with investors, incorporating market trends, competitor analysis, and customer behavior insights (Sen, 2024).

AI is also transforming financial modeling for startups. Machine learning algorithms are being employed to predict future revenue streams and cash flows with unprecedented accuracy. This allows startups to present a more realistic and granular picture of their business potential to investors, which is crucial for both the startup seeking funds and the investor looking to allocate capital wisely (Sen, 2024).

In the realm of investor matchmaking, AI-powered platforms such as Crunchbase and AngelList are streamlining the process of connecting startups with suitable investors. These platforms analyze factors such as the startup's business model, industry sector, and fundraising stage to identify and connect with investors best suited to the startup's unique needs, increasing efficiency and effectiveness in the fundraising process.

AI is also enhancing investor relationship management. Startups are using AI tools to automate the process of providing regular updates to investors, tracking critical performance indicators, and even forecasting potential issues (Jensen, 2024). This constant communication loop helps maintain transparency and trust between startups and their investors.

Furthermore, AI is being utilized for strategic decision-making in the fundraising process. Startups are leveraging AI-driven analytics to identify growth opportunities, foresee challenges, and make data-informed decisions about when and how to approach investors (Hubspot, 2023; Sen, 2024). This strategic use of AI helps startups present a more compelling case to potential investors.

Lastly, AI is helping startups refine their due diligence processes. By thoroughly analyzing large datasets, including financial documents and investors' social media behaviors, AI tools are helping startups identify potential risks and assess the credibility of potential investors more effectively, ensuring a more secure investment environment.

Startups are leveraging AI for financial planning and management. Zeni, for example, uses AI to handle bookkeeping, expense tracking, and financial reporting, allowing founders to focus on core business activities (Hubspot, 2023).

AI-powered platforms such as Crunchbase and Forge help identify the right investors based on industry and portfolio data. AI tools such as

ChatGPT for writing investor-ready emails and pitch decks. Understanding AI-based metrics that predict funding success (e.g., ML-powered scoring algorithms for business viability) are evolving quickly.

13. Human Resources

Startups are leveraging AI in innovative ways to transform human resources processes, making them more efficient and effective. In recruitment and talent acquisition, AI is revolutionizing the hiring process. Platforms such as HireVue use AI-driven video interviews and assessments to evaluate candidates beyond their resumes, reducing bias and accelerating hiring. Eightfold AI's talent intelligence platform, eightfold.ai, distinguishes between validated and likely skills, measuring an individual's true potential and using equal opportunity algorithms to avoid biases. These AI tools automate resume screening, analyze candidate data, and match applicants to job descriptions with greater precision.

For employee engagement and retention, startups are using AI to boost satisfaction and reduce turnover. Peakon.com, for instance, collects real-time employee feedback and uses AI to provide actionable insights, enabling HR teams to proactively address concerns. AI tools also analyze employee sentiment and predict potential attrition, allowing for targeted interventions.

In the realm of learning and development, AI is transforming how startups approach employee training. Platforms like Degreed.com use AI to personalize learning experiences based on individual employees' skills, interests, and career goals. AI assesses individual needs and uses personal performance data to deliver tailored internal upskilling or development programs.

Startups are also leveraging AI for HR analytics and decision-making. AI-powered analytics tools provide insights into workforce trends, helping HR professionals make informed decisions. These tools analyze data from various sources, such as employee surveys and performance reviews, to identify patterns and predict future outcomes.

Finally, AI is helping startups streamline HR operations by automating administrative tasks (Jensen, 2024). Chatbots such as those offered by Jobvite.com and XOR.ai engage with applicants, enhance the application process, and decrease drop-off rates. AI automates scheduling, employee updates, and other routine tasks, freeing up HR professionals to focus on more strategic initiatives.

Tools such as Mercor.com, an AI-based hiring platform, are helping startups streamline their recruitment processes, ensuring they can build strong teams efficiently as they scale (Jensen, 2024).

14. Operational Efficiency

By automating routine tasks, AI allows startups to allocate human resources more strategically. This automation can be seen in areas such as data entry and management, customer service inquiries, social media management, project management, and financial reporting. By handling these tasks, AI enables startups to operate with leaner teams and focus on their core business activities. AI significantly improves decision-making processes (Yadav *et al.*, 2024). AI-powered analytics tools provide startups with data-driven insights that are crucial for strategic planning. These tools can analyze market trends and consumer behavior, predict future outcomes using machine learning algorithms, optimize pricing strategies, and enhance product recommendations.

15. Conclusion

AI is revolutionizing the startup ecosystem, offering unprecedented opportunities for efficiency, data-driven decision-making, and rapid innovation. This transformation is creating new avenues for entrepreneurs while also challenging traditional startup models and funding approaches. However, integrating AI into startup operations is not without its challenges and potential pitfalls.

While AI tools can dramatically accelerate growth, reduce costs, and provide competitive advantages, they must be approached strategically rather than adopted blindly. Startups must carefully consider factors such as actual business needs, solution maturity, implementation costs and their own technical capabilities when deciding whether and how to implement AI. The goal should be to identify specific, high-impact areas where AI can provide measurable value rather than viewing it as a cure-all for business challenges.

The democratization of these AI tools has particularly benefited early-stage startups, allowing them to conduct sophisticated market research that was previously only accessible to larger companies with substantial research budgets.

It's crucial to remember that AI should augment human capabilities rather than replace human judgment, especially in areas such as product development, customer relationships, and strategic planning. Entrepreneurial success still requires human expertise to interpret results and make strategic decisions based on the insights generated. The most successful startups maintain a balanced approach, leveraging AI's strengths while recognizing its limitations and the continuing importance of human expertise. By focusing on creating real value for customers, aligning team skills with products or services, maintaining steady income streams, seeking mentorship, and managing expenses carefully, startups can improve their chances of success in this AI-driven landscape.

Here are 25 popular AI tools startups are using currently (https://foundershub.ai/ai-tools-every-startup-founder-use/; https://addlly.ai/blog/ai-tools-for-startups/; https://kipwise.com/blog/ai-tools-for-startups-small-businesses; https://lassonde.utah.edu/15-free-ai-tools-for-entrepreneurs/):

1. AIAR: AIAR is a self-paced, startup/business accelerator that leverages state-of-the-art artificial intelligence to take your idea from concept to revenue in 90 days or less. https://informulate.com/aiar/
2. ChatGPT: ChatGPT offers 24/7 customer support automation with AI-driven chatbots and enables personalized customer interactions with context-aware conversations.
3. Jasper AI: Jasper AI revolutionizes content creation by generating high-quality marketing copy, blogs, and social media posts while maintaining a consistent brand voice.
4. Notion AI: Notion AI streamlines productivity and collaboration by generating project summaries, meeting notes, and task descriptions while organizing workflows seamlessly.
5. GitHub Copilot: GitHub Copilot is a code-generation tool that uses AI to suggest code snippets and complete functions, significantly speeding up development processes.
6. HubSpot AI: HubSpot AI combines CRM, marketing, and sales automation with predictive lead scoring and automated email campaigns.
7. Grammarly: Grammarly ensures professional communication across all channels with AI-powered writing assistance, tone detection, and error correction.
8. Canva AI: Canva AI transforms design processes with AI-powered design suggestions, quick creation of marketing materials, and brand-consistent visuals.
9. TabNine: TabNine offers AI-powered code completion across multiple IDEs, enhancing developer productivity.

10. DataRobot: DataRobot automates machine learning model development and scales predictive analytics for businesses.
11. Azure DevOps: Azure DevOps provides comprehensive tools for version control, project management, and CI/CD automation.
12. Zapier: Zapier enables smart workflow automation and seamless integration between thousands of apps.
13. Otter.ai: Otter.ai delivers real-time meeting transcription and automated summaries for better meeting management.
14. Tableau: Tableau offers AI-powered data visualization and analytics for informed decision-making.
15. IBM Watson: IBM Watson provides comprehensive AI capabilities for natural language processing and decision optimization.
16. Codacy: Codacy automates code quality checks and provides insights into maintainability and security.
17. Snyk: Snyk focuses on security by identifying vulnerabilities in code and dependencies.
18. DVC: DVC manages large datasets and tracks experiments for machine learning projects.
19. Kite: Kite accelerates development with real-time code suggestions for Python and JavaScript.
20. Figma: Figma facilitates real-time collaboration on UI/UX mockups with AI-powered design assistance.
21. Prisma: Prisma simplifies database schema generation and supports scalable app development.
22. Zig: GoZigZag.com is an AI-powered platform designed to help entrepreneurs validate and develop their startup ideas more efficiently.
23. CodeScene: CodeScene identifies technical debt and detects code quality issues using AI analysis.
24. Synthesia: Synthesia creates professional-quality videos using AI avatars and text inputs.
25. Paradox: Paradox streamlines recruitment processes with AI-powered interview scheduling and candidate screening.

References

Anane-Simon, R. and Atiku, S. O. (2023). Artificial intelligence and automation for the future of startups. In *Ecosystem Dynamics and Strategies for Startups Scalability* (pp. 133–153). IGI Global.

Barsoux, L., Wade, M., and Bouquet, C. (2022). Identifying unmet needs in a digital age: A four-part framework for diversifying how and where you look. *Harvard Business Review*. Retrieved from: https://hbr.org/2022/07/identifying-unmet-needs-in-a-digital-age.

Bennett, P. (2023). How AI tools are impacting the startup Landscape. Hubspot.com. Retrieved from: https://www.hubspot.com/startups/startup-ai-tools.

Bezhovski, Z., Apasieva, T. J., and Temjanovski, R. (2024). Online methods for validating and testing entrepreneurial ideas: A new product development perspective. *Management Research and Practice*, 16(1), 26–45.

Bezhovski, Z., Janevski, Z., Apasieva, T. J., and Temjanovski, R. (2021). From traditional to online methods for generating business ideas. *Management Dynamics in the Knowledge Economy*, 9(3), 307–329.

Blank, S. (2023). AI and ChatGPT will revolutionize customer discovery. *Entrepreneur & Innovation Exchange*. Retrieved from: https://eiexchange.com/content/ai-and-chatgpt-will-revolutionize-customer-discovery.

Blank, S., and Dorf, B. (2020). The startup owner's manual: The step-by-step guide for building a great company. Wiley, 1st edition.

Bruno, A., McQuarrie, E., and Torgrimson, C. (1992). The evolution of new technology ventures over 20 years: Patterns of failure, merger, and survival. *Journal of Business Venturing*, 7(4), 291–302.

Bygrave, W., and Zacharakis, A. (2014). Entrepreneurship. John Wiley & Sons, Inc.

CB Insights (2019). The top 20 reasons startups fail. Report. Retrieved from: https://s3-us-west-2.amazonaws.com/cbi-content/research-reports/The-20-Reasons-Startups-Fail.pdf.

CB Insights (2024). Startup failure post-mortems 2024 first update. Report. Retrieved from: https://www.cbinsights.com/research/startup-failure-post-mortem/.

Coleman, K. (2024). How to improve go-to-market strategy in an AI world. Copy.ai. Retrieved from: https://www.copy.ai/blog/how-to-improve-go-to-market-strategy.

Copy.ai (2024). AI in Go-to-Market: Startup Success Guide. Copy.ai. Retrieved from: https://www.copy.ai/blog/ai-in-go-to-market-for-startups.

Crowne, M. (2002). Why software product startups fail and what to do about it. Evolution of software product development in startup companies. *Caring for The Ages*, 1, 338–343 vol 1.

Dias, A., and Teixeira, A. (2017). The anatomy of business failure: A qualitative account of its implications for future business success. *European Journal of Management and Business Economics*, 26(1), 2–20.

Eisenmann, T. (2021). Why startups fail: A new roadmap for entrepreneurial success. Crown Currency.

Edelman, D., and Abraham, M. (2022). Customer experience in the age of AI: The case for building "intelligent experience engines." *Harvard Business Review*. Retrieved from: https://hbr.org/2022/03/customer-experience-in-the-age-of-ai.

Gluggioli, G., and Pellegrini, M. (2023). Artificial intelligence as an enabler for entrepreneurs: A systematic literature review and an agenda for future research. *International Journal of Entrepreneurial Behavior & Research*, 29(4), 816–837.

Grigul, E. (2024). Disruption of the technology adoption curve: How AI is changing the game. *Forbes*. Retrieved from: https://www.forbes.com/councils/forbestechcouncil/2024/11/08/disruption-of-the-technology-adoption-curve-how-ai-is-changing-the-game/.

Haan, K. and Watts, R. (2023). How businesses are using artificial intelligence in 2024. *Forbes*. Retrieved from: https://www.forbes.com/advisor/business/software/ai-in-business/.

Horowitz, B. (2014). The hard thing about hard things: Building a business when there are no easy answers. Harper Business.

Hubspot (2023). 5 of the most disruptive AI tools for startups in 2024. Retrieved from: https://www.hubspot.com/startups/ai-tools-for-startups.

IBM (2022). IBM global AI adoption index 2022. Retrieved from: https://newsroom.ibm.com/2022-05-19-Global-Data-from-IBM-Shows-Steady-AI-Adoption-as-Organizations-Look-to-Address-Skills-Shortages,-Automate-Processes-and-Encourage-Sustainable-Operations.

Jensen, L. (2024). Generative AI landscape: Q3 2024 insights. Retrieved from: https://www.scalecapital.com/stories/generative-ai-landscape-q3-2024-insights.

Jansen, B. J., Jung, S., and Salminen, J. (2023). Employing large language models in survey research. *Natural Language Processing Journal*, 4, 100020. Elsevier.

Jones, H. (2024). How startups are using AI. Kruzeconsulting.com, Kruze Consulting. Retrieved from: https://kruzeconsulting.com/blog/how-startups-using-ai/.

Kamboj, A. (2024). Transform your start-up: Top generative AI tools and platforms for success. Retrieved from: https://binmile.com/blog/generative-ai-tools/.

Kenyon, T. (2021). Study: AI startup funding hits new high of US$17.9bn in Q3. *AI Magazine*. Retrieved from: https://aimagazine.com/ai-applications/study-ai-startup-funding-hits-new-high-usdollar179bn-q3.

Kim, C., and Mauborgne, R. (2015). Blue ocean strategy: How to create uncontested market space and make the competition irrelevant. Harvard Business Review Press.

Kipwise (2024). Top 15 AI tools for startups & small businesses in 2024. Kipwise. Retrieved from: https://kipwise.com/blog/ai-tools-for-startups-small-businesses.

Kitsios, F., and Kamariotou, M. (2021). Artificial intelligence and business strategy towards digital transformation: A research agenda. *MDPI Sustainability*, 13(4), 2025. https://doi.org/10.3390/su13042025.

Kollmann, T., Lomberg, C., and Peschl, A. (2021). AI startup business models. *Business & Information Systems Engineering*, 63, 747–758.

Lee, B., Kim, B., and Ivan, U. V. (2024). Enhancing the competitiveness of AI technology-based startups in the digital era. *Administrative Sciences*, 14(1), 6. https://doi.org/10.3390/admsci14010006.

Lerner, M. (2023). Worried about AI in the workplace? You're not alone. American Psychological Association. Retrieved from: https://www.apa.org/topics/healthy-workplaces/artificial-intelligence-workplace-worry.

Lu, C. (2024). Go-to-market strategy for startups: A guide to AI tools. Retrieved from: https://www.copy.ai/blog/go-to-market-strategy-for-startups.

McAlindon, P. (2024). Accelerating business model development and organizational decision making through the use of AI and Intuition. *Achieving Digital Transformation through Analytics and AI*. World Scientific.

Nielsen, J. (2023). AI improves employee productivity by 66%. Nielsen Norman Group. Retrieved from: https://www.nngroup.com/articles/ai-tools-productivity-gains/.

Nishar, D., Sullivan, A. (2024). AI adoptions in startups. Retrieved from: https://www.generalcatalyst.com/stories/ai-adoption-in-startups.

Oladigbolu, I. (2024). AI startup challenges: Unlocking innovation & success. Retrieved from: https://adamfard.com/blog/ai-startup-challenges.

Paliwal, G. (2024). How AI is transforming go-to-market strategies. *Forbes*. Retrieved from: https://www.forbes.com/councils/forbesbusinessdevelopmentcouncil/2024/08/09/how-ai-is-transforming-go-to-market-strategies/?t.

Perifanis, N. A., Kitsios, F. (2023). Investigating the influence of artificial intelligence on business value in the digital era of strategy: A literature review. *Information*, 14(2), 85.

Ries, E. (2011). The lean startup: How today's entrepreneurs use continuous innovation to create radically successful businesses. Crown Business.

Ries, E. (2017). The startup way: How modern companies use entrepreneurial management to transform culture and drive long-term growth. Crown Currency.

Rios-Campos, C., Guerrero Zambrano, E. O., Castro Vargas, D. J., Abanto Merino, L. A., Alejandría Vallejos, P. A., Ballena Alcantara, I. M., Diaz Rubio, D. E., Samillan Rodriguez, D., Huaman Tomanguilla, J., and Vega Calderón, E. (2024). Startups and artificial intelligence. *South Florida Journal of Development*, 5(2), 950–969.

Sen, S. (2024). Key funding trends in AI-driven startups. Analytics Insight. Retrieved from: https://www.analyticsinsight.net/artificial-intelligence/key-funding-trends-in-ai-driven-startups.

Singh, N. (2024). Case studies: Startups using AI to secure investor funding. MyStartup.ai. Retrieved from: https://www.mystartup.ai/post/case-studies-startups-using-ai-to-secure-investor-funding.

Sørensen, L. B., and Lahr, H. (2022). A scaling perspective on AI startups. CBS Research Portal. Retrieved from: https://research-api.cbs.dk/ws/portalfiles/portal/70078696/matthias_schulte_althoff_et_al_a_scaling_perspective_on_ai_startups_publishersversion.pdf.

Soroushian, J. (2024). Taking stock of AI adoption across the U.S. Economy. Bipartisan Policy Center. Retrieved from: https://bipartisanpolicy.org/blog/taking-stock-of-ai-adoption-across-the-u-s-economy/.

Statista (2024). Number of artificial intelligence (AI) tool users globally from 2020 to 2030. Retrieved from: https://www.statista.com/forecasts/1449844/ai-tool-users-worldwide.

Statista (2023). Usage of artificial intelligence (AI) tools weekly in 2023, by age range. Retrieved from: https://www.statista.com/statistics/1450290/weekly-ai-tool-usage-age-rangeweekly-ai-tool-usage-age-range/.

Statista (2023). Industry employment at risk of automation by artificial intelligence (AI) in the United States in 2023, by industry. Retrieved from: https://www.statista.com/statistics/1378599/industry-employment-automation-risk-us/.

Statista (2021). What is the stage of AI adoption in your organization? Retrieved from: https://www.statista.com/statistics/1225955/stage-of-ai-adoption-in-healthcare-worldwide/.

Thompson, N. (2024). How to build and scale go-to-market processes with AI. Retrieved from: https://www.copy.ai/guides/how-to-build-and-scale-go-to-market-processes-with-ai.

Tilo, D. (2023). How many hours are employees saving using AI each day? Human Resources Director Magazine. Retrieved from: https://www.hcamag.com/us/specialization/hr-technology/how-many-hours-are-employees-saving-using-ai-each-day/452315.

Verified Market Research (2022). Global artificial intelligence SaaS market size By organization size (large enterprise, small & medium enterprise), By Geographic Scope And Forecast. Retrieved from: https://www.verifiedmarketresearch.com/product/artificial-intelligence-saas-market/.

Walsh, G. S., and Cunningham, J. A. (2017). Regenerative failure and attribution: Examining the underlying processes affecting entrepreneurial learning. *International Journal of Entrepreneurial Behavior and Research*, 23(4), 688–707.

Walsh, G. S., and Cunningham, J. A. (2016). Business failure and entrepreneurship: Emergence, evolution and future research. *Foundations and Trends in Entrepreneurship*, 12(3), 163–285.

Weber, M., Beutter, M., Weking, J., Böhm, M., and Krcmar, M. (2021). AI Startup business models: Key characteristics and directions for entrepreneurship research. *Business & Information Systems Engineering*, 64(1), 91–109.

Wodecki, B. (2023). Half of businesses using AI report positive results. AI Business. Retrieved from: https://aibusiness.com/automation/half-of-businesses-using-ai-report-positive-results-.

Wodecki, B. (2023). Over two-thirds of employees back generative AI to help improve work. AI Business. Retrieved from: https://aibusiness.com/nlp/over-two-thirds-of-employees-back-generative-ai-to-help-improve-work.

World Economic Forum (2023). Future of jobs report 2023. Retrieved from: https://www3.weforum.org/docs/WEF_Future_of_Jobs_2023.pdf.

Yadav, M., Chandel, A., Quttainah, M. (2024). AI-driven decision-making in startups. *Improving Entrepreneurial Processes Through Advanced AI*, p. 217.

Zacharakis, A., Bygrave, W., and Corbett, A. C. (2017). Entrepreneurship. John Wiley & Sons, Inc.

https://doi.org/10.1142/9789819816347_0002

Chapter 2

AESOP: The AI Strategy Framework—Not a Fable

Casey Carnes and Jay Liebowitz

*Crummer Graduate School of Business,
Rollins College, Winter Park, Florida, USA*

1. Introduction

Artificial Intelligence (AI) is perhaps the most widely discussed new technology of the era. Many have even referred to innovations in AI as a 4th industrial revolution evoking images of disruption and growth as powerful as the advent of the steam engine in the first industrial revolution, a design still responsible for generating the world's power today.

AI technology has developed rapidly over the past ten years, and organizations have been scrambling to develop policies and processes to harness the profit-creating power of AI (Zhou, 2022). However, organizations often put the cart before the ox with overly ambitious goals and ill-conceived processes and procedures to try to ensure their initiatives yield results, are developed, and are implemented ethically, and they benefit the overall organization (Gartner, 2024). Even if profits can be made from these initiatives, there are many second-order consequences, such as loss of human capital, misinformation, knowledge deterioration, and large-scale environmental impact (National Telecommunications and Information Administration, 2024).

These ethical concerns and the practical problems they represent have not yet been sufficiently addressed in an organizational AI strategy. Though many attempts have been made at a "grand unified theory" of AI strategy, current frameworks fail to address ethical concerns as a primary concern, often treating them as an afterthought. Those current plans and strategies which do focus primarily on ethics are usually constrained to a specific industry or field and not designed to be easily translated from one organization to another. There is a need for an adaptable ethics-first AI framework for organizations to ensure their AI initiatives are implemented in a way which will ultimately benefit the organization in the long term.

2. Literature Review

The published literature discussing Artificial Intelligence (AI) technologies within a business strategy framework or policy perspective is relatively recent. For example, New York City, the European Union, and India have all launched their official AI strategies within the past five years (NITI Aayog, 2023; European Parliament, 2023; New York City Office of Technology and Innovation, 2021). Also, within the past five years, the United States Government Accountability Office released an AI Accountability Framework for responsible use by other federal agencies (U.S. Government Accountability Office, 2021). There are many similar features between these initiatives, and they can provide an excellent starting ground for both businesses and public entities in need of a framework to launch their own actionable AI strategies. Unfortunately, the question of how to ethically implement the AI policy is not sufficiently addressed and the problem of ensuring ethical AI outcomes remains a challenge for many large organizations. We highlight each of these major AI strategy plans, recognizing that many others have also been developed.

The New York AI Action Plan was published in October 2023 and proposes seven initiatives to be incrementally phased in. Several of these initiatives display features which will become recurring as we examine other plans both public and private. First, there is the desire for a governing authority, or committee in this case, to oversee the expansion of AI initiatives within the city. Next is the focus on measurable outcomes through metrics; the desire to quantify unquantifiable variables is a common theme in the emergence of AI technologies. Additionally, the desire to seek and formalize input from external expert organizations is seen in almost every other AI implementation strategy in one form or another. Last, the emphasis on building public awareness through engagement initiatives seems to be the solution for the widespread concerns regarding AI technologies within the community (New York City Office of Technology and Innovation, 2021).

The desire to promote awareness through public engagement is positive but ultimately does not address ethical concerns; it merely seeks to assuage them. One example of this failing is the rollout of the MyCity chatbot. The MyCity chatbot was designed to answer the questions of New Yorkers about local government, city codes, or ordinances and help register small businesses (Orland, 2024). The idea was this would free up city workers for meaningful concerns while the chatbot relayed menial details citizens needed. However, the chatbot garnered significant negative publicity after recommending New Yorkers break laws such as evicting renters without legal standing or taking tips from employees (Allen, 2024).

Polyviou (2023) discusses the dimensions of AI strategy as ecosystems, education, liability, data sufficiency, autonomy, and governance. The data sufficiency point refers to assurances of AI honesty and accuracy through Key Performance Indicators (KPIs). This represents an attempt to quantify AI ethics from a technical, not organizational, standpoint. The autonomy dimension focuses on maintaining ethical behavior from an organizational standpoint by identifying key areas where maintaining a human presence is necessary. Specifically, human resources is mentioned, and the research speculates an erosion of morale and trust in an organization would occur if the hiring and firing process was fully autonomous. Last, the governance dimension refers to establishing a central authority to control and regulate AI to ensure ethical practices and effective implementation. As mentioned, many of these themes also appeared in the New York AI Action Plan, specifically the elements of establishing a governing body, seeking outside expertise, and promoting awareness within the community. The same criticisms remain true for the effort to promote awareness to reduce concern as opposed to reducing the need for concern.

In June 2023, the European Union (EU) referred to the EU AI Act as the "first regulation on artificial intelligence" (European Parliament, 2023). Other governments, such as India, have also launched official AI strategies as far back as 2018 (NITI Aayog, 2023). India's initial plan, referred to as the *National Strategy for Artificial Intelligence*, was considered incomprehensive and in need of improvement (Chatterjee, 2020). India has since continued to grow and develop its AI initiatives with the Ministry of Electronics and Information Technology publishing its first report *IndiaAI* in October 2023 (Ministry of Electronics and Information Technology, 2021). Also, in 2020, India launched the *Global Partnership on Artificial Intelligence* seeking collaboration with at least 15 other countries. Their first summit took place in July of 2024 (Press Information Bureau Government of India, 2024).

Lastly, the U.S. Government Accountability Organization (GAO) developed the AI Accountability Framework as a guideline for other federal agencies and the U.S. Congress. This framework focuses on four key strategies identified by the GAO through its own literature review and panel of outside experts. These four elements are Monitoring, Data, Governance, and Performance: Both the performance and the governance aspects of the framework advocate for organizations to establish quantifiable metrics to measure. The framework does not mention public or organizational outreach but focuses on quantifiable metrics, data quality assurance, and establishing an intraorganizational governance group. These shared elements indicate the influential role of the outside expert opinions panel and extensive literature review in the framework's formulation. While borrowing from the same body of literature and outside experts lends this framework the strength of the other strategies, it also imports the same failures regarding front-end ethics.

Together, these four entities alone constitute a significant portion, around a quarter of the human population, with New York City containing around 8.8 million residents of the U.S total of more than 335 million, India possessing a population of over 1.43 billion, and the combined nations of the EU having a population of over 443 million people (U.S. Census Bureau, 2020; World Bank, 2024; O'Neill, 2022).

3. Gaps in Existing AI Strategy Frameworks

While existing AI strategies include many common features, they often lack a comprehensive framework for ensuring moral and ethical behavior by AI systems and organizations using AI. Attempts to address this gap have been made by various researchers through efforts to quantify the fairness or ethical nature of generative AI outputs going back to at least

2012 (Castelnovo, 2022). While these attempts have made progress in establishing metrics which may be useful for analyzing the effectiveness of individual AI systems, they do not provide an organizational framework to implement or utilize these "fairness" or data sufficiency metrics (Polyviou, 2023). When examining organizational strategies, particularly in the private sector, they often do not propose thorough implementation strategies for operationalizing ethics into their framework or model. The incorporation of ethics is treated more like an afterthought to be mentioned and vaguely enforced. The enforcement mechanism is often akin to a traditional research ethics board model which relies on committees and governing bodies to check for compliance with established principles at the end of an AI technology or project design. This does not solve ethical problems; it only mires research in a bog of tail-end bureaucracy.

One example of a project focused specifically on ensuring the ethical implementation of AI technology is the Verizon *Responsible AI Roadmap*, part of the Verizon *Ethical Artificial Intelligence* (EAI) plan (Verizon Communications, 2024). This project was initially called Ethical AI and focused on "operationalizing AI ethics at an enterprise scale" by incorporating ethics decisions into the research and development process (Verizon Communications, 2024). Verizon's EAI is different from the AI strategies of the European Commission and many others because it goes a step further than determining ethical considerations and checking products against them at the beginning and end of the design process (Cansu, 2019). The *Ethical AI roadmap* was later rebranded as a *Responsible AI roadmap* and implemented within the *Puzzle Solving in Ethics* (PiE) AI Ethics Strategy originally developed at the Northeastern University AI Ethics Lab in Cambridge, MA (Cansu, 2019). Cansu (2019) argued that simply listing ethical concerns at the beginning and end of the research process to determine if a project gets a rubber stamp of approval is not enough; she instead asserts addressing the ethical dilemmas as they arise in the design process is the only way to earnestly apply ethics to an organization's AI strategy.

Verizon's final strategy incorporated this roadmap alongside an *Ethics Risk Assessment Framework* and *Fairness Monitoring Methodology* all of which fell under Verizon's "Three-Legged Stool" of responsibility. The three legs of the stool are Technology, Governance, and Policy. The major contribution of this Verizon's AI strategy is asserting detecting ethical problems is not enough; they must be addressed at the beginning, using the roadmap, middle, using the Ethics Assessment Risk Framework, and end, using the Fairness Monitoring Methodology of the product life cycle

(Verizon Communications, 2024). This is certainly a step forward from earlier examples of AI strategies simply listing important principles to abide by, which is the traditional research ethics model. However, the PiE model approaches ethical concerns in AI from a product design standpoint, not an organizational or knowledge management perspective—meaning the model would be particularly difficult to implement for certain public projects which do not have a defined product design process.

Another approach is the AI4people model which most heavily inspired the European Commission's AI Ethics legislation (AI4People, 2018). This model successfully distills the growing list of AI ethics principles down to five high-level principles to ensure ethical AI behavior. However, defining ethical behavior is not necessary for an AI strategy as pointed out by the researchers at Northeastern University's AI Ethics Lab: "There is already thousands of years of ethics research out there" (Cansu, 2019). The European Commission's legislation inspired by the AI4People model admittedly leaves many ethical questions unanswered, such as cybersecurity and wartime concerns (Floridi, 2018). Regardless, the overall approach of listing principles to follow fails to incorporate ethics into the policy production process and leaves the model reliant upon end-of-process committee review and governance.

Modern AI plans, such as Verizon's EAI strategy, approach the problem of addressing ethical concerns throughout the entire implementation and design process. But they approach it from a purely enterprise perspective making the primacy their frameworks place on establishing, implementing, and then monitoring for ethical concerns difficult to transplant across industries, disciplines, and especially into the public sector. There is still a need for an organizational framework which is not hyper-focused on one industry and still treats ethical concerns as a primary and ongoing concern, not merely a principle to be established beforehand and checked for again upon completion of an AI initiative or product. The AESOP Framework, which we are proposing in the following section, hopefully fills this vacuum.

4. The AESOP Framework

4.1. *A for awareness*

Before an AI strategy can be developed, an organization needs to create an awareness of what AI can and cannot offer to its employees, management, and stakeholders. Creating and nurturing a culture whereby a human-centered AI approach is fostered helps ensure that employees aren't fearful that AI will replace them. In fact, a Brookings report (Fleming *et al.*, 2024) indicates that many jobs really aren't at risk because the AI system's value doesn't exceed the costs of development and implementation. Thus, one of the first steps is to assuage doubts and concerns of employees concerning the role of AI in the workplace and to be sure that they are an integral part of the conversation. This will help build trust among the employees and allow them to participate in the dialog for nurturing and building a human-centered AI culture. Additionally, the Harvard Business review article *Artificial Intelligence for the Real World* by Davenport (2018) states that the most efficient uses of AI are for easily automated tasks which have often already been outsourced overseas, further mitigating the risk of job loss to an organization's employees.

De Cremer (2024) talked about the importance of business leaders being AI-savvy but not to the point of necessarily being AI experts. He stresses that business leaders have to be knowledgeable enough to know what AI can and can't do to help establish a culture for "humanics" whereby people and machines work well together. (Talk about the importance of understanding efficient use cases. The example of the health industry investing billions in an AI model to diagnose cancer which was eventually scrapped compared to a cost-efficient AI use case of attempting to answer/diagnose IT tech support help desk tickets.)

Of course, before creating a human-centered AI culture, good trustworthy data and a thoughtful data strategy are needed for AI systems to be effective in the organization. The adage, "Garbage In, Garbage Out," could be apparent if the data isn't cleansed, reliable, and unbiased in which these AI systems are built for organizational use. Liebowitz (2024) pointed out that many executives often rely on their intuition versus analytics because they don't trust their internal data quality. Having reliable data will help bolster trust in the AI and related systems upon which they are built. This is especially true with SLMs (Small Language Models) which many companies are now building for domain-specific tasks in their organizations.

4.2. *E is for ethics*

Often, in reviewing AI frameworks, such as the AI4 People model, NYC AI Action Plan, and India's National Strategy for AI, we see ethics as an after-thought. Instead, AI Ethics should really be at the forefront of any AI strategy framework. Without ensuring transparency, fairness, and reliability, the development of an AI system based on "biased" data will be flawed.

Some people such as Salo-Pontinen (2021) discussed the need for several types of AI ethics. These include AI Deployment Ethics, AI Governance Ethics, AI Design Ethics, AI Embedded Ethics, and AI Data Ethics. Deployment ethics relate to the high-level goals of the AI system, and AI governance ethics are needed for incentivizing and supporting the integration of ethical frameworks into AI. Design ethics refers to the stage where abstractions and real use cases are to be combined together with data ethics. Embedded ethics represent the operationalizations of high-dimensional concepts and objectives described in the deployment ethics (Salo-Pontinen, 2021).

In Etzioni (2018), an interesting article was published on "Should AI Technology Be Regulated?" The author raises some of the following pertinent points:

- Set up regulations against AI-enabled weaponry and cyberweapons.
- AI should be subject to the full gamut of laws that apply to its human operator.
- AI shall clearly disclose that it's not human.
- AI should not retain or disclose confidential information without explicit prior approval from the source.
- AI must not increase any bias that already exists in our systems.

Even though the article was published in 2018, it is still very relevant today. Fast forward some years later, the National Institute for Standards and Technology (NIST) published the "AI Risk Management Framework" in January 2023 and the "AI Risk Management Framework: Generative AI Profile" in April 2024. Then, the US AI Safety Institute, under NIST, published its strategy in May 2024.

Most organizations have focused on the following attributes for AI Ethics, including being Responsible, Equitable, Reliable, Traceable, and Governable. The AI Ethics principles should focus on the following: Safe & Effective Systems; Algorithmic Discrimination Practices; Data Privacy; Notice and Explanation; and Human Alternatives, Consideration, and Fallback.

4.3. *S is for strategy*

The AI strategy should be aligned with the organizational strategic plan, goals, and objectives and should be integrated at the enterprise-wide level in concert with the data strategy for the organization.

There are various first- and second-order activities producing third-order themes in developing an AI strategy. Astrom *et al.* (2022) discussed these activities in connection with value creation and capture. The third-order themes focus on identifying prerequisites for AI value creation, matching value capture mechanisms, and developing an AI business model.

To better understand how best to develop the AI strategy, it is often helpful to see what core questions CEOs are asking in terms of how AI can contribute to value delivery, creation, and capture. The Boston Consulting Group (BCG, 2024) performed a study and found that 10% related to algorithms, 20% related to technology and data, and 70% related to people and processes. For example, the CEOs surveyed indicated some of their questions with respect to people and processes (BCG, 2024), which are as follows:

- How do I mobilize senior leaders to embrace and actively champion our (Gen)AI ambition?
- How must our roles, departments, and operating model adapt to capture value from AI?
- What are the best ways to fill the AI talent gap within my organization?
- How do I effectively manage change across my enterprise? How do I communicate our ambition and set the right expectations while promoting trust and preventing misconceptions?

For example, at the Crummer Graduate School of Business at Rollins College, we have established a new Center called AI-EDGE (Artificial Intelligence for Executive Decision-making, Governance, and Execution). The vision for AI-EDGE is to become internationally recognized as the "go to" place for executive AI education and for developing future leaders in applied AI. Its mission is to educate executives on improving their decision-making, governance, and execution through AI while enhancing their organization's value creation, capture, and delivery in responsible AI ways. Figures 1–4 highlight aspects of AI-EDGE's strategy.

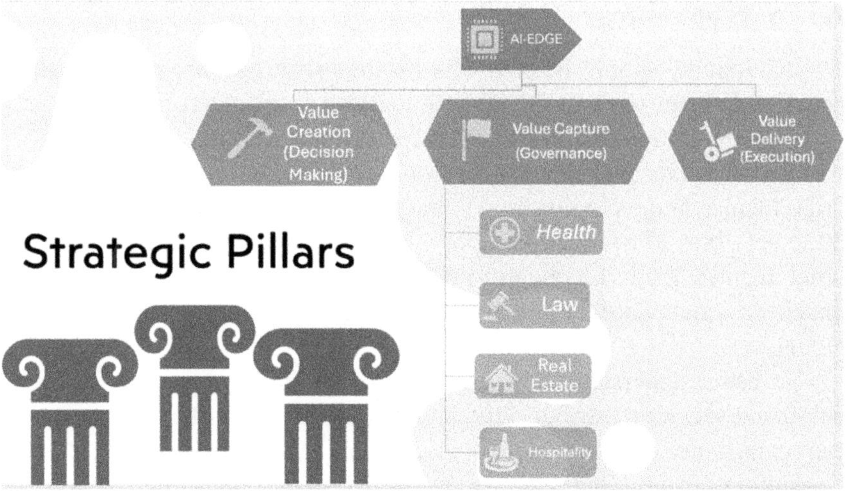

Figure 1. AI-EDGE strategic pillars.

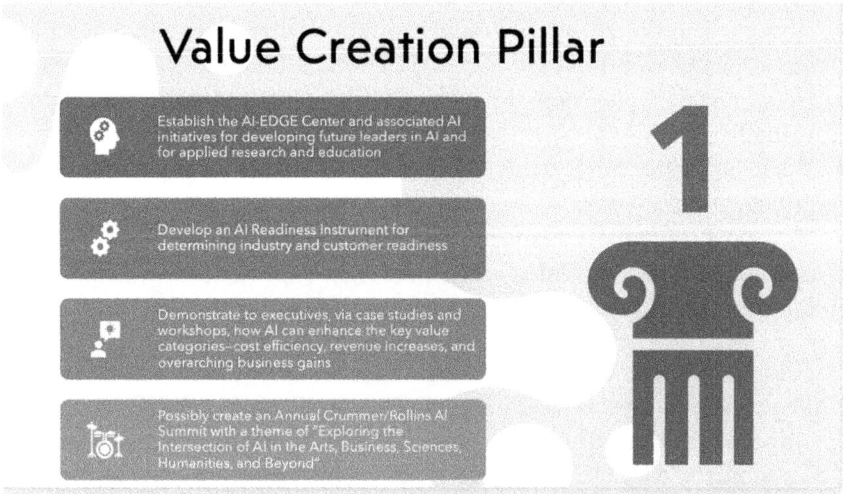

Figure 2. AI-EDGE value creation pillar.

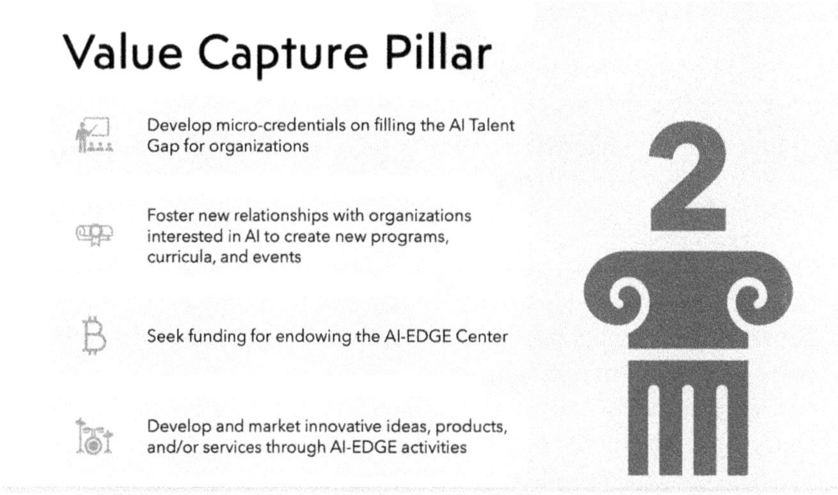

Figure 3. AI-EDGE value capture pillar.

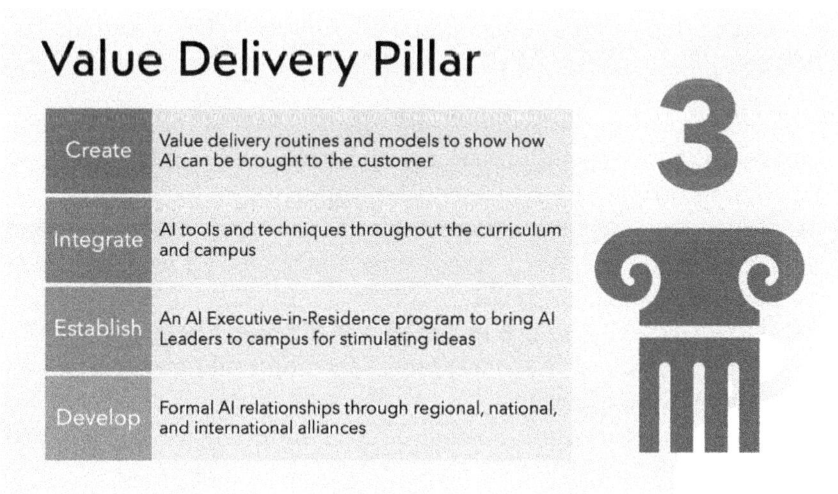

Figure 4. AI-EDGE value delivery pillar.

4.4. *O is for operationalization*

Once the AI strategy is defined, it must be operationalized in terms of governance. AI governance is a key part of the AI strategy and should focus on an AI Governance Operating Model, Policies and Standard Operating Procedures, and Regulatory Compliance (PwC, 2024). According to PwC (2024), the following insights are helpful in addressing AI governance:

- Good AI governance delivers value even before the use case starts.
- GenAI makes new demands of governance. With GenAI, enhanced governance is needed to deal with the multiple use cases, with different risk profiles, in different functions.
- An AI-focused risk taxonomy is fundamental. This can make governance decisions more consistent and repeatable.
- Good AI governance advances AI strategy. Perhaps give governance a seat at the table from the very start.
- Be tech-powered but human-led. Clear roles and responsibilities are needed for AI governance.

According to the NIST AI Risk Management Framework Playbook (2024), there are several components of "Govern." These include the following:

- Policies, processes, procedures, and practices across the organization related to the mapping, measuring, and managing of AI risks are in place, transparent, and implemented effectively.
- Accountability structures are in place so that the appropriate teams and individuals are empowered, responsible, and trained for mapping, measuring, and managing AI risks.
- Workforce diversity, equity, inclusion, and accessibility/belonging processes are prioritized in the mapping, measuring, and managing of AI risks through the lifecycle.
- Organizational teams are committed to a culture that considers and communicates AI risk.
- Processes are in place for robust engagement with relevant AI actors.
- Policies and procedures are in place to address AI risks and benefits arising from third-party software and data and other supply chain issues.

If these considerations are mapped into your AI strategy, governance, and operationalization framework, the organizations will reduce the risk of failure of AI initiatives.

4.5. *P is for performance*

Once operationalized, the AI initiatives should be measured for performance effectiveness and how well they contribute to the KPIs and strategic goals of the organization. When we talk about measures or metrics, we typically use system, output, and outcome measures. System metrics measure the functioning of the system itself. Output metrics measure the quantity or quality of what a process produces. Outcome measures, the most important, focus on the results and impact of the outputs and typically how they contribute to the organization's strategic mission, goals, and objectives. For example, in academe, we are interested in student learning outcomes rather than teaching delivery styles, although the two may certainly be correlated.

In performing a study (Shepherd University, 2024) looking at knowledge management (KM) metrics for a US Navy research and development lab, we looked at system, output, and outcome measures in terms of what we called the 3Ms: Measurable, the metric can be quantifiably measured; Meaningful, the metric can be closely aligned with the organization's strategic plan; Mature, the metric can be measured over time and is thus "enduring." Figure 5 shows the compiled results of one of the Knowledge Management experts who completed the survey.

The KM metrics provided some additional clarity in terms of the importance and performance characteristics for possible improvement in the future.

In the same manner, the resulting AI strategy, implementation plan, roadmap, and initiatives need to be measured on a periodic basis in order to be sure that the AI strategy doesn't go astray. As De Cremer (2024, p. 186) pointed out in his concluding sentences in his book:

"Be prepared to invest significant time and effort to master the art of leadership in a business world dominated by AI. Embrace your leadership responsibilities vigorously as if your life in the AI era depends on it. Because it most certainly does!"

5. AI in Central Florida Survey Results

Further evidence for the utility of ASEOP as an ethics-centered AI framework was discovered in the survey responses of C-level executives in Central Florida. The survey was adapted from the Global Center for Digital Business Transformation at IMD (Switzerland), and we received

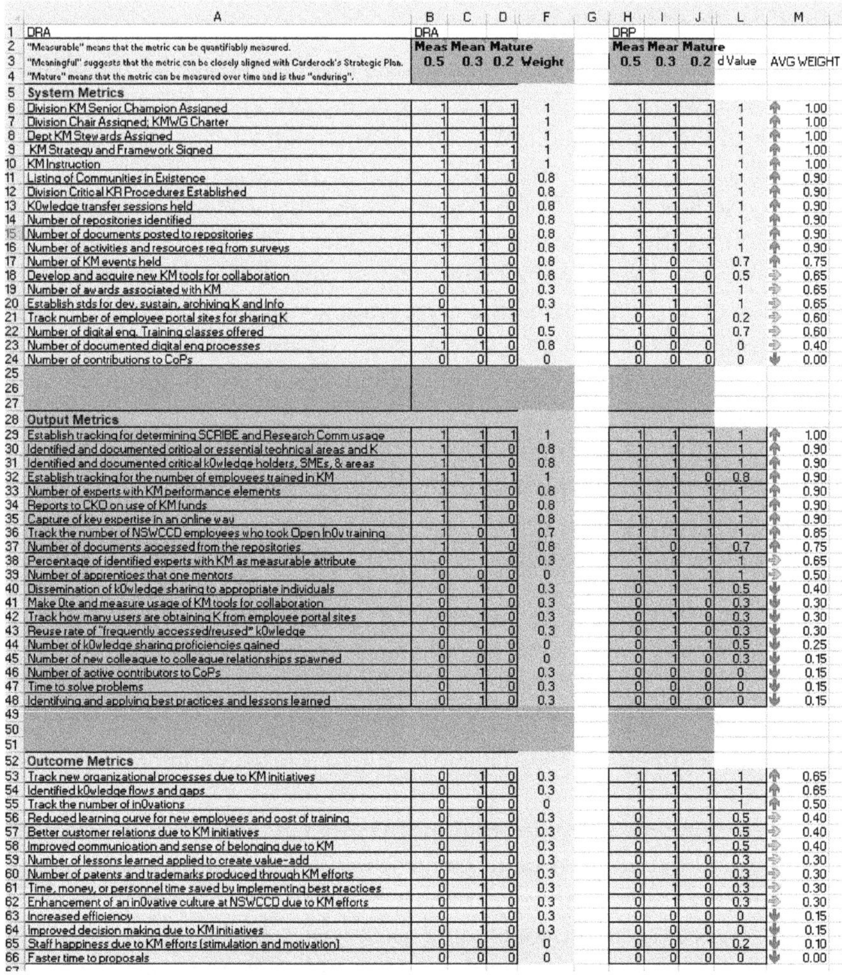

	A	B	C	D	F	G	H	I	J	L	M
1	DRA	DRA					DRP				
2	"Measurable" means that the metric can be quantifiably measured.	Meas	Mean	Mature			Meas	Mear	Mature		
3	"Meaningful" suggests that the metric can be closely aligned with Carderock's Strategic Plan.	0.5	0.3	0.2	Weight		0.5	0.3	0.2	d Value	AVG WEIGHT
4	"Mature" means that the metric can be measured over time and is thus "enduring".										
5	**System Metrics**										
6	Division KM Senior Champion Assigned	1	1	1	1		1	1	1	1	1.00
7	Division Chair Assigned; KMWG Charter	1	1	1	1		1	1	1	1	1.00
8	Dept KM Stewards Assigned	1	1	1	1		1	1	1	1	1.00
9	KM Strategy and Framework Signed	1	1	1	1		1	1	1	1	1.00
10	KM Instruction	1	1	1	1		1	1	1	1	1.00
11	Listing of Communities in Existence	1	1	0	0.8		1	1	1	1	0.90
12	Division Critical KR Procedures Established	1	1	0	0.8		1	1	1	1	0.90
13	K0wledge transfer sessions held	1	1	0	0.8		1	1	1	1	0.90
14	Number of repositories identified	1	1	0	0.8		1	1	1	1	0.90
15	Number of documents posted to repositories	1	1	0	0.8		1	1	1	1	0.90
16	Number of activities and resources req from surveys	1	1	0	0.8		1	1	1	1	0.90
17	Number of KM events held	1	1	0	0.8		1	0	1	0.7	0.75
18	Develop and acquire new KM tools for collaboration	1	1	0	0.8		1	0	0	0.5	0.65
19	Number of awards associated with KM	0	1	0	0.3		1	1	1	1	0.65
20	Establish stds for dev, sustain, archiving K and Info	0	1	0	0.3		1	1	1	1	0.65
21	Track number of employee portal sites for sharing K	1	1	1	1		0	0	1	0.2	0.60
22	Number of digital eng. Training classes offered	1	0	0	0.5		1	0	1	0.7	0.60
23	Number of documented digital eng processes	1	1	0	0.8		0	0	0	0	0.40
24	Number of contributions to CoPs	0	0	0	0		0	0	0	0	0.00
25											
26											
27											
28	**Output Metrics**										
29	Establish tracking for determining SCRIBE and Research Comm usage	1	1	1	1		1	1	1	1	1.00
30	Identified and documented critical or essential technical areas and K	1	1	0	0.8		1	1	1	1	0.90
31	Identified and documented critical k0wledge holders, SMEs, & areas	1	1	0	0.8		1	1	1	1	0.90
32	Establish tracking for the number of employees trained in KM	1	1	1	1		1	1	0	0.8	0.90
33	Number of experts with KM performance elements	1	1	0	0.8		1	1	1	1	0.90
34	Reports to CKO on use of KM funds	1	1	0	0.8		1	1	1	1	0.90
35	Capture of key expertise in an online way	1	1	0	0.8		1	1	1	1	0.90
36	Track the number of NSWCCD employees who took Open In0v training	1	0	1	0.7		1	1	1	1	0.85
37	Number of documents accessed from the repositories	1	1	0	0.8		1	0	1	0.7	0.75
38	Percentage of identified experts with KM as measurable attribute	0	1	0	0.3		1	1	1	1	0.65
39	Number of apprentices that one mentors	0	0	0	0		1	1	1	1	0.50
40	Dissemination of k0wledge sharing to appropriate individuals	0	1	0	0.3		0	1	1	0.5	0.40
41	Make 0te and measure usage of KM tools for collaboration	0	1	0	0.3		0	1	0	0.3	0.30
42	Track how many users are obtaining K from employee portal sites	0	1	0	0.3		0	1	0	0.3	0.30
43	Reuse rate of "frequently accessed/reused" k0wledge	0	1	0	0.3		0	1	0	0.3	0.30
44	Number of k0wledge sharing proficiencies gained	0	0	0	0		0	1	1	0.5	0.25
45	Number of new colleague to colleague relationships spawned	0	0	0	0		0	1	0	0.3	0.15
46	Number of active contributors to CoPs	0	1	0	0.3		0	0	0	0	0.15
47	Time to solve problems	0	1	0	0.3		0	0	0	0	0.15
48	Identifying and applying best practices and lessons learned	0	1	0	0.3		0	0	0	0	0.15
49											
50											
51											
52	**Outcome Metrics**										
53	Track new organizational processes due to KM initiatives	0	1	0	0.3		1	1	1	1	0.65
54	Identified k0wledge flows and gaps	0	1	0	0.3		1	1	1	1	0.65
55	Track the number of in0vations	0	0	0	0		1	1	1	1	0.50
56	Reduced learning curve for new employees and cost of training	0	1	0	0.3		0	1	1	0.5	0.40
57	Better customer relations due to KM initiatives	0	1	0	0.3		0	1	1	0.5	0.40
58	Improved communication and sense of belonging due to KM	0	1	0	0.3		0	1	1	0.5	0.40
59	Number of lessons learned applied to create value-add	0	1	0	0.3		0	1	0	0.3	0.30
60	Number of patents and trademarks produced through KM efforts	0	1	0	0.3		0	1	0	0.3	0.30
61	Time, money, or personnel time saved by implementing best practices	0	1	0	0.3		0	1	0	0.3	0.30
62	Enhancement of an in0vative culture at NSWCCD due to KM efforts	0	1	0	0.3		0	1	0	0.3	0.30
63	Increased efficiency	0	1	0	0.3		0	0	0	0	0.15
64	Improved decision making due to KM initiatives	0	1	0	0.3		0	0	0	0	0.15
65	Staff happiness due to KM efforts (stimulation and motivation)	0	0	0	0		0	0	1	0.2	0.10
66	Faster time to proposals	0	0	0	0		0	0	0	0	0.00

Figure 5. Compiled knowledge management expert results.

permission to use and modify it for our AI in Central Florida research. With 30 responses across 12 industry sectors, the results provide a small dataset for business organizations in our local area and indicated trends which, again, support the need for an ethics first AI framework. For example, less than a fifth of the respondents indicated they had at least some ethical guidelines established for AI development and use, and less than a fifth indicated their organization had a coordinated strategy to leverage value from AI. Additionally, 44% of respondents either answered "other" or "I don't know" when asked how AI is managed within their organization. Lastly, half of the respondents indicated their organizations do not measure the success of AI projects. The responses to these three questions alongside a few others asked in our survey all support the idea that most large organizations are under-prepared to implement AI, particularly in a safe and ethical manner.

Question #11, as shown in Figure 6, on whether organizations have established ethical guidelines for AI development and use, is the most directly related to the proposition of the ASEOP ethical AI framework. Forty percent of the respondents answered "No, we don't have any" and another 40% answered "No, but we are developing some" indicating a large majority of the Central Florida sample could benefit from a developed framework for Ethical AI. All but one of the remaining respondents replied "Yes, we have some" which still indicates room for improvements on existing ethical guidelines. As discussed previously, existing ethical guidelines are often more of an afterthought than a central fixture. In all, this question directly indicates that within our sample of Central Florida business organizations, a majority do not have adequate ethical guidelines for AI.

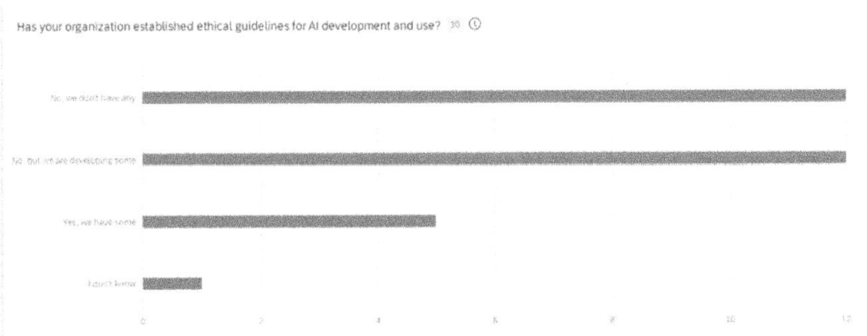

Has your organization established ethical guidelines for AI development and use?

Q011 - Has your organization established ethical guidelines for AI development and use?	Percentage	Count
No, we don't have any	40%	12
No, but we are developing some	40%	12
Yes, we have some	17%	5
I don't know	3%	1

Figure 6. Results for AI in Central Florida survey question #11.

We also looked at how AI is managed within organizations, as shown in Figure 7. Twenty-seven percent of the respondents replied "other," and 17% replied "I don't know" which could mean that many organizations do not use digital, IT, or a separate AI group to manage their AI policy. However, it may also imply many local organizations do not manage their AI initiatives structurally at all. This possibility is supported by the responses to question #12, as well. Given that "a separate group" was listed as one of the choices, it seems the choice to select "other" could be indicative of disorganized or *ad hoc* management of AI initiatives by executives themselves as opposed to an institutional organization. Again, the responses to question #12 support the idea that many organizations are not managing AI through a set of institutional policies at all since many individuals responded that they do not measure the success of their AI initiatives.

The responses to question #12 indicate more than a lack of institutional policies. Though half of those surveys said they did not measure the success of AI-related projects, 13% said they had developed specific KPIs to measure their success (Figure 8). According to Castelnovo (2022),

How is AI managed in your organization? 30

QID10 - How is AI managed in your organization? - Selected Choice	Percentage	Count
A separate AI group	17%	5
Part of Digital	20%	6
Part of IT	20%	6
I don't know	17%	5
Other	27%	8

Figure 7. Results for AI in Central Florida survey question #12.

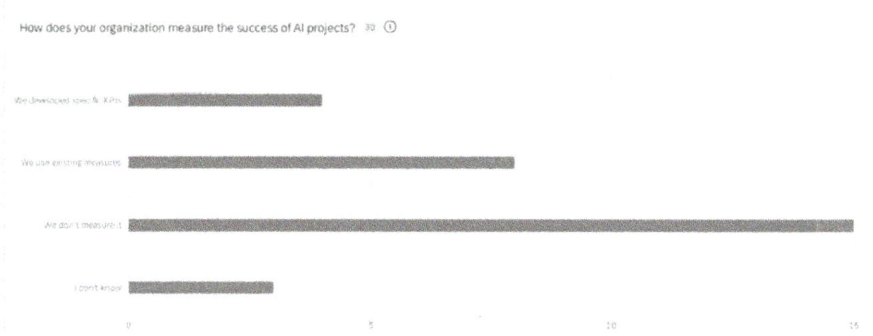

How does your organization measure the success of AI projects? 30

QID14 - How does your organization measure the success of AI projects?	Percentage	Count
We developed specific KPIs	13%	4
We use existing measures	27%	8
We don't measure it	50%	15
I don't know	10%	3

Figure 8. Results for AI in Central Florida survey question #13.

efforts to develop KPIs to measure fairness or biases of generative AI outcomes have been elusive and research is still ongoing. This means the 13% of organizations who developed their own KPIs along with the 27% who said they use existing metrics likely do not have a reliable quantitative system for accounting for ethics in their measurements despite having measurements for success.

Additionally, question #2 has only 19% of respondents indicate that they have a coordinated AI strategy, with 39% indicating their strategy was fragmented and another 39% saying theirs was non-existent. The survey indicates that 47% of respondents believe the level of AI maturity within their organizations is low and 7% believe there is none.

Ultimately, the survey results serve as a microcosm of the overarching themes and trends which have been observed in the literature review. Many organizations have only recently developed their artificial intelligence strategies, and those who have seldom account for ethics in their strategy. With this in mind, the utility of an ethics-centered AI framework, such as AESOP, is clear and would help organizations develop their AI strategies based on an existing model and measure success while ensuring compliance with ethical standards.

6. Summary and Recommendations

Most modern AI initiatives fail to adequately incorporate guardrails to protect against ethical concerns into the organization's AI policy. Given the prevalence of AI policy in current large-scale organizations, including large governments responsible for millions of citizens, it is essential these policies address ethical concerns as a top priority, not merely as an afterthought. The AESOP framework provides a way for organizations across industries and within both the private and public sectors to integrate ethics into the AI strategy as a front-end and continuous concern. Despite the significant resources being devoted to AI research and strategy development and the rapidly growing body of literature regarding AI ethics and strategies, both the literature review and the sample of data collected from business leaders in Central Florida suggest most organizations have not implemented adequate AI strategies.

Even the largest and most robust AI plans studied in the literature review have their shortcomings, largely due to the recent and still developing nature of scholarship on AI ethics and organizational strategies. For instance, even New York's *AI Action Plan* failed to safely and ethically implement a relatively simple AI use case, the My City Chatbot (Allen, 2024). This failure came even after the plan incorporated nearly all the suggested features of current AI strategies present in the existing scholarship and across leading public and private plans, including governance councils, outside expert panels, community outreach, and routine progress updates through measurable outcomes (New York City Office of Technology and Innovation, 2021). Additionally, even advanced ethics first initiatives, such as Verizon's Ethical Artificial Intelligence (EAI) plan, are industry-specific and may be difficult to translate from one use case to another since they approach the issue as a product development issue or concern (Verizon Communications, 2024).

Organizations sampled in the Central Florida region indicated far less preparedness than those observed in the literature review indicating even the inadequate levels of AI ethics policy which exists in developed AI strategies are not common in many organizations. Afterall, half of the organizations indicated they did not measure the success of their AI initiatives at all. While 80% of the organizations surveyed answered they either did not have ethical guidelines in their AI policy or are still developing their guidelines, in equal proportion. While the sample size was 30 local organizations, they included around a dozen different industries and were polled using the survey developed and tested by the Global Center for Digital Business Transformation at IMD in Switzerland. If the data collected from this sample is at all representative of the business world, then there is a clear need for an ethical AI implementation framework, such as AESOP.

We recommend that organizations adopt the AESOP framework to create an ethics first culture and strategy within their organizations. This will ensure future AI initiatives ultimately benefit the organization in the long run. Without ethics as a primary concern, an AI initiative could erode the trust of employees in the organization, cause knowledge deterioration within the organization, and result in false information or lack of data sufficiency in generated content (Polyviou, 2023). Many of these consequences can be mitigated or avoided entirely if an organization thoughtfully and carefully implements initiatives within an ethics-centered framework, such as AESOP.

References

Allen, J. (2024). New York City defends AI chatbot that advised entrepreneurs to break laws. *Reuters*. Retrieved from: https://www.reuters.com/technology/new-york-city-defends-ai-chatbot-that-advised-entrepreneurs-break-laws-2024-04-04/.

Astrom *et al.* (2022). Value creation and value capture for AI business model innovation: A three-phase framework. *Review of Managerial Science*. Retrieved from: https://link.springer.com/article/10.1007/s11846-022-00521-z.

Boston Consulting Group (BCG) (2024). CEO's Guide to Maximizing Value Potential from AI in 2024, July. Retrieved from: https://media-publications.bcg.com/BCG-Executive-Perspectives-CEOs-Guide-to-Maximizing-Value-from-AI-EP0-3July2024.pdf.

Castelnovo, A., Crupi, R., Greco, G. *et al.* (2022). A clarification of the nuances in the fairness metrics landscape. *Scientific Reports*, 12, 4209. Retrieved from: https://doi.org/10.1038/s41598-022-07939-1.

Chatterjee, S. (2020). AI strategy of India: Policy framework, adoption challenges, and actions for government. *Transforming Government: People, Process and Policy*, 14(5), 757–775. Retrieved from: https://doi.org/10.1108/TG-05-2019-0031.

Davenport, H. T. and Ronanki, R. (2018). Artificial intelligence for the real world. *Harvard Business Review*. Retrieved from: https://hbr.org/2018/01/artificial-intelligence-for-the-real-world.

De Cremer, D. (2024). The AI-Savvy Leader: Nine Ways to Take Back Control and Make AI Work. Harvard Business Review Press.

Etzioni, O. (2018). Point: Should AI Technology be Regulated? Yes, and Here's How. *Communications of the ACM*, December 1.

European Parliament. (2023, June 1). EU AI Act: First regulation on artificial intelligence. European Parliament. Retrieved from: https://www.europarl.europa.eu/topics/en/article/20230601STO93804/eu-ai-act-first-regulation-on-artificial-intelligence.

Fleming, M., Li, W. and Thompson, N. (2024). The Last Mile Problem in AI. Brookings, August 29. Retrieved from: https://www.brookings.edu/articles/the-last-mile-problem-in-ai/.

Gartner, D. and Chui, M. (2024). Achieving individual and organizational value with AI. *MIT Sloan Management Review*. Retrieved from: https://sloanreview.mit.edu/projects/achieving-individual-and-organizational-value-with-ai/.

Government Accountability Office (GAO). (2021). Artificial Intelligence: An Accountability Framework for Federal Agencies and Other Entities. Retrieved from: https://www.gao.gov/assets/gao-21-519sp-highlights.pdf.

Liebowitz, J. (ed.) (2024). Developing the Intuitive Executive: Using Analytics and Intuition for Success. Taylor & Francis.

Ministry of Electronics and Information Technology. (2021). India AI: Expert group report (First edition). Retrieved from: https://www.meity.gov.in/writereaddata/files/IndiaAI-Expert-Group-Report-First-Edition.pdf.

National Telecommunications and Information Administration. (2024). Requisites for AI accountability: Areas of significant commenter agreement — Recognize potential harms and risks. U.S. Department of Commerce. Retrieved from: https://www.ntia.gov/issues/artificial-intelligence/ai-accountability-policy-report/requisites-for-ai-accountability-areas-of-significant-commenter-agreement/recognize-potential-harms-and-risks.

New York City Office of Technology and Innovation. (2021). Artificial intelligence action plan. Retrieved from: https://www.nyc.gov/assets/oti/downloads/pdf/reports/artificial-intelligence-action-plan.pdf.

NIST (2024). NIST AI Risk Management Framework Playbook. Gaithersburg, Md. Retrieved from: https://airc.nist.gov/AI_RMF_Knowledge_Base/Playbook/Govern.

NITI Aayog. (2023). National Strategy for Transforming AI NITI Aayog: National Institution for Transforming India. Retrieved from: https://www.niti.gov.in/node/708.

O'Neill, A. (2022). European Union: total population from 2010 to 2022 (in million inhabitants). *Statista*. Retrieved from: https://www.statista.com/statistics/253372/total-population-of-the-european-union-eu/.

Orland, K. (2024). NYC's government chatbot is lying about city laws and regulations. *Ars Technica*. Retrieved from: https://arstechnica.com/ai/2024/03/nycs-government-chatbot-is-lying-about-city-laws-and-regulations/.

Polyviou, A. and Zamani, E. D. (2023). Are we nearly there yet? A desires & realities framework for Europe's AI strategy. *Information Systems Frontiers*, 25, 143–159. Retrieved from: https://doi.org/10.1007/s10796-022-10285-2.

PwC (2024). Good Governance for AI: 5 Real-World Insights for Risk Professionals. (J. Kosar, I. Golbin, and R. Sen), March 4. Retrieved from: https://www.pwc.com/us/en/tech-effect/ai-analytics/ai-governance-for-risk-leaders.html.

Salo-Pontinen, H. (2021). AI Ethics: Critical Reflections on Embedding Ethical Frameworks in AI Technology. In M. Rauterberg (ed.), *Culture and Computing: Design Thinking and Culure Computing*. Springer.

Shepherd University (2024). Establishing Knowledge Management Metrics and Supporting KM Activities for Naval Surface Warfare Center-Carderock Division. Final Report, Research Grant N00167-24-1-0002 (B. Martz, J. Liebowitz, Co-PIs), August 2.

U.S. Census Bureau. (2020). New York City, New York. Data.census.gov. Retrieved from: https://data.census.gov/profile/New_York_city,_New_York?g=160XX00US3651000.

World Bank. (2024). Population, total (India). Data.worldbank.org. Retrieved from: https://data.worldbank.org/indicator/SP.POP.TOTL?locations=IN.

Zhou, S., Zhao, R., Yuan, S., Ding, M., and Wang, Y. (2022). Tracing the evolution of AI in the past decade and forecasting the emerging trends. *Expert Systems with Applications*, 209, 118221. Retrieved from: https://doi.org/10.1016/j.eswa.2022.118221.

https://doi.org/10.1142/9789819816347_0003

Chapter 3

AI and Entrepreneurship

Rajiv Menon

Informulate, Orlando, Florida
AIAR, Orlando, Florida

1. Introduction

Humanity stands at the edge of an unprecedented transformation driven by Artificial Intelligence (AI), particularly Generative AI (GenAI) through Large Language Models (LLMs). Projections indicate that nearly a quarter of all jobs could be affected by AI systems (Future of Jobs Report, 2023), with robotics poised to bring another wave of disruption (Blakely & Sellman, 2024). While it is difficult to determine exactly when certain milestones will be reached, the current pace is already astonishing (Hu, 2023), driven by one of the fastest capital deployment cycles in history (Lynch, 2024).

AI is no longer merely a realm of research; it has transformed into a practical, accessible force that shapes industries, institutions, and individual careers. Individuals, organizations, and policymakers must take proactive steps to navigate this transitional phase, with insights from thinkers such as Nassim Taleb, Eric Ries, and Dr. Spencer Johnson providing clarity on what is required. Taleb, in his work on "antifragility," underscores the importance of emerging stronger from volatility and shocks, rather than just surviving them (Taleb, 2012). Ries' Lean Startup approach highlights the value of iterative, experimental problem-solving in the face of extreme uncertainty (Ries, 2011). Johnson, in his metaphorical work "Who Moved My Cheese?", emphasizes the need for individual adaptability—responding to change without nostalgia or resistance (Johnson, 1998). These principles together serve as a navigational compass for thriving in what is undeniably one of the most volatile yet opportunity-rich periods in modern history.

GenAI tools such as ChatGPT (OpenAI, 2024), Gemini (Google, 2024), and others generate texts, images, and codes based on prompted inputs for a variety of use cases. The surprisingly effective, accessible, and scalable nature of this technology is quickly reshaping workflows across industries, such as copywriting, design, and customer support. Like the Internet or the PC, this is no small change. It fundamentally shifts the landscape of strengths, weaknesses, opportunities, and threats (SWOT) for businesses across all sectors.

2. The Era of the AI Gold Rush

The closest historical analogy to today's AI zeitgeist is the dot-com boom of the late 1990s and the personal computing era of the 1980s. Comparisons to a "gold rush" are prevalent and rightly so. Big Tech firms have earmarked over $200 billion annually for AI investments, declaring these opportunities as "once in a lifetime" (Bloomberg, 2024). Meanwhile, VC firms have significantly increased their spending on AI by 20–30 times (OECD.AI, 2021), while overall startup investment has dropped to one-third during the same period (Glasner, 2024). Big Tech, startups, and venture capital (VC) firms are all vying for a foothold, driven by a palpable Fear of Missing Out (FOMO).

As with any market exuberance, questions arise. Is this the 1995 phase of the dot-com bubble or the 2000 phase? Is this NFT mania all over again? Time will tell, but while valuations are arguably high, today's AI-driven businesses seem to have clear value propositions and potential paths to profitability.

The reality is that the world economy has already made massive bets. As of 2024, there are over 83,000 AI-focused startups globally, marking an impressive 100% growth in just two years (Tracxn, 2023). VC allocations have heavily shifted toward AI ventures, while overall startup funding has declined. AI-focused companies now receive 35% of all startup investment (Glasner, 2024). This concentration of investment demonstrates a strong belief among entrepreneurs and investors that AI is the most critical frontier for value creation in the upcoming decade.

3. Entrepreneurship as a Vector of Innovation

Throughout the 19th century, there were dozens of literal gold rushes, along with similar events such as the dot-com boom, the intercontinental railroad, and personal computing. On the surface, these occurrences seem to have little in common aside from irrational exuberance and drama. But who are the actors in these dramas? Who are the prime movers taking risks, solving numerous challenges, and ultimately enjoying the rewards? Coders, miners, and engineers all play essential roles—every gold rush requires its unique set of technicians and specialists—but the role that *is always essential* is the risk-seeking entrepreneur.

Throughout history, the label of innovation has shifted among various groups. At one time, it belonged to the solitary scientist—uncovering discoveries and creating inventions. There was an era when this became the domain of renowned universities and their societies. For a period, innovation demanded significant investment, and developments emerged from large enterprises and even government. However, in the last generation or so, the baton has clearly been passed to startup entrepreneurs.

4. What is Entrepreneurship, Really?

In simple terms, entrepreneurship is the process of turning a business idea into reality. Startup founders embody the concept of pursuing unproven value propositions and innovative technologies. The startup environment is primarily defined by uncertainty, a state that Eric Ries famously captured in his definition of a startup as "a human institution designed to create something new under conditions of extreme uncertainty." (Ries, 2011)

5. The Entrepreneur's Edge

While large organizations can certainly act entrepreneurially, we will explore why the odds are against them. Small, resource-constrained startups are disproportionately active as drivers of innovative disruption.

Amazon, Tesla, Netflix, and Uber serve as examples of massively disruptive startups that are upending entire industries. Why? Startups do not need to protect existing cash flow since they have none, allowing them to pursue a vision based on first principles that refocus on the customer's true needs (Christensen *et al.*, 2015). Their small size also provides them with the agility to respond rapidly through continuous improvement or feedback/learning loops, such as Build-Measure-Learn, as described by Eric Ries (Ries, 2011).

Their contribution to the economy is also significant. About 16.5% of Americans are entrepreneurs (GEM, 2024). While large corporations are responsible for maintaining and *keeping* the majority of the workforce employed, new startups and small businesses account for the majority of *new job creation* in the United States (*Small Business Facts: Small Business Job Creation,* 2022).

6. Navigating the Waves of Disruption

The past generation has witnessed several waves of technological disruption—e-commerce, mobile, cloud computing, SaaS, and so forth. Each of these not only represented a significant disruption *on its own* but also built upon earlier waves. Take e-commerce, for example—it evokes images of retailers on the Internet, yet it has created value in numerous areas, including new media, e-learning, gaming, fintech, and more. Furthermore, as the Subscription as a Service (SaaS) business model evolved alongside e-commerce, it unlocked an entirely new level of value. Each innovation has also scaled more rapidly than the last. This mirrors the exponentially accelerating progress described by futurist Ray Kurzweil in his Law of Accelerating Returns (Kurzweil, 2005). AI is positioned to harness previous layers of technological foundation, and late adopters of AI are likely to face significant disruption.

7. Entrepreneurial Risk-Taking

Startup founders are celebrated in American society, and rightly so. Startup failure rates are estimated to be 90% (Startup Genome, 2022*),* with only 50% of startups making it to year 5 *(Frequently Asked Questions About Small Businesses, 2021*). Survival rates for startups are continuing to go down (Blum, 2023). VC and Angel investors are seen as risk-takers and, while that is true, their investments are diversified and more risk-mitigated. Entrepreneurs often take personal financial risk, investing their time and money into a single venture with a low chance of success. What makes this so hard?

8. Entrepreneurial Headwinds

Compared to other careers, entrepreneurs face many challenges on their lonely, risk-filled journeys, including the following list:

- **No set path:** Unlike traditional jobs, there is no defined career path for entrepreneurs, even though there are numerically more entrepreneurs than, for example, in white-collar professions, such as software development.
- **Financial risk:** Entrepreneurs typically invest time and money in a venture without any guarantee of success. In the initial stages, they are unlikely to be paid.
- **Body of knowledge:** Most jobs provide training, but entrepreneurs must start with either a wide-ranging body of knowledge or the ability to quickly acquire knowledge or both. A fundamental understanding of finance, leadership, accounting, compliance, hiring, and project management is often required.
- **Accountability:** Leadership bears the ultimate responsibility for success or failure. It is difficult for a single individual to possess the diverse range of skills needed. This is why multi-member founding teams are 300–600% more likely to succeed than solo founders (Startup Genome, 2023).
- **Unknown Risks:** To paraphrase Donald Rumsfeld, there are risks you know how to mitigate, risks you recognize but don't yet know how to address, and risks of which you are completely unaware. Entrepreneurship is filled with elements from all three categories, such as competition, regulation, technology, pricing, and so on.

Therefore, localities aspiring to build innovation ecosystems must find ways to support entrepreneurs. Accelerators, incubators, corporate programs, and many Entrepreneur Support Organizations (ESOs) exist. However, a serious supply–demand mismatch persists. Approximately 40 million Americans are considering entrepreneurship or are new founders (Bhattarai, 2023), over 30 million small businesses are already operating (U.S. Chamber of Commerce, 2023), and around 5 million new businesses are started each year (U.S. Chamber of Commerce, 2023). Small Business Development Centers, the largest ESO in America, serve about 300,000 individuals annually (The SBA's Small Business Development Centers Program, 2023), while the thousands of incubator and accelerator programs across the country assist roughly 30,000 per year (*2.7K+ Accelerators & Incubators in United States—Tracxn,* 2024). Consequently, there is an order of magnitude gap between demand for startup support and supply. Therefore, most entrepreneurs don't receive the help they need.

Accelerators perform exceptional work—startups participating in their programs raised 50–170% more funding (Cohen *et al.*, 2024) and experienced a 23% increase in survival rates on average (Butz & Mrożewski, 2021). With this context, let us consider how AI can serve as a resource for entrepreneurs.

9. AI: A Superpower for Entrepreneurs

As with other domains, AI will disrupt entrepreneurship as well. GPTs such as Co-Founder AI, Your Startup Buddy, and Y Combinator Startup Assistant can serve an unlimited number of entrepreneurs. AI tools for startups and businesses cover a wide range of functions, including sales, marketing, customer support, accounting, idea generation, strategy development, content generation (text, audio, images, and now even video), project management, code generation, and more. Not only are these tools accessible, but they are also context-aware and tailored to the end user's needs. However, we are still in the early stages of AI deployment. Some story-telling will help better visualize entrepreneurial use cases for generative AI.

10. Meet Jill, the Entrepreneur

On a lazy Saturday morning, Jill finishes breakfast and ponders what to do next. She has a job but has always wanted to be her own boss. She doesn't have a specific idea, but she is passionate about the environment. She could prompt an LLM with "I would like some business ideas in the area of climate advocacy and resilience. My technical skills include web development, and I have a solid social media following. What business ideas could I pursue?" The LLM then generates a list of ideas.

In the future, it is highly likely that she will have an AI assistant/agent (let's call it Aldo) who understands her background. She might simply say, "Given what you know about me, what is a good business idea that I would enjoy and profit from?" Aldo responds with options such as planning events focused on sustainability, a climate education podcast, environmental consulting, and more. Jill reviews the options and selects one. She then discusses the investment required, the risks, competitors, and other considerations.

She can also specify how much time she can devote to this part-time exploration of entrepreneurship in the next month or so. Within an hour, she could define an outreach campaign to assess customer demand for what she offers. Aldo scans LinkedIn or other social media, identifies targets for customer discovery, automatically reaches out with a custom-crafted message to request a meeting, and simply schedules it for her. Over the next few weeks, Jill will have open-ended conversations with targets and ask non-biasing questions per Aldo's recommendations.

Assuming this phase goes well, Aldo moves her into a validation phase to truly assess demand. It writes copy for a web-based landing page and marketing message. It crafts a call to action and scrapes targets to share this with, creating Google or social media ads to drive traffic to a pre-registration or sign-up page. Within a couple of weeks, Jill gains hundreds of registrations that confirm her idea has demand. These are paid pre-registrations (an approach akin to Kickstarter) that provide her with some capital to build her solution.

In the next phase, Jill and Aldo decide what her Minimum Viable Product (MVP) features should be. Being context-aware, Aldo generates use cases and estimates costs based on low-code solutions while connecting her to co-founders and other resources. At the same time, Aldo coordinates with third-party services to create her LLC, gives her instructions on filing for an EIN, and uses an API to open a bank account for her. Jill employs another AI tool for her bookkeeping. In a month or two, Jill launches her MVP. Real users begin paying. Aldo reviews her website analytics, survey feedback, and usage statistics, generating ideas to increase conversion and engagement.

At this point, Jill decides to transition to a part-time role at her job. She realizes she can scale her business while Aldo identifies potential corporate partners. He also points her toward grants and funding sources. Jill feels more fulfilled in her mission in ways she never has before. By giving Aldo access to her email, she can easily juggle vendors, tasks, ideas, and follow-ups. With Aldo handling the tedious work, she frees up time to improve quality. She stays on top of everything by reviewing and approving a prioritized list of items. The AI agent is the perfect employee; no issue is raised without several potential solutions.

One day, Jill catches the flu, so she informs Aldo, who then takes the necessary steps to reschedule meetings. For an important client, Aldo orders a cookie as an apology. Priorities are rearranged, and while Jill recuperates, Aldo provides her with a first draft of a major proposal that is approaching a deadline, highlighting areas she should focus on more closely. Suddenly, a significant corporate partner changes its policy, which shocks Jill since she has already quit her job. Aldo acknowledges the situation and sends her a personalized message, reminding her of the reasons she began this journey and the impact she has made. Aldo then creates a new list of potential partners and, with Jill's approval, messages them directly. We could continue the story, but the picture is clear.

We reviewed an ideal outcome for our story, knowing—based on the statistics we examined earlier—that it is highly likely Jill will fail on her first attempt at entrepreneurship. However, even in that scenario, Jill will reach that endpoint faster and with less investment thanks to Aldo's assistance.

Jill is still the driver, focusing on a problem she cares about. She connects the dots and builds personal relationships and a network. She learns about the problem she intends to solve, understands what her users really want, and thinks about the big picture in a way that only a passionate human can. Aldo does everything else that is a chore but, also encourages Jill and holds her accountable to her own vision.

While that may sound like science fiction, everything in that story is *already possible* with the technologies available *today*. We can explore how this can be achieved in the case study.

11. Innovation Methodology

Innovation methodology offers tools and frameworks to reduce the risks associated with product development and entrepreneurship. One of the major challenges for an entrepreneur is Confirmation Bias (Entrepreneur, 2016). Every individual is shaped by their inherent personality, skills, and experiences. A software developer brings a technical perspective, while a marketer provides a storytelling angle, and so on. Unfortunately, this leads people to overemphasize what they understand and underestimate what they don't, according to research conducted by Dunning and Kruger (1999).

Successful entrepreneurs must do two opposing things: they must be committed optimists and harsh pessimists. Without optimism, passion, and problem-solving energy, nothing can be created. Without recognizing potential failure points, they may overlook competitors, evolving technology, negative customer feedback, and other risks. AI agents can apply innovation methodology to mitigate biases. They can foster and create energy, as well as identify risks and mitigations. This is especially powerful for solopreneurs without a founding team. While there are no guarantees of business success, the AI-enabled use of innovation methodology can reveal the quickest path to learning—whether through success or failure.

12. Case Study: Meet AIAR

As previously mentioned, all the groundwork and technology needed for Jill's hyper-powered AI agent is already available. AIAR.co (short for AI AcceleroR) is a product that provides the foundation for just such a solution. It is a mobile application (in public beta as of this writing) that is positioned as the world's first self-paced, AI-driven startup accelerator. Users are presented with a path to progress from an idea to generating revenue in 90 days. That may seem unfeasible for some capital-intensive or highly regulated industries. However, if we recognize pre-registration fees (*à la* Kickstarter) as revenue, this is possible even in the domains with a lot of up-front costs.

This is achieved through four modules: Value Proposition Design, Customer Discovery, Validation, and MVP. A powerful notifications system sends in-app messages to keep users accountable and motivated to continue. Let's examine the functional experience.

13. Functionality and Use Cases

Once a user downloads the mobile app and completes registration, the first mobile task they must complete is **Orientation**. They are first asked a few demographic questions, followed by inquiries about their "Why," i.e., their motivation for pursuing this, and finally about their business idea. After that, they are introduced to their mentors (AI agents): Aria and Aiden. Aria specializes in user behavior and possesses an empathetic nature, while Aiden focuses on business models and monetization, exhibiting a more task-oriented personality. They then watch a training video in which Aria and Aiden explain how the app will work, and the user has the option to chat. From that point on, the interactions resemble those of a user in a startup accelerator consuming training and then discussing ideas/action items with their mentors. They can ask questions, and the mentors help keep them focused and progressing to the next module.

Unlike traditional LLM interactions, where users must type a request (input prompt) to receive a response (output), AIAR exemplifies *objective-driven AI.* The app proactively asks questions, politely navigates away from distractions, and guides users along a pathway to accomplish tasks. See the following illustration.

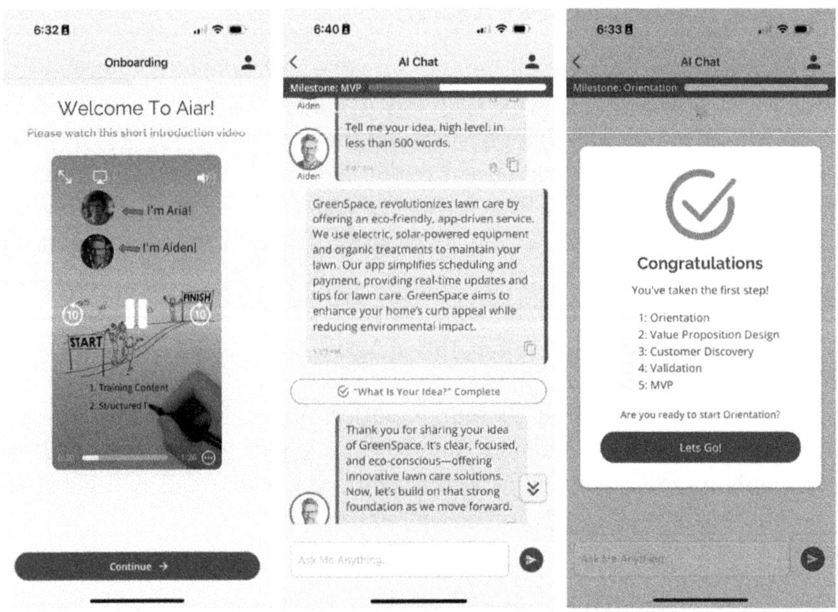

Once that is completed, the next module is **Value Proposition Design**. Once again, a training video is presented. Then they are asked further questions including the type of business (B2B, B2C, etc.), Customer Segments, Problem Statement, and Solution Statement. All of these interactions happen within the chat module, using auto-generated recommendations that the user can accept, edit, or delete. Clicking on the magic wand icon generated new suggestions. Following is the illustration.

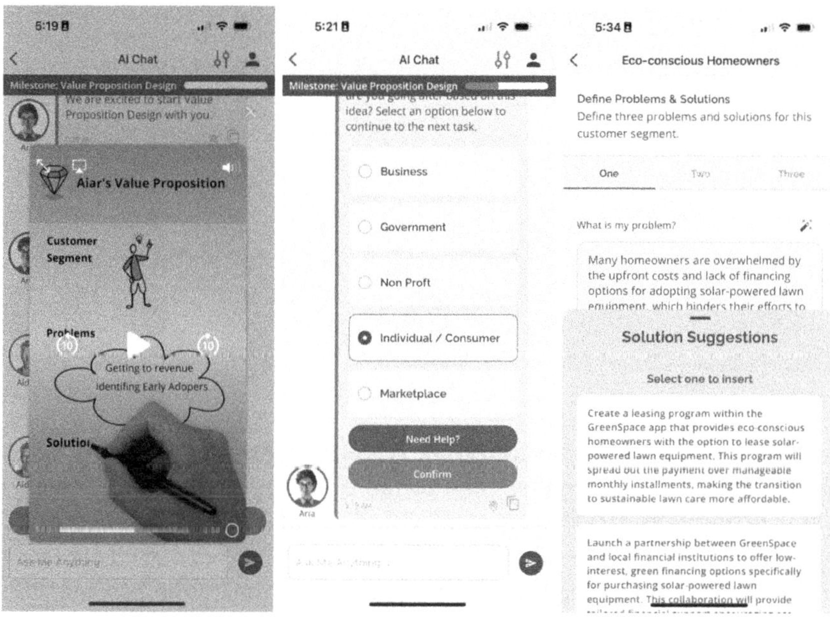

Next is the **Customer Discovery** module, where users graduate to doing real-world tasks *outside* of the app. They begin by watching a training video for the module that emphasizes the importance of unbiased conversations. Afterward, users are presented with a set of questions to conduct customer discovery for their target segment, based on best practices, which they can modify. Upon completion, Aria and Aiden assist users in finding targets and encourage them to reach out for these crucial conversations. Users then carry out the task and report back to the app, which determines whether sufficient validation has been achieved. The app also allows users to adjust or change their problem/solution statement. If satisfied, users can proceed to the next module. Following are the illustrations.

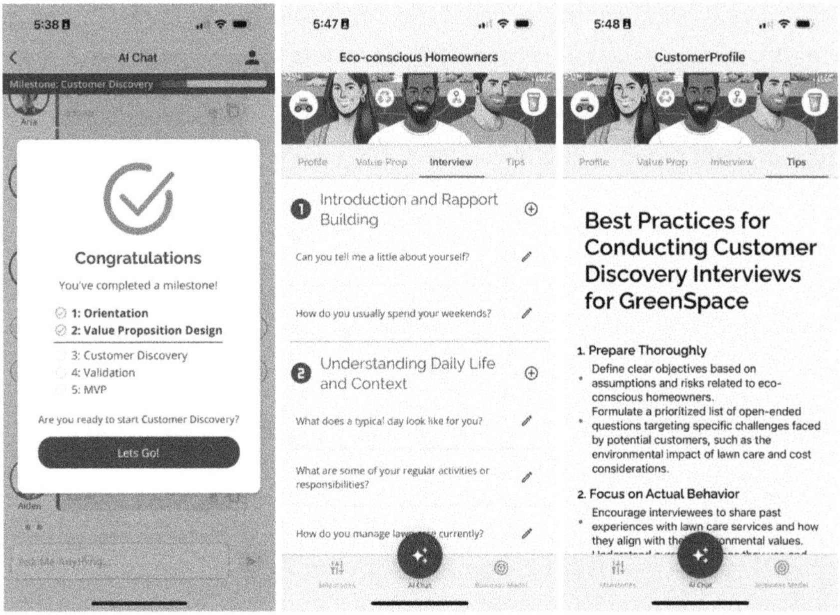

The next module is **Validation**. Once the training video is completed, the user must conduct one or more live, real-world experiments that will mitigate risks associated with their idea. Accordingly, the AI agents will present and review various risks the entrepreneur may encounter and assist them in developing mitigations. One primary risk for any business is inadequate demand, so the validation typically involves conducting a pre-registration drive or a similar initiative. The app offers options for outreach channels, sample messages, landing page copy, and any other tasks where the user seeks assistance. They are encouraged to charge users for pre-registrations to demonstrate genuine demand. After completion, the user reports back with the results, and if the AI agents are satisfied that sufficient validation has been achieved, they are allowed to progress to the final milestone. Following are the illustrations.

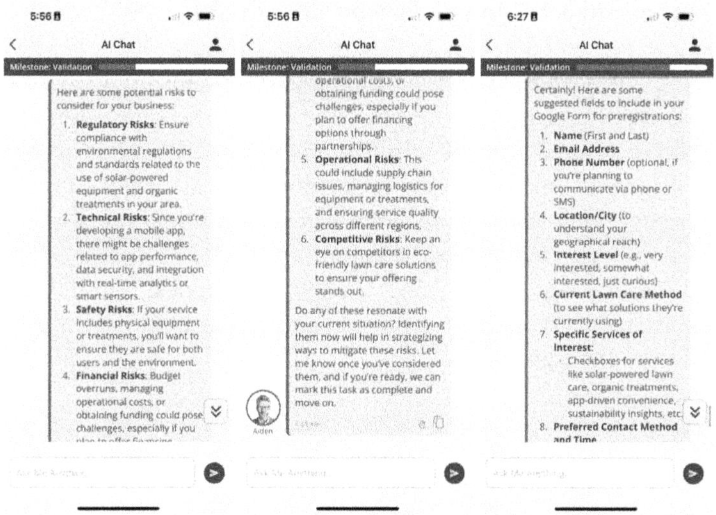

The final milestone in the AIAR app (as of this writing) is **the Minimum Viable Product or MVP**, which begins with the training video. The AI agents then assist the user in articulating the features and use cases of the product/service they are looking to build, offering recommendations on tools and options to find co-founders or resources. As always, mentors are available to answer any questions the user may have as they work to build their MVP. The app keeps them on task and helps them move forward with notifications and reminders. See the following illustrations.

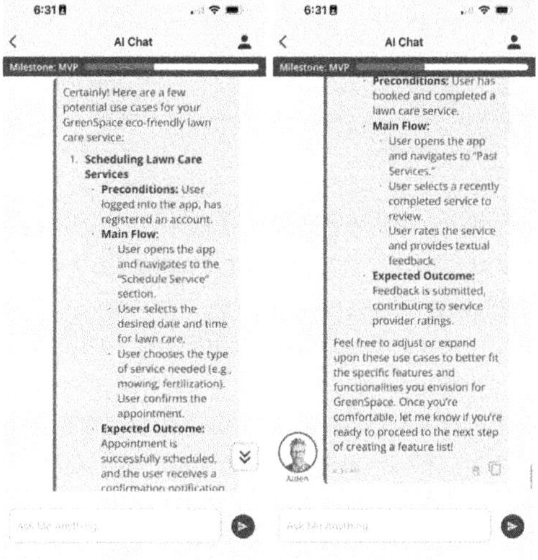

A user can thus progress in a short time from idea to revenue. While the example presented here is of a lawn care business, there are no limits on the types of business ideas, or the industry domains covered. Ideas as diverse as SaaS and rocket engines have been tested, resulting in high-quality responses and guidance. In partnership with existing Entrepreneur Support Organizations, it is easy to envision a wide array of real-world resources becoming available to users such as funding sources, peers, first customers, subject matter experts, and more.

As the user progresses through the app milestones, it builds out their business model and customer segments and tracks their overall progress. See the following illustration.

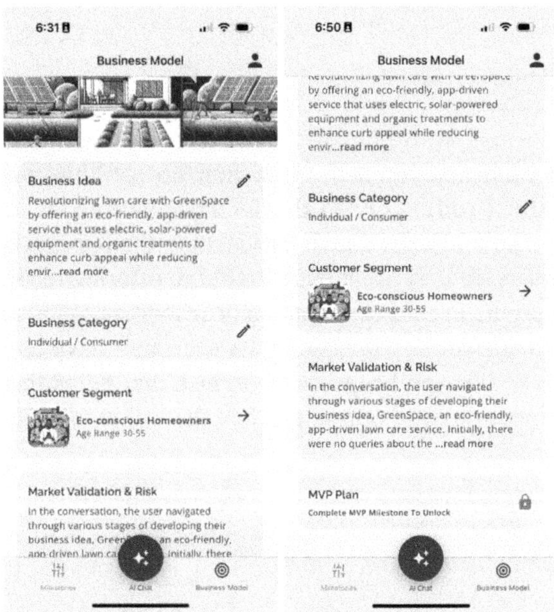

In this manner, the user is guided step by step through a predefined workflow designed to ensure success and minimize foreseeable risks, supported by an underlying knowledge base and innovative best practices. Thus, the AI agents propel the process forward while providing expertise in innovation methodology. Traditional accelerators advise members and teach concepts using online or live content. However, with a product such as AIAR, the value proposition can be richer and scalable. Content, best practices, and real-world actions are integrated to train users and assign them small, context-specific tasks. Objective-driven AI takes on one of the most challenging tasks—entrepreneurship—and presents it to first-time founders in a way that simplifies and potentially gamifies a highly complex workflow with significant uncertainty.

14. Under the Covers

For the tech-savvy reader, several architectural decisions and design features have been made to support the functionality described earlier. Highlights are provided in the following:

- **User experience simplification:** Chat serves as the main interaction, and being familiar with this interface reduces the cognitive load on the user.
- **Eliminate the blank-slate problem:** Apart from the Orientation module, most questions are accompanied by recommendations or ideas to unblock the user.
- **Retrieval-Augmented Generation (RAG):** It helps eliminate Gen AI "hallucinations" or poor responses by leveraging a custom knowledge base in vectorized format. By providing this knowledge base as input along with pre-crafted prompts, it maximizes the quality of responses.
- **Accountability through nudges:** The app monitors progress and sends personalized and contextual notifications based on the user's idea and progress.
- **On-the-fly lists and forms:** AI will generate editable forms, including recommendations for problem statements, solution ideas, and more.

Holistically, these features tackle the challenge of educating, encouraging, and guiding first-time founders through the most uncertain of journeys—entrepreneurship.

15. The Roadmap

While this lays the groundwork for an entrepreneur to start their journey on a solid foundation, future possibilities are limited only by the imagination:

1. **MVP generator:** Direct integration with AI-driven tools to build working software.
2. **AI-simulated training:** Used for real-world scenarios, such as customer discovery, sales, pitch presentations, interviewing, and negotiating.

3. **Agent-driven automation of admin tasks:** Accounting, legal, compliance, etc.
4. **Chatbot generator:** Create a chatbot for the idea that leverages internal or external knowledge base or provides online sales assistance.
5. **Multimodal interaction:** Voice, text, or video.
6. **Gamification:** Incentive-based tracking of actions using points and rewards.
7. **Peer collaboration:** A social network for entrepreneurs with AI-guided networking.
8. **Meeting support:** The app could join meetings to play different roles such as strategy, sales support, AI CTO, or co-founder while being contextually aware.
9. **Predictive modeling:** Analyze user progress and predict success probabilities based on market conditions, idea feasibility, and customer feedback.
10. **Resource finder:** Match users with potential co-founders, freelancers, advisors, or investors based on their needs and progress stage.

16. The Future of AI and Entrepreneurship

We have already imagined how Jill and entrepreneurs like her could leverage today's AI technologies to achieve five to ten times more than previously possible. But this is just the beginning. Much like it was impossible to predict Blockchain in 1995, we cannot fully envision the future evolutions and convergences of AI with other technologies. The possibilities, however, are vast.

17. Conclusion: The Dawn of AI-Enabled Entrepreneurship

Entrepreneurship has driven transformative change over the past century and is poised for an even greater revolution. As discussed in this chapter, it is both the engine of global progress and one of the most challenging professions, marked by high risk and high reward. Paired with AI's disruptive potential, this field is poised for unparalleled growth and impact.

Here are the main points from this chapter:

1. **A Golden Opportunity:** AI presents a once-in-a-generation "gold rush" for entrepreneurs. By lowering barriers to entry and minimizing friction, AI makes entrepreneurship more accessible than ever.

2. **Superpowers for Founders:** Agentic and workflow-based architectures enable entrepreneurs to accomplish significantly more with fewer resources, streamlining tasks and optimizing results.
3. **Room for Innovation:** Although core Large Language Models (LLMs) might consolidate into a few dominant players, the applications of these models will need customized, user-oriented solutions—creating endless opportunities for entrepreneurs to develop "last mile" tools that meet specific needs.
4. **The App Store Parallel:** Just as the mobile app boom took advantage of large hardware install bases, a similar surge is occurring with AI-powered applications. Entrepreneurs can leverage the backend capabilities of LLMs to provide diverse, high-impact solutions for end users.

18. The Age of AI-Driven Entrepreneurship

Several socio-economic and tech trends are accelerating, such as skyrocketing college costs, diminishing returns on traditional white-collar jobs, and the commoditization of skills by AI. At the same time, barriers to entrepreneurship continue to fall, and with AI rising to support entrepreneurs, many will see this as a practical career choice.

If those trend lines hold true, it is possible to envision a future where 30% or even 50% of the population is entrepreneurial—compared to the current 16%. This democratization of entrepreneurship has the potential to drive unprecedented prosperity and innovation. To compare and contrast this with our previous metaphor: entrepreneurs contributed to the literal Gold Rushes of the 19th century, but their reward was confined to financial success. In the "AI Gold Rush," however, there is the promise of a chain reaction where AI can help cultivate better entrepreneurs with greater capabilities and reduced risks, while entrepreneurs themselves push the boundaries of AI technology and adoption. With the added catalyst of massive amounts of liquidity, there is no telling how quickly and how far this self-propelling feedback loop could extend.

We'll conclude this chapter by embracing uncertainty—both the promising and the intimidating aspects that come with it. Consider the possibility that we may witness, in our lifetimes, the emergence of the world's first self-made trillionaire—leading an AI-first enterprise entirely devoid of employees. While this may seem speculative, it represents an increasingly plausible extrapolation of the unprecedented advancements we have seen and, perhaps, a glimpse into a future where AI is truly ubiquitous.

References

2.7K+ Accelerators & Incubators in United States - Tracxn. (2024, January 1). Tracxn.com. Retrieved from https://tracxn.com/d/investor-lists/accelerators-incubators-in-united-states/__ipYdkLo_FgbzV1gMFal2rWv-EyhedJX0mEbP-IXdRgs

Bhattarai, A. (2023, September 14). American entrepreneurship is on the rise. *Washington Post*. Retrieved from https://www.washingtonpost.com/business/2023/09/14/small-business-entrepreneurship-gem-report/

Blakely, R., and Sellman, M. (2024, October 11). Robots are coming for our jobs. Will we welcome them? Thetimes.com. Retrieved from https://www.thetimes.com/uk/technology-uk/article/robots-are-coming-for-our-jobs-will-we-welcome-them-h0vq6bz2m

Bloomberg. (2024, November). Tech giants are set to spend $200 billion this year chasing AI. *The Economic Times*. Retrieved from https://economictimes.indiatimes.com/news/international/business/tech-giants-are-set-to-spend-200-billion-this-year-chasing-ai/articleshow/114860492.cms

Blum, S. (2023, July 18). Startup Failures Have Doubled Over the Past 12 Months. There Are Ways to Ensure Yours Won't Suffer the Same Fate. *Inc.* Retrieved from https://www.inc.com/sam-blum/startup-failures-have-doubled-there-are-ways-to-ensure-yours-wont-suffer-the-same-fate.html

Butz, H., and Mrożewski, M. J. (2021). The Selection Process and Criteria of Impact Accelerators. An Exploratory Study. *Sustainability*, Vol. 13(12), 6617. Retrieved from https://doi.org/10.3390/su13126617

Christensen, C. M., Raynor, M. E., and McDonald, R. (2015). What is disruptive innovation? *Harvard Business Review*, Vol. 93(12), 44–53.

Cohen, S., Hallen, B., and Bingham, C. (2024, March 12). What Sets Successful Startup Accelerators Apart. *Harvard Business Review*. Retrieved from https://hbr.org/2024/03/what-sets-successful-startup-accelerators-apart

Entrepreneur. (2016). Entrepreneurs should watch out for cognitive biases and the errors they bring. Retrieved from https://www.entrepreneur.com/growing-a-business/entrepreneurs-should-watch-out-for-cognitive-biases-and-the/252499

Frequently Asked Questions about Small Businesses. (2021). *U.S. Small Business Administration Office of Advocacy*. Retrieved from https://advocacy.sba.gov/wp-content/uploads/2021/12/Small-Business-FAQ-Revised-December-2021.pdf

Future of Jobs Report 2023: Up to a Quarter of Jobs Expected to Change in Next Five Years. (2023, April 30). *World Economic Forum*. Retrieved from https://www.weforum.org/press/2023/04/future-of-jobs-report-2023-up-to-a-quarter-of-jobs-expected-to-change-in-next-five-years/

GEM Global Entrepreneurship Monitor. (2024). GEM Global Entrepreneurship Monitor. Global Report: 25 Years and Growing. *London: GEM.* Retrieved from https://www.gemconsortium.org/report/global-entrepreneurship-monitor-gem-20232024-global-report-25-years-and-growing

Glasner, J. (2024, September 4). AI Gobbled A Record Share Of Startup Funding This Year. *Crunchbase News*. Retrieved from https://news.crunchbase.com/ai/record-share-startup-funding-2024-xai-anthropic/

Google DeepMind. (2024). Gemini 2.0: Advanced AI for multimodal applications [Large language model]. Retrieved from https://gemini.google.com/app

Google. (2024). Gemini. *Gemini.google.com*. https://gemini.google.com/app

Hu, K. (2023, February 2). ChatGPT sets record for fastest-growing user base. *Reuters*. Retrieved from https://www.reuters.com/technology/chatgpt-sets-record-fastest-growing-user-base-analyst-note-2023-02-01/

Johnson, S. (1998). Who moved my cheese? An amazing way to deal with change in your work and in your life. *G.P. Putnam's Sons*.

Kruger, J., and Dunning, D. (1999). Unskilled and unaware of it: How difficulties in recognizing one's own incompetence lead to inflated self-assessments. *Journal of Personality and Social Psychology*, Vol. 77(6), 1121 1134. Retrieved from https://doi.org/10.1037/0022-3514.77.6.1121

Kurzweil, R. (2005). The singularity is near: When humans transcend biology. *Viking Press*.

Lynch, S. (2024, April 15). AI Index: State of AI in 13 Charts. Hai.stanford.edu. Retrieved from https://hai.stanford.edu/news/ai-index-state-ai-13-charts

OECD.AI. (2021). A sharp increase in AI-related venture capitalist investments could transform global economies and shape the future of artificial intelligence (2012-2020). Retrieved from https://oecd.ai/en/vc

OpenAI. (2024). ChatGPT. *Chat.openai.com*. Retrieved from https://chat.openai.com/chat

Ries, E. (2011). The lean startup: How today's entrepreneurs use continuous innovation to create radically successful businesses. *Crown Business*.

Small Business Facts: Small Business Job Creation. (2022, April 26). *SBA's Office of Advocacy*. Retrieved from https://advocacy.sba.gov/2022/04/26/small-business-facts-small-business-job-creation/

Startup Genome (2023). What Makes a Startup Succeed? Identifying Scaling Success Factors. *Startup Genome*. Retrieved from https://startupgenome.com/article/what-makes-a-startup-succeed-identifying-scaling-success-factors

Startup Genome. (2022). The State of the Global Startup Economy. *Startup Genome*. Retrieved from https://startupgenome.com/article/the-state-of-the-global-startup-economy

Taleb, N. N. (2012). Antifragile: Things that gain from disorder. *Random House.*

The SBA's Small Business Development Centers Program (2023, May). *Congressional Research Service*. Retrieved from https://crsreports.congress.gov/product/pdf/IF/IF12402

Tracxn. (2023, August 2). Artificial Intelligence. *Tracxn.com*. Retrieved from https://tracxn.com/d/sectors/artificial-intelligence/__cbMnXfS2GfFo-4Vi2dxZyUy7l4O8WyzVYLseb9keW5cI/companies

U.S. Chamber of Commerce. (2023, April 10). The State of Small Business in America. *Www.uschamber.com*. Retrieved from https://www.uschamber.com/small-business/state-of-small-business-now

https://doi.org/10.1142/9789819816347_0004

Chapter 4

AI Unlocked: Proven Frameworks for Implementation Success

Isar Meitis

Multiplai, USA

1. Introduction

Artificial Intelligence (AI) is no longer a futuristic concept; it's a transformative force reshaping industries across the globe. For business leaders, the question is no longer "if" but "how" to integrate AI effectively. This chapter provides a comprehensive guide to demystify AI implementation and outlines actionable steps to ensure success. By leveraging AI strategically, businesses can drive innovation, optimize operations, and create unparalleled value.

AI's integration into business requires not only understanding its capabilities but also a paradigm shift in how processes are viewed and executed. This chapter explores proven strategies and frameworks that can help businesses unlock the potential of AI, ensuring both immediate gains and long-term adaptability.

2. The Five Laws for Success in the AI Era

2.1. *Stop thinking efficiency; Start thinking outcome*

Traditional business practices often focus on optimizing each step of a process. However, AI enables businesses to leapfrog these incremental improvements and achieve transformative outcomes. For example, companies such as Klarna use AI to replace entire customer service processes, drastically reducing resolution times and enhancing customer satisfaction.

Focusing on outcomes requires a mental shift. Instead of asking how each step in a workflow can be improved, leaders must ask what the end goal is and how AI can directly achieve it.

Let's use customer service as an example. Traditionally, customer service processes involve multiple steps, including the following:

- **Customer Intake:** Collecting inquiries through phone calls, emails, or ticketing systems, often requiring customers to navigate complex menus or fill out forms.
- **Categorization:** Filtering and categorizing issues into topics such as technical support, billing, or general inquiries.
- **Assignment:** Routing inquiries to the appropriate team or individual based on expertise and availability.
- **Analysis:** Investigating the problem, gathering necessary details, and diagnosing the issue.
- **Resolution:** Providing solutions, answers, or fixes to the customer, sometimes requiring multiple follow-ups.
- **Feedback and Closure:** Documenting the resolution, gathering customer feedback, and officially closing the case.

Each of these steps is traditionally handled by separate systems or staff, making the process lengthy and prone to delays. AI-driven customer service tools such as advanced chatbots and natural language processing platforms revolutionize this by bypassing many of these steps. They seamlessly handle inquiries, categorize issues, and even provide resolutions autonomously. These systems adapt and improve with each interaction, enhancing their accuracy and efficiency. These systems operate 24/7, 365 days a year, providing uninterrupted support without the limitations of human staff. They never get sick, never experience frustration or fatigue, and don't require shift changes due to personal emergencies, such as when a child is unwell at home. Additionally, these AI-driven systems can seamlessly integrate with company platforms such as billing systems, customer relationship management (CRM) tools, and enterprise resource planning (ERP) software. This connectivity ensures that customer interactions are informed by real-time data, enabling accurate, personalized, and efficient responses. These systems also scale effortlessly to handle surges in customer queries during peak times, offering a level of reliability and adaptability that traditional methods cannot match.

For example, Klarna's AI-powered support eliminated the need for multi-step processes, reducing resolution times significantly while managing millions of inquiries with minimal human intervention. These systems not only handle customer inquiries faster but also learn and adapt from each interaction, improving their accuracy and efficiency over time.

This shift transforms the entire paradigm of customer service by eliminating redundant steps and focusing solely on delivering the desired outcome—improved customer satisfaction. An excellent example is Klarna's AI-powered customer support, which replaced the need for traditional multi-step processes. Within the first month of implementation, Klarna's AI handled 2.3 million conversations, accounting for two-thirds of all customer service chats. This achievement equated to the workload of 700 full-time agents, reducing average resolution times from 11 minutes to under 2 minutes. Additionally, the AI assistant achieved comparable customer satisfaction scores to human agents while reducing repeat inquiries by 25%. These impressive results underscore the transformative potential of AI in not just improving efficiency but redefining the scope and scale of customer service entirely. The emphasis here is not on marginally enhancing existing workflows but on rethinking the fundamental approach to achieve transformative results.

2.2. *From profession to skills*

AI is transforming professions into skills. Historically, many roles that once required specialized expertise have evolved into widely accessible skills due to technological advancements. For instance, in the 17th and 18th centuries, "computer" was a job title for individuals skilled in mathematical calculations. Similarly, the profession of typist emerged in the 20th century, as few people knew how to type efficiently. Over time, as calculators, typewriters, and later computers became commonplace, these roles transformed into skills that virtually everyone could learn and apply.

Today, AI is driving a similar shift on an even larger scale. Tasks that once demanded extensive training, such as graphic design, coding, and even legal research, are increasingly becoming skills accessible to anyone willing to leverage AI tools. This democratization of expertise not only expands opportunities but also challenges traditional notions of work and specialization. Tasks that once required specialized expertise, such as graphic design or coding, can now be executed by leveraging AI tools.

This shift necessitates a fundamental rethinking of HR strategies. Companies must focus on identifying the specific AI skills required for each role and integrating them into job descriptions. This ensures that new hires or reskilled employees align with the evolving demands of the workplace. For instance, leveraging tools such as Canva combined with AI capabilities can reduce the need for external graphic designers, enabling tasks to be completed faster and more cost-efficiently. Businesses should evaluate whether to reskill existing employees or hire new talent to bridge identified skills gaps. Providing targeted training programs, fostering hands-on experience with AI tools, and embedding AI proficiencies into ongoing professional development plans are critical. These steps not only democratize expertise but also enable smaller businesses to compete effectively by reducing reliance on costly external experts, creating a workforce equipped to fully harness AI's potential.

2.3. *Three ways to win: Better strategy, proprietary data, and optimization*

AI success hinges on three pillars:

- **Improved Business Strategy:** AI provides every decision-maker in the company with her or his advisory board. When provided with relevant information about the company, the market, competitors, industry, the person's role, etc., this advisory board allows any leader to brainstorm ideas quickly and effectively.

  It even allows us to evaluate business dilemmas through known frameworks such as EOS, category design, or concepts by Jim Collins (Good to Great).

  Using AI for brainstorming is a superpower. It fosters and accelerates innovation, through the generation of new ideas and approaches, while at the same time allowing us to make better decisions.
- **Proprietary Data:** Your company's unique data is an invaluable asset. Organize and structure this data to create competitive advantages. Proprietary data allows businesses to train AI models tailored to their needs, delivering customized solutions that competitors cannot replicate.

Contrary to popular belief, one does not need to be a tech giant such as Google or Amazon to have valuable proprietary data. Every company generates and possesses unique data, such as customer interactions, sales records, operational workflows, and product feedback. Emails, invoices, customer service transcripts, and even internal documents form a rich reservoir of proprietary information.

When organized and structured, this data can be leveraged to develop AI-driven insights and solutions that are specific to your business. Recognizing and utilizing this data is key to creating competitive advantages in the AI era. For instance, a lighting design company optimized its processes by leveraging its well-documented proprietary data to automate services, enabling them to deliver the same quality of work at half the time.

- **Optimization:** Use AI to streamline operations, increasing efficiency. Even modest improvements can significantly impact competitiveness and profitability.

Opportunities to utilize proprietary data and optimize processes exist in every department and every company, regardless of size or budget. These do not require significant investments but instead leverage resources already available within the organization. Examples include the following:

- **Sales and Marketing:** Analyze customer behavior data to personalize campaigns and improve lead generation.
- **Customer Service:** Use chat transcripts to train AI systems for faster, more accurate responses.
- **Operations:** Optimize inventory management by analyzing historical sales patterns.
- **Finance:** Automate expense tracking and reporting with AI-powered tools.
- **Human Resources:** Streamline recruitment by analyzing resumes and matching candidates to roles.
- Etc.

These examples demonstrate how every business can unlock value by identifying and applying AI to existing datasets and processes. By starting with these manageable initiatives, organizations can gain confidence and experience while achieving immediate benefits.

When these two elements are combined—leveraging unique data while optimizing processes—businesses gain a dual advantage that positions them for sustained success in a competitive marketplace.

2.4. *Continuously improving compromise*

AI systems are imperfect but rapidly improving. Adopting AI now allows businesses to benefit from incremental gains and build organizational "muscle" for when systems become more advanced. On the other hand, waiting for an issue-free AI solution, risks falling behind and facing a steeper learning curve later.

Leaders must embrace AI's current limitations while recognizing its potential. By starting early, businesses can refine their strategies and workflows, ensuring they are prepared for more advanced capabilities as AI evolves. Incremental improvements in areas such as task automation, customer interaction, and predictive analytics provide immediate value and lay the groundwork for future success.

2.5. *Infinite scalability*

While infinite scalability is unattainable, AI can dramatically increase your operational capacity. By identifying and addressing bottlenecks with AI tools, businesses can achieve exponential growth in marketing, sales, fulfillment, and customer service, maximizing throughput without proportionally increasing resources.

For example, AI-driven marketing tools can personalize campaigns at scale, reaching a larger audience with tailored messaging. This increase in lead generation creates a new challenge: ensuring the sales team can handle the higher volume of leads effectively. AI solutions such as automated lead nurturing and qualification tools can address this bottleneck by scoring and categorizing leads, enabling sales teams to prioritize their efforts on high-potential prospects and close deals faster. It can also assist in writing more and better proposals.

Once sales processes are optimized, the business may encounter a surge in customer onboarding and support needs. Here, AI-driven customer service tools, such as chatbots and voice agents, can manage these increased demands by handling routine inquiries and providing instant support 24/7 and in any language. Chatbots integrated with CRM and ERP systems ensure customer interactions are informed by real-time data, offering seamless support.

The cycle continues into operations, where AI can streamline supply chain logistics or automate various aspects of order fulfillment. AI-powered inventory management tools can predict stock levels based on demand patterns, reducing delays and overstock situations. Similarly, AI-driven hiring systems can help scale and train the workforce efficiently to manage the increased load by automating job description creation, candidate screening, and interview processes.

This interconnected approach demonstrates how addressing one bottleneck, such as marketing, often creates new challenges in sales, customer service, and operations. However, AI offers solutions at every stage, allowing businesses to scale their processes holistically and maintain growth without sacrificing efficiency.

3. Roadmap for Successful AI Implementation

AI is evolving at an unprecedented pace, transforming the way businesses operate and compete. While in the first part of this chapter we focused on mindsets and concepts, in the second half of the chapter, we provide you the blueprint for AI implementation success. The steps outlined here are drawn from extensive experience in helping hundreds of businesses implement AI effectively through courses and consulting engagements. These proven strategies are designed to address real-world challenges and ensure success in navigating the complexities of AI adoption.

Step 1: Continuous Education

AI evolves rapidly. Ensure leadership and staff stay informed through ongoing education. Encourage following thought leaders, participating in courses, and attending workshops. Divide responsibilities so different team members track various aspects of AI developments, ensuring a well-rounded understanding across the organization.

Education should extend beyond the initial stages of AI adoption. Regularly scheduled training sessions and knowledge-sharing initiatives can keep the organization aligned with emerging trends. Encourage employees to experiment with AI tools and share their findings, fostering a culture of learning and innovation.

It is also essential to follow the right people in the AI field to stay updated. Look for thought leaders and practitioners across various platforms, such as LinkedIn, X (formerly Twitter), TikTok, or specialized podcasts. Follow individuals who provide the following:

- **News and Updates:** Experts who share the latest AI advancements and tools.
- **Visionary Insights:** Leaders who discuss the future implications of AI and provoke strategic thinking.
- **Practical Applications:** Practitioners who demonstrate hands-on examples of AI in action, offering step-by-step guidance.

By curating a diverse mix of these voices, organizations can ensure their teams remain informed and inspired, ready to leverage AI effectively.

Step 2: Form an AI Committee

3.1. *Forming an AI committee*

To ensure a successful AI implementation, businesses need a dedicated group to oversee and guide their AI initiatives. An AI committee not only centralizes decision-making but also ensures alignment across departments, helping organizations achieve a cohesive and effective strategy.

3.2. *Who needs to be in the committee and why*

- **Representatives from all Departments:** Include members from each department (marketing, finance, sales, operations, HR, etc.) to ensure diverse perspectives and tailored AI solutions. People from different departments are required for several reasons:
  - They provide inputs for different needs in the organization.
  - They represent different opinions that make the brainstorming sessions more productive.
  - They would be the AI champions in each department.
- **Volunteers with Enthusiasm for AI:** Choose individuals who are passionate about exploring AI and willing to invest time in learning and experimenting. The "geeks" of the company will spend their personal time exploring tools and use cases because they find it to be fun, and the entire company will benefit from it.
- **Senior Leadership Member/s:** Ensure alignment with overall business goals and facilitate swift decision-making. The goal is to move

fast. When the committee makes a decision they should be able to execute it without waiting for additional approval.
- **IT and Data Security Specialists:** Provide technical expertise, ensure proper integration of AI systems, and provide data security guidance.

3.3. *Roles of the committee*

- **Define AI Policies and Ethical Guidelines:** Establish boundaries and best practices to ensure responsible AI use. These guidelines should define the do's and don'ts from data security, brand and reputation management, and ethical considerations that should align with the company's core values and culture.
- **Stay Updated on AI Developments:** Monitor emerging tools, trends, and advancements in AI, distill the information, and share it with the entire company in easy-to-digest ways. You can use AI tools such as NotebookLM from Google to help you with summarizing the information in various formats, including a short podcast.

  The committee is in charge of continuous education and needs to find ways to make it relevant and engaging.
- **Evaluate and Select AI Tools:** Conduct due diligence on potential solutions to identify the best fit for business needs. Tools recommendations can come from anyone in the company.

  The committee (or a sub-committee) will evaluate the tool/s for specific use cases, and if they find it effective and safe, they need to develop the process to maximize the tool/s benefit for a defined use case. Once the process and the tools are defined, the committee needs to deliver training to the relevant people in the company.
- **Oversee Training and Adoption:** Facilitate company-wide education and encourage AI experimentation within defined parameters. This is an evergreen effort—by completing the three tasks above, the committee should always have fresh and relevant training for the entire company, or specific groups.
- **Maintain a Centralized Prompt Library:** Standardize and manage AI prompts to ensure consistency and efficiency. Break it down by department and use cases, and make it easily searchable for anyone.

  The goals are Speed, getting it right the first time, and Consistency, since everyone will use the same prompts and the same tools.
- **Data security and data preparation:** Data, more specifically proprietary data, is the jet fuel of AI success. The committee plays two roles

in relation to company data. On one hand, the committee needs to make sure that the right data, in the right format, is available to the relevant AI solutions. On the other hand, they need to establish the right processes, IT solutions, and tools to protect the company's sensitive data.

- **Support Cross-Functional Collaboration:** Act as a bridge between departments to identify synergies and shared opportunities for AI implementation.

3.4. *Committee resources*

For the AI committee to operate effectively and drive meaningful impact, it must be equipped with the right resources. These include the following:

- **Budget Allocation:** Ensure there is adequate funding for purchasing tools, building infrastructure, and supporting experimentation. This includes subscriptions to AI tools, data storage, external consultants and trainers, computational resources, etc.
- **Dedicated Time:** Allocate specific time blocks in committee members' calendars to focus on committee activities. This ensures that committee members can actively participate without compromising their primary responsibilities.
- **IT Infrastructure:** Provide necessary technical support, including the following:
    - Compute resources for running AI models and training algorithms.
    - Robust security measures to protect sensitive data during AI experimentation.
    - A sandbox environment for safe testing and prototyping of AI use cases.
    - Installation and access control for both humans and data for various AI tools.

The AI committee acts as the central hub for AI strategy and implementation. By bringing together diverse expertise, the committee ensures that AI adoption is holistic and addresses the unique needs of each department. This collaborative approach also helps in identifying potential synergies between departments, enhancing overall efficiency.

Step 3: Conduct Assessments

1. **Strategic Assessment:** Identify how AI will change customer needs and industry dynamics. Analyze potential risks and opportunities.
   - **Assess Impact on Existing Products and Services:** Evaluate which current offerings may become less appealing or obsolete due to AI advancements. For example, services such as basic copywriting or graphic design may face declining demand as AI tools become more accessible and efficient. Maybe it will not impact your entire business, but it may still have a significant impact on your revenue and profitability. As an example, paralegal hours would most likely be reduced. If you are a law firm and paralegal hours generate 30% of your revenue, you need to start planning for a significant reduction of that part of your revenue. Similar examples exist in many businesses.
   - **Explore New Opportunities for Current Clients:** Identify innovative products or services that can now be offered to existing customers because AI makes them cost-effective. This may take different forms in different companies, but this might include advanced analytics, personalized recommendations, enhanced customer engagement, custom-tailored services or SaaS products, etc.
   - **Identify New Client Segments:** Determine potential markets or niches that can be served with the assistance of AI capabilities, that you couldn't profitably serve before. This could involve developing new solutions tailored to industries or customer groups that were previously out of reach due to high costs or technological barriers.
2. **Skills Gap Analysis:** The rapid pace of AI advancements has widened the gap between the current capabilities of most teams and the skills required to fully leverage AI's benefits. Addressing this gap involves a collaborative effort between HR and the AI committee to map these discrepancies and develop a clear strategy to bridge them.
   - **Map Existing Skills vs. Required Skills:** Identify the AI-specific skills your organization needs but currently lacks. For example, proficiency in using generative AI tools, data analysis, or creating AI workflows.
   - **Options for Closing the Gap:**
     - **Training Existing Employees:** Invest in reskilling programs to equip your current workforce with essential AI knowledge and tools. This approach retains institutional knowledge and strengthens organizational loyalty.

  - **Hiring New Talent:** Bring in specialized talent with pre-existing AI expertise to fill critical gaps quickly. This can be through hiring employees or through relationships with consultants and fractional team members.
  - **A Mix of Both:** Combine training and hiring strategies to balance the benefits of retaining experienced employees while introducing fresh perspectives.
- **Optimize Workforce Structure:** Re-evaluate roles and responsibilities in light of AI capabilities. This may involve letting go of redundant roles but could also mean retaining employees and using AI to enhance their productivity. For instance, retaining skilled workers while scaling up growth can outpace cost savings achieved by downsizing, leading to a stronger long-term position.
- **Plan for Industry-Specific Realities:** Certain industries may face more abrupt transitions, leading to sharper impacts on workforce needs. The sooner these challenges are addressed, the more profit margins and operational stability can be preserved.

3. **Low-Hanging Fruit:** Identify quick wins with high ROI, such as automating repetitive tasks or enhancing internal processes. Here are some guidelines on how to identify tasks that are well positioned to benefit from AI:
   - **Focus on Low-Risk Tasks:** Start with areas that are not consumer-facing or do not involve sensitive data or strategic decisions. These provide a safe environment for testing and implementation without major repercussions.
   - **Prioritize High Value:** Look for tasks that directly impact the bottom line by increasing revenue, reducing costs, or removing tedious work that improves employee satisfaction. Examples include automating reporting, streamlining internal communication, or reducing repetitive manual inputs.
   - **Repetitive Processes:** The more repetitive a task, the greater the benefit from automation. For example, categorizing customer reviews, archiving files, or generating routine performance reports are ideal for AI-driven automation.
   - **Leverage Data Analysis:** Identify tasks involving data synthesis or prediction, as AI excels in analyzing patterns and providing actionable insights. Examples include forecasting sales trends or identifying customer churn risks.

- **Tasks That Require Some Human Input:** Focus on tasks that require human judgment or oversight, as these are where AI truly shines compared to traditional automation or RPA (Robotic Process Automation). For example:
    - **Tasks Needing Contextual Understanding:** Use AI to assist with writing SEO content, summarizing documents, or categorizing customer reviews, where human insight ensures accuracy and relevance.
    - **Processes Involving Nuance:** AI can draft responses to complex customer queries or prepare proposals.
    - **Iterative Decision-Making and Brainstorming Tasks:** Leverage AI tools for recommendations or analysis in areas like prioritizing leads or suggesting improvements, while final decisions remain with a person.

By addressing these criteria and focusing on tasks that meet two or more of them, organizations can identify and implement impactful AI solutions that drive efficiency and effectiveness from day one.

One should start a shared document using the recommendations above as the initial outline of one's review. Hold brainstorming sessions with relevant people from different departments, and continue to refine the document until you feel it is mature enough to start execution.

Remember, it does not need to be perfect, it needs to be good enough and fast.

Assessments should be revisited periodically to ensure alignment with evolving business goals, market conditions, and advancement in AI. By continually refining these analyses, businesses can adapt their AI strategies to maximize value.

Step 4: Develop a Plan

Developing a comprehensive AI implementation plan is essential after completing the assessments. This plan should account for tools, processes, training, and measurable outcomes to ensure successful implementation. The key elements include the following:

- **Selecting AI Tools Based on Defined Needs:** Identify tools that address your specific use cases but avoid locking into long-term subscriptions as the landscape evolves rapidly. Instead, prioritize flexibility to adopt newer, better tools as they emerge. Ensure employees

understand how these tools work so transitioning to new ones is seamless.
  - Example: Choose tools for current needs such as automating customer queries but remain adaptable to replace them if better options arise.
- **Establishing Processes for Effective Tool Usage:** Frameworks and processes should accompany tools to maximize their impact. A common mistake is to provide all employees with access to specific AI tools such as Microsoft Co-Pilot or ChatGPT but without defining clear use cases and without proper training. This rarely leads to a positive ROI.

  Define how each tool fits into existing or new workflows and train teams on these processes. This ensures consistent and scalable use across the organization:
  - Example: Develop standardized workflows for using AI in generating marketing content, analyzing customer feedback, defining new product requirements, or writing code.
- **Training and Hiring to Address Skills Gaps:** Determine the balance between training existing employees and hiring new talent. Continuous education programs ensure teams stay proficient while hiring AI-savvy individuals can accelerate adoption:
  - Example: Train marketing teams on generative AI tools while hiring data analysts familiar with predictive modeling.
- **Defining Leading and Lagging KPIs (Key Performance Indicators):** Establish clear metrics to measure AI's effectiveness. Leading indicators, the number of implemented use cases or tools evaluated, track progress in the short term. Lagging KPIs, such as increased revenue or reduced costs, measure long-term outcomes:
  - Example: Track whether the AI committee meets weekly and defines five use cases per quarter as leading indicators. Monitor the cost savings or time efficiencies achieved as lagging indicators.

A well-crafted plan provides clarity and reduces the risk of missteps during implementation. It serves as a reference point for evaluating progress, making adjustments, and aligning efforts with business objectives.

Step 5: Encourage AI Usage

AI implementation is first and foremost a change management process. And like every change management process it lives and dies by the people who are on board or not. This means that as a business leader you need to create excitement around the opportunities that AI presents for every employee.

You can encourage AI usage and promote adoption by doing the following:

- Leading by example—showcase leadership's use of AI.
- Talk about it—have an AI item in every all-hands and every weekly team meeting.
- Celebrating successes—highlight team and individual achievements with AI.
- Building a culture of experimentation within clearly defined guidelines. Showcase what people are working on. Share it even if it doesn't work yet. Share the lessons learned and the next steps.
- Incorporate gamification elements to encourage AI experimentation and reward employees who excel in AI adoption. Recognize achievements through incentives, such as bonuses, public acknowledgment, and PTOs. This motivates employees to engage with AI tools enthusiastically and fosters a competitive yet collaborative environment.

Encouraging usage involves not only providing access to AI tools but also fostering an environment where experimentation and innovation are valued. Celebrate successes and provide constructive feedback on failures, creating a safe space for learning and growth. Depending on your industry and the level of sensitivity of your data, this may require creating a sandbox for experimentation as well as generating synthetic data for training and testing.

Step 6: Build and Manage a Prompt Library

Standardize and refine prompts to ensure consistency and efficiency in AI interactions. A centralized library saves time, improves results, and builds trust in AI's capabilities.

A well-maintained prompt library is a living resource that evolves with the organization's needs. Encourage employees to contribute to the library and share insights on what works best for specific tasks, fostering a collaborative approach to AI usage.

The AI committee is responsible for managing the centralized prompt library, ensuring it remains a living resource that evolves with the organization's needs. This includes testing prompt suggestions submitted by employees to validate their effectiveness, consistency, and alignment with organizational goals. By maintaining and refining this library, the committee enables employees to maximize AI's potential while ensuring high quality and consistency across all use cases.

Step 7: Prioritize Human Connections
Based on MIT research (https://mitsloan.mit.edu/sites/default/files/2023-10/SSRN-id4573321.pdf), AI helps lower performers more than it helps to performers. This means that the gap between people's ability to execute different tasks effectively is shrinking. And it will shrink further as AI tools get better. If one aggregates this to the company level, it means that the gap between great companies and mediocre companies will shrink.

As AI levels the playing field, human relationships become a key differentiator. Invest in building strong connections with clients, partners, and employees through events, personalized interactions, and thoughtful communication.

Strengthening human connections goes beyond traditional relationship-building activities. In other words, leverage AI to enhance personalization and responsiveness in interactions, ensuring that technology supports rather than replaces genuine human engagement.

4. Summary

Implementing AI successfully requires a clear strategy, organizational buy-in, and a willingness to adapt. This chapter outlined the Five Laws for Success in the AI Era and provided a step-by-step roadmap for implementation. Key takeaways include the following:

- Focus on outcomes, not processes.
- Shift from hiring for professions to training for skills.
- Leverage proprietary data and optimize operations.
- Adopt AI early and continuously improve.
- Scale by addressing bottlenecks systematically.
- Establish an AI committee that will drive AI innovation and implementation.
- Focus on employee training and specific use cases rather than on a specific technology or tool.

By following these principles and steps, business leaders can position their organizations to thrive in the AI era, unlocking unparalleled opportunities for growth and innovation. The journey to succcssful AI implementation is iterative, requiring ongoing evaluation and adaptation, but the rewards are well worth the effort. With the right mindset and approach, businesses can harness AI to achieve transformative success.

https://doi.org/10.1142/9789819816347_0005

Chapter 5

The AI Revolution in New Product Development

Robert G. Cooper

McMaster University Business School, Canada

1. Introduction

1.1. *AI's dramatic results*

Early adopters of AI for new product development (NPD) report dramatic performance results and are now accelerating their investment in AI (Cooper, 2024a,b; IBM, 2024). Companies such as Siemens, GE, Nestlé, and Pfizer have experienced reductions in development times of 50% or more, better optimization of product designs, and breakthrough discoveries (Cooper and McCausland, 2024). While businesses have adopted AI for productivity improvements and cost reductions, the top benefit realized is increased innovation (Jyoti and Kuppuswamy, 2023).

Despite the promise that AI offers, McKinsey reported that by early 2024, *only 23% of firms globally had adopted AI for NPD* (Singla *et al.*, 2024). A 2024 study by Cooper and Brem found that this adoption rate was 31% in Germany but only 18% in the US (Cooper and Brem, 2024a).

1.2. *AI for business defined*

Just what is AI when it comes to business? The question was put to artificial intelligence itself:

"AI refers to the simulation of human intelligence in machines programmed to think, reason, and perform tasks that typically require human intelligence. AI enables computers or machines to mimic cognitive functions such as learning, problem-solving and reasoning, perception, and decision-making. The goal of AI is to create systems that can perform tasks independently, adapt to new situations, and improve their performance over time without explicit programming.

AI can be implemented through various techniques and technologies, including machine learning (ML), natural language processing (NLP), computer vision, deep learning, robotics, and expert systems" (Cooper, 2024a; Brem *et al.*, 2023).

A simpler definition is that AI is simply a "prediction technology that reduces the cost of predictions" (Agrawal *et al.*, 2018). Where humans make predictions today—for example, market forecasting—AI makes them faster, better, and cheaper. For problems that do not involve prediction, AI will take the traditional problem, such as creating drawings for a new concept car, and turn it into a prediction challenge: AI will predict how a creative auto designer would draw the car, given specific instructions.

1.3. *AI's role in the NPD process*

AI silently assists at every stage of NPD. While autopilots and driver assistance systems are the most visible signs of AI in the auto sector, AI extends much further into the actual engineering design and development of the car, for example, facilitating concept car design and predicting consumer reactions (Cooper, 2024a,b). From ideation to market research and engineering design, AI streamlines the innovation process (McKinsey, 2024b; Mendes and Vitari, 2024).

A positioning map illustrating the multifaceted landscape of AI applications in NPD offers valuable insights into the diverse array of possibilities (Figure 1; Cooper, 2024a). This visual representation delineates the "where" and "how" dimensions, mapping out where AI interventions occur in the NPD process, from ideation to product launch. The vertical axis delineates the role of AI as either an *originator*, fueling creative and inventive processes, or a *facilitator*, enhancing the NPD process for

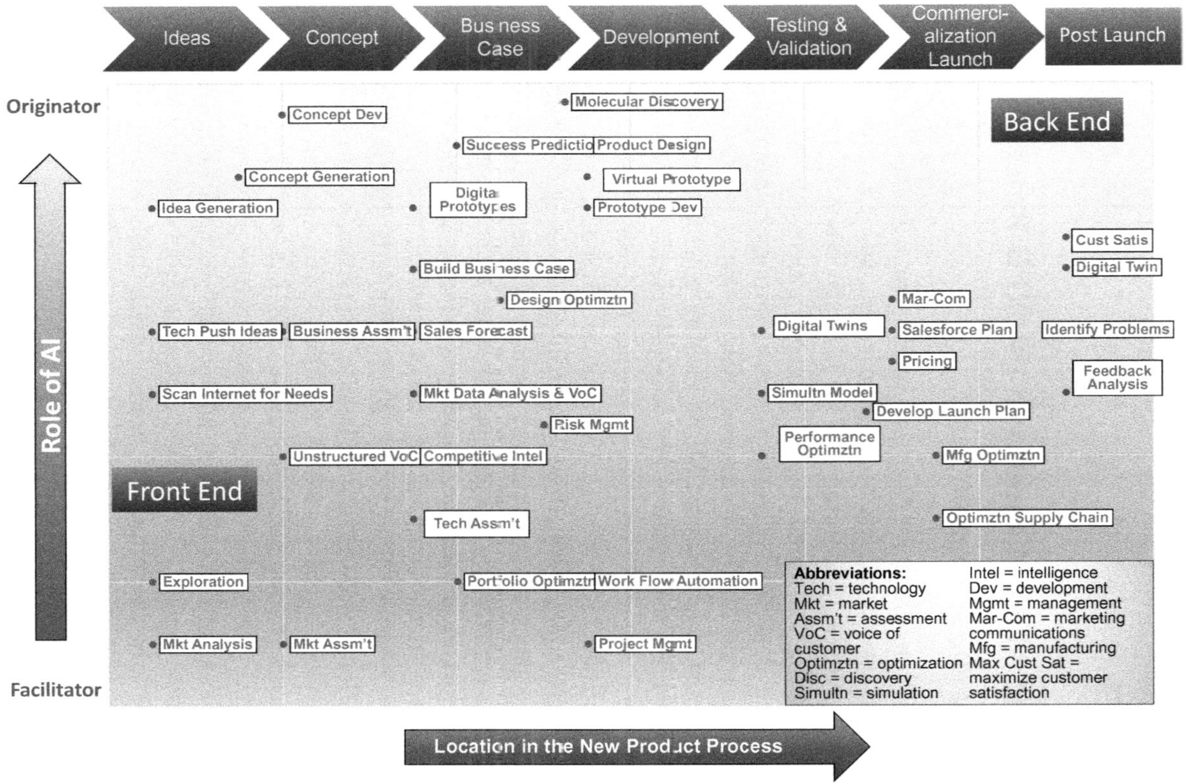

Figure 1. The AI-NPD model positions AI in NPD—where AI is used in the NPD process and the role of AI as a facilitator or originator.

heightened efficiency and efficacy. This conceptualization of AI's role draws from a framework proposed by Brem *et al.* (2023), providing a comprehensive understanding of AI's impact across the NPD continuum. The horizontal axis is based on a standard idea-to-launch NPP process model such as *Stage-Gate*.

2. Specific AI Applications in the NPD Process

2.1. *AI and idea generation*

NPD project teams are using AI to gain market and customer insights and enhance ideation and creativity (Marion *et al.*, 2024; Cooper, 2025a). Companies increasingly leverage AI for idea generation by tapping into machine learning (ML) and natural language processing (NLP). These tools analyze data from diverse sources—customer feedback, social media, and market trends—to uncover new customer needs and market gaps. For instance, LEGO uses ML to identify potential product growth areas by analyzing user interactions on social media, including likes on trending videos and clicks on popular memes (Cooper, 2024a).

Social media AI scanners such as YouScan, Brand24, and Birdeye are popular for extracting product-relevant insights, assessing customer sentiment, demographics, and competitors' activity (Capterra, 2024). By analyzing trends, preferences, and pain points, these tools help generate ideas for new products. For example, Unilever's skincare line was influenced by AI-powered trend identification, which revealed evolving customer needs and preferences (Dominguez, 2023). Similarly, Nestlé's "concept engine," developed with AI firm Ai Palette, uses scanning insights to propose new product concepts, which are then tested internally and with target consumers (Palzer, 2022; Ai Palette, 2023).

NLP further aids in analyzing open-ended text responses from various channels, such as product reviews, surveys, and social media. Platforms such as Upsiide employ NLP to extract insights from customer feedback and pinpoint key challenges or needs, which fuels idea generation. Similarly, Applied Marketing Science developed an AI tool to scan online user comments on forums and blogs to detect unmet needs (AMS, 2023). When applied to a US snowplow manufacturer, AMS's app analyzed thousands of comments to identify pain points, such as poor visibility while turning. This insight led to a product innovation that filled a market gap and achieved commercial success.

Given the right prompts, generative AI even *generates original new product ideas*. A study comparing the use of ChatGPT for ideation versus human ideation (brainstorming and TRIZ) showed promising results (Filippi, 2023). From a "novelty" perspective, ChatGPT performed quite well but proved less helpful in suggesting "useful concepts." Technology-driven opportunities can also be identified by AI. Nestlé, for example, uses data mining to leverage its extensive research archives for new discoveries, maximizing the value of past technical research (Palzer, 2022).

AI applications also include CRM data analysis (customer relationship management), where tools like Salesforce Einstein use sales and customer interaction data to identify trends and new product opportunities, such as identifying high-risk customers or spotting upselling prospects (Salesforce, 2023). This enables companies to anticipate and fulfill emerging needs within their market.

2.2. *AI's role in the concept stage*

In the concept stage, AI aids in defining product concepts, preliminary design, and early market assessments, which are crucial steps in the NPD front end (Figure 1; Cooper, 2024a; Cooper, 2025a):

Market assessment: AI analyzes market data to provide a comprehensive understanding of customer behavior, trends, and competitors. This allows teams to scope projects accurately by automating data collection and analyzing user stories or customer feedback from concept tests. Tools such as ChatGPT also assist in performing PESTEL analysis (examining political, economic, social, technological, environmental, and legal factors) to inform early planning (Bilgram & Laarmann, 2023).

Concept design: AI algorithms assist with product design by analyzing data to generate insights and support decision-making (Mailey, 2023). Gen AI accelerates concept development by transforming expert prompts into novel images. Designers can quickly visualize ideas by inputting sketches, research insights, and customer preferences, enabling faster iteration and more distinctive concepts (McKinsey, 2024b). Generative AI can create 3D renderings and adjust design parameters based on feedback. For example, Mattel uses OpenAI's DALL-E to develop Hot Wheels car designs, adjusting models with simple prompts such as "Make it a convertible." This functionality enables real-time visualization, facilitating quick iterations and enabling concept tests with stakeholders or customers (Roach, 2022).

Technical assessment: AI evaluates the technical feasibility of new product concepts by analyzing existing technologies, potential challenges, and the resources needed. This evaluation helps teams make informed decisions about moving forward with concepts based on their technical viability.

Financial and risk assessments: AI models can rapidly generate cost estimates, revenue projections, and profitability forecasts for early concept validation. By running risk assessments, AI identifies potential pitfalls, like market or technical risks, helping to guide concept selection.

Regulatory and legal: AI also assists teams by researching relevant regulations and patents associated with the product concept, ensuring compliance and minimizing potential legal issues.

2.3. *Building the business case*

As the concept matures, AI's role extends to building a more robust business case by providing in-depth market, financial, and competitive analyses (Cooper, 2024a; Cooper, 2025a):

Market analysis: AI is used to understand the size of the market, the competition, and target customer segments. AI tools analyze market data from sources such as online reviews, social media, and sales data to gain insights into the market (Columbus, 2020). Many software tools exist that seek market data and undertake market analysis: Examples include *Statista* (accesses reliable statistics), *Usetiful* (provides user feedback and product insights), *Brand24* (tracks mentions of products and competitors), *Radarly* (provides real-time insights into consumer preferences), *GWI* (*Global Web Index;* gives access to views, behaviors, and interests of consumers in 53 countries), and many more—see the works of Laurinavicius, 2024; Lasota and Sadowski, 2024; and Capterra, 2024. AI tools also make predictions: market, sales, pricing, and costs.

Voice-of-customer research (VoC): AI can accelerate VoC interviews. For example, the *AIM Blueprinter* can *identify the main user problems* in the target market *before the VoC interviews even start*, thus greatly reducing the number of interviews needed (Adams, 2023). AI also identifies key challenges that users face while using a product and can even generate a first draft of a customer interview guide (Bilgram and Laarmann, 2023).

Competitive intelligence: Tools such as *Crayon* use AI-powered algorithms to monitor competitors' activities: product launches, pricing changes, and marketing campaigns (Van Houtven, 2023). AI also provides real-time insights into competitors' strategies, market positioning, and customer targeting, thus helping project teams make informed decisions on product differentiation and market opportunities.

Technology assessment: AI software provides real-time insights into technology trends, investment activities, and technology disruptions (e.g., *CB Insights*). *ChatGPT* also answers questions on the fly and rapidly pulls together facts on a specific technical subject.

Financial analysis: AI-powered financial tools undertake financial analysis, forecasting, and optimization. Such AI models analyze historical data, project product revenue, and estimate profitability (Helrish, 2022). They also simulate various scenarios, helping the team assess how changes in factors such as pricing or competition might affect the product's success. By examining data patterns, AI offers more precise forecasts than traditional methods.

Creating the business case: AI solutions exist that *will even write the business case*, using prompts along the way (Upmetrics, 15MinutePlan, and My Business Case Hub) (Cooper, 2024b).

Risk assessment and management: One of the most developed applications of AI in business, risk assessment tools utilize big data and ML to identify potential risks, offering proactive mitigation strategies. Some tools are evolving to the point where they may eventually adjust project plans autonomously to avoid or reduce certain risks (Nieto-Rodriguez and Vargas, 2023; Cooper, 2025b).

2.4. *Decision to go to development*

The "Go to Development" decision is one of the most critical resource commitment points in the NPD process. This decision often involves evaluating extensive data to determine which projects have strong potential for market success, making AI an invaluable tool. By analyzing large volumes of data and detecting patterns that may go unnoticed by human evaluators, AI can assess which projects are development-ready, remove human biases, and predict potential product success or failure with more accuracy (Nieto-Rodriguez and Vargas, 2023). Through neural network analysis, AI-based decision models identify factors most likely to influence success, enabling project teams to make more informed choices.

While many organizations hesitate to entrust AI with final NPD investment decisions, AI-based project selection is gaining ground in fields such as finance. For example, Hong Kong-based venture capital firm Deep Knowledge Ventures employs an AI algorithm, "Vital," to make investment decisions, even crediting it with saving the firm from bankruptcy (Burridge, 2017). In the context of NPD, AI models can recommend decisions based on large, unbiased data sets, suggesting potential for future applications.

2.5. *AI in the development stage*

AI significantly impacts the development stage, enhancing four primary activities: product design, iterative testing, design optimization, and discovery of innovative products (Cooper, 2024a).

Product design: AI-driven design tools accelerate and streamline product design by automating tasks such as generating 3D models, creating technical drawings, and simulating design modifications (Nieto-Rodriguez and Vargas, 2023). Autodesk, for instance, enables companies to direct AI prompts to generate, test, and refine designs tailored to specific customer segments. AI simulations help run complex tests such as stress and thermal flow analyses, allowing for quick adjustments based on test results. In collaboration with General Motors, MIT researchers developed a generative AI model to create new car designs based on designer input, such as color, style, or body type. Using a predictive AI model, the designs were rated for consumer appeal, helping GM reduce costs by eliminating concepts unlikely to resonate with buyers before entering expensive physical testing.

Rapid, iterative product testing: AI-driven virtual prototypes make iterative testing faster and more cost-effective by reducing the need for physical models. Digital twins—virtual models of physical products—offer advanced testing capabilities by mirroring real-world performance. This type of digital twin, called the *product twin*, is a representation of a product that allows the designer to get *live, real-time data on a product as if it is in service* (McKinsey, 2024a).

Such digital twins allow for simulated testing, which can identify potential flaws or performance issues before the product is built. For example, Siemens' *Simcenter* (a specialized tool for in-depth simulation and testing) combines simulation data and physical test data to create a digital twin, a virtual representation of the physical product (Brandstetter, 2023); *Simcenter* allows engineers to model the exact physical behavior of products or processes, replacing physical prototypes and test beds with digital ones. The firm also created HiSimcenter using a GenAI-based interface to handle tasks from simple queries about selecting the right engineering tool to fully automated generative design, resulting in a more than 50% increase in modeling efficiency.

Similarly, GE's digital twin technology, which has generated over $1 billion in value, enables virtual testing of products such as turbines, medical devices, and automotive parts under simulated real-world conditions (GE, 2023b). GE has further applied AI in diesel engine development, using its DT4D (Digital Thread for Design) model to optimize piston designs. Through this model, GE evaluated nearly a million design variations in under 15 minutes—a task that previously required days with a team and a supercomputer. The optimal piston design achieved a 7% increase in fuel efficiency while reducing emissions, demonstrating AI's potential for rapid iterative testing and optimization (GE, 2023a).

In a different industry, biotech company Moderna uses AI to develop and test thousands of mRNA-based medicines and vaccines (Overby, 2023). Drug companies often spend a billion dollars per drug with a typical success rate of just 15%, but AI increases that success rate to 50% and accelerates the time to market. Moderna created a web-based drug-design application to streamline inputting information for synthetic mRNA molecules: These AI algorithms support molecular design by predicting the best code sequences to use. This AI approach enabled Moderna to develop a leading COVID-19 vaccine in record time (Euchner, 2023; Iansiti and Lakhani, 2020).

Design optimization: AI's ability to optimize structural and material design offers significant cost and time savings, particularly in industries such as automotive and aerospace. Generative AI can create optimized designs that meet stringent requirements for strength, weight, and durability while using minimal material. Across various applications, AI-driven generative design has reduced part weight by up to 50% and slashed development times by 30–50% (Brossard *et al.*, 2020). For example, a tool manufacturer leveraged AI to achieve up to a 38% reduction in weight and 15% in cost for forged steel components by optimizing its structure through AI-driven analysis.

Discovery of new products: AI accelerates product discovery, particularly in pharmaceutical and biotech sectors, by screening millions of compounds to identify promising candidates for drug development (Satoh *et al.*, 2024). Major firms such as Pfizer and Lilly partner with AI firms such as Atomwise, whose ML discovery engine scans massive chemical libraries to find active compounds likely to treat specific diseases (Atomwise, 2022).

Formulating new or improved chemical, polymer, food and beverage, and materials products has traditionally involved lengthy experimentation in a laboratory or pilot plant. However, recent AI advancements in data acquisition and analytics (predictive modeling) greatly increase the pace of NPD by being able to identify molecules with the right properties and predict their performance—the *physics of chemistry*—thereby eliminating much experimental (trial-and-error) work (Schmidt and Kristin, 2024).

Unilever worked with Arzeda to develop *a new enzyme for laundry products* that uses 50% fewer ingredients but has increased stability and performance. By applying physics-based AI design to proteins, Unilever cut development time from the typical five years to just 18 months, underscoring AI's power in accelerating product discovery (Unilever, 2023). Similarly, BASF developed *Emollient Maestro* to identify sustainable emollients with the right properties to replace existing emollients in clients' skin care products (Rivard, 2022).

2.6. *Validation and testing*

The Validation and Testing stage is crucial for ensuring that products meet specifications and perform as expected under real-world conditions. AI enhances both physical and digital testing, expediting prototype development and optimizing product performance:

Building physical prototypes: AI-driven design accelerates the transition from concept to prototype, allowing teams to create 3D-printed models or nearly final product versions based on AI-optimized designs. Unilever's Materials Innovation Factory (MIF) uses AI and robotics to rapidly prototype products, with AI handling tasks such as testing and refining chemical formulations. MIF's contributions to Unilever's portfolio include Dove Intensive

Repair Shampoo, demonstrating the value of AI-enhanced prototyping in accelerating the company's innovation pipeline (Dominguez, 2023).

Digital twins for user tests: While much iterative testing occurs in the Development stage with virtual products and digital twins, many firms also conduct rigorous user tests of the *pre-production physical prototype* or MVP product: field trials, beta tests, or in-home consumer tests. Such "data digital twins" are useful for field testing physical products. Algorithms analyze *data from sensors in the test product* to identify potential defects or product quality issues. For example, road-testing of new-product vehicles is done with digital twins (Dilmegani, 2023). In the development of self-driving vehicles, the test cars contain numerous sensors that collect on-the-road data, which they feed to the digital twin.

User feedback analysis: AI-driven natural language processing (NLP) tools enhance the analysis of user feedback by converting *unstructured data into actionable insights.* Traditionally, feedback from field trials is captured in interviews or notes, often leaving valuable insights untapped (Forsey, 2023). NLP transforms this qualitative feedback into structured data, such as charts and trend lines, helping teams identify common themes in customer preferences and validate product features. AI can also analyze responses from in-home product tests, field trials, and digital surveys, allowing project teams to gain deeper insights into user acceptance and satisfaction.

AI has become especially useful for testing IoT-connected and complex products that require rigorous system integration. Advanced system testing tools are evolving to detect potential defects early and even initiate self-correcting processes. This capability ensures that final products are more robust and reduces post-launch defects, streamlining the path to market (Nieto-Rodriguez and Vargas, 2023).

2.7. *AI in commercialization and launch*

AI significantly enhances new product marketing effectiveness. It guides project teams in creating marketing launch plans and streamlines the process through AI-driven tools like *Taskaid*. AI also assists in executing various elements of the marketing mix (Goyal, 2023):

Marketing communications: A majority of B2B (78%) and B2C (65%) firms use generative AI for creating advertising content (Deeb, 2023).

Google employs AI for targeted advertising, while Amazon leverages AI-powered product recommendations to boost customer engagement and revenue.

Salesforce and distribution: AI automates lead scoring and salesforce routing, predicting customer behavior and suggesting the next best actions (Dataconomy, 2023). Procter & Gamble utilizes machine learning algorithms to optimize product assortment and analyze in-store availability.

Pricing: Companies such as Netflix use AI to personalize pricing based on viewing habits, while Uber implements dynamic pricing using AI to analyze real-time demand (Obviously.AI, 2023).

Manufacturing: The limitless applications and inroads that AI has made into manufacturing and supply-chain management go far beyond NPD and are beyond the scope of this chapter. Marr (2023) provides a good summary.

2.8. *Post-Launch*

AI and NLP algorithms analyze customer feedback and market data to identify issues and areas for improvement in newly launched products. This analysis guides future product development efforts.

Tesla, for example, creates digital twins for each new vehicle, collecting performance data from embedded sensors. GE implements digital twins for its GE90 engines on Boeing 777 aircraft, enabling predictive maintenance (Preface, 2023). Siemens introduced ATOM, a virtual model for gas turbines and compressors, demonstrating AI's role in product lifecycle management.

2.9. *More AI tools for NPD*

Project management: AI project management tools have revolutionized scheduling, resource allocation, and progress tracking, enabling project teams to manage NPD tasks more efficiently. Tools such as Asana, Trello, and Albert Invent leverage AI to automate data collection, scheduling, and reporting. With automated systems, teams gain real-time visibility into project metrics, such as progress toward milestones, achieved benefits, and potential slippages (Reddi, 2023).

Portfolio management: Here, AI provides support to the PMO by tracking projects in the portfolio, identifying potential problems, and preparing project reports. For example, Sopheon's *Accolade* allows firms to prioritize their portfolio of projects based on strategic goals and balance factors, such as risk, value, and innovation potential. Similarly, Planview's strategic portfolio management solution provides a single view into all projects across the organization, with accurate, real-time data and analyses; it effectively plans, aligns, and adapts the firms' resources and projects to realize strategic objectives.

Natural language processing: NLP analyzes unstructured data such as customer reviews, survey responses, and social media comments to extract insights and trends. For instance, platforms such as Upside leverage AI to generate new product ideas by interpreting open-ended feedback from surveys and interviews.

3. AI Adoption in New Product Development

3.1. *Current adoption rates and trends*

Despite the many proven applications for AI in NPD, and the positive results achieved by early adopters, *the adoption rate of AI in NPD has been sluggish.* Only 23% of firms had adopted AI for NPD by early 2024 (McKinsey, 2024a; Cooper and Brem, 2024a,b), and none of the firms in the Cooper–Brem study reported "extensive use of AI" in NPD.

3.2. *Adoption for specific NPD applications*

AI adoption rates for specific NPD applications outlined above—from idea generation to pre-launch product testing—were investigated (Cooper and Brem, 2024a,b). Here is a snapshot of the results:

Front-end applications: AI usage in front-end innovation, such as market analysis and idea generation, is limited, with less than 10% adoption for most applications (Figure 2). However, there's optimism for future growth, with intentions to adopt AI averaging 36% across these applications within the next year. This signals an expected 5.6-fold increase in adoption.

The limited use of AI in the front end of NPD is surprising, especially considering the abundance of commercially available tools outlined

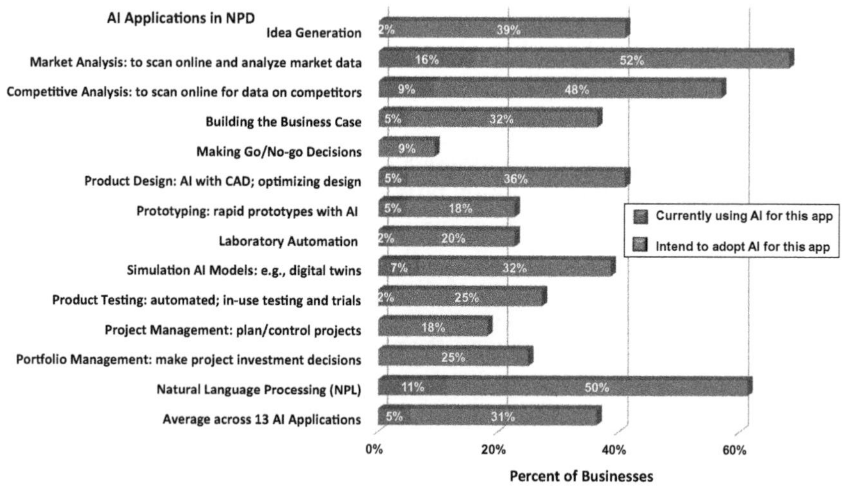

Figure 2. Current and expected adoption of AI for various applications in NPD (percent of businesses that are now using AI or intend to use it).

above. ChatGPT generates original new product ideas, while many off-the-shelf software products outlined in the section titled "Building the business case" aid in market data acquisition and analysis, even building business cases complete with financial analyses (Cooper, 2025a).

Development and Testing: AI adoption in the Development and Testing stages is even lower, averaging only a 4.2% usage rate (Figure 2). AI-enhanced CAD for product design shows the highest current adoption in this category. Intentions to adopt AI in these stages average 25%, suggesting a potential 6.2-fold increase in adoption.

The low usage in these Development and Testing stages is unexpected, given the availability of AI-powered solutions such as Siemens' Xcelerator and Simcenter for physical product design, Tessent for integrated circuit testing, and Altair TwinActivate for both data-driven and physics-based digital twins (Grace, 2024).

Other AI tools for NPD: Natural Language Processing (NLP) stands out with 11% current usage and 50% intention to adopt, the highest future adoption intention of any AI application studied. NLP's potential to analyze unstructured text from various sources, including customer feedback and field trials, makes it a valuable tool for identifying market needs and pain points. The adoption rates for both portfolio and project management AI tools were zero.

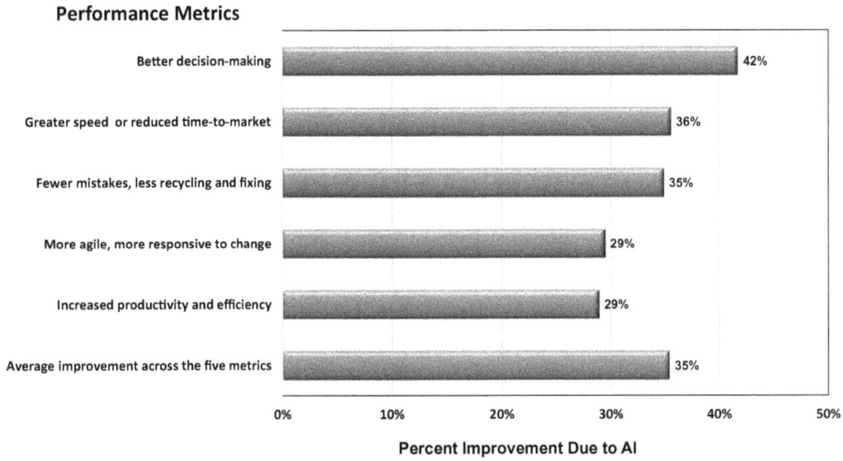

Figure 3. Improvement realized by using AI for NPD across five performance metrics.

3.3. *Positive impact of AI on NPD performance*

For the 23% of firms that have adopted at least one AI application for NPD, *the outcomes are very positive*. Performance *improvements average a solid 34%* across five important metrics, from better decision-making (42% improvement) to increased productivity (29% improvement) (Figure 3). Several high-impact applications driving NPD performance were identified:

1. *AI for product testing and validation*: Significantly accelerates development and enhances decision-making.
2. *AI for product design*: Project acceleration, improved decision-making, error reduction, and higher productivity.
3. *AI for prototyping*: Strongly affects project acceleration.
4. *Extensive AI usage overall in NPD*: Leads to project acceleration and improved decision-making.

3.4. *Firms' readiness to adopt AI*

Despite interest in AI, *many businesses remain hesitant to adopt it* extensively (Figure 4). This readiness assessment reveals several challenges (Cooper and Brem, 2024b):

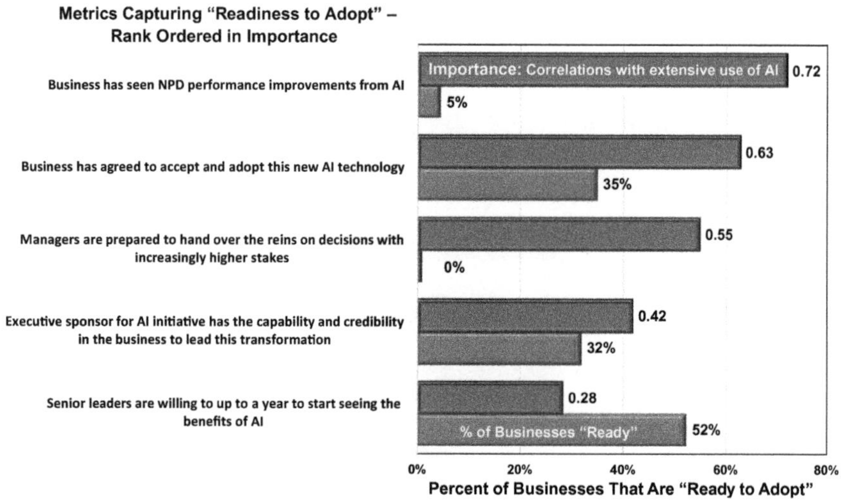

Figure 4. Businesses' "readiness to adopt" AI for NPD and the importance (0-1 correlations) of each for the adoption of AI.

- Only 5% of firms have seen visible performance improvement that demonstrated value from AI in NPD.
- Two-thirds of firms have not fully committed to moving forward with AI for NPD.
- Trust in AI is lacking. In none of the firms is management willing to turn over the reins of NPD decision-making to AI.
- In most cases, the executive sponsor lacks the credibility or capability to lead the AI transformation.

These four factors are the strongest drivers of readiness to adopt AI for NPD, but management struggles with all four. The most important—a lack of demonstrated value—is likely caused in part by the high failure rate of AI adoption projects. Note that larger early adopter firms mentioned above, with deeper pockets and more professionalism, *achieved dramatic performance improvements—the difference between high performers and typical firms is how AI was implemented.*

3.5. *Roadblocks to AI adoption in NPD*

Despite the potential benefits, many *companies hesitate to adopt AI for NPD*. Our investigations identify five roadblocks:

1. *Low business value*: Business value is the most important driver of adoption, but companies struggle to achieve it. Only 18–36% of organizations report achieving expected benefits from AI (Mittal *et al.*, 2024).

   This *low business value* occurs because some AI projects are simply *poor-value applications* and others *just fail in execution*. The "pilot paralysis" phenomenon, where companies successfully undertake pilot projects but struggle to scale up, is epidemic (Gregory, 2021). Some estimates place *the failure rate as high as 80%*, almost double the failure rate of corporate IT projects a decade ago (Bojinov, 2023).
2. *Lack of leadership commitment*: Senior management commitment is crucial for AI adoption in NPD, yet not all leadership teams are ready to embrace it (Cooper and Brem, 2024b). A lack of executive buy-in is the major obstacle to scaling up in 50% of businesses (Deloitte, 2022). A significant disconnect exists between CEO optimism and other executives' outlook on AI readiness: While 74% of CEOs express optimism about their organizations' AI readiness, only 29% of other executives share this view (Marshall, 2023).

   Many executives lack AI literacy and understanding, which contributes to their hesitancy (Pinski *et al.*, 2024). Fear of the unknown and the potential for AI to upend business as we know it are also factors in senior management's reluctance.
3. *Lack of trust*: Trust is a significant barrier to AI adoption within NPD (Nylund *et al.*, 2023; Mittal *et al.*, 2024). In none of the firms in the AI adoption study above was senior management prepared to hand over decision-making to AI (Figure 4). Trust issues revolve around the quality and reliability of AI output. The prevalence of AI-generated garbage content on the Internet may further complicate trust-building. However, executives and managers need to understand AI and trust its data and decision-making processes (Nunez, 2021).
4. *High infrastructure and adoption costs*: Companies often overlook comprehensive expenses, including infrastructure and skills acquisition (Peeler, 2023). Many lack the necessary infrastructure to process and handle required data, hindering full adoption. A Gartner study (2019) found that approximately 64% of organizations cite a lack of skills as a major obstacle to successful AI projects. A talent shortage exists for AI, making it challenging to attract and reskill tech-savvy executives challenging (LaBerge *et al.*, 2022). This shortage contributes to the overall cost and difficulty of AI adoption.

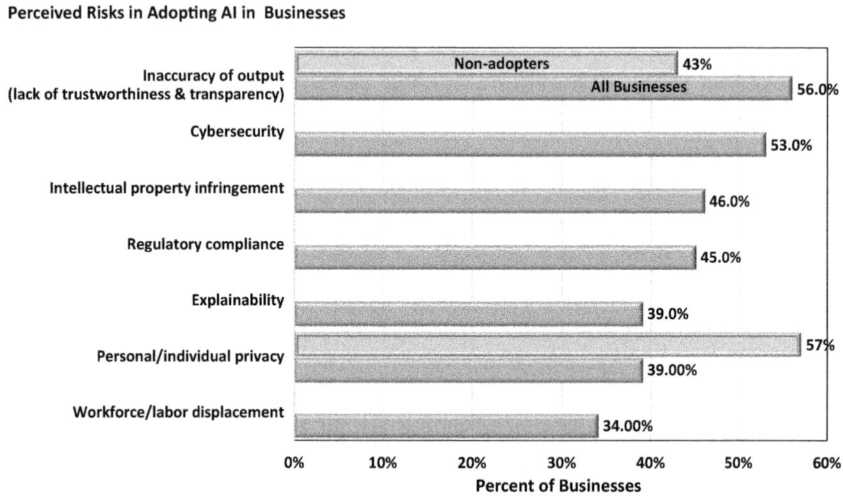

Figure 5. Percentage of businesses citing each risk in the adoption of AI in their business (McKinsey, 2023; IBM, 2024).

5. *Risks and ethical issues*: Managing AI-related risks is a key challenge in 50% of businesses (Mittal *et al.*, 2024). Major concerns are in Figure 5 (McKinsey, 2023). Interestingly, output inaccuracy is more frequently cited as a risk than both cybersecurity and regulatory compliance, which were the most common risks from AI overall in previous years.

Ethical concerns, particularly job displacement, are significant. However, *AI is expected to have the least impact on job numbers in NPD* compared to other functions and departments (McKinsey, 2023). AI is seen as complementing and augmenting rather than replacing human creativity in NPD. In marketing, while AI can generate content and analyze data, it raises concerns about deceptive practices. Deepfakes and overly intrusive personalization can erode trust and raise concerns about customer manipulation (Lawyers, 2023).

4. Why Most AI Projects Fail

AI adoption projects share striking similarities with NPD initiatives (Cooper, 2024c). Both aim to deliver solutions that meet the needs of end-users or customers, whether internal or external. The activities involved in

AI and NPD projects often mirror each other, including building business cases, developing products or solutions, conducting field trials, beta tests or pilots, and scale-up or launch.

4.1. *Common reasons for AI project failure*

While personal opinions are many, the reasons for AI failure have *yet to be revealed by robust research studies of large samples of AI failure cases.* However, evidence from the few but limited studies of AI projects, augmented by expert opinion, enabled the creation of a list of the important AI project failure reasons (see Figure 6; Cooper, 2024c). They are (unranked):

1. *Failure to understand users' needs*: Many AI projects begin with a *technology-first orientation*, referred to as the "shiny things disease" (RAND Corp., 2024; Overby, 2023). Instead of starting with a solution looking for a problem, companies must first investigate specific user problems and then determine which AI tool can solve them (Lamarre, 2023; Dilmegani, 2023). A lack of understanding of users' needs frequently results in ill-defined project objectives and solutions that miss the mark.
2. *Unrealistic expectations*: AI Ops Teams often *overestimate the capabilities of AI* or have unrealistic expectations about its potential impact (Schlegel *et al.*, 2023). This stems from a lack of understanding of the technology's limitations (Korolov, 2023), overly optimistic projections, or a desire to showcase the project favorably to secure management's approval and resources. When expectations are set too high, there is a risk of disappointment, loss of stakeholder support, and project cancelation, particularly during the pilot stage (Westenberger *et al.*, 2022).
3. *Technical issues with the AI solution*: According to an IDC study, the top reason for AI failure is that the model did not perform as promised (35% of firms; Jyoti and Kuppuswamy, 2023). Delivering inaccurate results can be due to various technical reasons, such as *inadequate data quality*, algorithmic limitations, or unforeseen outlier cases (Westenberger *et al.*, 2022).
4. *Poor data quality*: AI systems rely heavily on high-quality, relevant, and properly labeled data for both training and operation (RAND Corp., 2024; Overby, 2023). Lack of data availability for training the model is often a key reason for failure. Many companies struggle with poor data quality, insufficient data volume, or lack of proper data

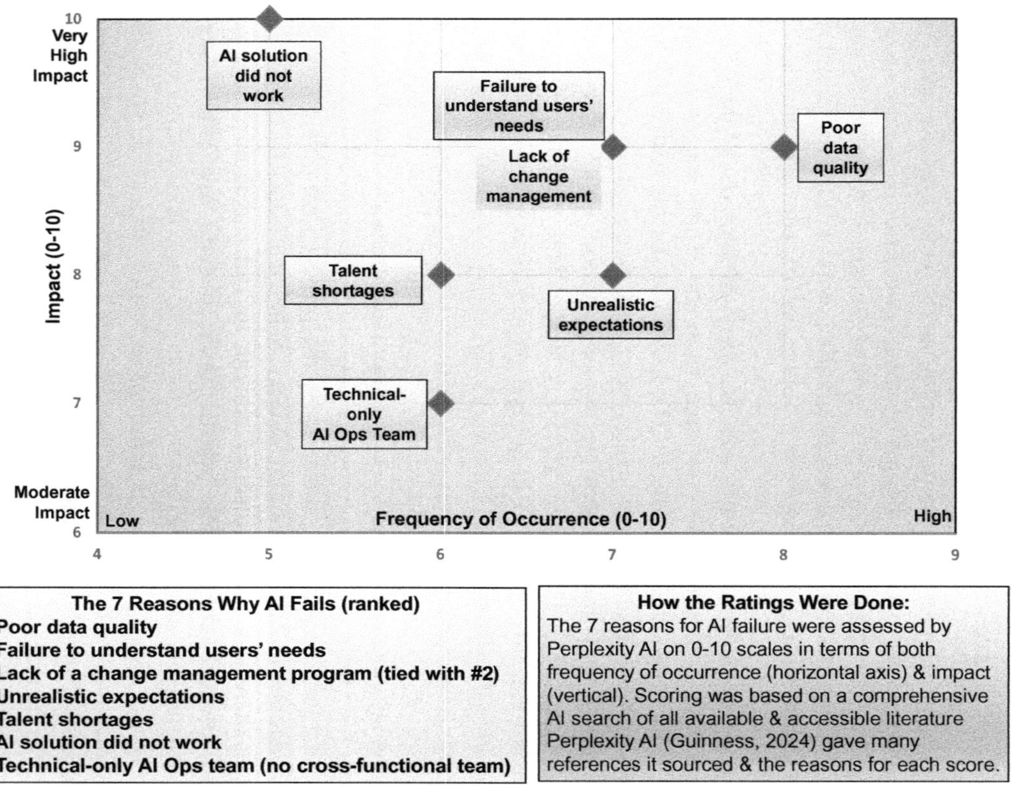

Figure 6. The 7 failure reasons for AI in business (box, top left) plus a positioning map showing AI failure reasons in terms of both impact and frequency of occurrence.

governance, leading to inaccurate models, biased outputs, and ultimately, project failure (Tadiparthi, 2024; Dilmegani, 2023; Brem and Riviecco, 2024).

5. *A technical-only AI Ops Team*: Having a data science team working in isolation on an AI project is not a recipe for success. Successful AI projects require *collaboration across various functional areas*, including data science, IT, and relevant business functions (Bratton and Glynn, 2024). Teams composed solely of technical personnel are likely to result in solutions disconnected from real user needs and operational realities (Dilmegani, 2023).
6. *Talent shortages*: The shortage of skilled professionals with expertise in AI is a significant challenge, cited as a major failure reason by 29% of firms (Jyoti and Kuppuswamy, 2023). Without strong data scientists and IT engineers, AI projects suffer from sub-optimal execution, lack of technical depth, and failure to realize the full potential of the technology (Westenberger *et al.*, 2022).
7. *Lack of change management*: Implementing AI requires *significant organizational, mindset, and cultural changes*. Failure to implement a comprehensive change management program, address ethical and job concerns, and foster a data-driven culture leads to resistance and hinders the effective integration of AI solutions (AIM, 2023; Overby 2023).

Table 1 shows mitigation strategies to avoid these common pitfalls, many taken from the field of NPD.

4.2. *RAPID: A roadmap for AI acquisition and deployment*

The high failure rate of AI projects has become a significant concern for businesses attempting to integrate artificial intelligence into their operations. To address these challenges, the *RAPID* (Roadmap for AI Procurement, Implementation, and Deployment) process has been developed. Inspired by Technology Development (TD) models (Aristodemou *et al.*, 2019), *RAPID* offers a structured process model designed to avoid common pitfalls and mitigate risk in AI adoption projects in much same way that *Stage-Gate* was deployed in the 1980s to deal with the high failure rate in NPD. *RAPID* employs a gated, stage-based roadmap that focuses on iterative validation, user-centric design, and a focus on value to the company (Cooper, 2024d).

Table 1. Recommended best practices to avoid AI project failures.

Failure Reason	Mitigating Actions to Avert AI Project Failures
1. Failure to Understand Users' Needs, a Lack of Clear Objectives	• Use a proven *technology adoption and deployment process*, similar to Technology Development frameworks—a combination of Stage-Gate, Agile & Lean methodologies—for driving projects forward, with: ◦ clearly defined stages, tasks, deliverables with best practices built in, and ◦ gates with go/no-go (investment) decision criteria (see Section 5.0) • Begin AI projects by gathering insights from users to identify their needs, problems & wants. • Involve end-users throughout the development process using iterative feedback loops with demo validations • Define *project objectives*: the problem to be solved, the expected outcomes, & measurable success criteria.
2. Unrealistic Expectations	• Conduct a thorough technical *feasibility assessment* early in the AI project ◦ Vet the *AI vendor* & the *technical solution* • Create a *business case* with realistic financial expectations & timelines. • Ensure open communication with management at go-no-go gate decision points re. project benefits & risks. • Hold the AI Ops team *accountable for the results* vs. their business case, & build in a *post-implementation review*.
3. The AI Solution Did Not Work	• Vet the vendor & solution—a technical assessment • Conduct thorough technical test ing & validation of the AI solution: alpha testing & pilot trials, before scale-up • Implement disciplined methods to assess accuracy, manage bias & deal with incorrect output with human oversight • Establish clear acceptance criteria to evaluate the AI's effectiveness. • Continuously monitor the AI's performance, accuracy & reliability once in operation.
4. Poor Data Quality	• Prioritize data readiness, quality & governance. • Implement *robust data governance practices*: data quality checks, data labeling & data management processes. • Continuously monitor & update the data used by t he AI system to maintain accuracy over time.

Table 1. (*Continued*)

Failure Reason	Mitigating Actions to Avert AI Project Failures
5. No Cross-Functional AI Ops Team	• Establish a *cross-functional AI Task Force*: members from data science, IT & data engineering, plus members from key user group, such RD&E, Marketing, Operations to ensure that the AI solution ... ○ aligns with organizational goals, and ○ focuses on high-value user applications & integrates seamlessly with technological architecture & existing workflows.
6. Talent Shortages	• Invest in *training & upskilling existing employees in* AI. include managers. • Invest in *talent acquisition*—competitive compensation, growth opportunities; foster a culture that attracts top AI talent. • Explore partnerships with academic institutions, research labs, or specialized AI firms. • Leverage cloud-based AI services & vendors' platforms & services to supplement in-house capabilities.
7. Lack of Change Management	• Develop a *change management strategy* to address the organizational & cultural shifts needed with AI {Creasey, 2023}. • Focus on the *new mindset*: a culture of data-based decision-making & learning, experimenting & adapting. • Undertake employee *training, education & communication.*

4.3. *The details of the RAPID process*

RAPID consists of four main stages, each stage followed by a gate review (Figure 7):

Vision and purpose: This initial stage begins with a clear commitment from top management, establishing the vision and goals for the AI initiative. A cross-functional task force is created, reporting directly to senior management and ideally composed of dedicated members from various departments, including potential user departments, not just IT and AI specialists. A high-level plan for the next stage is crafted. This stage culminates in Gate 1, where management reaffirms the vision and commits resources for the next stage.

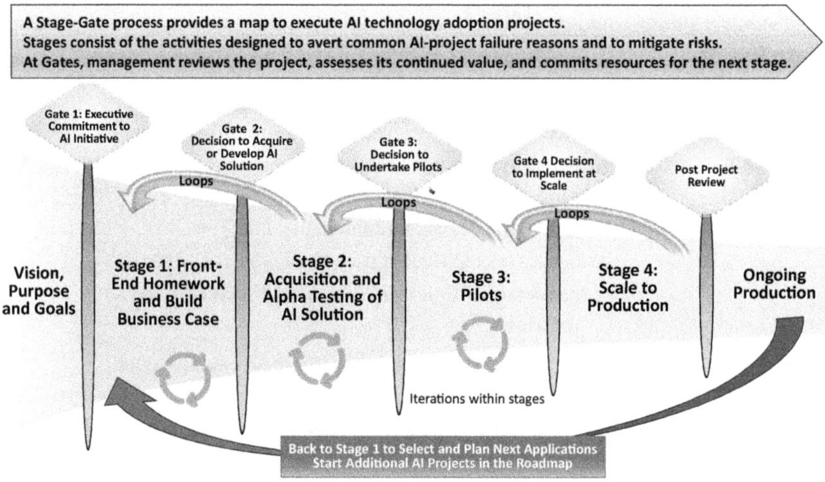

Figure 7. The RAPID technology acquisition and deployment process map for AI projects for NPD.

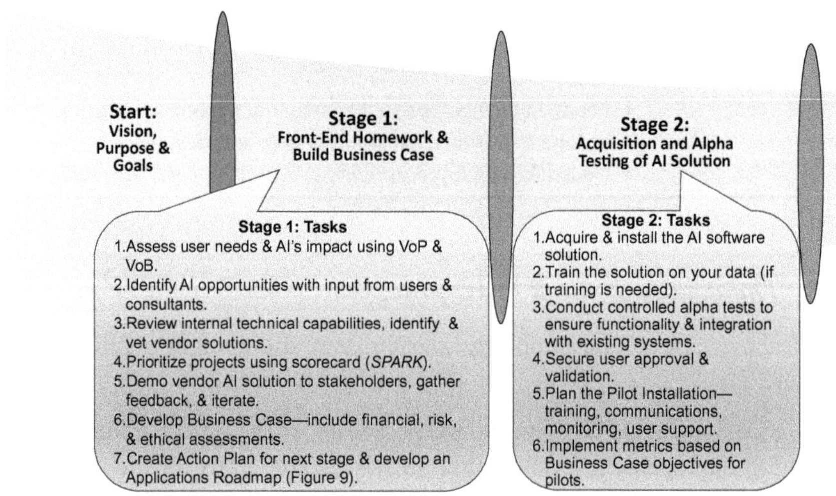

Figure 8. Key tasks in the first half of the RAPID process: Business Case and AI Acquisition.

Build business case: The task force begins by researching user needs using Voice of Process (VoP) and Voice of Business (VoB) to identify high-impact AI applications (Figure 8). They conduct a technical assessment, examine internal capabilities, and vet possible AI solutions and vendors (see the vetting model in the work of Cooper, 2024d). If possible, vendors demo their AI products to internal users who provide feedback on potential value. The task force determines the business value of relevant for each application—creates business cases for each—"sub-projects" of the main AI initiative—and proposes project teams for the individual AI projects.

The outcome is a set of recommended AI applications and an AI Application Projects Roadmap guiding future efforts (Figure 9). A Gate 2 review determines whether to proceed with the proposed AI projects, using tools such as the *SPARK* scorecard (see the following) for guidance.

Solution acquisition and alpha testing: Once the business case is approved, the project team acquires the AI solution, by either purchasing or leasing it. Data preparation, often the most time-consuming task, also takes place, and the model is trained.

Many firms choose off-the-shelf solutions, but 47% either develop or heavily customize the software (Singla *et al.*, 2024). If development is required, the project shifts to an internal IT project.

Controlled Alpha Tests verify functionality and system integration. Test-and-revise cycles assess technical performance and validate user acceptance before piloting. Deliverables to Gate 3 include a Pilot Action Plan, an updated business case, and an Applications Roadmap.

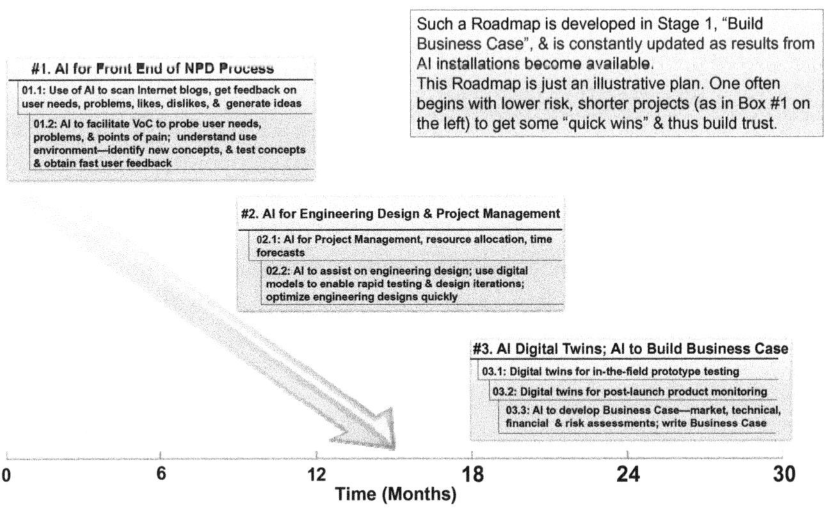

Figure 9. The Application Projects Roadmap is a tentative plan for future AI application projects.

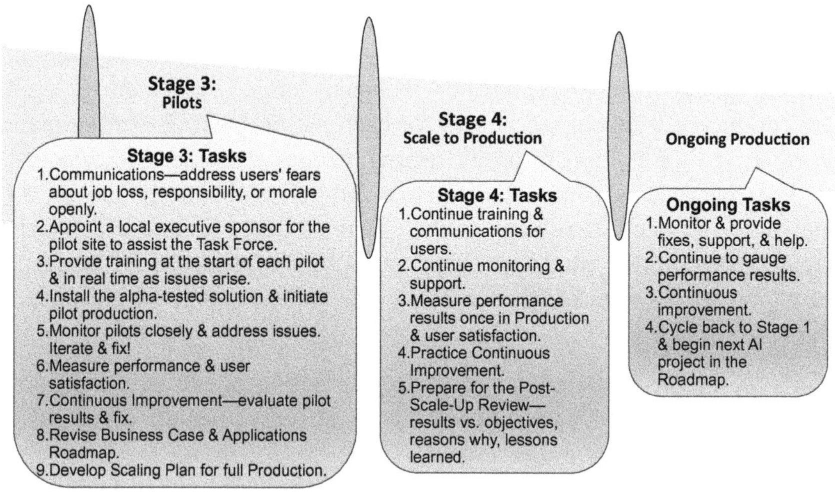

Figure 10. Key tasks in the back half of the *RAPID* process—Pilots and Scale-Up.

Pilots: The pilot(s) are crucial for testing the solution in a real-world setting and addressing any user concerns (Figure 10). The project team executes the Pilot Plan, which includes training and communications to address employee concerns about job security. They closely monitor the pilot, make improvements based on feedback, and measure performance against business case metrics.

After the pilot, results are reviewed, and the business case and Applications Roadmap are updated. A Scaling Plan is developed for full production, incorporating lessons from the pilot.

Scale to production: Scaling transitions the AI solution from pilot to full production, ensuring it handles real-world data, operates reliably, and integrates with existing systems. Key tasks include communications, training, installation, and start-up. Once in full production, the focus shifts to monitoring, performance measurement, and continuous improvement.

A Post Project Review concludes the project, evaluating results against objectives. The cycle then repeats with the next AI project in the Applications Roadmap.

4.4. *Gate reviews and decision-making*

Throughout the *RAPID* process, *go/no-go decisions are made at each gate* to kill weak projects and commit resources to better ones. While financial metrics such as NPV are commonly used in making project go/no-go

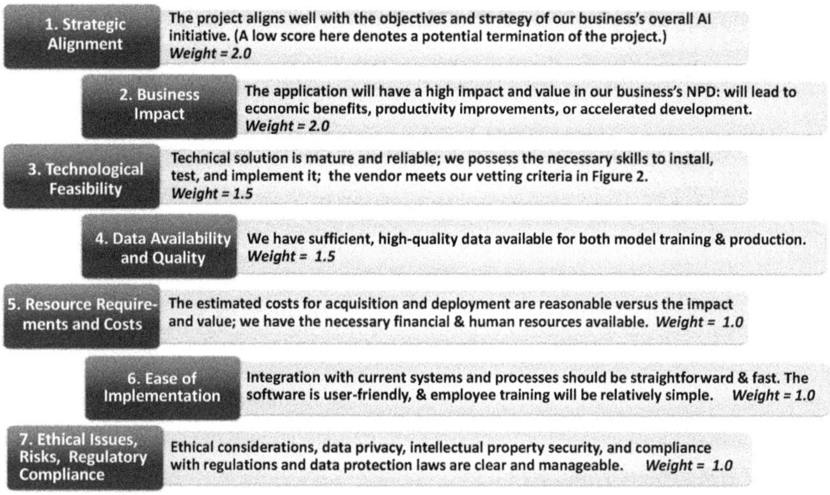

Figure 11. The SPARK scoring model for rating AI project attractiveness at Gate decision points in the RAPID process model.

decisions, *financial metrics can be unreliable for AI projects due to high uncertainty*. As an alternative, consider using a scoring model; for highly uncertain NPD projects, they have proved very effective.

SPARK is a seven-factor AI-evaluation scoring model that helps management distinguish potential winning AI projects from losers (Figure 11) (*SPARK*: Scoring Projects for AI R&D Knowledge; Cooper, 2024d). At gates, senior managers each rate the AI project on the seven criteria (0–10 scales), which are added in a weighted fashion to yield a Project Score out of 100. A score of 60–65 typically is adequate to proceed while 80+ indicates an exceptional project.

The true value of SPARK, however, lies not in the Project Score but in *the decision-making process* it facilitates. By guiding management teams through a structured evaluation, *SPARK* leads to better performance compared to traditional intuitive decision-making (Mitchel *et al.*, 2022).

4.5. *The Value of a Roadmap Like RAPID*

By following the *RAPID* framework and utilizing tools such as *SPARK*, firms can overcome common barriers and move through AI pilots to scalable, impactful AI applications in NPD. This approach offers RD&E leaders a proven method to drive successful AI integration, addressing the high failure rates and "pilot paralysis" that have plagued many AI initiatives.

5. The AI Wave Is Coming Fast

The AI revolution in business and in NPD is approaching rapidly, and its impact is expected to be transformative. Historical data on technological adoption reveals a clear trend: *Each successive industrial revolution has seen an accelerated pace of adoption*, with shorter "adoption windows" for new technologies. The First Industrial Revolution, characterized by steam power and mechanization, took approximately 85 years for widespread adoption. In contrast, the Third Revolution, the Information Age, had a significantly shorter adoption period of just 28 years (Figure 12). This pattern of accelerating adoption rates is remarkably consistent and predictive.

5.1. *AI adoption forecast*

Based on this historical trend in Figure 12, the adoption window for the current Industry 4.0 wave, led by AI, is predicted to be about 22 years. An adoption curve for AI in NPD has been constructed in Figure 13 based on Rogers' diffusion-of-innovation curve (Rogers, 1962) and using the

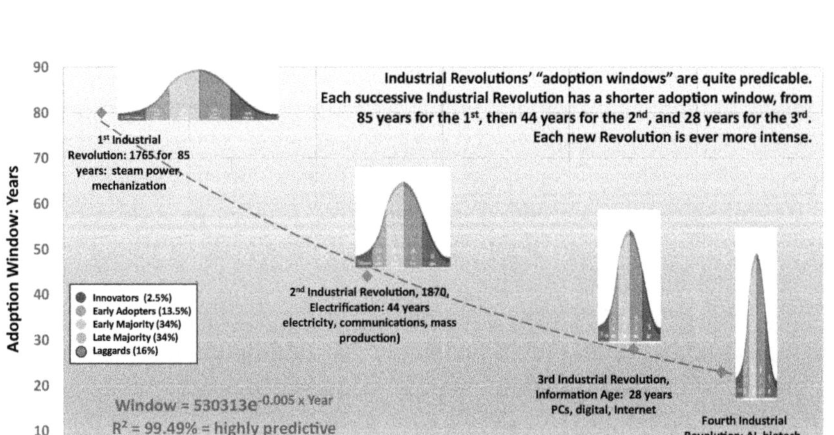

Figure 12. The duration of the Adoption Window for successive industrial revolutions—an ever-shorter but very predictable time period (figure created with help from Evan C. Thomas).

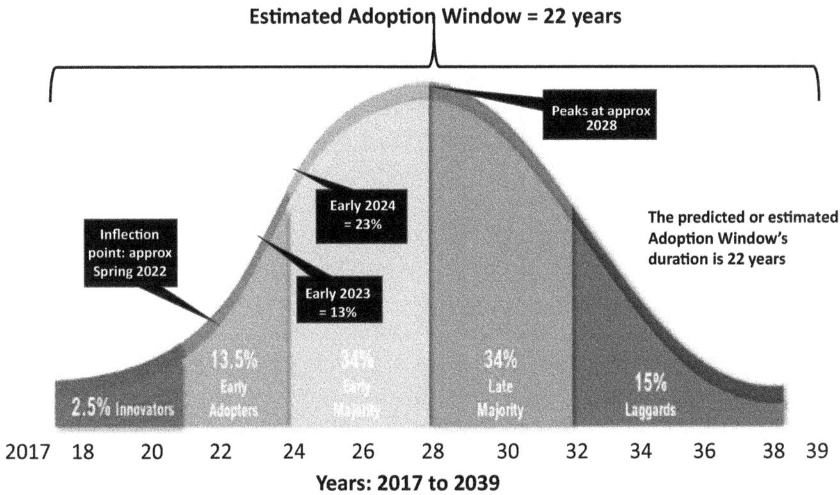

Figure 13. The estimated adoption curve for AI for NPD, using the Adoption Window duration from Figure 16 plus other data points (dates are approximate).

predicted 22-year window and available adoption data; its peak is expected around 2028.

The inflection point likely occurred in early 2022 (Jafari, 2022), and adoption rates of 13% and 23% were observed in early 2023 and 2024, respectively. Not only is the peak not far away, but the intensity of adoption (the slope of the AI adoption curve) in Figures 12 and 13 is much higher than for previous technology revolutions.

6. Conclusion

The pace of AI adoption in NPD presents both opportunities and challenges for businesses. However, as a *Forbes* article warns, "The ramifications for non-action will be swift: You either jump on board, or prepare to eat the dust of the other AI first-movers" (Deeb, 2023). Now is the time for action but not piece-meal and directionless without a strategy. Thus, *follow a rational deployment process!* History has shown that those who have hesitated too long when technological revolutions occur do not fare well. And AI is the most significant innovation of our lifetime, perhaps of all time.

References

AIM. (2023, June 13). Culture key to successful AI transformation: Empowering organizations for the future. *AIM Research*. (aimresearch.co). https://aimresearch.co/cdo-insights/culture-key-to-successful-ai-transformation-empowering-organizations-for-the-future.

AMS (Applied Marketing Science). (2023). Machine learning uncovers key insights for snow removal. *AMS Insights*. https://ams-insights.com/case-study/machine-learning-uncovers-key-insights-for-snow-removal/.

Adams, D. (2023, December 1). Accelerate VoC interviews with AI. *The AIM (Advanced Innovation Marketing) Institute*. The AIM Institute. https://theaiminstitute.com/blog/accelerate-voc-interviews-with-ai-and-6-other-tips/?utm_campaign=Monthly%20Newsletters&utm_medium=email&_hsmi=285464035&_hsenc=p2ANqtz-_PbKiCoL6weaISY37fepAifDLIx0bNvzJzxxErs_HVc5H5ZwvcusC4Mn4iRSmQ-e1nMv3BYHx9wx3jYAA4fYida_MP-s4mLGx8Po_ypPVbVU_H_rU&utm_content=284839761&utm_source=hs_email.

Agrawal, A., Gans, J., and Goldfarb, A. (2018). Prediction Machines—The Simple Economics of Artificial Intelligence. *Harvard Business Review Press*. ISBN:978-1-63369-567-2.

Ai Palette. (2023). Crafting a best-selling flavor: Pringles gastronomic triumph in South Korea. *Ai Palette Case Study*. https://www.aipalette.com/resources/customer-stories/pringles-case-study-renovation/.

Aristodemou, L., Tietze, F., O'Leary, E., and Shaw, M. (2019, January). A literature review on technology development process (TDP) models. *Innovation and IP Management. IIPM Lab*. https://doi.org/10.17863/CAM.35692.

Atomwise. (2022, August 17). Atomwise signs strategic multi-target research collaboration with Sanofi for AI-powered drug discovery. *Atomwise Press Release*. https://www.atomwise.com/category/press-release/page/5/.

Bilgram, V., and Laarmann, F. (2023). Generating innovation with generative AI: AI augmented digital prototyping and innovation methods. *IEEE Engineering Management Review*, Vol. 51(2), 18–25. https://ieeexplore.ieee.org/document/10115412.

Bojinov, I. (2023, Nov.–Dec.). Keep your AI projects on track. *Harvard Business Review Magazine*. https://hbr.org/2023/11/keep-your-ai-projects-on-track#:~:text=Sadly%2C%20beneath%20the%20aspirational%20headlines,increase%20the%20odds%20of%20success.

Bratton, A., and Glynn, K. (2024). Why your AI project is going to fail. *Lextech*. https://www.lextech.com/get-up-to-speed/why-your-ai-project-is-going-to-fail.

Brem, A.M., Giones, F., and Werle, M. (2023). The AI digital revolution in innovation: A conceptual framework of artificial intelligence technologies for the management of innovation. *IEEE Transactions on Engineering Management*, Vol. 70(2), 770–776. https://ieeexplore.ieee.org/document/9590499.

Brem, A., and Rivieccio, G. (2024). Artificial Intelligence and cognitive biases: A viewpoint. *Journal of Innovation Economic & Management*, Vol. 2(44), 223–231. https://www.cairn.info/revue-journal-of-innovation-economics.htm.

Brandstetter, M. (2023, August 25). Digital twins—successfully combining simulation and test. *Siemens*. https://blogs.sw.siemens.com/simcenter/digital-twins-simulation-and-test/.

Brossard, M., Gatto, G., Gentile, A., Merle, T., and Wlezien, C. (2020, February 5). How generative design could reshare the future of product development. *McKinsey and Company Report*. https://www.mckinsey.com/capabilities/operations/our-insights/how-generative-design-could-reshape-the-future-of-product-development.

Burridge, N. (2017, May 10). Artificial Intelligence gets a seat in the boardroom. *NikkeiAsia*. https://asia.nikkei.com/Business/Artificial-intelligence-gets-a-seat-in-the-boardroom.

Capterra. (2024). Social media scanning tools software. *Social Media Scanning Tools Software*. https://www.capterra.com/sem-compare/social-media-monitoring software/?utm_source=bing&utm_medium=cpc&utm_campaign=:1:CAP:2:COM:3:All:4:INTL:5:BAU:6:SOF:7:Desktop:8:BR:9:Social_Media_Monitoring:11:WCI&network=o.

Columbus, L. (2020, July 9). 10 ways AI is improving new product development. *Forbes*. https://www.forbes.com/sites/louiscolumbus/2020/07/09/10-ways-ai-is-improving-new-product-development/?sh=27a90ce45d3c.

Cooper, R.G. (2024a). The Artificial Intelligence revolution in new product development. *IEEE Engineering Management Review*, Vol. 52(1), 195–211. https://doi.org/10.1109/EMR.2023.3336834.

Cooper, R. (2024b). The coming AI wave: The Impact on product development in engineering management. *IEEE Engineering Management Review*, Vol. 52(3), 17–26. https://doi.org/10.1109/EMR.2024.3378536.

Cooper, R.G. (2024c). Why AI projects fail: Lessons from new product development. *IEEE Engineering Management Review*. https://doi.org/10.1109/EMR.2024.3419268

Cooper, R.G. (2024d). Adopting Artificial Intelligence for new product development: The RAPID process. *PDMA Online Journal, kHUB*. https://community.pdma.org/knowledgehub/bok/product-innovation-process/adopting-artificial-intelligence-for-new-product-development-the-rapid-process.

Cooper, R.G., and Brem, A.M. (2024a). The adoption of AI in new product development: Results of a multi-firm study in the US and Europe. *Research-Technology Management*, Vol. 67(3), 44–53. https://doi.org/10.1080/08956308.2024.2324241

Cooper, R.G., and Brem, A.M. (2024b). Insights for Managers About AI Adoption in New Product Development. *Research-Technology Management*, Vol. 67(6), 39–46. https://doi.org/10.1080/08956308.2024.2418734
Cooper, R.G., and McCausland, T. (2024). AI and new product development. *Research-Technology Management*, Vol. 67(1), 70–75. https://doi.org/10.1080/08956308.2024.2280485
Cooper, R.G. (2025a). The NPD game is won or lost in the first five plays: How AI can help in product innovation. *IEEE Engineering Management Review*, February. https://doi.org/10.1109/EMR.2025.3540373
Cooper, R.G. (2025b). A new AI model shows promise in predicting new product success. *Research-Technology Management*, July–August. https://doi.org//10.1080/08956308.2025.2496109
Creasey, T. (2023, June 23). A point of view on AI, change, and change management. *Change Success Insights*. https://www.linkedin.com/pulse/point-view-ai-change-management-tim-creasey/.
Dataconomy. (2023, August 31). How does Salesforce use artificial intelligence to transform businesses? *Artificial Intelligence*. https://dataconomy.com/2023/08/31/how-does-salesforce-use-artificial-intelligence-to-transform-businesses/
Dilmegani, C. (2023, May 9). Digital twin applications: Use cases by industry in 2023. *AIMultiple*. https://research.aimultiple.com/digital-twin-applications/.
Deeb, G. (2023, September 6). Artificial Intelligence is taking over marketing. *Forbes*. https://www.forbes.com/sites/georgedeeb/2023/09/06/artificial-intelligence-is-taking-over-marketing/?sh=7af778df5588.
Deloitte. (2022, October 18). State of AI in the enterprise' fifth edition uncovers four key actions to maximize AI value. *Deloitte*. Deloitte Announces State of AI in the Enterprise 5th Edition Report—Press Release. Deloitte US. https://www2.deloitte.com/us/en/pages/about-deloitte/articles/press-releases/deloitte-state-of-ai-fifth-edition-report.html.
Dominguez, L. (2023, April). How Unilever expedites product innovation with AI, automation, and robots. *Consumer Goods*. https://consumergoods.com/how-unilever-expedites-product-innovation-ai-automation-and-robots
Euchner, J. (2023). ChatGPT and generative AI. *Research-Technology Management*, Vol. 66(3), 71–74. https://doi.org/10.1080/08956308.2023.2188861.
Filippi, S. (2023, August 21). Measuring the impact of ChatGPT on fostering concept generation in innovative product design. *Electronics*, Vol. 12(16). https://doi.org/10.3390/electronics12163353.
Forsey, C. (2023, June 26). How AI will revolutionize product development, and how to prepare. *HubSpot*. https://blog.hubspot.com/marketing/how-ai-will-revolutionize-product-development.
GE. (2023a). Digital Thread for Design (DT4D). *GE Research*. https://www.ge.com/research/initiative/industrial-ai.
GE. (2023b). Accelerating the breadth & depth of AI in a physics+world. *GE Research*. https://www.ge.com/research/initiative/industrial-ai.

Gartner. (2019, July 9). Gartner survey reveals leading organizations expect to double the number of AI projects in place within the next year. *Gartner Press Release.* https://www.gartner.com/en/newsroom/press-releases/2019-07-15-gartner-survey-reveals-leading-organizations-expect-t#:~:text=The%20top%20challenges%20to%20adopting%20AI%20for%20respondents,and%20concerns%20with%20data%20scope%20or%20quality%20%2834%25%29.

Goyal, C. (2023, July 3). How to create an AI marketing strategy? *Analytics Vidhya.* https://www.analyticsvidhya.com/blog/2023/03/ai-marketing-strategies/#Best_AI_Marketing_Tools_and_their_Use_Cases.

Grace, R. (2024, February 23). Leveraging AI to speed product design simulations. *Plastics Engineering.* https://www.plasticsengineering.org/2024/02/leveraging-ai-to-speed-product-design-simulations-003848/#!.

Gregory, R. (2021, April 27). Overcoming pilot paralysis in digital transformation. *Weatherhead School of Management, Case Western Reserve University.* https://case.edu/weatherhead/xlab/about/news/overcoming-pilot-paralysis-digital-transformation.

Helrish, T. (2022, August 12). 10 ways to use AI for a successful product launch. *Forbes.* https://www.forbes.com/sites/forbestechcouncil/2022/08/12/10-ways-to-use-ai-for-a-successful-product-launch/?sh=65faa1ea74b1.

IBM. (2024, January 10). Data suggests growth in enterprise adoption of AI is due to widespread deployment by early adopters, but barriers keep 40% in the exploration and experimentation phases. *IBM Newsroom.* https://newsroom.ibm.com/2024-01-10-Data-Suggests-Growth-in-Enterprise-Adoption-of-AI-is-Due-to-Widespread-Deployment-by-Early-Adopters.

Iansiti, M., and Lakhani, K. (2020). Competing in the Age of AI: Strategy and Leadership When Algorithms and Networks Run the World. *Harvard Business Review Press.* https://www.hbs.edu/faculty/Pages/item.aspx?num=56633.

Jafari, A. (2022, July 7). How far are we from Artificial General Intelligence (AGI)? The experts weigh in.... *AI Future.* https://aifuture.substack.com/p/how-far-are-we-from-artificial-general.

Jyoti, R., and Kuppuswamy, R. (2023, February 27). Create more business value from your organizational data. *IDC Research InfoBrief.* http://idcdocserv.com/download/US49981822-IB.pd.

Korolov, M. (2023, March 4). 4 reasons why gen AI projects fail. *CIO.* https://www.cio.com/article/220445/6-reasons-why-ai-projects-fail.html.

LaBerge, L., Smaje, K., and Zemmel, R. (2022, June 15). Three new mandates for capturing a digital transformation's full value. *McKinsey Digital.* https://www.mckinsey.com/capabilities/mckinsey-digital/our-insights/three-new-mandates-for-capturing-a-digital-transformations-full-value.

Lamarre, E. (2023, November). In digital and AI transformations, start with the problem not the technology. *McKinsey Strategy & Corporate Finance*

Practice. https://www.mckinsey.com/capabilities/strategy-and-corporate-finance/our-insights/in-digital-and-ai-transformations-start-with-the-problem-not-the-technology.

Lasota, M., and Sadowski, M. (2024, August 22). The 8 best review monitoring tools for your business. *Brand24*. https://brand24.com/blog/review-monitoring-tools/.

Laurinavicius, T. (2024, July 29). 9 Best Market Research Tools for 2024. *Marketful*. https://marketful.com/blog/best-market-research-tools/.

Lawyers. (2023, May 14). Ethical concerns of AI in marketing. *Lawyers Blog*. https://4legalleads.com/blog/ethical-concerns-of-ai-in-marketing/.

Mailey, K. (2023, May 31). How generative AI is streamlining the concept phase in new product development. *Fast Company*. https://www.fastcompany.com/90902288/how-generative-ai-is-streamlining-the-concept-phase-in-new-product-development.

Marion, T.J., Srour, M., and Piller, F. (2024). When generative AI meets product development. *MIT Sloan Management Review*, Vol. 66(1), 14–15. https://shop.sloanreview.mit.edu/store/when-generative-ai-meets-product-development.

Marr, B. (2023, July 25). The future of manufacturing: Generative AI and beyond. *Forbes*. https://www.forbes.com/sites/bernardmarr/2023/07/25/the-future-of-manufacturing-generative-ai-and-beyond/?sh=377a3b4851fa.

Marshall, A. (2023, September). Uncertainty and the future—Hybrid AI. *IBM Institute for Business Value*. Pennsylvania State University Institute for the Study of Business Markets (ISBM) Members' Conference AI in B2B Marketing. https://www.youtube.com/embed/L8bL_sOtSBU.

McKinsey. (2023, August 21). The state of AI in 2023: AI's breakout year. *Quantum Black by McKinsey*. https://www.mckinsey.com/capabilities/quantumblack/our-insights/the-state-of-ai-in-2023-generative-AIs-breakout-year.

McKinsey. (2024a, August 26). What is digital twin technology? *McKinsey & Company*. https://www.mckinsey.com/featured-insights/mckinsey-explainers/what-is-digital-twin-technology.

McKinsey. (2024b, March 5). Generative AI fuels creative physical product design but is no magic wand. *McKinsey Digital*. https://www.mckinsey.com/capabilities/mckinsey-digital/our-insights/generative-ai-fuels-creative-physical-product-design-but-is-no-magic-wand.

Mitchell, R., Phaal, R., Athanassopoulou, N., Farrukh, C., and Rassmussen, C. (2022). How to build a customized scoring tool to evaluate and select early-stage projects. *Research-Technology Management*, Vol. 65(3), 27–38. https://doi.org/10.1080/08956308.2022.2026185.

Mittal, N., Perricos, C., Schmidt, K., Sniderman, B., and Jarvis, D. (2024, April). Now decides next: Getting real about Generative A. *The Deloitte AI Institute™ Report*. https://www.nationalcoalition.gov.gr/wp-content/uploads/2024/05/us-state-of-gen-ai-report-q2.pdf.

Nieto-Rodriguez, A., and Vargas, R.V. (2023, February 2). How AI will transform project management. *Harvard Business Review*. https://hbr.org/2023/02/how-ai-will-transform-project-management.

Nunez, S. (2021, Nov 15). Why AI investments fail to deliver. *InfoWorld*. https://www.infoworld.com/article/3639028/why-ai-investments-fail-to-deliver.html.

Nylund, P.A, Ferràs-Hernández, X., and Brem, A. (2023). A trust paradox may limit the application of AI-generated knowledge. *Research-Technology Management*, Vol. 66(5), 44–52. https://doi.org/10.1080/08956308.2023.2236475.

Obviously.AI. (2023, May 14). Using data predictions to apply Uber-like dynamic pricing. *Obviously AI Blog*. https://www.obviously.ai/post/using-data-predictions-to-apply-uber-like-dynamic-pricing.

Overby, S. (2023). 8 examples of Artificial Intelligence in action. *SAP*. https://www.sap.com/norway/insights/viewpoints/eight-examples-of-artificial-intelligence-in-action.html.

Palzer, S. (2022, November 29). Meaningful innovation to unlock growth. *Nestlé Investors Seminar, Barcelona, Spain*. https://www.nestle.com/sites/default/files/2022-12/investor-seminar-2022-innovation-transcript.pdf.

Peeler, R. (2023, August 31). The hidden costs of implementing AI in enterprise. *Forbes*. https://www.forbes.com/sites/forbestechcouncil/2023/08/31/the-hidden-costs-of-implementing-ai-in-enterprise/?sh=6deba3474d5c.

Roach, J. (2022, Oct 12). From Hot Wheels to handling content: How brands are using Microsoft AI to be more productive and imaginative. *Microsoft News*. https://news.microsoft.com/source/features/ai/from-hot-wheels-to-handling-content-how-brands-are-using-microsoft-ai-to-be-more-productive-and-imaginative/.

Pinski, M., Tarafdar, M., and Benlian, A. (2024, April 9). Why executives can't get comfortable with AI. *MIT Sloan Management Review*. https://sloanreview.mit.edu/article/why-executives-cant-get-comfortable-with-ai/#:~:text=AI%20will%20require%20continuous%20learning%3A%20Leaders%20need%20to,it%20and%20to%20productively%20interact%20with%20IT%20professionals.

Preface. (2023). What is a 'Digital Twin'? An introduction to the NASA technology. *Preface (technology education)*. https://www.preface.ai/blog/digital-twin-technology/.

RAND Corporation editorial team. (2024, August 14). New RAND Research—Why Do AI projects fail? *Inside AI News*. https://insideainews.com/2024/08/14/new-rand-research-why-do-ai-projects-fail/.

Reddi, L.T. (2023, March 25). How AI will help project planning. *Project Management Institute report*. https://www.projectmanagement.com/wikis/849920/how-ai-will-help-project-planning#_=_.

Rivard, D. (2022, February 17). BASF introduces Emollient Maestro, a digital service powered by AI to calculate ideal emollient mixes in cosmetics and personal care. *Industry Intel.* https://www.industryintel.com/transformation-and-innovation/news/basf-introduces-emollient-maestro-a-digital-service-powered-by-ai-to-calculate-ideal-emollient-mixes-in-cosmetics-and-personal-care-156927573024.

Rogers, E.M. (1962). Diffusion of Innovations, 1st ed. *Free Press of Glencoe*: OCLC 254636. https://search.worldcat.org/title/diffusion-of-innovations/oclc/254636.

Salesforce. (2023, March 7). Salesforce announces Einstein GPT, the world's first generative AI for CRM. *Salesforce press release.* https://www.salesforce.com/news/press-releases/2023/03/07/einstein-generative-ai/.

Satoh, H., Funatsu, K., and Yamamoto, H. (2024). Drug development supported by Informatics. *Springer Nature Singapore.* ISBN: 9789819748280. https://link.springer.com/book/10.1007/978-981-97-4828-0.

Schlegel, D., Schuler, K., and Westenberger, J. (2023). Failure factors of AI projects: Results from expert interviews. *International Journal of Information Systems and Project Management*, Vol. 11(3), 25–40. https://doi.org/10.12821/ijispm110302.

Schmidt, A., and Kristin, W. (2024). *The Digital Transformation of Product Formulation: Concepts, Challenges, and Applications for Accelerated Innovation.* 1st edition. CRC Press (New edition: 2025, Taylor and Francis). https://doi.org/10.1201/9781003385974.

Singla, A., Sukharevsky, A., Yee, L., Chui, M., and Hall, B. (2024). The state of AI in early 2024: Gen AI adoption spikes and starts to generate value. *Quantum Black by McKinsey.* https://www.mckinsey.com/capabilities/quantumblack/our-insights/the-state-of-ai.

Tadiparthi, G. (2024). Why AI projects fail. *InsiteAI.* https://www.insite.ai/why-ai-projects-fail/.

Unilever. (2023, June 12). Unilever and Arzeda use AI to develop performance-boosting enzymes. *Unilever News.* https://www.unilever.ca/news/2023/unilever-and-arzeda-use-ai-to-develop-performanceboosting-enzymes/.

Van Houtven, C. (2023, May 5). How artificial intelligence is accelerating digital product development. *LinkedIn.* https://www.linkedin.com/pulse/how-artificial-intelligence-accelerating-digital-van-houtven/.

Mendes, V.Z., and Vitari, C. (2024, June). A systematic literature review on the use of Artificial Intelligence in new product development. *R&D Management Conference, R&D Management; KTH Royal Institute of Technology, Stockholm, Sweden.* https://hal.science/hal-04627520/document.

Westenberger, J., Schuler, K., and Schlegel, D. (2022). Failure of AI projects: Understanding the critical factors. *Procedia Computer Science*, Vol. 196, 69–76. https://creativecommons.org/licenses/by-nc-nd/4.0.

https://doi.org/10.1142/9789819816347_0006

Chapter 6

Language Models as Tools of/in/by/for Thought

Steve J. Bickley

School of Economics and Finance, Queensland University of Technology, 2 George St, Brisbane, QLD 4000, Australia

Australian Research Council (ARC) Training Centre for Behavioural Insights for Technology Adoption (BITA), 2 George St, Brisbane, QLD 4000, Australia

Panalogy Lab Pty Ltd, Brisbane, QLD, Australia

1. Introduction

Recent advancements in Artificial Intelligence (AI) have ushered in an era where machines are evolving from passive tools of automation into dynamic, integrated partners within human creative and decision-making processes. Among these advancements, Large Language Models (LLMs) and Augmented Language Models (ALMs) stand out due to their unprecedented ability to understand, generate, and reason about information in ways that approach human-like complexity and to do so across a wide spectrum of domains.

In this chapter, I explore how LLMs and ALMs can extend beyond processing or generating text to serve as cognitive partners—*tools of thought*—creativity, problem-solving, and decision-making. With these models, individuals and organizations can better understand and communicate complex information, generate and evaluate innovative ideas, and simulate scenarios that might otherwise be inaccessible. However, the integration of ALMs into enterprise environments has delivered mixed outcomes, illustrating the need for context-specific approaches to AI adoption.

To address these complexities, I introduce a conceptual framework (Table 1) that adapts the "in/by/for" approach found in established responsible AI and ethics frameworks (Dignum, 2019; Bickley & Torgler, 2023). Table 1 outlines the integration of ALMs (Augmented Language Models) as Tools of/in/by/for Thought, providing a multi-dimensional lens for understanding their cognitive and ethical roles. Specifically, Tools in Thought focus on embedding ALMs into human and organizational workflows to enhance knowledge access, problem-solving, and decision-making. Tools by Thought emphasize the internal reasoning of ALMs, embedding structured logic, curated tasks, and value-aligned heuristics to ensure transparency and alignment with human objectives. Tools for Thought broaden this perspective by situating ALMs within a wider societal and stakeholder ecosystem, ensuring their deployment aligns with strategic, ethical, and regulatory standards. In doing so, we re-contextualize existing topics—previously organized around applications, ethics, safety, deployment, and refinement—within these new conceptual domains.

When mapped alongside the Ethics in/by/for Design framework, strong parallels emerge: Ethics in Design aligns with Tools in Thought by embedding ethical principles and processes at the outset, ensuring responsible integration into existing human workflows. Ethics by Design complements Tools by Thought, embedding ethical reasoning into ALM's decision-making and self-reflection processes. Finally, Ethics for Design mirrors Tools for Thought, establishing governance structures, accountability mechanisms, and ecosystem-wide oversight to ensure ALMs act in compliance with societal expectations and regulatory frameworks. By situating ALM workflows and ethical considerations within these interconnected dimensions, Table 1 provides a comprehensive foundation for responsibly integrating ALMs as tools of thought across diverse human, organizational, and societal contexts.

2. From Traditional NLP to Advanced Models

Understanding language is not merely about grammatical structures but fundamentally concerns how humans process, interpret, and communicate experience through narratives. Drawing from cognitive science and

Table 1. Comparison of frameworks for integrating ALMs as tools of/in/by/for thought and ethical principles in/by/for AI design and deployment.

Core Focus	**Tools in Thought:** Integration of ALMs into human cognitive and organizational workflows, shaping how people access, process, and produce knowledge.	**Tools by Thought:** Defining how (and what) ALMs (can) internally think, reason, and decide; embedding curated data and tasks, cognitive architectures, value-aligned heuristics, and structured reasoning frameworks.	**Tools for Thought:** Contextualizing ALM's broader ecosystem of stakeholders, standards, and societal expectations; guiding strategic decisions about selection, deployment, and management.
	Ethics in Design: Ensuring ethical and responsible AI principles are considered from the start (e.g., transparency and accountability), by defining responsible engineering processes, rules, and methodologies at the outset; translating values into technical requirements.	**Ethics by Design:** Designing algorithms and embedding ethical reasoning into AI so it can reason ethically, override simple rules, if necessary, continuously align with moral obligations, and allow adaptation for situational ethics.	**Ethics for Design:** Establishing governance frameworks, codes of conduct, regulatory requirements, professional guidelines, certification processes, and other oversight mechanisms and accountability structures that ensure adherence to ethical principles throughout the AI lifecycle, maintain public trust, and prevent harm.

(*Continued*)

Table 1. *Continued*

Desired Outcomes	**Tools in Thought:** Responsibly augmented human cognition and workflows, enhanced problem-solving, insight generation, and strategic decision-making.	**Tools by Thought:** ALMs that can self-reflect, maintain logical coherence, remain transparent, valid, and aligned with human preferences and organizational values.	**Tools for Thought:** Context-sensitive and well-informed use of ALMs across various industries, supported by strategic ecosystem awareness, responsible/ethical AI principles, and acts in compliance with regulations, via a proactive, risk-oriented approach.
	Ethics in Design: AI systems developed with ethical considerations "baked-in" to prevent harm, promote fairness, and maintain stakeholder trust from inception.	**Ethics by Design:** AI systems capable of autonomous ethical reasoning and moral adaptation, supporting complex, value-sensitive decisions.	**Ethics for Design:** Ensuring that AI developers and organizations uphold ethical principles, maintain public trust, and align with societal well-being through transparent governance and compliance.

narrative psychology, researchers such as Ferretti (2022) and Winston (2011) argue that storytelling is fundamental to human cognition, positioning humans as inherent "narrative processors", shaping our understanding of the world and its history through storytelling (MacMullen, 2003). Anthropological evidence by Brown (1991) reveals the narrative's universal role in explaining existential phenomena across diverse cultures, while Mueller (1990) extends this understanding to dream states, suggesting narratives permeate even our subconscious meaning-making processes.

The history and evolution of predictive language models (LMs) more specifically trace a journey from static probabilistic frameworks to the dynamic, neural architectures of modern LLMs (Hadi *et al.*, 2023; Wang *et al.*, 2024; Zhao *et al.*, 2023; Zhou *et al.*, 2024). Early statistical language models employed probabilistic methods to predict word sequences, relying on, e.g., n-gram models, with inherent limitations in capturing contextual nuances and long-range dependencies due to sparsity in data. While contributing significantly to tasks such as speech recognition and text retrieval, these models were fundamentally constrained by their static probability distributions and computational limitations at the time. The 'curse of dimensionality,' where the computational complexity grew nonlinearly with increased context window sizes, rendered comprehensive linguistic modeling extremely challenging (Goodman, 2001), if not intractable. The exponential growth of possible n-gram combinations meant that even with large corpora, many potential word sequences could remain unobserved, leading to unreliable probability estimates which translate into higher error rates.

The advent of Neural Language Models (NLMs) marked a pivotal paradigm shift, fundamentally reimagining probabilistic reasoning through neural network architectures. By embedding words into continuous vector spaces, NLMs enabled more dynamic and semantically rich representations. Models such as Word2Vec introduced semantic relationships through vector arithmetic, demonstrating how distributed representations could capture complex linguistic patterns beyond localized contexts. Pre-trained Language Models (PLMs) such as BERT and ELMo, in particular, represented a critical stage in NLM development, introducing pivotal techniques that would later define LLMs.

2.1. *Large language models (LLMs)*

LLMs have brought forward "emergent abilities," such as in-context learning, where the models could adapt to tasks with minimal to nil fine-tuning and often using only in-context prompting to steer model behavior. Unlike earlier models, LLMs exhibit general-purpose capabilities, leveraging massive pre-trained datasets to address a broad spectrum of complex real-world problems and tasks, ranging from conversational AI to multi-modal applications.

At their core, LLMs rely on autoregressive mechanisms to predict the next token in a sequence based on prior context. Each input word is encoded into a high-dimensional vector, capturing its semantic and syntactic relationships. The transformer architecture then utilizes multi-head attention to weigh the relevance of each token in the input sequence, enabling models to process long-range dependencies. Fine-tuning, with common techniques including reinforcement learning with human feedback (RLHF) and instruction tuning, can then enhance LLMs' utility for specific downstream applications—such as chatbots or recommendation systems—by aligning models with task-specific objectives and human preferences, for example.

But as Mitchell and Krakauer (2023) and Mahowald *et al.* (2024) highlight, formal linguistic competence (knowledge of language rules and patterns) and functional linguistic competence (using language in real-world contexts) are distinct capabilities, both in human cognition and in LLMs. The authors argue that while LLMs demonstrate near-human levels of formal linguistic competence, they fall short of functional linguistic competence, which requires broader cognitive abilities like reasoning, social understanding, and world knowledge. This distinction challenges misconceptions conflating linguistic ability with cognitive reasoning and highlights the need for empirical research that independently evaluates both competences.

Similarly, Messeri and Crockett (2024) caution that over-reliance on AI systems may foster "illusions of understanding," where users perceive AI outputs as inherently objective or exhaustive, overlooking the limitations embedded in their training and operational frameworks. Fundamentally, LLMs are shaped by their primary training objective (McCoy *et al.*, 2024): statistical next-word prediction. While this enables diverse downstream applications, it also introduces limitations, such as sensitivity to the probability of input/output tasks, or constraints of the models' context window and/or encoding or decoding processes.

2.2. *Augmented language models (ALMs)*

Addressing these gaps requires, among other approaches, various augmentation techniques to enhance both the technical and cognitive dimensions of LLMs in more complex, real-world applications. Mialon *et al.* (2023) provide a comprehensive and landmark review of techniques that augment and extend the capabilities of LLMs through reasoning and the integration of external tools, collectively termed as ALMs. This includes techniques such as chain-of-thought prompting and recursive decomposition, retrieval-augmented generation, and reinforcement learning techniques, as well as integrating external modules such as search engines, code interpreters, symbolic processors, and multi-modal capabilities.

These augmentations enable ALMs to perform tasks more effectively, including complex computations and multi-step reasoning (breakdown tasks into subtasks), and use tools as external modules that interact with the ALM to retrieve information (e.g., web search, document/file, and database operations) or act on the virtual or physical world (e.g., database operations, code interpreters, and call APIs through functions to push/pull information to the Internet). Therefore, helping overcome limitations of traditional LLMs, such as hallucinations, static/old knowledge bases, computational inefficiencies, and errors in reasoning.

3. Understanding ALMs as Tools of Thought

Since these models derive their capabilities from massive corpora of human-generated text—often drawn from a multitude of online sources—they are, in effect, collective knowledge bases shaped by the cultural, historical, and ideological contours of their training data. As a result, ALMs can often mirror or even amplify societal biases, norms, and assumptions. And may even nudge users toward specific perspectives and solutions or subtly frame problems in particular ways, thereby influencing not just individual decisions but also patterns of thought and discourse within organizations and entire social ecosystems. For example, systems such as Agent4Rec (Zhang *et al.*, 2024) showcase how generative agents can emulate user behavior to refine (manipulate) recommendation algorithms and study phenomena such as (human) filter bubbles which reinforce existing biases and limit exposure to diverse viewpoints. "Tools of Thought" addresses these broader social and societal implications of integrating ALMs into everyday decision-making processes.

This dimension prompts us to study ALMs from a social science perspective—examining how they propagate and reinforce certain values, how they interact with diverse cultural contexts, and how they may privilege some voices or viewpoints over others. Recognizing them as culturally situated artifacts can inform strategies for more inclusive and equitable model development. For example, ongoing research into ALM outputs can help identify biases and understand the tendencies toward "Western, educated, industrialized, rich, and democratic" (WEIRD) frames and value systems (Abdurahman *et al.*, 2024; Deshpande *et al.*, 2023). Addressing these biases involves refining training methodologies, carefully curating data sources, and implementing safety guardrails and alignment techniques.

Cultural differences in cognition reveal significant population-level variations shaped by environment, experience, and cultural routines, further highlighting the challenges of relying on WEIRD perspectives as universals (Henrich *et al.*, 2010). For example, in folkbiological reasoning, WEIRD populations often exhibit anthropocentric patterns (human-centered thinking), while small-scale societies emphasize ecological relationships, reflecting deeper integration with their natural environments. Similarly, in spatial cognition, Western populations favor egocentric reasoning (self-referenced spatial orientation), whereas many non-Western groups adopt allocentric or geocentric frames of reference (landscape- or earth-fixed systems). In modes of reasoning, Westerners often prioritize analytic thinking, characterized by isolating objects from their context and applying categorical rules for classification. In contrast, East Asian and other non-Western populations emphasize holistic reasoning, focusing on relationships and interdependencies within a broader contextual framework. These patterns underscore how ALMs trained predominantly on WEIRD-influenced data risk amplifying these biases, thereby shaping global applications of the technology in ways that may not reflect or respect broader human diversity and the pluralistic realities of human cognition and society.

This homogenization risk extends beyond cultural and cognitive biases to the centralization of knowledge and control within organizations and society. The increasing computational power and reach of ALMs enable unprecedented scalability in knowledge processing and decision-making, which may tempt some organizations to consolidate control, streamline processes, and centralize decision-making structures. However, as Helbing *et al.* (2019) argue, such centralization, particularly when embedded in surveillance systems and recommendation infrastructures, erodes individual autonomy, increases manipulation, and risks fragmenting societal cohesion by concentrating power in the hands of a few entities—whether governments, corporations, or influential individuals. These systems, through personalized information streams, nudging techniques, and recommender algorithms, can manipulate human behavior, thoughts, and decision-making at scale.

By creating "filter bubbles" that reinforce existing beliefs, they can polarize opinions, stifle creativity, and narrow the diversity of thought necessary for collective intelligence. This becomes particularly concerning as LLMs are increasingly applied as tools of learning and exploration since these filter bubbles risk constraining the knowledge spaces we search and explore. By limiting exposure to diverse perspectives, ideas, and problem-solving approaches, they may inadvertently restrict intellectual growth, reduce innovation, and inhibit the discovery of novel solutions. Therefore, underlining that without safeguards—such as decentralization, transparency, and informational self-determination—AI systems could transform humanity into passive consumers of predetermined narratives, undermining both individual agency and the resilience of pluralistic societies.

Building on these concerns, decentralization emerges not only as a safeguard against the risks of centralized systems but as an essential enabler of adaptability and inclusivity. Hayek (1945) argued that decentralized systems thrive by leveraging local, context-specific knowledge—insights that centralized entities often overlook or decontextualize, leading to a disconnect from on-the-ground realities. Likewise, Polanyi (1966) demonstrated that much of human expertise is tacit, learned through practice and experience, and inherently resistant to codification into explicit rules or datasets. ALMs trained on global, aggregated data thus often generalize patterns at the expense of these fine-grained insights, missing critical variability and specificity in localized environments; mirroring the pitfalls of centrally planned economies, where decision-makers erroneously assume they possess sufficient knowledge but lack the nuanced, context-specific insights critical for effective action. To address this, embedding decentralization into AI workflows—such as integrating ALMs with domain-specific data and human-in-the-loop oversight—enables organizations to retain and activate the tacit and local knowledge necessary for context-aware decision-making. Such a strategy not only ensures that tacit, local knowledge is activated within relevant bounds but also resists the homogenizing tendencies of centralized AI systems.

3.1. *ALMs as (Expanding) knowledge bases*

As AlKhamissi *et al.* (2022) highlight, LLMs have played a role in reshaping knowledge bases by functioning as dynamic, adaptive repositories of implicit and explicit knowledge. Unlike traditional Knowledge Bases (KBs), which rely on manually curated schemas and rule-based relationships, ALMs integrate vast structured and unstructured datasets during pretraining, encoding knowledge across distributed parameters in a deep neural network. This transition allows ALMs to perform reasoning, update facts dynamically, and generate contextually enriched outputs that extend beyond strict factual retrieval. Moreover, ALMs have demonstrated significant capabilities in transforming unstructured or less-structured data into structured, analyzable formats. For instance, ALMs can automate thematic coding in large-scale text datasets (Dai, Xiong & Ku, 2023; Drápal, Westermann & Savelka, 2023), extracting key patterns and insights without requiring manual annotation. Similarly, multi-modal models can extract and organize information from scanned documents, images, or handwritten texts, further bridging the gap between unstructured data and structured knowledge. However, as AlKhamissi *et al.* (2022) highlight, the diffused nature of knowledge within model parameters still poses challenges for access, consistency, and updateability, underscoring the need for methods that ensure transparency and validation during these transformation processes.

ALMs' conceptual framing as "style engines" (Riemer & Peter, 2024) emphasizes their application as tools that encode and blend patterns—be it linguistic, visual, or conceptual styles. This conceptualization dissolves the traditional distinction between an object and its appearance, reframing generative AI-generated content as representations of encoded "styles" that capture the essence or "thing-ness" of their training data. In other words, highlighting that LLMs encode data patterns probabilistically, allowing them to render more creative, stylistic outputs rather than storing or replicating data in a conventional sense.

By integrating external knowledge graphs, vector databases, and ontologies, ALMs can form layered knowledge ecosystems that bridge the generative flexibility of AI with the structured precision of traditional KBs. At one layer, the model provides fluent, human-like generation; at another layer, well-curated data sources ensure factual correctness and domain specificity. As Zhu *et al.* (2024) highlight, LLMs perform well in tasks like reasoning over knowledge graphs (KGs) and retrieving domain-specific information when supplemented with external data sources. This dynamic integration facilitates "retrieval-augmented generation" or RAG, where models such as GPT-4 use external KGs (and/or semantic datasets) for improved accuracy and contextual relevance, blending human-like fluency with reliable knowledge retrieval.

4. Integrating ALMs as Tools in Thought

"Tools in Thought" emphasizes how ALMs are integrated into human cognitive and organizational workflows. Some common task goals/objectives include programming support (e.g., code generation and debugging assistance), knowledge access (e.g., internal document retrieval and compliance checks), content creation (e.g., generating marketing copy and product descriptions), translation and tagging (e.g., multi-lingual support and domain-specific taxonomies), summarization and explanation (e.g., executive summaries of technical reports), creative ideation (e.g., brainstorming new product concepts), and scenario simulation/planning (e.g., forecasting market trends, evaluating policy impacts, or testing crisis response strategies). But rather than just existing as external utilities, taking a complex systems' perspective, these models become embedded elements that actively shape how individuals and teams access, process, and produce knowledge within the organization.

4.1. *ALMs as assistants and multi-agent systems*

Riemer and Peter (2024) introduce four primary archetypes of ALM-based agent systems, which can help guide the use-case ideation, design, and implementation process: *creative assistants*, *knowledge advisors*, *social companions*, and *task agents*. These archetypes distinguish between discrete, transactional uses (e.g., summarizing text or creating reports) and continuous, agent workflows and systems (e.g., AI companions or autonomous task agents), which can help organizations understand and frame the focus and extent of their AI use-cases.

Creative assistants assist with tasks ranging from summarizing or refining existing materials to generating original or exploratory content, leveraging humans' creativity and human–machine interactions with LLMs' capacity to encode and combine patterns as "styles." Knowledge advisors are more task-focused and function primarily as a more factual, reliable source of information or guidance in knowledge-intensive domains such as medicine or law (both as more extreme cases requiring strict knowledge retrieval). Social companions aim to mimic human conversation styles and emotional responsiveness, typically designed for ongoing, open-ended interactions, providing companionship, support, or entertainment over time. Lastly, task agents are single- and multi-agent systems specially designed to carry out ongoing, goal-directed, and knowledge-intensive tasks by combining generative capabilities with tools and process automation to complete complex, multi-step workflows.

4.2. *Applications of synthetic research in academia and industry*

In academia, generative agents offer important computational capabilities. For instance, in epidemic modeling (Williams *et al.*, 2023), these agents simulate human behaviors such as quarantine and risk perception, creating realistic feedback loops between disease dynamics and societal responses. This leads to more accurate projections and better-informed policy decisions. Similarly, in social sciences, simulated societies generated by ALMs allow researchers to explore complex social behaviors (Liu *et al.*, 2023; Park *et al.*, 2023), games, and systems (Gong *et al.*, 2023; Wang *et al.*, 2024; Xu *et al.*, 2024); for example, to test and refine community design strategies before real-world deployment (Park *et al.*, 2022), particularly useful in high-risk domains. Generative agents can also automate entire tasks and workflows, even ones as complex as chemical synthesis planning (Boiko, MacKnight, & Gomes, 2023).

In industry, generative agents enhance decision-making through scenario planning, risk assessment, and synthetic dataset generation. In other words, enabling organizations to explore at-scale various "what-if" scenarios with generative agents to, for example, stress-test different business strategies or brand/marketing communications, and help with identifying potential risks and testing different mitigation strategies through simulation. These so-called "silicon samples" are revolutionizing consumer research by mimicking diverse human responses, streamlining pretesting and pilot studies, hypothesis testing, and public opinion research; reducing costs (Argyle *et al.*, 2023; Bickley *et al.*, 2024; Sarstedt *et al.*, 2024), albeit acknowledging the difficulties in capturing behaviors or judgments driven by deep cultural or experiential context (Dillion *et al.*, 2023). Yet the capacity of generative agents to create high-quality synthetic data also addresses critical challenges in model training, improving representation across diverse tasks and demographics.

5. Designing ALMs as Tools by Thought

"Tools by Thought" encompasses several key activities: *teaching ALMs "How to Think"* by embedding structured reasoning paradigms and guiding principles into their inference processes; *deciding "What and How the ALM Thinks About"* by providing access to tools or external knowledge bases, curating prompts and training examples, defining task objectives, and specifying contextual boundaries; *"Evaluating the Alignment of ALM Reasoning"* through ongoing assessments, metrics, and feedback loops that ensure the model's logic remains transparent, valid, and values-aligned; and *providing "Human Oversight and Guidance"* to fine-tune outputs, adjust reasoning strategies, and maintain alignment with evolving organizational goals and ethical standards.

Deciding how ALMs can think requires mapping the ALM-based use cases and workflows to their mechanisms and types of data required. After defining clear, measurable objectives tied to broader goals, ensure data suitability and set transparent metrics for success (e.g., reduced resolution times, improved inventory turnover, and fewer false negatives). These criteria naturally guide small-scale pilots, enabling teams to validate assumptions, fine-tune model performance, and continually track key indicators—such as accuracy, fairness, and user satisfaction—using real-time monitoring and feedback loops. Table 2 provides examples of the augmentation techniques often used in ALM integrations, detailing their roles, mechanisms, workflow examples, and the types of data they can leverage.

Fine-tuning LLMs with expert data, as demonstrated in this paper that developed a philosopher-mimicking model (Schwitzgebel *et al.*, 2024), further extends their utility in producing domain-specific outputs for knowledge-intensive applications. Meanwhile, the modular nature of KG construction, as seen in frameworks such as AutoKG (see, e.g., Zhu *et al.*, 2024), can enhance automation and scalability, allowing businesses to dynamically adapt to evolving data landscapes.

As discussed in the work of Bickley and Torgler (2023), cognitive architectures are frameworks designed to mimic human cognitive processes, enabling artificial agents to perform complex reasoning, learning, and decision-making tasks. They are useful in this context because they provide structured approaches for integrating diverse cognitive functions, allowing agents to adaptively interact with their environments and execute sophisticated tasks. For Xi *et al.* (2023), the architecture comprises three core components: a "brain" or "planner" (LLM core), "perception" (multi-modal inputs), and "action" (interaction capabilities and task/workflow execution). The framework by Sumers *et al.* (2024) leverages a "brain" or decision procedure (again, LLM core) that interacts also with procedural, semantic, and episodic memory. Such modular approaches

Table 2. Augmentation techniques and their roles, mechanisms, and examples in workflows and data for ALM integrations.

Technique	Role in ALM Workflows	Mechanism	Workflow Examples	Example Data Types
Reinforcement Learning (RL)	Refines model behaviors by maximizing alignment with specific goals and values.	Uses iterative feedback to prioritize high-value actions and refine outputs.	• Optimizing customer support ALMs for satisfaction ratings. • Enhancing recommendation systems.	• User interaction logs. • Feedback surveys. • Operational performance metrics.
RAG with Knowledge Graphs	Enhances context and accuracy by integrating external structured and unstructured knowledge sources.	Retrieves relevant information from knowledge graphs and repositories to provide accurate contextual responses.	• Generating financial analysis using real-time market data. • Legal document summarization.	• Knowledge bases. • Document repositories. • FAQ datasets. • Real-time transactional systems.
Fine-Tuning	Customizes ALMs for specific industries, domains, or tasks.	Adapts general-purpose models by training them on domain-specific datasets.	• Training ALMs to assess patent applications. • Developing fraud detection systems in finance.	• Domain-specific datasets (e.g., healthcare, legal). • Historical task records. • Risk management case studies.

Codex	Automates code generation and validation for software development and computational workflows.	Uses natural language prompts in combination with in-built code interpreters, to generate, debug, and validate executable code.	• Automating logistics operations scripts. • Generating algorithms for supply chain optimization.	• API calls. • Process automation workflows. • Software development repositories.
Multi-modal Analysis	Integrates text, image, and video data for comprehensive analysis and output.	Combines insights from multiple data types to provide richer, context-aware results.	• Designing marketing campaigns using text and visuals. • Analyzing video content for defect detection.	• Textual feedback. • Visual media files. • Drone imagery and sensor data.
Multi-lingual Analysis	Expands global reach by supporting multi-language interactions and outputs.	Translates content and interactions across languages using specialized multi-lingual corpora.	• Translating corporate documents for multi-national use. • Multi-lingual customer support systems.	• Multi-language datasets. ○ Regional news articles. ○ Technical manuals.

allow the agent to execute a decision cycle, integrating retrieval, reasoning, and learning to adaptively propose, evaluate, and select actions.

However, harnessing "Tools by Thought" also calls for vigilance in maintaining human agency. Just as a driver who over-relies on an autonomous vehicle's self-driving features may lose situational awareness and relinquish too much control, organizations risk ceding critical decision-making power to ALMs. In doing so, human judgment and domain expertise can atrophy, allowing the model's probabilistic reasoning—trained on past patterns, not future possibilities—to shape outcomes unchecked. Such a dynamic may lull decision-makers into a passive stance, assuming the ALM's outputs are inherently valid and inevitably correct. To prevent this erosion of oversight and strategic discernment, it is essential to keep humans actively "behind the wheel": regularly interrogating the reasoning paths, stress-testing the model's assumptions, and proactively managing the division of cognitive labor. A continued emphasis on human-guided appraisal and intervention helps ensure that ALMs serve as thought partners rather than covertly becoming the sole navigators of complex organizational landscapes.

6. Contextualizing ALMs as Tools for Thought

"Tools for Thought" considers the interplay among model developers, model architectures, training data providers, companies, investors, customers, end users, research institutions, regulatory bodies, open-source communities, and standardization organizations.

Each of these entities influences the models' evolution and adoption, from funding research and guiding ethical standards to shaping deployment platforms and integration policies. Therefore, it is important to consider this broader context in which your prompt is embedded because the viability, trustworthiness, and long-term impact of ALMs are determined not solely by their technical performance but also by the diverse interests, constraints, and values of the ecosystem participants. This contextualization encompasses entire value chain and stakeholder network and can help in guiding strategic decisions about selecting, configuring, and managing ALMs across various industries.

Think of this as defining context as painting a vivid picture of where your organization stands—what it does, who it serves, what rules it must follow, what pressures it faces, and what opportunities it aims to seize—before you even start planning your AI systems. This "context" is not just about geography or industry; it's about the organization's values, its long-term goals, the interests of the people it affects, and the rules (legal, ethical, or societal) it must abide by. Understanding this broader picture ensures that when you implement AI, it aligns with your strategic objectives, respects the needs of stakeholders, and operates smoothly within all the internal and external conditions influencing your business.

6.1. *Legal and regulatory compliance*

The rapid advancements in AI, particularly in large language models (LLMs), clearly raise significant questions about the ownership and attribution of AI-generated outputs. Most existing Intellectual Property (IP) laws, such as copyright, patent, and trademark laws, are designed for human creators without explicitly addressing AI-generated works. While AI can assist in creating inventions, determining ownership of AI-assisted inventions may depend on the degree of human involvement in the creative process. For firms leveraging AI to create content (e.g., marketing materials, product designs, or research insights), the inability to claim exclusive ownership over AI-generated outputs could clearly impact competitive advantages.

AI models, particularly those trained on large-scale datasets, risk infringing on IP rights by incorporating copyrighted material or proprietary knowledge. Local and global data protection and privacy regulations, such as the General Data Protection Regulation (GDPR) in the European Union and the California Consumer Privacy Act (CCPA) in the United States, also impose strict requirements on how personal data is collected, stored, processed, and shared in different regressions. Hence, increasing the transaction costs for multi-national firms. While safety-critical sectors such as finance, healthcare, and aviation often have additional, more stringent regulatory requirements that can significantly impact AI implementations. And for good reason, AI decision-making that could have significant negative consequences for human livelihoods, such as misdiagnosing a patient or approving a fraudulent transaction, needs to be traceable so the right parties can be held accountable.

6.2. *Quality management and safety standards*

AI management (IEC/ISO 42001) does not operate in a vacuum (see, e.g., Table 3). Standards such as IEC/ISO 9001 (for quality), IEC/ISO ISO

Table 3. Frameworks and roles in guiding ALM safety, standards, and knowledge management.

Domain	Role	Impact on ALMs and Workflows
Functional Safety	Ensures systems operate predictably, avoiding harm.	Guides ALM development with protocols to prevent harmful outputs and errors in decision-making.
Quality Management Standards	Defines frameworks for consistency, reliability, and compliance.	Aligns ALM workflows with industry standards (e.g., ISO 9001) to ensure robust and auditable processes.
Document Engineering	Creates and manages structured, traceable documents.	Supports ALM workflows with transparent documentation for datasets, training processes, and outputs.
Knowledge Engineering	Structures and operationalizes knowledge within systems.	Embeds safety rules, task hierarchies, and domain-specific knowledge into ALMs for informed tool use.

61508 (for safety-critical systems), and IEC/ISO 27001 (for cybersecurity) provide complementary frameworks that can help organizations address the unique challenges of AI systems. Functional safety focuses on preventing harmful outputs through risk-oriented planning and implementation of safety controls, while quality management emphasizes consistency and compliance through systematic processes. Document engineering plays a critical, though often underemphasized, role by creating structured, traceable documentation for datasets, training workflows, and outputs. Finally, knowledge engineering operationalizes rules and task hierarchies within organizations. Together, these standards form a cohesive foundation for developing trustworthy and adaptive ALMs, capable of addressing evolving risks while maintaining operational integrity through transparent development, updates, and audits.

In practice, IEC/ISO 9001's PDCA model provides a systematic structure for iterative development and deployment. During the *Plan* phase, organizations define both quality objectives and functional safety requirements, such as implementing failover protocols for autonomous decision-making systems. These objectives are operationalized in the *Do* phase through actionable steps such as integrating diagnostic checks to ensure operational integrity. The *Check* phase incorporates regular audits and validation tests, leveraging functional safety practices to assess system robustness under varying conditions, while the *Act* phase uses these insights to refine both the AI system and its governance practices.

Functional safety standards, such as those outlined in IEC/ISO 61508, extend this lifecycle by addressing the evolving risks of dynamic AI systems, where updates to models or data pipelines may introduce new vulnerabilities. For instance, a hazard and operability study (HAZOP) can identify potential failure modes in AI algorithms, such as decision-making biases or real-time inference errors, ensuring mitigation strategies are implemented during the planning and execution phases.

ALMs can even be integrated within the quality/safety workflow itself (see Table 4 for examples). For instance, an organization which operates a facial recognition system in a public setting might assess risks such as potential invasion of privacy or misidentification of minority groups, using ALMs to explore the potential societal-, ethical-, and individual-level consequences through scenario-based simulations. With a slight pivot, the same ALMs can help the organization identify controls—technical (e.g., bias detection algorithms), organizational (e.g., policies against certain prohibited uses), and procedural (e.g., human-in-the-loop review of edge cases)—mapping them directly to the specific scenarios they simulate. They can then test (at scale) different possible variations on how best to implement these controls (via simulations), document their

Table 4. ALM Applications across domains for enhanced workflow and decision-making.

Domain	How ALMs Enhance Workflows	Example Use Case
Functional Safety	• Simulate and explore failure scenarios. • Generate solutions for risk mitigation in workflows.	Creating a fault tree analysis for autonomous vehicle systems.
Quality Management Standards	• Automate quality checks on outputs (e.g., ensuring ethical alignment in generated content).	Validating HR chatbot outputs for bias-free hiring processes.
Document Engineering	• Summarize, validate, and organize large volumes of structured and unstructured documents.	Generating safety reports for AI-powered manufacturing systems.
Knowledge Engineering	• Encode domain-specific knowledge into ALMs for operational tasks. • Enhance human–AI interaction.	Training ALMs to assist engineers with troubleshooting systems.

rationale (via content generation), and regularly review their effectiveness (via automated social/environmental sensing and aggregation).

6.3. *Hallucinations and misinformation in ALMs*

The dual capabilities of LLMs—as powerful tools for information processing and as potential vectors for misinformation—underscore the need for lifecycle- and systems-based thinking when integrating ALMs into human workflows and societal frameworks. As explored in the survey on hallucinations in LLMs (Zhang *et al.*, 2023), these models occasionally deviate from their input, context, or factual knowledge, resulting in "hallucinations" that may propagate incorrect or misleading information. This presents a pressing need for robust detection and mitigation strategies that can identify and address these deviations before they cause harm, particularly in high-stakes applications such as healthcare, finance, or public policy.

Simultaneously, as discussed in the misinformation landscape (Chen & Shu, 2024), the reasoning and multi-modal abilities of LLMs position them as transformative tools for detecting, attributing, and intervening against misinformation, as well as generating it. Their capacity to analyze vast datasets for patterns and inconsistencies makes them invaluable in combating fake news, rumors, and propaganda. However, these same abilities can be exploited to craft sophisticated misinformation, amplifying the risks of their misuse. This dual-edged nature of ALMs calls for carefully designed safeguards that limit the scope for generating harmful content while maximizing their potential to support truth and transparency.

A key challenge lies in constraining how ALMs think, reason, and behave in ways that are trustworthy, bias-free, and aligned with ethical principles while simultaneously fostering creativity and innovation. Achieving this balance is critical, as it reflects a broader paradox of AI development again, ensuring models adhere to strict ethical standards while enabling them to produce novel, insightful, and valuable outputs.

References

Abdurahman, S., Atari, M., Karimi-Malekabadi, F., Xue, M. J., Trager, J., Park, P. S., Golazizian, P., Omrani, A., and Dehghani, M. (2024). Perils and opportunities in using large language models in psychological research. *PNAS Nexus*, Vol. 3(7), 245. https://doi.org/10.1093/pnasnexus/pgae245.

AlKhamissi, B., Li, M., Celikyilmaz, A., Diab, M., and Ghazvininejad, M. (2022). A review on language models as knowledge bases. *arXiv preprint arXiv:2204.06031*. https://doi.org/10.48550/arXiv.2204.06031.

Argyle, L. P., Busby, E. C., Fulda, N., Gubler, J. R., Rytting, C., and Wingate, D. (2023). Out of one, many: Using language models to simulate human samples. *Political Analysis*, Vol. 31(3), 337–351. https://doi.org/10.1017/pan.2023.2.

Bickley, S. J., Chan, H. F., Dao, B., Torgler, B., Tran, S., and Zimbatu, A. (2024). Comparing human and synthetic data in service research: Using augmented language models to study service failures and recoveries. *Journal of Services Marketing*. https://doi.org/10.1108/JSM-11-2023-0441.

Bickley, S. J., and Torgler, B. (2023). Cognitive architectures for artificial intelligence ethics. *AI & Society*, Vol. 38(2), 501–519. https://doi.org/10.1007/s00146-022-01452-9.

Boiko, D. A., MacKnight, R., and Gomes, G. (2023). Emergent autonomous scientific research capabilities of large language models. *arXiv preprint arXiv:2304.05332*. https://doi.org/10.48550/arXiv.2304.05332.

Chen, C., and Shu, K. (2024). Combating misinformation in the age of llms: Opportunities and challenges. *AI Magazine*, Vol. 45(3), 354–368. https://doi.org/10.1002/aaai.12188.

Brown, D. E. (1991). Human Universals. *Boston: McGraw-Hill*. ISBN: 978-0070082090.

Dai, S. C., Xiong, A., and Ku, L. W. (2023). LLM-in-the-loop: Leveraging large language model for thematic analysis. *arXiv preprint arXiv:2310.15100*. https://doi.org/10.48550/arXiv.2310.15100.

Deshpande, A., Murahari, V., Rajpurohit, T., Kalyan, A., and Narasimhan, K. (2023). Toxicity in chatgpt: Analyzing persona-assigned language models. *arXiv preprint arXiv:2304.05335*. https://doi.org/10.48550/arXiv.2304.05335.

Dignum V (2019) Responsible artificial intelligence: How to develop and use AI in a responsible way. *Springer Nature*. https://doi.org/10.1007/978-3-030-30371-6.

Dillion, D., Tandon, N., Gu, Y., and Gray, K. (2023). Can AI language models replace human participants? *Trends in Cognitive Sciences*, Vol. 27(7), 597–600. https://doi.org/10.1016/j.tics.2023.04.008.

Drápal, J., Westermann, H., and Savelka, J. (2023). Using Large Language Models to Support Thematic Analysis in Empirical Legal Studies. In *JURIX 2023: The 36th Annual Conference* (pp. 197–206), Maastricht, the Netherlands. https://doi.org/10.3233/faia230965.

Ferretti, F. (2022). Narrative persuasion. A cognitive perspective on language evolution. *Springer Nature*. https://doi.org/10.1007/978-3-031-09206-0.

Gong, R., Huang, Q., Ma, X., Vo, H., Durante, Z., Noda, Y., Zheng, Z., Zhu, S., Terzopoulos, D., Fei-Fei, L., and Gao, J. (2023). Mindagent: Emergent gaming interaction. *arXiv preprint arXiv:2309.09971*. https://doi.org/10.48550/arXiv.2309.09971.

Goodman, J. T. (2001). A bit of progress in language modelling. *Computer Speech & Language*, Vol. 15(4), 403–434. https://doi.org/10.1006/csla.2001.0174.

Hadi, M. U., Qureshi, R., Shah, A., Irfan, M., Zafar, A., Shaikh, M. B., Akhtar, N., Hassan, S., Shoman, M., Wu, J., Mirjalili, S., and Shah, M. (2023). A survey on large language models: Applications, challenges, limitations, and practical usage. *Authorea Preprints*. https://doi.org/10.36227/techrxiv.23589741.v1/.

Hayek, F. A. (1945). The use of knowledge in society. *American Economic Review*, Vol. 35(4), 519–530. https://www.jstor.org/stable/1809376.

Helbing, D., Frey, B. S., Gigerenzer, G., Hafen, E., Hagner, M., Hofstetter, Y., van den Hoven, J., Zicari, R.V., and Zwitter, A. (2019). Will democracy survive big data and artificial intelligence? In D. Helbing (Ed.): *Towards digital enlightenment: Essays on the dark and light sides of the digital revolution* (pp. 73–98). Cham, Germany: Springer. https://doi.org/10.1007/978-3-319-90869-4_7.

Henrich, J., Heine, S. J., and Norenzayan, A. (2010). The weirdest people in the world? *Behavioral and Brain Sciences*, Vol. 33(2-3), 61–83. https://doi.org//10.1017/S0140525X0999152X.

Liu, R., Yang, R., Jia, C., Zhang, G., Zhou, D., Dai, A. M., Yang, D., and Vosoughi, S. (2023). Training socially aligned language models on simulated social interactions. *arXiv preprint arXiv:2305.16960*. https://doi.org/10.48550/arXiv.2305.16960.

MacMullen, R. (2003). Feelings in history, ancient and modern. *California, US: Regina Books*. ISBN: 978-1479379835.

Mahowald, K., Ivanova, A. A., Blank, I. A., Kanwisher, N., Tenenbaum, J. B., and Fedorenko, E. (2024). Dissociating language and thought in large language models. *Trends in Cognitive Sciences*, Vol. 28(6), 517–540. https://doi.org/10.1016/j.tics.2024.01.011.

McCoy, R. T., Yao, S., Friedman, D., Hardy, M. D., and Griffiths, T. L. (2024). Embers of autoregression show how large language models are shaped by the problem they are trained to solve. *Proceedings of the National Academy of Sciences (PNAS)*, Vol. 121(41), e2322420121. https://doi.org/10.1073/pnas.2322420121.

Messeri, L., and Crockett, M. J. (2024). Artificial intelligence and illusions of understanding in scientific research. *Nature*, Vol. 627(8002), 49–58. https://doi.org/10.1038/s41586-024-07146-0.

Mitchell, M., and Krakauer, D. C. (2023). The debate over understanding in AI's large language models. *Proceedings of the National Academy of Sciences (PNAS)*, Vol. 120(13), e2215907120. https://doi.org/10.1073/pnas.2215907120.

Mueller, E. T. (1990). Daydreaming in Humans and Machines: A Computer Model of the Stream of Thought. *New York, US: Ablex Publishing Corp.* ISBN: 978-0-89391-562-9.

Polanyi, M. (1966). The Logic of Tacit Inference. *Philosophy*, Vol. 41(155), 1–18. https://doi.org/10.1017/S0031819100066110.

Riemer, K., and Peter, S. (2024). Conceptualizing generative AI as style engines: Application archetypes and implications. *International Journal of Information Management*, Vol. 79, 102824. https://doi.org/10.1016/j.ijinfomgt.2024.102824.

Mialon, G., Dessì, R., Lomeli, M., Nalmpantis, C., Pasunuru, R., Raileanu, R., ... and Scialom, T. (2023). Augmented language models: A survey. *arXiv preprint arXiv:2302.07842*. https://doi.org/10.48550/arXiv.2302.07842.

Park, J. S., O'Brien, J., Cai, C. J., Morris, M. R., Liang, P., and Bernstein, M. S. (2023). Generative agents: Interactive simulacra of human behavior. In *UIST '23: Proceedings of the 36th Annual ACM Symposium on User Interface Software and Technology* (pp. 1–22). https://doi.org/10.1145/3586183.3606763.

Park, J. S., Popowski, L., Cai, C., Morris, M. R., Liang, P., and Bernstein, M. S. (2022). Social simulacra: Creating populated prototypes for social computing systems. In *UIST '22: Proceedings of the 35th Annual ACM Symposium on User Interface Software and Technology* (pp. 1–18). https://doi.org/10.1145/3526113.3545616.

Sarstedt, M., Adler, S. J., Rau, L., and Schmitt, B. (2024). Using large language models to generate silicon samples in consumer and marketing research: Challenges, opportunities, and guidelines. *Psychology & Marketing*, Vol. 41(6), 1254–1270. https://doi.org/10.1002/mar.21982.

Schwitzgebel, E., Schwitzgebel, D., and Strasser, A. (2024). Creating a large language model of a philosopher. *Mind & Language*, Vol. 39(2), 237–259. https://doi.org/10.1111/mila.12466.

Sumers, T. R., Yao, S., Narasimhan, K., and Griffiths, T. L. (2023). Cognitive architectures for language agents. *arXiv preprint arXiv:2309.02427*. https://doi.org/10.48550/arXiv.2309.02427.

Wang, Z., Chu, Z., Doan, T. V., Ni, S., Yang, M., and Zhang, W. (2024). History, development, and principles of large language models: An introductory survey. *AI and Ethics*, 1–17. https://doi.org/10.1007/s43681-024-00583-7.

Wang, L., Ma, C., Feng, X., Zhang, Z., Yang, H., Zhang, J., Chen, Z., Tang, J., Chen, X., Lin, Y., Zhao, W., Wei, Z., and Wen, J. (2024). A survey on large language model based autonomous agents. *Frontiers of Computer Science*, Vol. 18(6), 186345. https://doi.org/10.1007/s11704-024-40231-1.

Williams, R., Hosseinichimeh, N., Majumdar, A., and Ghaffarzadegan, N. (2023). Epidemic modelling with generative agents. *arXiv preprint arXiv:2307.04986*. https://doi.org/10.48550/arXiv.2307.04986.

Winston, P. H. (2011). The Strong Story Hypothesis and the Directed Perception Hypothesis. In *2011 AAAI (Association for the Advancement of Artificial Intelligence) Fall Symposium Series* (FS-11-01), November 4-6, United States, Virginia.

Xi, Z., Chen, W., Guo, X., He, W., Ding, Y., Hong, B., Zhang, M., Wang, J., Jin, S., Zhou, E., Zheng, R., Fan, X., Wang, X., Xiong, L., Zhou, Y., Wang, W., Jiang, C., Zou, Y., Liu, X., Yin, Z., Dou, S., Weng, R., Cheng, W., Zhang, Q., Qin, W., Zheng, Y., Qiu, X., Huang, X., and Gui, T. (2023). The rise and potential of large language model based agents: A survey. *arXiv preprint arXiv:2309.07864*. https://doi.org/10.48550/arXiv.2309.07864.

Xu, X., Wang, Y., Xu, C., Ding, Z., Jiang, J., Ding, Z., and Karlsson, B. F. (2024). A survey on game playing agents and large models: Methods, applications, and challenges. *arXiv preprint arXiv:2403.10249*. https://doi.org/10.48550/arXiv.2403.10249.

Zhang, Y., Li, Y., Cui, L., Cai, D., Liu, L., Fu, T., Huang, X., Zhao, E., Zhang, Y., Chen, Y., Wang, L., Luu, A. T., Bi, W., Shi, F., and Shi, S. (2023). Siren's song in the AI ocean: A survey on hallucination in large language models. *arXivpreprintarXiv:2309.01219*.https://doi.org/10.48550/arXiv.2309.01219.

Zhang, A., Chen, Y., Sheng, L., Wang, X., and Chua, T. S. (2024, July). On generative agents in recommendation. In *SIGIR '24: Proceedings of the 47th International ACM SIGIR Conference on Research and Development in Information Retrieval* (pp. 1807–1817). https://doi.org/10.1145/3626772.3657844.

Zhao, W. X., Zhou, K., Li, J., Tang, T., Wang, X., Hou, Y., Min, Y., Zhang, B., Zhang, J., Dong, Z., Du, Y., Yang, C., Chen, Y., Chen, Z., Jiang, J., Ren, R., Li, Y., Tang, Z., Liu, Z., Liu, P., Nie, J., and Wen, J. (2023). A survey of large language models. *arXiv preprint arXiv:2303.18223*. https://doi.org/10.48550/arXiv.2303.18223.

Zhou, C., Li, Q., Li, C., Yu, J., Liu, Y., Wang, G., ... and Sun, L. (2024). A comprehensive survey on pretrained foundation models: A history from bert to chatgpt. *International Journal of Machine Learning and Cybernetics*, 1–65. https://doi.org/10.1007/s13042-024-02443-6.

Zhu, Y., Wang, X., Chen, J., Qiao, S., Ou, Y., Yao, Y., Deng, S., Chen, H., awnd Zhang, N. (2024). LLMs for knowledge graph construction and reasoning: Recent capabilities and future opportunities. *World Wide Web*, Vol. 27, 58. https://doi.org/10.1007/s11280-024-01297-w.

https://doi.org/10.1142/9789819816347_0007

Chapter 7

Generative AI and Multi-Agent Systems in Management

Andrzej Wodecki

Warsaw University of Technology, Department of Management, Warsaw, Poland

1. Introduction

Generative technologies are becoming increasingly widespread. Most likely, no other contemporary technology has seen such rapid adoption as solutions such as ChatGPT (Cromwell *et al.*, 2023). This growth is mainly due to their ease of use, the speed with which they deliver results, and the breadth of tasks they can address: Large language models can respond to queries quickly and accurately, solve complex problems almost instantaneously, and image generation systems produce increasingly sophisticated visuals.

It is, therefore, not surprising that people of all ages, from primary school students to retirees, are embracing these tools in their daily lives, uncovering new use cases along the way. Naturally, these tools have also begun infiltrating workplaces, sparking growing interest from organizations (Bick *et al.*, 2024; Davis & Li, 2024). Unlike other AI methods (e.g., regression models, classification, or segmentation), which often demand large, high-quality datasets, data science teams, and complex deployments, generative technologies typically require far fewer resources upfront. Usually, it is sufficient to procure access to these systems, allowing employees to integrate them organically into their workflows. The result: a low entry barrier, satisfied employees, and rapid productivity improvements.

However, the reality of widespread adoption is more nuanced. First, these technologies can fall victim to their own simplicity: Users, pleased with the initial, surface-level results, may believe they have mastered the tools (an "illusion of competence"). This phenomenon is not new; similar assumptions have long existed for office suites or search engines, where most people feel that knowing the basics is enough. Yet, unlocking the true potential of generative AI—whether through advanced prompt engineering, specialized model fine-tuning, or workflow integration—often demands greater awareness, education, and skill development.

Second, the ease of adoption can mask significant legal and compliance concerns. Only when IT departments restrict access to open systems such as ChatGPT do legal teams sometimes recognize the importance of confidentiality and data privacy. Addressing these issues demands a sophisticated understanding of regulatory frameworks and the variety of technological architectures offered by different vendors to ensure secure and compliant implementations.

Third, companies implementing generative technologies often discover their transformative potential only after initial deployment. While these solutions can streamline individual tasks, they can reshape entire business processes, influence organizational structures, and redefine value creation. In other words, what may start as a simple productivity aid can evolve into a catalyst for broad organizational transformation.

Indeed, research increasingly highlights the substantial role of generative AI in driving innovation and digital transformation. Venture capital firms have invested over 1.7 billion USD in generative AI solutions, underscoring their confidence in this technology's potential (Mariani & Dwivedi, 2024). Far beyond simple automation, generative AI is emerging as a transformative force that reshapes innovation management landscapes. It compels organizations to rethink strategies, restructure operations, and maintain human-centric approaches to harness these systems effectively. As these models advance, they enable the automation of complex creative tasks previously requiring significant human intellect, thereby redefining innovation processes and fostering digital transformation across numerous industries (Felicetti *et al.*, 2024).

It is, therefore, not surprising that the impact of generative technologies on organizational activities is becoming a focal point of intense study. On the one hand, researchers concentrate on the evolution and refinement of the technologies themselves; on the other, they examine their current and potential impacts across various organizational areas, entire sectors, and the models through which companies generate new value. In this chapter, we outline this landscape: briefly presenting generative technologies and their capabilities, exploring their influence on business operations, evaluating costs and benefits, identifying challenges and best practices for implementation, and finally, discussing the most promising avenues for future research.

2. Generative Technologies and Their Capabilities

The concept of "generative technologies" is very ambiguous. This one term includes systems that analyze and generate not only text, but also voice (audio), images, or video, but also systems that enable data analysis, advanced reasoning, and inference. And multi-agent systems, composed of many agents equipped with various tools, can often solve very complex problems.

2.1. *A bit of history*

Naturally, many different technologies developed for many years form the foundations of such systems. These technologies depend on the modality: We use various methods for analysis, processing, and text generation, and others for similar operations on images or inference and decision-making. The dynamic development of generative technologies in the modern sense of the word is mainly due to the transformer technology (Vaswani *et al.*, 2023). Simply put, so-called attention mechanisms make it possible to train and improve systems that allow for the continuation of the text. In this sense, generative models are "predictive" once: They allow identifying the most probable sequences of words following the entered phrase and thus "generate" new texts.

Large language models that provide such functionalities are, as the name suggests, "large" (often containing more than 1 trillion (10^{12}) parameters) neural networks (Gadre *et al.*, 2024). Such large network sizes require enormous computing resources to train them (for example, the cost of training a GPT-4 model is estimated at tens of millions of dollars (Cottier *et al.*, 2024)), as well as the so-called inference (answers to users' questions). As a result, only a few organizations are able to train and serve large language models on their own, and in practice, it is less likely to offer them in a free formula.

Conversely, the growing capabilities of generative technologies are capturing increasing interest from both individual users and organizations. While the following section delves into their potential economic impact and market dynamics, this section focuses on the technical aspects of generative technologies that are critical for successful organizational implementation. The following points aim to address the most frequently asked questions and concerns raised by managers and decision-makers.

2.2. *There are many different generative models*

The diversity of generative models is vast. Understanding this differentiation is very important from an implementation perspective, so we'll present it from several dimensions in the following.

The first dimension of the differentiation of generative models is the so-called modality. Generative models can specialize in analyzing, processing, and generating texts (so-called language models), images (e.g., diffusion models), videos, or sounds. Multi-modal models (e.g., Google Gemini or GPT-4V) are also becoming increasingly popular, allowing, e.g., understanding an image or a video (a text description of the situation in the image) or generating an image based on text messages (Song *et al.*, 2023).

Another dimension is size. Large language models are neural networks with more than trillions of parameters. As already mentioned, such structures require vast resources (hardware, energy, and specialists) both for training and inference. However, medium-sized models (from 9 to 80 billion parameters) and small ones (the so-called small or specialized language models, with less than 2 billion parameters), are already appearing on the market (Nguyen *et al.*, 2024). These models can often run on relatively weak devices (small servers, PCs, notebooks, or even mobile phones). They can not only be used to solve simple, general problems but also be trained to solve narrow, specialized ones. Finally, they can be configured into complex multi-agent frameworks that are slowly starting to compete in quality with large language models.

The next dimension is the license for use. Models can be closed (e.g., the OpenAI, Google, or Anthropic model family) and open (e.g., the Llama model family offered by Meta (*Llama*, 2024)). Open models can often be downloaded and run on local devices and used for research and commercial purposes (Minaee *et al.*, 2024). Although the issue of model openness is currently the subject of much discussion, such solutions undoubtedly broaden the spectrum of strategies for launching them in organizations.

This brings us to another aspect of generative technologies: runtime options.

2.3. *Language models can be hosted on internal providers, in the public cloud, on premise, and edge devices*

Organizations interested in implementing generative technologies most often face the problem of data confidentiality. The most popular option: using free and/or paid access to services such as OpenAI, ChatGPT, Anthropic Claude, or Google Gemini to analyze documents containing confidential or personal data boils down to sharing this information with unauthorized third parties. How to prevent this? The simplest solution is to use the so-called "public cloud": language models made available as part of dedicated to a given organization, secure (both technically and from a legal perspective) cloud solutions offered by companies such as Microsoft, Google, or Amazon. It is currently (2024) the safest and most economically effective option for access to generative technologies.

Suppose the organization cannot share its data with other entities (e.g., particularly sensitive medical, financial, or defense data). In that case, there is still the option of hosting generative models on its infrastructure; however, this solution requires obtaining a relatively expensive infrastructure.

2.4. *Generative models have much more possibilities than just "generating" content*

When formulating a business case for an AI-based solution, it is worth being as fully aware as possible of the possibilities and limitations of these methods and techniques. Naturally, we identify generative technologies with content (texts, images, or videos) "generation." Sometimes, we also note elements of "reasoning," especially when AI allows us to solve complex, e.g., mathematical, problems.

However, the capabilities of these technologies go far beyond "generation." In fact, there are so many of them that it is worth developing a framework that allows us to move quickly in this dynamic reality. In the following, we present such heuristics for single models (tentatively called "assistants"), models equipped with tools ("agents"), and multi-agent structures ("Agentic AI").

Let's start with individual language models. Their capabilities can be divided into three groups: generation, transformation, and analysis (Figure 1).

Generation is the most commonly used functionality. Generative systems allow us to generate not only text (e.g., a poem) but also a computer program, synthetic data, image, or video. The user enters text on the input and receives the desired object on the output.

In the case of **transformation**, the input can contain plain text and other types of objects: program, image, or data. Transformation can involve changing the style, translating into another language (including programming), or transforming an image.

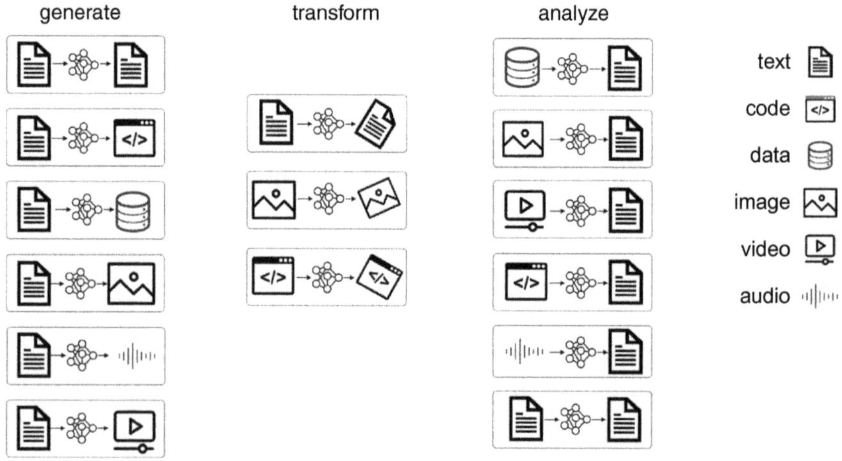

Figure 1. Schematic depiction of generative AI capabilities. The blocks above may be used to model a data pipeline in the GenAI software development analysis stage.

Analysis capabilities are essential in business applications. As in the case of transformation, we can analyze text, data, computer programs, images, video, or voice. In particular, extract keywords, identify sentiment, recognize situations, etc.

2.5. *The quality of the answer strongly depends on the quality of the question*

As already mentioned, generative models are, in a nutshell, predictive models. The vast number of connections in these neural networks makes their answers (1) unpredictable and (2) strongly dependent on the questions introduced at the input. Awareness of this fact has driven the rapid evolution of prompt engineering—a collection of methods and techniques designed to enhance the quality of responses (and even reasoning processes) of generative models. Notably, this encompasses both the "soft" skill of crafting effective queries and the "hard" technical strategies employed by programmers. As a result, a subtle yet significant shift has occurred: Queries have emerged as a new form of knowledge, complementing the established categories of explicit and implicit knowledge. To support this development, engineers have created innovative methods for storing them, such as prompt libraries.

As we demonstrate next, this development could have intriguing implications for the future of both knowledge management and project management.

2.6. *Hallucinations of generative technologies can be reduced*

"Hallucinations" are inherent in generative technologies. Let's remember that, in a sense, these are predictive systems: They generate their answers in a "stochastic" way. This raises natural concerns among users. How can I be sure that the answers given by, for example, my virtual assistant are grounded in facts?

Fortunately, this problem is recognized and addressed, with better or worse results, by a large part of the community involved in the development of GenAI. Retrieval Augmented Generation (RAG) systems enable generative models to obtain the information necessary to provide answers from trusted sources, e.g., public or private knowledge bases (Gao *et al.*, 2024). Technologies such as Pydantic not only force generative models to respond in a specific format but also give these models prompts on how to achieve it. On the other hand, extensive evaluation systems such as RAG triads or RAGAS enable advanced statistical analysis of the correctness of the answers given by such systems (Yu *et al*., 2024). Finally, advanced techniques such as Graph RAG not only enable the extraction of knowledge structures (graphs) from large text or multimedia sets but also, in conjunction with RAG systems, the creation of Question-and-Answer systems that provide answers based on information scattered throughout the knowledge corpus (so-called multi-hop questions) (Edge *et al*., 2024). It is, therefore, not surprising that generative models are only a part, sometimes small, of systems based on them. More interestingly, the quality of such comprehensive solutions is primarily influenced by the "higher-level" methods used in them and the architecture as a whole, and not necessarily by the generative models themselves. This brings us to the next observation.

Generative models can be an integral part of other applications—they do not always have to be available in the form of conversational interfaces (e.g., assistants or chat).

In the public sphere, generative technologies are frequently accessed through conversational interfaces, which are commonly associated with this technology. However, in professional applications, generative models are more often integrated into programming pipelines, serving roles akin to advanced computational functions or machine learning models. In this capacity, they remain "invisible" to end users while delivering significant value. Recognizing the role of generative technologies within IT system architectures is often the first step toward designing truly transformative use cases.

2.7. *We can create semi-autonomous structures equipped with the ability to reason*

In addition to the above-mentioned "basic" abilities, generative systems are also often equipped with higher-order skills, both "acquired" in the training process (e.g., arithmetic reasoning, common-sense reasoning), or different types of logical reasoning (e.g., deductive, inductive, or abductive reasoning), as well as solutions indicated by the designer using prompt-engineering (e.g., chain-of-thought or tree-of-thought) (Plaat *et al*., 2024). The field of improving the methods of "thinking" machines by equipping them with various "thinking tools" is developing very dynamically and has great potential for use in business, particularly in strategic management.

The next phase in the development of generative technologies, particularly significant for their application in management, involves the emergence of so-called agent structures (Guo *et al.*, 2024a; Li *et al.*, 2024; Yang *et al.*, 2024). An agent is a generative model equipped with tools such as the ability to search for information on the Internet, query internal knowledge bases or databases, run computer scripts, and integrate with office suites or even with computer operating systems (Figure 2).

The functioning of an agent equipped with a set of tools can be described as follows: Upon receiving a complex task from a user, the language model breaks it down into smaller, more manageable subtasks. It then identifies the tools within its set that are best suited to handle each subtask. The agent executes these subtasks using the selected tools, integrates the results into a cohesive final response, and presents it to the user (or forwards it if it is part of a larger development pipeline).

The virtually unlimited potential of these systems stems from the fact that any computer function designed by the system creator can serve as a tool. In practice, this means that anything implementable within an IT system can be made available as a tool for the agent.

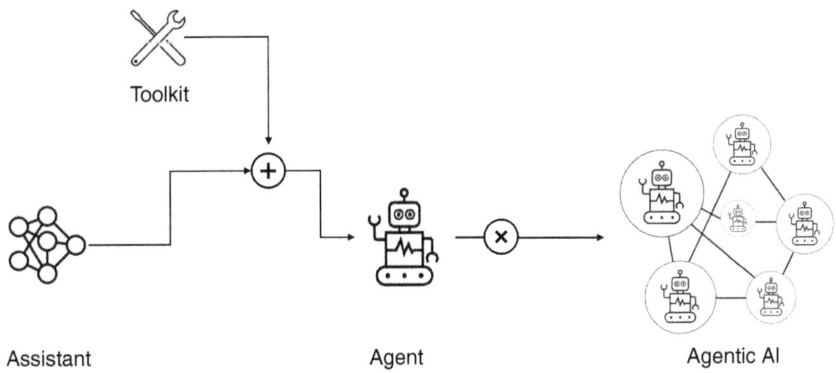

Figure 2. Schematic representation of the evolution of generative AI systems, from the generative model (assistant), via agent (generative model equipped with tools) to agentic AI (multi-agent, generative model-based system). Since generative models may be multimodal, we try to avoid LLMs (Large Language Models) here.

Agents are capable of handling complex tasks, but as problem complexity increases, the quality of their responses often diminishes. To overcome this limitation, significant research in recent years has focused on developing multi-agent structures. These systems consist of multiple agents collaborating within hierarchical or non-hierarchical frameworks to address highly complex problems (Figure 3). Leveraging distributed decision-making, coordinated problem-solving strategies, and adaptive learning mechanisms, these multi-agent systems have demonstrated exceptional effectiveness, prompting a growing number of organizations to adopt them in (Guo *et al.*, 2024b; Li *et al.*, 2024; Yang *et al.*, 2024). This adoption, in turn, drives not only further research but also the creation of increasingly sophisticated IT environments that facilitate their design, such as Langgraph, Microsoft AutoGen, CrewAI, OpenAI Swarm, and Amazon Bedrock Agents. These advancements strongly suggest that the future of artificial intelligence lies in agentic AI.

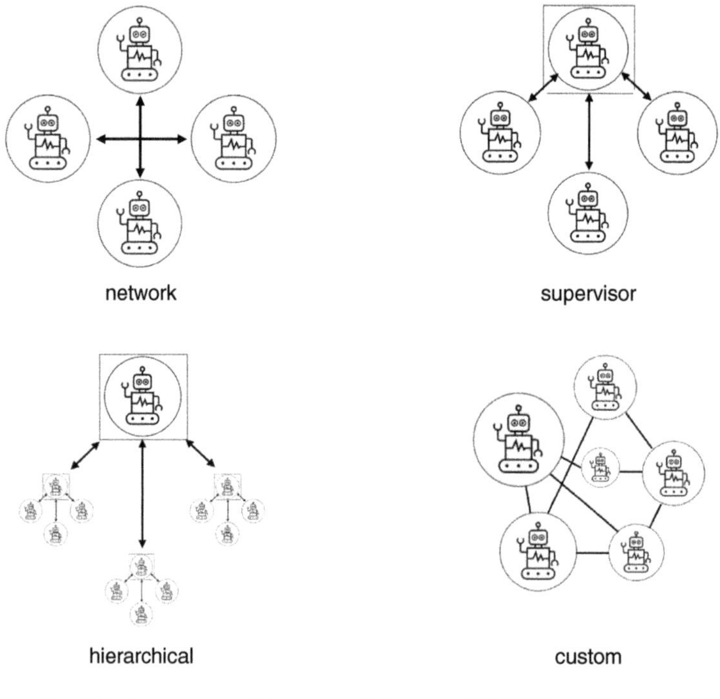

Figure 3. Most common multi-agent architectures (Multi-Agent Systems, 2024).

Having provided a basic overview of key technologies and their core capabilities, we can now turn to a brief discussion of their current and potential impact on organizational operations and management.

3. Impact

The rapid advancements in generative artificial intelligence (AI), notably large language models (LLMs), are reshaping a wide spectrum of business domains. Emerging evidence suggests that generative AI can significantly enhance productivity and streamline operations, influencing industries ranging from software development and manufacturing to marketing, supply chain management, and professional services. While these technologies show immense potential in augmenting human capabilities, they also raise new operational, strategic, and ethical questions that warrant careful consideration.

3.1. *Productivity and work dynamics*

Generative AI-driven tools are increasingly deployed to augment knowledge work, particularly in software development and related domains. Empirical evidence indicates that LLMs can significantly improve task efficiency and reshape workflows, enabling individuals and teams to focus on higher-level problem-solving (Eloundou *et al.*, 2023). For instance, research on GitHub Copilot demonstrates that generative AI can influence task allocation among software developers, accelerating coding processes and improving output quality (Hoffmann *et al.*, 2024). These findings underscore the potential of LLMs to not only assist in routine tasks but also foster organizational innovation and knowledge-intensive work.

In corporate meeting environments, generative AI and other natural language processing tools can enhance productivity by summarizing discussions, identifying key decision-makers, and promoting balanced participation. Morgan Stanley's Debrief, developed in collaboration with OpenAI, illustrates how generative AI applications can summarize video meetings and generate follow-up communications, streamlining workflows and improving efficiency (*Morgan Stanley Has a New OpenAI-Powered Assistant for Its Financial Advisors*, 2024).

3.2. *Project and process management*

Project and process management is another domain undergoing rapid transformation due to generative AI's capabilities. Scholars have proposed the notion of "Large Process Models" (LPMs) that combine LLMs with knowledge-based systems to offer context-specific recommendations for process improvement (Kampik *et al.*, 2023). Similarly, "ProcessGPT" has been introduced as a model trained on extensive business process data to enhance decision-making and improve data-centric workflows (Beheshti *et al.*, 2023). These approaches have the potential to optimize resource allocation, refine project timelines, and enhance decision-making accuracy (Badmus, 2023).

3.3. *Product and service development*

Generative AI has shown remarkable promise in product and service development, particularly in manufacturing, design, and pharmaceuticals. For example, Toyota's integration of generative AI in vehicle design reportedly reduced design cycle times by 50%, optimizing both materials and costs (Mast, 2023). In the pharmaceutical sector, LLM-driven methods are expediting drug discovery and molecular design, with projections suggesting that by 2025, approximately 30% of new drugs and materials could be discovered using generative AI techniques (Mariani & Dwivedi, 2024). Such advancements signal a shift toward more rapid, data-informed innovation processes.

Beyond manufacturing and pharmaceuticals, creative industries are leveraging generative AI to enhance content production. Gaming company Ubisoft uses AI to assist in writing non-playable characters' dialogs, enriching player experiences (*The Convergence of AI and Creativity*, 2024). Media organizations such as *Forbes*, *The New York Times*, and *The Washington Post* employ LLMs to generate articles with minimal human editing, though these applications raise questions about editorial standards, ethics, and the responsible use of training data (Brigham *et al.*, 2024).

3.4. *Software development*

The software development sector has embraced generative AI to bolster productivity and address talent shortages. Studies from MIT Technology Review (2024) outline how generative AI can automate routine coding tasks, facilitate rapid prototyping, and improve software quality (*Transforming Software with Generative AI*, 2024; *Unleash Developer Productivity with Generative AI | McKinsey*, 2023). These tools can potentially reduce time-to-market and enhance developer satisfaction, ultimately transforming software engineering practices (Jedlitschka, 2024).

3.5. *Supply chain management and back-office processes*

General AI-driven multi-agent systems, such as InvAgent, increasingly influence supply chain management, which leverages LLMs to optimize inventory management and improve overall supply chain resilience (*InvAgent*, 2024). In finance, generative AI enhances budget forecasting, real-time fraud detection, and risk management while providing more accurate stock and earnings predictions than human analysts (Kim *et al.*, 2024). The legal sector also integrates generative AI tools for contract drafting, opinion formulation, and rapid legal research. Firms such as Gilbert + Tobin and MinterEllison have introduced AI functionalities that ensure reliable, secure, and efficient legal processes (Huber, 2024).

3.6. *Sales, marketing, and customer experience*

Generative AI is transforming marketing strategies and customer engagement. Kshetri describes how generative AI can create new content, enhance marketing initiatives, and improve strategic decision-making (Kshetri *et al.*, 2024). Fashion brands use AI-generated images for promotional campaigns, reducing production costs and time while expanding creative possibilities. Similarly, in hospitality, Remountakis demonstrates that generative AI can craft tailored marketing content in hotel marketing, resonating with target audiences and improving engagement (Remountakis *et al.*, 2023). Moreover, innovative applications in e-commerce have integrated LLMs into conversational recommender systems, enhancing user interaction and satisfaction (Liu *et al.*, 2023).

3.7. *Strategic decision-making and education*

Generative AI's role extends to strategic decision-making and innovation management. Multi-agent systems powered by LLMs have shown the capacity to handle complex business problems and provide actionable strategic insights (Nguyen & Tulabandhula, 2023). In education, LLMs may foster collaborative learning, improve feedback mechanisms, and encourage knowledge convergence, although ethical and practical challenges must be addressed (Yan *et al.*, 2024; Zheng *et al.*, 2023).

3.8. *Labor market implications*

As generative AI technologies diffuse across industries, labor market dynamics are shifting. Unlike previous waves of automation, which often targeted routine tasks, generative AI can potentially affect a broad range of knowledge-based occupations. While some roles may be redefined, research suggests that generative AI could enhance freelancers' output and popularity in creative sectors (Hui *et al.*, 2023; *Research: How Gen AI Is Already Impacting the Labor Market*, 2024). Thus, the technology's impact involves both the transformation of existing jobs and the emergence of new capabilities and roles.

3.9. *Business models of LLM providers*

The potential applications of generative technologies in management are undeniably vast, which explains the growing demand for such services from both individuals and organizations. However, as previously noted, the high cost of training and deploying large generative models creates a notable tension between increasing demand and significant expenses. This dynamic yields several interesting outcomes.

First, companies developing LLMs continue to face challenges in establishing sustainable business models, partly due to the rapid expansion of the market for open, high-quality generative models. Second, there is a parallel surge in the development and adoption of small (or specialized) language models, further reshaping the competitive landscape.

As a result, SLMs are becoming a viable alternative to large language models, which may have major consequences for the adoption of such solutions among smaller organizations and the business models of LLM providers on the one hand. Companies interested in maintaining generative solutions on their own infrastructure see more and more potential in multi-agent solutions based on SLMs—they are not only cheaper to operate but also (potentially) better suited to their own needs.

Finally, it is important to remember the very high environmental costs of maintaining large language models (reference needed). This is a cost to not only suppliers but also societies. Therefore, there are many indications that multi-agent structures and small, specialized generative models have a very high potential for development and use in the future. And they are naturally an attractive direction for future research.

Generative AI represents a transformative force in business and management, offering increased productivity, improved decision-making, and the potential to drive innovative product and service development. From project management and supply chain optimization to personalized marketing and strategic decision-making, these tools are reshaping how organizations operate.

What value can the implementation of these solutions generate in practice?

The first category of benefits is the reduction of operating costs (*601 Real-World Gen AI Use Cases from the World's Leading Organizations*, 2025). Automation of processes, especially those related to the processing of large amounts of text data, reduces the time of completing tedious tasks and their costs. This is directly linked to improving employee productivity. Generative technologies not only reduce the time of text or data analysis but also make it possible to improve the quality of the tasks performed, which, combined with the acceleration of processes, translates into improved service quality and, as a result, increased customer satisfaction. Generative technologies also make it possible to not only accelerate the processes of designing new solutions but also generate qualitatively new ideas. Finally, multi-agent structures create opportunities to solve complex problems, laying the foundation for qualitatively new forms of human–machine collaboration (Yang *et al.*, 2024).

The summary of the potential value added of generative AI is presented in Table 1.

4. Implementation

As can be seen, generative technologies can generate a wide variety of values. How to implement them effectively?

Implementations of generative technologies are subject to "laws" similar to the implementations of IT systems or other methods of artificial intelligence. Here, too, it is crucial to design a portfolio of potential

Table 1. A summary of GenAI value added. Source: Own elaboration, basing on a literaturȩ review, specifically (601 Real-World Gen AI Use Cases from the World's Leading Organizations, 2025)

Category	Value	Examples
Strategic Decision-Making and Insights	Faster scenario planning, data-driven strategy formulation	Multi-agent LLMs reducing M&A due diligence from weeks to days; board-level decision support tools improving strategic investment decisions
Project and Process Management	Optimized resource allocation, accelerated workflows, higher operational efficiency	"Large Process Models" cutting project planning times by 60%; ProcessGPT enabling real-time process adjustments, leading to faster product rollouts
Product and Service Development	Shortened R&D cycles, improved product quality, enhanced innovation	Toyota's 50% reduction in automotive design cycles; LLM-driven molecular discovery enabling quicker drug candidate identification (Mariani & Dwivedi, 2024)
Software Development	Increased developer productivity, higher code quality, rapid prototyping	30% boost in developer productivity at Turing; AI-assisted debugging reducing defect rates by 20% and speeding up code integration (Hoffmann *et al.*, 2024)
Supply Chain and Back-Office Operations	Improved inventory management, better forecasting, reduced manual processes	InvAgent optimizing inventory levels, cutting stockouts by 20%; automated invoice processing reducing financial close times from days to hours
Marketing and Customer Engagement	Personalized campaigns, higher conversion rates, enhanced customer experiences	AI-generated marketing content increased hotel booking conversions by 15%; Conversational recommenders boosted user engagement and retention (Liu *et al.*, 2023)

Table 1. (*Continued*)

Category	Value	Examples
Education and Knowledge Management	Faster skill acquisition, improved training efficiency, collaborative learning	LLM-driven onboarding reducing new employee training by 40%; AI-assisted course materials enabling quicker understanding and knowledge transfer (Zheng *et al.*, 2023)
Compliance and Risk Management	Accurate legal research, efficient regulatory checks, lower risk exposure	AI-enabled contract analysis streamlining review times from days to hours; Finance teams improving fraud detection accuracy by 30% (Kim *et al.*, 2024)
Sustainability and Environmental Impact	Reduced energy consumption, greener operations, efficient resource usage	Smaller, domain-specific LLMs lowering GPU utilization by 30%, shrinking carbon footprints and data center costs
Ethical and Responsible AI Use	Greater trust, adherence to guidelines, minimized bias and misinformation	Integrated bias detection reducing discriminatory outputs; Compliance frameworks ensuring responsible data usage and alignment with privacy regulations
Operational Efficiency and Employee Empowerment	Time savings, improved workforce productivity, better allocation of human talent	80% reduction in manual captioning time (Warner Bros. Discovery); AI-enabled assistants enabling caseworkers to save 25 hours/week (Bayes Impact)

projects, taking into account their difficulty of implementation and impact on the business, properly formulate goals, and measures of success and then plan, implement, monitor, and maintain the project. “Nihil novi sub sol.”

In projects of this type, however, special attention should be paid to the 1. data management, 2. proper preparation of employees, and 3. possible ethical consequences of implementing such systems.

As in any other AI projects, data quality sits at the heart of GenAI effectiveness. Successful implementations rely on zero or first-party data, regular data updates, and proper labeling processes that maintain model accuracy and reliability. Establishing robust data pipelines, validation processes, and continuous monitoring helps organizations mitigate the risks of biased outputs and incorrect predictions. By embedding data stewardship into GenAI initiatives from the outset, companies reinforce model integrity and ensure that the insights generated can guide informed decision-making.

An important problem, probably most often indicated by practitioners, is the issue of data privacy and, more broadly, compliance with regulations. This applies both to the issue of data confidentiality (personal, sensitive, or simply secret data) but also to the processing of large amounts of publicly available data or the generation of own content using generative models. While the first issue is relatively easy to solve, the next ones can be more challenging.

Generative technologies enable the creation of vast amounts of synthetic data, posing significant challenges to the data governance systems within organizations. Moreover, the ability to generate new content—particularly multimedia—using models trained on publicly available online resources has long been met with resistance from creators whose works have been utilized in this manner. The absence of clear regulations in this area presents a dilemma not only for creators but also for producers, such as major computer game companies. For instance, interpreting image-generation systems such as Midjourney as tools in the hands of artists employed by publishers can be a double-edged sword. While it provides some protection, it falls short of adequately safeguarding creators' works from being exploited by others. In this context, organizational leaders face the critical responsibility of ensuring compliance with evolving regulations, protecting user privacy, and maintaining transparent data-handling practices. Without strong oversight and robust compliance frameworks, organizations risk severe consequences, including reputational harm, legal liabilities, and a loss of stakeholder trust, all of which can undermine their long-term success.

The possibilities of generative technologies raise not only hopes but also many concerns, much of them ethical. That is why organizations should develop governance models to guide GenAI initiatives. Responsible innovation requires frameworks that uphold ethical standards, ensure transparency in algorithmic decision-making, and incorporate mechanisms for regular oversight. Recent Harvard Business Review discussions emphasize the necessity of balancing innovation with responsibility by setting clear guidelines, monitoring compliance, and conducting ethical audits. These governance structures foster trust among stakeholders and reduce the risk of reputational damage or unintended negative consequences (Baxter & Schlesinger, 2023).

Robust GenAI deployments require a workforce prepared to interpret and act on machine-generated insights. Upskilling staff and cultivating new capabilities ensure that employees can fully leverage GenAI's potential. Training programs, workshops, and integrated learning experiences—where teams learn on the job—empower employees to navigate GenAI tools confidently. Beyond technical skills, workers benefit from developing critical thinking abilities and acquiring competencies that enable them to integrate GenAI outputs into strategic decision-making processes.

In this area, a slightly less obvious challenge is the very dynamic development of generative technologies (Liebowitz, 2024). Virtually every key programming library in this market provides new, important features on a monthly basis, and makes fundamental changes on an annual basis. This development is of course positive in itself (it allows problems to be solved in a new, better way), but it generates several new challenges. To keep up with the capabilities of these systems, developers need to spend a lot of time learning, naturally spending less time on work. On the other hand: Involvement almost exclusively in work (often in the case of IT specialists overloaded with duties) generates a large technical debt (implementation of projects based on old, ineffective solutions). As a result, a dilemma arises: How to find a balance between work and learning? What proportions should be maintained between these activities? It turns out to be a remarkable challenge in a regime of many projects and tight deadlines...

Fortunately, generative technologies can partially help solve this dilemma. They support programmers in not only designing, producing, and testing good-quality code but also learning. Therefore, it is possible to imagine a situation in which properly implemented generative technologies will cause the implemented IT project also to become a situation that allows learning the latest technologies. The methodologies of such a generative technology-supported learning-by-doing process are a very interesting direction for future research.

The complexity of multi-agent architectures can challenge traditional software engineering methods. As already mentioned, multi-agent architectures are teams of generative models equipped with different sets of tools organized to perform respective tasks for a given organization with a high degree of complexity. Their design largely comes down to mapping heuristics and human workflows and, to a lesser extent, to the software itself. This, in turn, requires different skills than code development. For this reason, "flow engineering" can be an interesting alternative to programming skills, which will soon be able to be more or less automated by generative technologies. In this context, the implementation of multi-agent structures can be a challenge for modern organizations: It will force a new look at the processes of software development and maintenance and will generate the need to develop new strategies for integrating business processes with IT systems (here, semi-automatic multi-agent structures).

Additionally, research indicates that the aforementioned multi-agent systems introduce new layers of complexity, including the need for well-defined communication protocols, decision-making transparency, and reliable orchestration mechanisms (Li *et al.*, 2024). Ensuring each agent can communicate effectively, maintain internal consistency, and align with overarching business objectives requires carefully designed agent profiling and capacity-building processes. The reliability of such systems depends on performance evaluation frameworks that can assess individual agent efficacy and collective outcomes. These frameworks must incorporate metrics for coordination efficiency, error resolution, and long-term adaptability, thereby offering organizations insights into the holistic functioning of the multi-agent environment.

Finally, as GenAI lowers content creation, knowledge generation, and software development barriers, organizations must reconsider their traditional roles and value propositions. For instance, advisory firms that previously relied on expert analysis and guidance may need to reshape their offerings, focusing more on meta-level competencies such as curating knowledge flows, verifying outputs, and refining strategic directions. Similarly, knowledge workers may find their roles transforming into orchestrators of AI-driven processes rather than direct producers of content. In academic and research settings, for example, the principal investigator or scientist might function as a conductor, defining the research question, shaping the methodology, and verifying the outputs generated by GenAI agents. In this evolving scenario, the human expert's value lies in conceptualizing problems, ensuring intellectual rigor, and maintaining ethical and methodological standards amidst an abundance of automated, AI-generated advisory materials.

5. Thoughts, Trends, and Future Research Directions

Generative technologies, perhaps more than any other human-created innovation, encroach upon domains traditionally considered the exclusive realm of human activity. Unsurprisingly, this raises profound questions about the future role of humans within organizations. In the following section, we aim to highlight several compelling research areas—topics that, when explored, not only offer significant cognitive insights but also provide practical guidance for organizations seeking to integrate generative AI more effectively.

Let's start with an inspiring area at the intersection of knowledge management and project management. A very interesting issue is the emergence of questions as a new form of knowledge. Organizations have so far focused on collecting and codifying knowledge already acquired. In the context of effective use of generative technologies, it is equally important, if not more important, to collect "prompts": questions formulated in such a way that the generative model's answer addresses the user's intentions in the best possible way. Since the potential of generative technologies in management is so great, and their effectiveness strongly depends on questions, why not add a new stage to project management methodologies: one whose goal is to formulate questions that will form the basis for subsequent actions? For example, precede the Product Breakdown Structure > Work Breakdown Structure (PBS > WBS) sequence often found in projects with a Question Breakdown Structure (QBS) session. Either way, in the context of the development of generative technologies, one can expect a renaissance of the art of questioning ("Quizzics") or prompt skilling.

The significant potential of multi-agent structures deserves particular attention. In this area, the disparity between the rapid advancement of methods and techniques and their adoption in management is especially pronounced. Particularly compelling research topics include exploring advanced mechanisms for cooperation, efficient task delegation, and communication among agents, as well as investigating how these structures can be integrated with existing business processes and workflow engineering. Another critical challenge lies in addressing the scalability of such systems in corporate environments and their broader application across diverse industries. Moreover, viewing agents as virtual employees equipped with specific skills and tools opens an intriguing line of inquiry. This perspective invites an examination of how traditional human resource management practices could be adapted to select and assign agents to specific tasks—a concept that might be described as "AI Resource Management."

Now, let's turn to the impact of GenAI on innovation. Early studies have indicated that GenAI can augment human innovation teams during the new product development process, e.g., by facilitating larger problem-solving spaces and enhancing innovation performance. Mariani and Dwivedi go even further, identifying 10 major research themes that can guide future research developments at the intersection of GenAI and innovation management (Mariani & Dwivedi, 2024b). In the context presented in this chapter, however, another research question naturally arises: to what extent might generative technologies not so much enhance as impair human capacity to create innovative solutions? How will humans behave when technologies provide them with the ability to generate not only new content but also innovative ideas or breakthroughs quickly and in practice effortlessly? How will this affect the role of humans in the whole process? And, at a slightly higher level, how do we manage innovation processes so that contact with the machine strengthens us rather than weakens us?

Finally, it will be necessary, as perhaps never before, to develop methods for evaluating the impact of GenAI on organizational performance. Generative technologies are excellent at rapidly generating solutions, often with multiple variants. However, organizations do not have the resources and space to implement them all. Thus, a rational choice is key: deciding what to implement and how. Due to the innovative nature of these technologies, many companies are forced to make such decisions based on intuition. However, it is definitely better to build it upon experience, preferably acquired in a scientific "regime." For this reason, it is worth considering refining experimental methods to assess the actual impact of generative technologies on operational efficiency and accumulating this knowledge in a way that allows the best optimization of processes in the future.

6. Conclusions

We live in interesting times. The concept of innovation is naturally evolving: from the "classic" era with Schumpeter's theory of creative destruction and innovation as a linear process through the era of systems thinking (innovation as a complex system), the beginnings of technology management, the network era (knowledge networks, collaborative environments), to the current era of digital transformation (platform-based, user-driven innovation supported by agile and lean methodologies). Nowadays, generative technologies may become a force that, once again in history, will change innovation processes and perhaps even redefine the concept of creativity. It is, therefore, worth leaning into these new possibilities, balancing the development of technologies and the study of their impact not only on organizations but also on the human condition and our environment as a whole.

And a final thought. Modern children have access to an array of powerful tools, enabling them to answer almost any question or solve virtually any problem. Yet, this remarkable capability comes with a risk—they may miss out on one of the most critical factors in human development: surprise. The gap between what is expected and what is experienced has long been a driver of learning and innovation. In a world where nearly everything is known and can be explained in an instant, how do we foster surprise-driven learning and spark genuine innovation? This is why the science of surprise and human engagement is not only timely but also essential.

References

601 real-world gen AI use cases from the world's leading organizations. (2025). *Google Cloud Blog*. Retrieved June 29, 2025, from https://cloud.google.com/transform/101-real-world-generative-ai-use-cases-from-industry-leaders

Badmus, O. F. (2023). Transforming Program Management through Generative Artificial Intelligence. *International Journal of Latest Engineering and Management Research (IJLEMR)*, Vol. 8(12).

Baxter, K., and Schlesinger, Y. (2023). Managing the Risks of Generative AI. Retrieved December 10, 2024, from https://hbr.org/2023/06/managing-the-risks-of-generative-ai

Beheshti, A., Yang, J., Sheng, Q. Z., Benatallah, B., Casati, F., Dustdar, S., Nezhad, H. R. M., Zhang, X., and Xue, S. (2023). ProcessGPT: Transforming Business Process Management with Generative Artificial Intelligence (No. arXiv:2306.01771). *arXiv*. https://doi.org/10.48550/arXiv.2306.01771

Bick, A., Blandin, A., and Deming, D. J. (2024). The Rapid Adoption of Generative AI (Working Paper No. 32966). *National Bureau of Economic Research*. https://doi.org/10.3386/w32966

Brigham, N. G., Gao, C., Kohno, T., Roesner, F., and Mireshghallah, N. (2024). Breaking News: Case Studies of Generative AI's Use in Journalism (No. arXiv:2406.13706; Version 1). *arXiv*. https://doi.org/10.48550/arXiv.2406.13706

Cottier, B., Rahman, R., Fattorini, L., Maslej, N., and Owen, D. (2024). The rising costs of training frontier AI models (No. arXiv:2405.21015). *arXiv*. https://doi.org/10.48550/arXiv.2405.21015

Cromwell, J. R., Harvey, J.-F., Haase, J., and Gardner, H. K. (2023). Discovering Where ChatGPT Can Create Value for Your Company. *Harvard Business Review*. Retrieved December 9, 2024, from https://hbr.org/2023/06/discovering-where-chatgpt-can-create-value-for-your-company?t

Davis, J. P., and Li, J. B. (2024). Early Adoption of Generative AI by Global Business Leaders: Insights from an INSEAD Alumni Survey (No. arXiv:2404.04543). *arXiv*. https://doi.org/10.48550/arXiv.2404.04543

Edge, D., Trinh, H., Cheng, N., Bradley, J., Chao, A., Mody, A., Truitt, S., and Larson, J. (2024). From Local to Global: A Graph RAG Approach to Query-Focused Summarization (No. arXiv:2404.16130). *arXiv*. https://doi.org/10.48550/arXiv.2404.16130

Eloundou, T., Manning, S., Mishkin, P., and Rock, D. (2023). GPTs are GPTs: An Early Look at the Labor Market Impact Potential of Large Language Models (No. arXiv:2303.10130). *arXiv*. https://doi.org/10.48550/arXiv.2303.10130

Felicetti, A. M., Cimino, A., Mazzoleni, A., and Ammirato, S. (2024). Artificial intelligence and project management: An empirical investigation on the appropriation of generative Chatbots by project managers. *Journal of Innovation & Knowledge*, Vol. 9(3). https://doi.org/10.1016/j.jik.2024.100545

Gadre, S. Y., Smyrnis, G., Shankar, V., Gururangan, S., Wortsman, M., Shao, R., Mercat, J., Fang, A., Li, J., Keh, S., Xin, R., Nezhurina, M., Vasiljevic, I., Jitsev, J., Soldaini, L., Dimakis, A. G., Ilharco, G., Koh, P. W., Song, S., and Schmidt, L. (2024). Language models scale reliably with over-training and on downstream tasks (No. arXiv:2403.08540). *arXiv*. https://doi.org/10.48550/arXiv.2403.08540

Gao, Y., Xiong, Y., Gao, X., Jia, K., Pan, J., Bi, Y., Dai, Y., Sun, J., Wang, M., and Wang, H. (2024). Retrieval-Augmented Generation for Large Language Models: A Survey (No. arXiv:2312.10997). *arXiv*. https://doi.org/10.48550/arXiv.2312.10997

Guo, T., Chen, X., Wang, Y., Chang, R., Pei, S., Chawla, N. V., Wiest, O., and Zhang, X. (2024a). Large Language Model based Multi-Agents: A Survey of Progress and Challenges (No. arXiv:2402.01680). *arXiv*. https://doi.org/10.48550/arXiv.2402.01680

Guo, T., Chen, X., Wang, Y., Chang, R., Pei, S., Chawla, N. V., Wiest, O., and Zhang, X. (2024b). Large Language Model Based Multi-agents: A Survey of

Progress and Challenges. *Proceedings of the Thirty-Third International Joint Conference on Artificial Intelligence*, 8048. https://doi.org/10.24963/ijcai.2024/890

Hoffmann, M., Boysel, S., Nagle, F., Peng, S., and Xu, K. (2024). Generative AI and the Nature of Work. *Harvard Business Review*. https://www.hbs.edu/ris/Publication%20Files/25-021_49adad7c-a02c-41ef-b887-ff6d894b06a3.pdf

Huber, N. (2024, May 17). Law firms start generative AI rollout, with safeguards. *Financial Times*. https://www.ft.com/content/a3be653f-2563-4e65-a64c-c2f31a4f8bf7

Hui, X., Reshef, O., and Zhou, L. (2023). CESifo Working Paper no. 10601.

InvAgent: A Large Language Model based Multi-Agent System for Inventory Management in Supply Chains | AI Research Paper Details. (2024). Retrieved December 9, 2024, from https://aimodels.fyi

Jedlitschka, D. J. S., Dr Andreas. (2024, November 25). Generative AI in Software Engineering: Scenarios and Challenges Ahead—Blog des Fraunhofer IESE. *Fraunhofer IESE*. https://www.iese.fraunhofer.de/blog/generative-ai-in-software-engineering-scenarios-and-challenges/

Kampik, T., Warmuth, C., Rebmann, A., Agam, R., Egger, L. N. P., Gerber, A., Hoffart, J., Kolk, J., Herzig, P., Decker, G., Aa, H. van der, Polyvyanyy, A., Rinderle-Ma, S., Weber, I., and Weidlich, M. (2023). Large Process Models: Business Process Management in the Age of Generative AI (No. arXiv: 2309.00900). *arXiv*. https://doi.org/10.48550/arXiv.2309.00900

Kim, A. G., Muhn, M., and Nikolaev, V. V. (2024). Financial Statement Analysis with Large Language Models. *SSRN*. https://doi.org/10.2139/ssrn.4835311

Kshetri, N., Dwivedi, Y. K., Davenport, T., and Panteli, N. (2024). Generative Artificial Intelligence in Marketing: Applications, Opportunities, Challenges, and Research Agenda. *International Journal of Information Management*, Vol. 75. https://eprints.lancs.ac.uk/id/eprint/206556/

Li, X., Wang, S., Zeng, S., Wu, Y., and Yang, Y. (2024). A survey on LLM-based multi-agent systems: Workflow, infrastructure, and challenges. *Vicinagearth*, Vol. 1(1), 9. https://doi.org/10.1007/s44336-024-00009-2

Liebowitz, J. (ed.) (2024). Regulating Hate Speech Created by Generative AI. *Taylor & Francis*.

Liu, Y., Zhang, W., Chen, Y., Zhang, Y., Bai, H., Feng, F., Cui, H., Li, Y., and Che, W. (2023). Conversational Recommender System and Large Language Model Are Made for Each Other in E-commerce Pre-sales Dialogue. In H. Bouamor, J. Pino, and K. Bali (Eds.), *Findings of the Association for Computational Linguistics: EMNLP 2023* (pp. 9587f the Association for Computational Linguistics. https://doi.org/10.18653/v1/2023.findings-emnlp.643

Llama. (2024). Meta Llama. Retrieved December 9, 2024, from https://www.llama.com/

Mariani, M., and Dwivedi, Y. K. (2024). Generative artificial intelligence in innovation management: A preview of future research developments. *Journal of Business Research*, Vol. 175, 114542. https://doi.org/10.1016/j.jbusres.2024.114542

Mast, G. (2023, June 20). Toyota Research Institute Unveils New Generative AI Technique for Vehicle Design. *Toyota USA Newsroom*. https://pressroom.toyota.com/toyota-research-institute-unveils-new-generative-ai-technique-for-vehicle-design/

Minaee, S., Mikolov, T., Nikzad, N., Chenaghlu, M., Socher, R., Amatriain, X., and Gao, J. (2024). Large Language Models: A Survey (No. arXiv:2402.06196). *arXiv*. https://doi.org/10.48550/arXiv.2402.06196

Morgan Stanley has a new OpenAI-powered assistant for its financial advisors. (2024, June 26). *Quartz*. https://qz.com/morgan-stanley-openai-debrief-ai-chatbot-genai-1851561076

Multi-agent Systems. (2024). Retrieved December 10, 2024, from https://langchain-ai.github.io/langgraph/concepts/multi_agent/

Nguyen, C. V., Shen, X., Aponte, R., Xia, Y., Basu, S., Hu, Z., Chen, J., Parmar, M., Kunapuli, S., Barrow, J., Wu, J., Singh, A., Wang, Y., Gu, J., Dernoncourt, F., Ahmed, N. K., Lipka, N., Zhang, R., Chen, X., and Nguyen, T. H. (2024). A Survey of Small Language Models (No. arXiv:2410.20011). *arXiv*. https://doi.org/10.48550/arXiv.2410.20011

Nguyen, S. T., and Tulabandhula, T. (2023). Generative AI for Business Strategy: Using Foundation Models to Create Business Strategy Tools (No. arXiv:2308.14182). *arXiv*. https://doi.org/10.48550/arXiv.2308.14182

Plaat, A., Wong, A., Verberne, S., Broekens, J., Stein, N. van, and Back, T. (2024). Reasoning with Large Language Models, a Survey (No. arXiv:2407.11511). *arXiv*. https://doi.org/10.48550/arXiv.2407.11511

Remountakis, M., Kotis, K., Kourtzis, B., and Tsekouras, G. E. (2023). ChatGPT and Persuasive Technologies for the Management and Delivery of Personalized Recommendations in Hotel Hospitality (No. arXiv:2307.14298). *arXiv*. https://doi.org/10.48550/arXiv.2307.14298

Research: How Gen AI Is Already Impacting the Labor Market. (2024). Retrieved December 9, 2024, from https://hbr.org/2024/11/research-how-gen-ai-is-already-impacting-the-labor-market?t

Song, S., Li, X., Li, S., Zhao, S., Yu, J., Ma, J., Mao, X., and Zhang, W. (2023). How to Bridge the Gap between Modalities: A Comprehensive Survey on Multimodal Large Language Model (No. arXiv:2311.07594). *arXiv*. https://doi.org/10.48550/arXiv.2311.07594

The Convergence of AI and Creativity: Introducing Ghostwriter. (2024). Retrieved December 9, 2024, from https://news.ubisoft.com/en-us/article/7Cm07zbBGy4Xml6WgYi25d/the-convergence-of-ai-and-creativity-introducing-ghostwriter

Transforming software with generative AI. (2024). *MIT Technology Review*. Retrieved December 9, 2024, from https://www.technologyreview.com/2024/10/17/1105295/transforming-software-with-generative-ai/

Unleash developer productivity with generative AI | McKinsey. (2023). Retrieved December 9, 2024, from https://www.mckinsey.com/capabilities/mckinsey-digital/our-insights/unleashing-developer-productivity-with-generative-ai?utm_source=chatgpt.com

Vaswani, A., Shazeer, N., Parmar, N., Uszkoreit, J., Jones, L., Gomez, A. N., Kaiser, L., and Polosukhin, I. (2023). Attention Is All You Need (No. arXiv: 1706.03762). *arXiv*. https://doi.org/10.48550/arXiv.1706.03762

Yan, L., Sha, L., Zhao, L., Li, Y., Martinez-Maldonado, R., Chen, G., Li, X., Jin, Y., and Gaa., D. (2024). Practical and Ethical Challenges of Large Language Models in Education: A Systematic Scoping Review. *British Journal of Educational Technology*, Vol. 55(1), 90 https://doi.org/10.1111/bjet.13370

Yang, Y., Peng, Q., Wang, J., and Zhang, W. (2024). Multi-LLM-Agent Systems: Techniques and Business Perspectives (No. arXiv:2411.14033). *arXiv*. https://doi.org/10.48550/arXiv.2411.14033

Yu, H., Gan, A., Zhang, K., Tong, S., Liu, Q., and Liu, Z. (2024). Evaluation of Retrieval Augmented Generation: A Survey (No. arXiv:2405.07437). *arXiv*. https://doi.org/10.48550/arXiv.2405.07437

Zheng, L., Long, M., Chen, B., and Fan, Y. (2023). Promoting knowledge elaboration, socially shared regulation, and group performance in collaborative learning: An automated assessment and feedback approach based on knowledge graphs. *International Journal of Educational Technology in Higher Education*, Vol. 20(1), 46. https://doi.org/10.1186/s41239-023-00415-4

https://doi.org/10.1142/9789819816347_0008

Chapter 8

The Role of AI in Corporate Learning

José A. Fernández-Calvo

AI Center, Miami Dade College, Miami, Florida, USA

1. The Shift from Corporate Training to Corporate Learning

The rapid evolution of technology has ushered in a new era of learning, one where Artificial Intelligence (AI) makes the most of existing Learning Management Systems (LMSs) and is changing the way organizations approach corporate training. This chapter explores the transformative impact of AI on corporate training programs, highlighting key areas where it empowers organizations to enhance learning effectiveness, personalize experiences, and optimize outcomes with detailed tracking of learners' progress.

Corporate learning has become an integral aspect of organizational growth and employee development in today's fast-paced business landscape. With the increasing complexity of job roles and the rapid evolution of technology, corporations recognize the need to foster a culture of continuous learning to maintain a competitive edge (Kirkpatrick & Kirkpatrick, 2016). As companies strive for adaptability and innovation, the traditional methods of training and development are being scrutinized and upgraded to meet these new demands (Noe *et al.*, 2014; Shurygin *et al.*, 2021).

The adoption of Learning Management Systems (LMSs) in corporate training has steadily increased over the past few decades, driven by the need for scalable, flexible, and efficient solutions for employee development (Shurygin *et al.*, 2021). These systems have allowed organizations to streamline training processes, standardize content delivery, and provide employees with the ability to access learning materials anytime, anywhere. As digital transformation became a key strategic priority across industries, LMS platforms evolved to include features such as personalized learning paths, analytics for tracking progress, and integrations with other corporate tools, further solidifying their role in modern training strategies (Al-Fraihat *et al.*, 2020).

The onset of the COVID-19 pandemic in 2020 acted as a catalyst for this ongoing trend, forcing educational and corporate institutions to transition from in-person to online training in a matter of weeks (Crawford *et al.*, 2020). This rapid shift highlighted the critical importance of LMS platforms and required organizations to familiarize themselves with online learning tools and the pedagogical frameworks necessary for effective digital instruction (Malureanu *et al.*, 2021; Hodges *et al.*, 2020). The pandemic not only underscored the value of LMS in ensuring business continuity but also revealed gaps in digital literacy and instructional design that many organizations had to address quickly (Dwivedi *et al.*, 2020). As a result, LMS adoption and the understanding of best practices in online pedagogy became essential components of organizational resilience and workforce development.

2. Evolution of Corporate Training Models: Transition from Traditional to Modern Approaches

The field of corporate training has undergone a significant transformation over the years, shifting from traditional, instructor-led methods to more modern, technology-driven solutions. This evolution reflects broader trends in organizational learning and development, driven by advancements in technology, changes in workforce demographics, and the need to adapt to rapidly evolving business environments (Noe *et al.*, 2014). Traditional corporate training models, often characterized by static, one-size-fits-all content delivered through in-person lectures, have given way

Table 1. From corporate training to corporate learning.

	Old Model	**New Model**
Modality	In-Person	Blended
Tools	PowerPoint	LMS + AI Tools
Duration	Multiple Hours per Session	Short Modules (approx. 15 min)
Delivery Format	In-Person Presentation	Multi-Format (video, audio, text)
Generational Style	Classroom	YouTube, Podcasts
Content Creation	SME/Trainer	SME + AI Tools
Content Changes	Manually by SME/Trainer	Centrally updated, instant rollout
Objective	Gain Skills	Gain Skills, improve KPIs
Onus	Trainer	Learner
Evaluation	Satisfaction Survey	Testing Dashboard, KPIs

to more dynamic, interactive, and personalized approaches facilitated by digital tools and platforms (Zhang *et al.*, 2004).

The emergence of blended learning models, which combine the flexibility of online modules with the interactivity of in-person sessions, has become a defining feature of modern corporate training (Garrison & Vaughan, 2008). These models allow organizations to tailor learning experiences to individual needs, incorporate real-time feedback, and create scalable solutions that accommodate a global workforce (Bersin, 2004). Furthermore, the use of data-driven insights, powered by Learning Management Systems (LMSs) and Artificial Intelligence (AI), enables organizations to continuously refine and improve their training strategies (Al-Fraihat *et al.*, 2020).

This transition to technology-driven solutions has not only improved accessibility and engagement but also aligned training initiatives with broader organizational goals, such as enhancing employee performance and achieving measurable business outcomes (Kirkpatrick & Kirkpatrick, 2016). By leveraging these modern approaches, organizations can foster a culture of continuous learning that meets the demands of a fast-paced, innovation-driven economy (see Table 1).

1. **Modality:** In the traditional model, training was conducted exclusively in person, requiring employees to be physically present in a

designated classroom or training center. This format, while effective in fostering interpersonal interaction, often posed logistical challenges, including scheduling conflicts and limited scalability (Garrison & Vaughan, 2008). In contrast, the new model embraces a blended modality, combining in-person training with online components. This hybrid approach offers greater flexibility, allowing learners to engage with training materials remotely while still benefiting from occasional face-to-face interactions. The blended model ensures a more adaptable and inclusive training environment that caters to diverse learner needs (Bersin, 2004).

2. **Tools:** Historically, PowerPoint was the primary tool used to deliver training content, with trainers relying heavily on static slide presentations. While effective for basic information sharing, this tool lacked interactivity and adaptability to individual learning preferences (Zhang *et al.*, 2004). The modern training paradigm leverages Learning Management Systems (LMS) and advanced AI tools. These platforms provide a centralized hub for managing, delivering, and tracking training programs. AI tools enhance the process by offering personalized learning paths, automating administrative tasks, and analyzing learner performance in real time (Bassi *et al*, 2016). This integration of technology has elevated the training experience, making it more engaging, efficient, and data-driven (Shurygin *et al*, 2021).
3. **Duration:** Traditional training sessions were typically lengthy, often spanning several hours in a single sitting. While this format allowed for deep dives into complex topics, it often led to cognitive overload and reduced learner retention (Sweller, 1988). The new model addresses this issue by adopting short modules, each lasting approximately 15 minutes. These microlearning sessions are designed to fit seamlessly into employees' busy schedules, enabling them to absorb information in manageable chunks. This approach not only improves knowledge retention but also encourages continuous learning (Bersin, 2004).
4. **Delivery Format:** In the old model, training was primarily delivered through in-person presentations, with trainers leading sessions in a lecture-style format. While this method allowed for real-time interaction, it often lacked the versatility to accommodate different learning styles (Noe *et al.*, 2014). The new model employs a multi-format delivery system, incorporating video, audio, and text-based content.

This diverse approach ensures that learners can access materials in the format that best suits their preferences, fostering greater engagement and inclusivity of people with disabilities (Nguyen *et al.*, 2020). Platforms such as YouTube and podcasts are also increasingly utilized, making learning more accessible and relatable.

5. **Generational Style:** The traditional classroom setup was designed for structured, instructor-led learning, often mirroring the educational environments familiar to older generations. While effective for some, this approach did not always resonate with younger, tech-savvy learners (Prensky, 2001; Shurygin *et al*, 2021). In response, the new model integrates modern generational styles, leveraging platforms such as YouTube and podcasts that align with contemporary consumption habits. These formats appeal to a broader audience by offering on-demand access and an informal learning experience (Oblinger, 2003).
6. **Content Creation:** Content in the traditional model was developed manually by Subject Matter Experts (SMEs) or trainers. While this ensured a high degree of expertise, the process was time-consuming and often lacked scalability (Bersin, 2004). The new model combines the expertise of SMEs with the capabilities of AI tools, streamlining content creation. AI can assist in generating training materials, automating repetitive tasks, and even suggesting improvements based on learner feedback (Nguyen *et al.*, 2020). This partnership between human expertise and artificial intelligence enhances the quality and efficiency of content development (Dwivedi *et al.*, 2020).
7. **Content Changes:** In the past, updates to training content were made manually by SMEs or trainers, often resulting in delays and inconsistencies across training programs. This reactive approach made it challenging to keep materials current, especially in fast-paced industries (Noe *et al.*, 2014). The new model adopts a centrally updated system, enabling instant rollout of changes across all platforms. This ensures that learners always have access to the most up-to-date information, improving the relevance and effectiveness of training programs (Kirkpatrick & Kirkpatrick, 2016).
8. **Objective:** The primary goal of traditional training programs was to impart skills to employees, focusing on specific tasks or knowledge areas. While effective in skill development, this approach often lacked alignment with broader organizational goals (Noe *et al.*, 2014). The new model expands its objectives to include not only skill acquisition

but also the improvement of Key Performance Indicators (KPIs). By aligning training outcomes with organizational metrics, this approach ensures that learning initiatives directly contribute to business success (Phillips & Phillips, 2016).

9. **Onus:** In the old model, the responsibility for learning largely fell on the trainer, who was expected to deliver content, answer questions, and ensure learner understanding. This trainer-centric approach often placed a heavy burden on the facilitator. The new model shifts the onus to the learner, empowering individuals to take ownership of their learning journey. With the support of LMS platforms and AI tools, learners can access resources, track their progress, and engage in self-directed learning. This learner-centric approach fosters greater accountability and motivation.
10. **Evaluation:** Traditional training programs primarily relied on satisfaction surveys to gauge their effectiveness. While useful for gathering immediate feedback, this method provided limited insights into long-term learning outcomes or business impact (Kirkpatrick & Kirkpatrick, 2016). The new model employs a more robust evaluation framework, using testing dashboards and KPIs to measure performance. These tools provide detailed analytics on learner progress, knowledge retention, and the impact of training on organizational goals (Phillips & Phillips, 2016). This data-driven approach enables continuous improvement and ensures that training initiatives deliver measurable results.

In summary, the shift from traditional to modern corporate training models reflects a broader transformation in how organizations approach learning and development. By leveraging technology, embracing flexibility, and aligning training objectives with business goals, the new model addresses the limitations of its predecessor while meeting the demands of a rapidly changing workforce.

3. The KPI-Centric Approach to Corporate Learning: A Continuous Improvement Cycle

The evaluation and justification of corporate learning programs have undergone a paradigm shift in recent years. Traditional evaluation methods, such as satisfaction surveys, are increasingly being replaced by data-driven learning dashboards that provide real-time insights into training effectiveness (Kirkpatrick & Kirkpatrick, 2016; Phillips & Phillips., 2016). These dashboards enable organizations to track program progress with remarkable granularity, offering detailed breakdowns by business unit, country, or other relevant metrics. This transition underscores the growing demand for measurable outcomes and the integration of corporate learning into broader operational and strategic frameworks (Bassi *et al.*, 2016).

At the heart of this new approach is a continuous improvement cycle that aligns corporate learning initiatives with Key Performance Indicators (KPIs). This cycle ensures that learning programs are directly tied to measurable business outcomes, fostering accountability and maximizing return on investment (ROI) (Phillips & Phillips, 2016). The cycle typically includes three interconnected phases: identifying opportunities for KPI improvement, developing and deploying tailored corporate learning programs, and measuring ROI alongside the impact on organizational performance metrics (Noe *et al.*, 2014). By leveraging these data-driven methodologies, organizations not only improve the precision and relevance of their learning initiatives but also create a robust framework for aligning training with strategic goals. This paradigm shift represents a significant evolution in how corporate learning is evaluated and justified, moving beyond anecdotal evidence to deliver tangible, quantifiable results.

The cycle can be broken down into three interconnected phases (see Figure 1) :

1. **Identify Opportunities for Improvement of KPIs:** The process begins with identifying areas where KPIs can be improved. This step involves analyzing organizational data to uncover performance gaps and pinpointing specific metrics that need enhancement. For example, a sales team may struggle to achieve monthly revenue targets, or a customer service department may fall short in customer satisfaction scores. By focusing on KPIs that directly impact business performance, organizations can prioritize training initiatives that address the most critical needs. This step ensures that learning efforts are targeted and relevant, laying the foundation for meaningful improvement.
2. **Develop and Deploy a Corporate Learning Program to Improve KPIs:** Once opportunities for KPI improvement are identified, the next step is to design and implement a corporate learning program tailored to those needs. This phase leverages modern learning tools such as Learning Management Systems (LMS) and AI-driven

platforms to create highly customized training solutions. These tools enable the delivery of diverse content formats, including videos, interactive modules, and simulations, ensuring that training is engaging and accessible to all learners. The deployment process also incorporates real-time learning dashboards, which allow managers to monitor program progress and adjust as needed. These dashboards provide visibility into participation rates, knowledge retention, and other key metrics, enabling a proactive approach to training management.

3. **Measure ROI and the Impact on KPIs:** The final phase involves evaluating the impact of the training program on the identified KPIs. Unlike traditional methods that rely on vague claims of "training our people," this step focuses on clear, quantifiable outcomes. Using data from learning dashboards, organizations can measure improvements in performance metrics, such as increased sales revenue, reduced error rates, or higher customer satisfaction scores. Critically, this phase also assesses the ROI of the training program. By comparing the costs of implementation with the tangible benefits achieved, organizations can determine whether the program delivered value. This data-driven evaluation not only justifies the investment in corporate learning but also informs future training strategies.

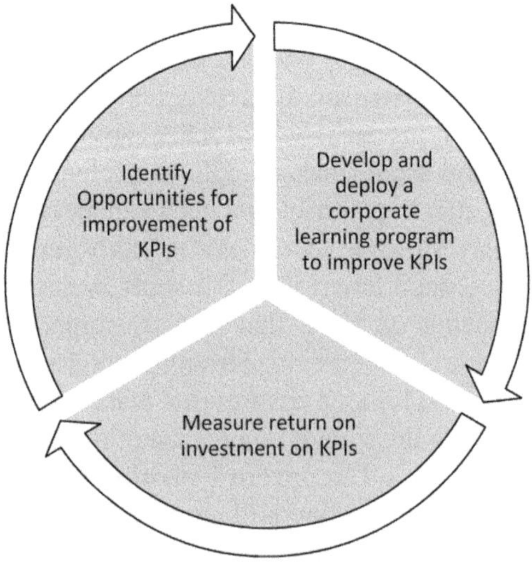

Figure 1. The lifecycle of KPI-focused learning programs.

4. A Shift in Ownership and Accountability

One of the most significant changes in this new approach is the shift in responsibility for corporate learning. Traditionally managed by Human Resources (HR), learning programs are now becoming a shared priority across departments, such as sales, operations, and customer service. Every manager, regardless of their functional area, has a vested interest in developing training programs that improve the KPIs tied to their personal performance metrics. This decentralization of corporate learning fosters a culture of continuous improvement, where training is not viewed as a standalone HR initiative but as an integral part of achieving organizational success. By aligning learning with operational goals, organizations can ensure that every training program contributes directly to business outcomes (Phillips & Phillips, 2016).

In summary, the KPI-centric approach to corporate learning represents a significant evolution in how organizations design, implement, and evaluate training programs. By focusing on measurable outcomes, leveraging advanced learning tools, and fostering cross-departmental ownership, this approach transforms corporate learning from a cost center into a strategic driver of performance and growth. This continuous improvement cycle ensures that training initiatives remain relevant, effective, and aligned with the ever-changing needs of the business.

5. Application of the Flipped Classroom Model to Corporate Training

The flipped classroom model, originally popularized in educational institutions, has emerged as a transformative approach in corporate training. This model reverses the traditional training structure by shifting the initial learning phase to pre-session activities, allowing participants to engage with foundational content before attending in-person or live virtual sessions. In corporate training, this approach addresses the challenges of limited time and resources while fostering deeper engagement and collaboration during face-to-face interactions.

In the flipped corporate training model, employees access pre-training materials such as instructional videos, readings, or interactive modules through Learning Management Systems (LMSs). These materials are tailored to individual learning needs and can include AI-generated content for enhanced personalization. By consuming this content at their own pace, employees build a baseline understanding of the subject matter, ensuring they are better prepared for in-depth discussions and activities during live training sessions. This approach supports diverse learning styles and accommodates varying levels of prior knowledge, making it particularly effective for a heterogeneous workforce (Hedden, 2017).

During the live sessions, trainers focus on higher-order learning activities, such as case studies, group projects, role-playing, and problem-solving exercises. This collaborative environment allows employees to apply their pre-learned knowledge to real-world scenarios, reinforcing their understanding while promoting critical thinking and teamwork. Trainers, empowered by AI tools, can use real-time analytics to identify gaps in understanding and adapt session content accordingly. For example, AI-powered dashboards can highlight areas where participants struggled during pre-training assessments, enabling trainers to address specific challenges effectively.

The flipped classroom model also enhances retention and engagement in corporate training. By shifting passive learning to pre-session activities, employees can dedicate live session time to active, hands-on experiences that promote knowledge application and skill development. Moreover, this model fosters a culture of accountability, as employees take greater ownership of their learning journey (Lo, 2023).

Organizations adopting the flipped classroom model have reported improvements in training efficiency and effectiveness. The model's flexibility supports global teams by providing consistent pre-training resources accessible across time zones, while the collaborative live sessions build a cohesive learning culture (Hedden, 2017). As AI and digital technologies continue to evolve, the flipped classroom model will remain a cornerstone of innovative corporate training strategies, aligning with the needs of modern businesses and their dynamic workforces (Lo, 2023).

6. The New Learning Process: A Blended Approach to Online and In-Person Training

In the evolving landscape of corporate learning, organizations are increasingly adopting a blended approach that seamlessly integrates online and in-person learning methodologies. This model leverages the best of both worlds, providing flexibility and scalability while ensuring hands-on

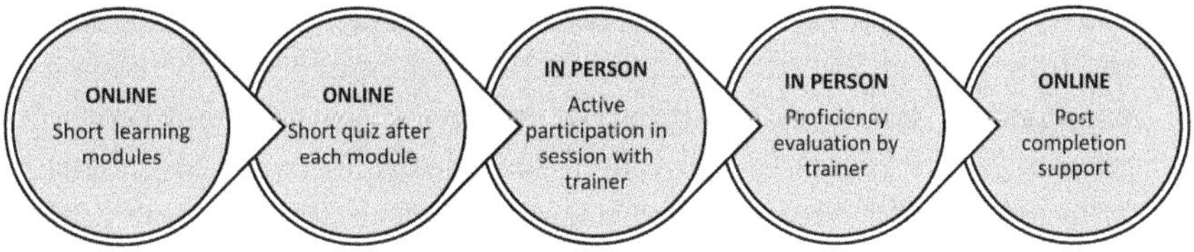

Figure 2. Blended learning steps

engagement and accountability. The process unfolds in a structured, step-by-step sequence designed to maximize learner engagement, retention, and overall effectiveness. As shown in Figure 2:

1. **Short Online Learning Modules:** The learning journey begins with short, focused online modules that cover specific topics or skills. These modules are designed for microlearning, allowing employees to consume content in manageable segments that fit into their busy schedules. The concise nature of these sessions ensures that learners remain engaged and retain critical information. This step also supports self-paced learning, empowering individuals to progress at a comfortable speed while balancing other professional responsibilities.
2. **Short Quiz After Each Module:** To reinforce learning and assess comprehension, a short quiz follows each online module. These quizzes serve multiple purposes: They provide immediate feedback to learners, help solidify the material covered, and identify areas where additional support may be needed. This formative assessment approach ensures continuous learning and prepares participants for subsequent steps in the training process. Additionally, quiz results feed into a centralized dashboard, which provides granular data on learner performance. This enables trainers and managers to monitor progress by individual, division, or even geographical region, ensuring that no participant is left behind (Kirkpatrick & Kirkpatrick, 2016).
3. **Active Participation in Sessions with Trainer:** Once learners have completed the online modules and quizzes, they transition to in-person sessions led by trainers. These sessions are designed to foster active participation, allowing employees to engage in discussions, hands-on activities, and real-world applications of the concepts they have learned online. The in-person element of the training ensures that learners can

clarify doubts, collaborate with peers, and deepen their understanding through guided instruction. Active participation not only enhances engagement but also significantly improves learning outcomes by encouraging learners to apply their knowledge in practical scenarios, bridging the gap between theoretical concepts and on-the-job performance. Additionally, these in-person sessions provide employees with a valuable opportunity to bond with their colleagues and expand their professional networks. The collaborative environment helps build a sense of community, strengthens team spirit, and fosters a cohort-based approach to learning, which can translate into improved collaboration and morale in the workplace. This shared learning experience promotes a culture of teamwork and mutual support, further amplifying the impact of the training program (Bersin, 2004).

4. **Proficiency Evaluation by Trainer:** The next step in the process is a proficiency evaluation, conducted by the trainer during the in-person session. This evaluation ensures that participants have effectively absorbed and can apply the training content. Trainers use a variety of assessment tools, including role-playing, problem-solving exercises, and direct observation, to gauge learners' competencies. This step is critical for maintaining accountability, as it validates the effectiveness of the training program and identifies any remaining knowledge gaps. Feedback provided during this stage allows learners to refine their skills and ensures that they are prepared to implement their new knowledge in their roles (Bersin, 2004).
5. **Post-Completion Support:** Learning does not end with the completion of formal training sessions. The final step in the blended process emphasizes post-completion support, delivered through online platforms. This support may include access to additional resources, discussion forums, or follow-up sessions to address ongoing questions or challenges. Post-completion support ensures that learners continue to apply and build on what they have learned, promoting long-term retention and sustained performance improvement. This step also fosters a culture of continuous learning, where employees feel supported in their development journey.

7. Data-Driven Insights with Learning Dashboards

Throughout the entire process, data plays a pivotal role in optimizing the learning experience. A learning dashboard collects and displays detailed information about each learner's progress, offering insights into performance trends by individual, team, division, or country. This data empowers managers and trainers to

- **identify learners who require additional support** and intervene early,
- **pinpoint opportunities to improve training content** based on patterns of misunderstanding or low scores,
- **measure the effectiveness of the training program** by linking learning outcomes to organizational KPIs,
- **calculate the ROI of training initiatives**, ensuring alignment with business objectives.

By providing real-time data, the dashboard facilitates continuous improvement and ensures that training programs remain aligned with organizational goals.

8. A Holistic, Flexible, and Outcome-Oriented Approach

The blended learning process represents a significant advancement in corporate training methodologies. By combining online and in-person elements, incorporating real-time assessments, and leveraging data-driven insights, this approach ensures that learning is both effective and measurable. The integration of post-completion support further underscores the commitment to sustained employee growth and organizational success.

9. How AI is Transforming Every Aspect of Corporate Learning

Artificial Intelligence (AI) has become a transformative force in corporate learning, revolutionizing how content is created, modified, delivered, and evaluated (Dwivedi *et al.*, 2020). By automating routine processes, enhancing personalization, and providing actionable insights through advanced analytics, AI has significantly increased the efficiency, engagement, and outcome orientation of corporate training (Al-Fraihat *et al.*, 2020).

AI-powered tools enable organizations to design dynamic, scalable learning experiences tailored to individual needs while continuously adapting to organizational requirements (Nguyen *et al.*, 2020). In the following, we explore how AI is applied across six critical stages of the corporate learning lifecycle, demonstrating its impact on reshaping training methodologies and aligning them with strategic business goals (see Figure 3).

1. **Content Creation:** The foundation of any training program lies in its content. AI plays a pivotal role in creating dynamic, tailored training materials (Kirkpatrick & Kirkpatrick, 2016). From designing program structures to developing syllabi, AI-powered tools help generate engaging resources, including videos, audio (with avatars), texts, and images. These tools can analyze existing training needs, suggest relevant topics, and even create interactive multimedia content to enhance learner engagement (Shurygin *et al*, 2021). AI accelerates the content creation process, ensuring materials are comprehensive, up-to-date, and tailored to the target audience.
2. **Content Modification:** Corporate training content must evolve to meet the needs of a diverse, global workforce. AI facilitates content modification by supporting translations, localizations, and updates (Al-Fraihat *et al.*, 2020). It ensures that content aligns with regional languages, cultures, and compliance requirements. AI-driven version control systems allow organizations to track changes and maintain consistency across training materials. Additionally, AI identifies outdated or irrelevant content, recommending updates to ensure materials remain accurate and impactful (Dwivedi *et al.*, 2020).
3. **Learner Support:** AI has transformed learner support by providing 24/7 assistance through teaching assistant chatbots (Shurygin *et al.*, 2021). These chatbots answer learner queries, provide motivational nudges, and offer tailored support for individuals who may be falling behind, ensuring no one is left behind in their learning journey. AI also enables mock quizzes and feedback, giving learners a safe environment to test their understanding and improve their skills. Personalized nudges encourage consistent participation and help learners stay on track with their training goals (Shurygin *et al*, 2021).
4. **Learner Evaluations:** AI enhances learner evaluations by automating the grading process and providing detailed feedback (Zawacki-Richter *et al.*, 2019). Quizzes and assessments powered by AI can

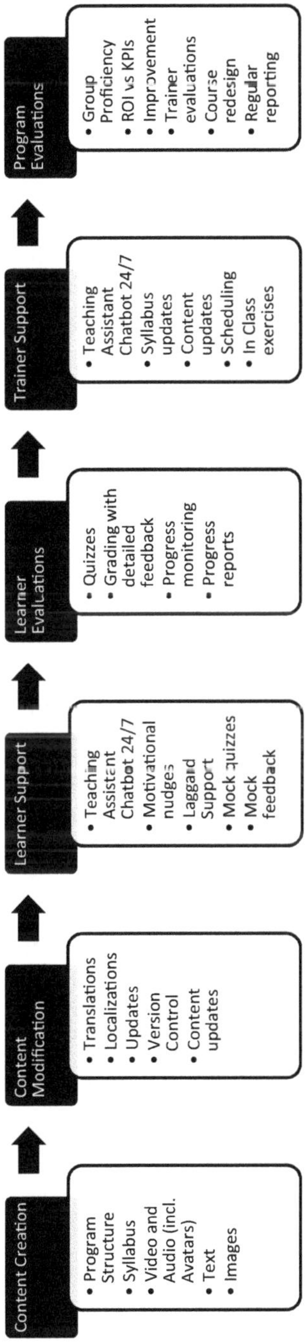

Figure 3. Artificial intelligence applications at each step of the corporate learning journey.

analyze responses, identify areas for improvement, and offer personalized recommendations for further study. AI-driven progress monitoring tools track each learner's development over time, highlighting trends and identifying potential challenges early. Additionally, AI generates comprehensive progress reports, offering valuable insights for both learners and trainers (Shurygin *et al*., 2021).

5. **Trainer Support:** AI does not just support learners—it also empowers trainers. AI-driven teaching assistant chatbots provide trainers with instant access to resources, scheduling tools, and updated syllabi. By automating routine administrative tasks, AI allows trainers to focus on delivering high-quality instruction. In addition, AI can suggest in-class exercises tailored to the specific needs of a group, ensuring that training sessions are both relevant and engaging. Trainers also receive content updates generated by AI, keeping them informed of the latest trends and best practices (Kumar, 2023).
6. **Program Evaluations:** The final stage of the learning process involves evaluating the program's overall effectiveness. AI provides advanced analytics to measure group proficiency, track ROI against KPIs, and assess areas for improvement (Phillips & Phillips, 2016). By analyzing data from multiple sources, AI generates insights that guide course redesign and optimization. Regular reporting powered by AI ensures that organizations have a clear understanding of training outcomes and their alignment with business objectives. Trainer evaluations are also streamlined, providing actionable feedback to improve future sessions (Kumar, 2023).

10. Conclusion: The Role of AI in Corporate Learning

The integration of Artificial Intelligence (AI) in corporate learning marks a profound shift in how organizations approach training and development. This transformation, driven by technology, has redefined every stage of the learning process: content creation, delivery, support, and evaluation. The transition from traditional methods to a KPI-centric, blended learning approach not only enhances the learning experience but also aligns it with strategic business objectives (Kirkpatrick & Kirkpatrick, 2016; Phillips & Phillips, 2016).

The journey begins with AI-driven content creation, where advanced tools generate dynamic, personalized materials tailored to the unique needs of diverse learners (Nguyen *et al.*, 2020). AI simplifies content modification, ensuring that learning materials remain relevant, localized, and up to date. By automating translations and updates, organizations can maintain consistency and scalability in their training initiatives.

In learner and trainer support, AI empowers stakeholders with 24/7 teaching assistant chatbots, real-time progress monitoring, and personalized feedback (Kumar, 2023). These innovations foster a culture of continuous improvement, enabling employees and trainers to achieve their learning goals effectively. Proficiency evaluations and post-completion support further enhance this process, bridging gaps between theoretical knowledge and practical application (Ciavaldini-Cartaut, 2024).

Most importantly, AI transforms program evaluations, providing granular insights into training effectiveness through advanced analytics and real-time dashboards. These tools not only measure ROI but also inform data-driven decisions to improve future programs, ensuring alignment with organizational KPIs. By embedding AI into the corporate learning framework, organizations can ensure their workforce remains competitive in a rapidly evolving global landscape.

Ultimately, the incorporation of AI fosters an ecosystem of learning that is adaptive, personalized, and result-oriented. AI's ability to adapt and optimize makes it an indispensable tool in the modern corporate learning ecosystem. As AI continues to evolve, its potential to enhance corporate learning will only grow, making it an essential driver of organizational success.

References

Al-Fraihat, D., Joy, M., and Sinclair, J. (2020). Evaluating E-learning systems success: An empirical study. *Computers in Human Behavior*, Vol. 102, 67–86. https://doi.org/10.1016/j.chb.2019.08.004

Bassi, L., McMurrer, D., and Van Buren, M. (2016). Human capital analytics: How to harness the potential of your organization's greatest asset. *SHRM Foundation.*

Bersin, J. (2004). The blended learning book: Best practices, proven methodologies, and lessons learned. *Pfeiffer.*

Ciavaldini-Cartaut, S., Métral, JF., Olry, P., Guidoni-Stoltz, D., and Gagneur, CA. (2024). Artificial Intelligence in Professional and Vocational Training. In: Urmeneta, A., Romero, M. (eds) *Creative Applications of Artificial Intelligence in Education. Palgrave Studies in Creativity and Culture.* Palgrave Macmillan, Cham. https://doi.org/10.1007/978-3-031-55272-4_11

Crawford, J., Butler-Henderson, K., Rudolph, J., Malkawi, B., Glowatz, M., Burton, R., Magni, P., and Lam, S. (2020). COVID-19: 20 countries' higher education intra-period digital pedagogy responses. *Journal of Applied Learning & Teaching*, Vol. 3(1), 1–20. https://doi.org/10.37074/jalt.2020.3.1.7

Dwivedi, Y. K., Hughes, D. L., Coombs, C., Constantiou, I., Duan, Y., Edwards, J. S., Gupta, B., Lal, B., Misra, S., Prashant, P., Raman, R., Rana, N. P., Rowe, F., and Slade, E. L. (2020). Impact of COVID-19 pandemic on information management research and practice: Transforming education, work, and life. *International Journal of Information Management*, Vol. 55, 102211. https://doi.org/10.1016/j.ijinfomgt.2020.102211

Garrison, D. R., and Vaughan, N. D. (2008). Blended learning in higher education: Framework, principles, and guidelines. *Jossey-Bass.*

Hedden, G. (2017). Applications of Flipped Instruction in the Corporate Training Environment. In J. Johnston (Ed.) *Proceedings of EdMedia 2017* (pp. 817–826).

Hodges, C., Moore, S., Lockee, B., Trust, T., and Bond, A. (2020). The difference between emergency remote teaching and online learning. *Educause Review*, Vol. 27. https://er.educause.edu/articles/2020/3/the-difference-between-emergency-remote-teaching-and-online-learning

Kirkpatrick, D. L., and Kirkpatrick, J. D. (2016). Evaluating training programs: The four levels (3rd ed.). *Berrett-Koehler Publishers.*

Kumar, N. (2023, October 28). Corporate training AI: Use cases and best practices. *eLearning Industry.* Retrieved from https://elearningindustry.com/how-is-ai-changing-the-face-of-corporate-training

Lo, C. K. (2023). Strategies for enhancing online flipped learning: A systematic review of empirical studies during the COVID-19 pandemic. *Interactive Learning Environments*, Vol. 32(7), 3517–3545. https://doi.org/10.1080/10494820.2023.2184392

Malureanu, A., Panisoara, G., and Lazar, I. (2021). The relationship between self-confidence, self-efficacy, grit, usefulness, and ease of use of eLearning platforms in corporate training during the COVID-19 pandemic. *Sustainability*, Vol. 13(12), 6633. https://doi.org/10.3390/su13126633

Nguyen, Q., Gardner, L. A., and Sheridan, D. (2020). A framework for applying learning analytics in serious games for people with intellectual disabilities. *British Journal of Educational Technology*, Vol. 51(2), 497–514. DOI: 10.1111/bjet.12625

Noe, R. A., Clarke, A. D. M., and Klein, H. J. (2014). Learning in the twenty-first-century workplace. *Annual Review of Organizational Psychology and Organizational Behavior*, Vol. 1(1), 245–275. https://doi.org/10.1146/annurev-orgpsych-031413-091321

Oblinger, D. (2003). Boomers, Gen-Xers, and Millennials. *Educause Review*.

Phillips, J. J., and Phillips, P. P. (2016). Handbook of training evaluation and measurement methods (4th ed.). Routledge.

Prensky, M. (2001). Digital natives, digital immigrants. *On the Horizon*, Vol. 9(5), 1–6.

Shurygin, V., Saenko, N., Zekiy, A., Klochko, E., and Kulapov, M. (2021). Learning management systems in academic and corporate distance education. *International Journal of Emerging Technologies in Learning (iJET)*, Vol. 16(11), 121–139. https://doi.org/10.3991/ijet.v16i11.20701

Sweller, J. (1988). Cognitive load during problem solving. *Cognitive Science*, Vol. 12(2), 257–285.

Zawacki-Richter, O., Marín, V. I., Bond, M., and Gouverneur, F. (2019). Systematic review of research on artificial intelligence applications in higher education–where are the educators? *International Journal of Educational Technology in Higher Education*, Vol. 16(1), 39. https://doi.org/10.1186/s41239-019-0171-0

Zhang, D., Zhou, L., Briggs, R. O., and Nunamaker, J. F. (2004). Instructional video in e-learning: Assessing the impact of interactive video on learning effectiveness. *Information & Management*, Vol. 41(1), 15–27. https://doi.org/10.1016/j.im.2005.01.004

https://doi.org/10.1142/9789819816347_0009

Chapter 9

Artificial Intuition in Management Decision-Making: Are We There Yet?

Leonie Hallo

The University of Adelaide, Adelaide, South Australia, Australia

1. Introduction

The development of artificial intelligence (AI) is proceeding at an incredible pace. AI is embedded in all aspects of our lives. For many people, this will not be apparent. Peter and Reimer (2024) presented a framework describing the seven basic kinds of capability of AI existing in a stack, with each capability building on the one below it. Some of these capabilities are now present in our everyday life and they certainly make life much more convenient. At the lowest level, there is the capability of pattern recognition, and we can think, for instance, of facial recognition. At the next level, there is classification; for instance, consider your photo app in which your gallery of photos is organized into albums. Such capabilities operate seamlessly without us being necessarily aware of them. Beyond these levels, there are capabilities of prediction of future outcomes based on past patterns, recommendations of the most suitable option, automation with a degree of autonomy, generation of original content that mimics the training data, and interaction such as we see with chatbots. The impact of AI is huge, including in the world of management decision-making and this is transforming business strategies (Kaggwa *et al.*, 2024). Managers were already coping with vastly increased complexity before the arrival of the pandemic. This event, of course, brought additional burdens of rapidly advancing digitization and massive changes in ways of working (Hanzis and Hallo, 2024). Since that time, there have been several other occurrences affecting management decision-making and one of the most impactful is the rapidly devolving implementation of AI into organizations, both large and small. The range of AI tools available seems to increase week by week.

This rapid evolution presents a massive quandary for managers. The exposure of most managers to AI will be via large language models (LLMs). How exactly can AI tools and particularly LLMs be used for optimal effectiveness to support managers? Many are beguiled by LLMs, particularly chatGPT, and readily accept the output arising from that LLM as correct, probably more often than they should. There is a kind of mystery as to how these tools work, but a wise person would bear in mind the old aphorism "lies, damned lies and statistics" and apply a vetting process to the output of LLMs. Statistics may be mathematical truths, but how humans choose to interpret them is important. There is also a growing understanding of the importance of prompt engineering in obtaining suitable responses (Meskó, 2023). Human oversight in this domain should consist of both an analytic and an intuitive assessment. How these models work is not well understood. Some have mused about whether such models could ever be intuitive in the way of people. This question has not been fully addressed and certainly not in the management decision-making literature. To date, most appreciations of intuitive behavior by LLMs have indicated a kind of pattern matching, rather like what an expert might do in applying a seemingly intuitive process. The ability of LLMs and AI in general to act in a truly intuitive way is a question that is not resolved.

This chapter is concerned with management decision-making. Decision-making as discussed within psychology and organizational behavior is closely related to problem-solving, which is generally viewed as more of an umbrella term within human cognition and more holistic in nature (Sinclair, 2011, 2020). Thus, problem-solving occurs at a more strategic level while decision-making is a more constrained activity involving identifying and choosing alternatives, evaluating the outcome of those alternatives, and then selecting the most appropriate. Problem-solving is a more comprehensive process focusing on identifying and understanding the problem in a more holistic way, analyzing the root causes, devising potential solutions, and evaluating those before implementation. Problem-solving utilizes decision-making as one of its components. Kanfer and Busemeyer (1982) presented a model of the use of these cognitive frames within the field of behavioral self-regulation showing that problem-solving occurs first and is followed by decision-making.

The role of intuition versus analysis in decision-making and problem-solving has been the focus of much research over the years. Intuition has also been researched in the field of creative behavior (Sadler-Smith and Akstinaite, 2022). At the present time, the speed of requirements of decision-making in the light of the big data available for managers presents a quandary. The pressure for speed and the sheer amount of data almost necessitates the use of AI. Firms that resist this pressure will quickly become uncompetitive. Managers are aware that many firms are using AI to significantly increase their productivity, particularly through LLMs, but are overwhelmed about how to best bring these new capabilities into their company and work with them. There may be a fear of missing out, but it is not exactly clear how to join in. There seem to be more and more LLMs being developed weekly. How can managers choose? Having chosen an LLM that they think will be suitable, they will need to become familiar with how that model works and with the optimal method of prompt engineering to obtain the best results. Various other organizational adjustments will need to be made, including the preparation of both workers and data for this change in direction.

Standing back and looking at this situation from a distance, there are many arguments about the benefits and costs of AI at the societal level. Indeed, there is a deep chasm in views about whether AI will be beneficial, catastrophic, or somewhere in between. Many take the view that AI will create a whole new set of opportunities for people to hand over the drudgery work to the machines, and instead pursue things that they have always wanted to do; or at the very least spend their time in the work setting performing more meaningful activities that require higher capabilities (Bankins and Formosa, 2023). Some have predicted that fourth-generation AI will be capable of intuition-based learning that can mirror human intuition (Akinci and Sadler-Smith, 2023). Sadler-Smith (2022) applied the term "artificial intuition" to discuss the possibility of fourth-generation AI being able to emote in a human fashion and make inroads into areas that we currently ascribe only to human capabilities.

At the other end of the dimension, there are those who warn that AI has the potential to overtake its human creators (Buttazzo, 2023). The role of people within the loop is an important and timely discussion. Human-in-the-loop (HITL) optimization maintains human judgment and oversight in AI systems with the human as a supervisor or decision-maker at critical points (Slade *et al.*, 2024). Paydas Turan and Sadler-Smith (2023) propose a hybrid intelligence model that combines the cognitive and information-processing functions of human intelligence and AI. They propose that AI and human intelligence operate in an interactive and synergistic fashion, with iterative decisions that can produce outcomes better than either type of decision-maker alone. They also refer to the unique sensing and translating features that only humans can bring, referring to "cognitive augmentation."

There are many debates now about to what extent AI can be left in charge and how much a person must maintain control, and the circumstances of this assessment. What is the contribution of people that is different from what machines can contribute? In the end, will the machines be able to learn how to act just like people? The thesis of the paper is that discussions about whether machines can act in an intuitive way have been truncated to date and should be expanded. The research aim is to investigate the degree to which intuition is present within AI. The research objective is to examine literature in the field of management decision-making in the particular instance of commercially successful visual artists. The research hypothesis is that current understandings of intuition as it operates within AI are limited to one type of intuition termed expert intuition. If that is true, by extension, the relationship between AI and people can never be equal within the decision-making/problem-solving space.

2. Literature Review

2.1. *Decision-making fundamentals*

It is now well accepted that there are two quite dissimilar methods of decision-making: analysis and intuition. Analysis is the use of rationality in a conscious fashion to break down the whole into its constituent parts to better understand a problem in a step-by-step fashion and is based on disembodied knowledge (Julmi, 2024). Intuition on the other hand is an unconscious process, holistic in its nature and rapid, being embodied and implicit (Meziani and Cabantous, 2020), and producing outcomes that are tacit, holistic, and about which the intuitor feels confident (Dörfler and

Ackermann, 2012). Debates have raged for many decades within psychology about the comparative merits of these two techniques and how they operate together, either in sequence or in parallel (Evans, 2008). This understanding of the counterpoint between intuition and analysis is demonstrated within the Myers–Briggs Typology Index (MBTI) with two ends of one dimension being labeled intuition versus sensation, which is data collection through the senses (King and Mason, 2020). Much earlier, the discipline of philosophy discussed the nature and role of intuition. Greek philosophers, for example, Aristotle, opined that "noesis" or holistic, immediate, and direct appreciation contrasts favorably with "dianoia" or analytical thought (Henden, 2004). Ancient wisdom dictated that intuition will always be superior to analysis because it gives us access to ultimate reality, whereas analytical thought, based as it is upon unquestioned assumptions held by the decision-maker, will be bound to be inferior and fallible (Westcott, 1968).

Within psychology, this discussion started largely through the proposed process of dual process thinking, in which the two parallel and complementary cognitive systems of analysis and intuition operate (Epstein *et al.*, 1996). Most people will probably incline either to analysis or to intuition. Earlier writers in psychology were strongly of the view that analysis will always be superior to intuition, in line with the Western mindset that rationality is superior (Wang *et al.*, 2021). According to this way of thinking, intuition can give us a quick solution, but it may not be well thought out and analysis will be needed to check its veracity. Many people still believe that intuition is nothing more than an immediate and possibly untrustworthy emotional response. Another major approach to understanding intuition has been presented by the work of Kahneman and others in the field of heuristics, suggesting that intuition is a form of mental shortcut that we employ when we do not have the time or mental bandwidth to analyze properly. Heuristics are used to quickly come to a decision taking account of only what are considered relevant aspects. This process is of course efficient but may not be accurate.

On the other hand, there has been an increasing recognition that analysis has many limitations in the way it is applied to human judgment (Sinclair *et al.*, 2009). The work of Gigerenzer (Gigerenzer and Gaissmaier 2015; Gigerenzer, 2020) talks about fast and frugal heuristics that can sometimes lead to better decisions than strategies that are much more complex. The adaptive toolbox proposed by Gigerenzer indicates that having a range of intuitive strategies at hand can produce better outcomes with less information in conditions of uncertainty, including the recognition heuristic (name recognition), the "take the best" heuristic (using the most important cue), and the satisficing heuristic, first publicized by Simon (Simon, 1991, in which the decision-maker chooses the first option that reaches a pre-set threshold. The study of decision-making within management also has a very long history, with scholars showing interest in how decisions are made (Sterman, 1989), and more recently how technology can support managerial decision-making (Jarrahi, 2018).

Important work by Sinclair (Sinclair 2011) differentiated three types of intuition. Unfortunately, this useful categorization has not been picked up substantially in the literature on management decision-making, as was noted by Walsh *et al.* (2022). The typology has immediate relevance to the conjunction of intuition and AI. Sinclair's categories are as follows. Intuitive expertise draws upon patterns that an individual has accumulated within their domain of expertise and knowledge. This is a decision-making method in which matching the present scenario with one's experience reveals overlaps and similarities that can be helpful. Such an approach is not effortful and does not seem to necessarily involve affect or emotion. The approach bears resemblance to recognition-primed decision-making (RPD) models such as those advocated by Klein (Klein, 2011), where experts or experienced people rely upon their experience to pick up an element of familiarity in current decision space and can use this to quickly come up with a suitable action strategy and evaluate their selection through a mental simulation process. There may be a need for simulation in advance of the decision where there is a lack of clarity for the expert. In this approach, decision-makers would be drawing upon experience-based knowledge and external cues in the environment, including body based sensory cues and environmental cues. This approach has been well investigated in emergency situations (Okoli and Watt, 2018) and in stock market trading (Sukhov *et al.*, 2021).

The second type of intuition proposed by Sinclair is intuitive creation. Here there may be only cursory exposure and general experience to support the decision-maker. This approach to decision-making is a more creative style. Entrepreneurial research has hinted that seeing the future in a marketing sense could be part of intuitive creation (Baldacchino *et al.*, 2015). Others have named this approach "insight": a sudden new understanding which sometimes arrives with an accompanying solution. Sobkow *et al.* (2018) termed this kind of intuition "coherence and insight," where coherence suggests congruity. In this process, we connect knowledge in novel ways, akin to what has been called the "aha" experience (La Pira, 2011). There will likely be a sense of surprise and excitement when this new understanding arrives (Shen *et al.*, 2016). Creative intuition is useful in seeing the big picture within complex contexts where there are many interconnected elements and cause-and-effect relationships are not discernible. Creative intuition is often extremely successful where analytical approaches would not be (Tabesh and Vera, 2020).

A third category of intuition proposed by Sinclair is that of intuitive foresight. This concerns the ability to anticipate the future and is a type of intuition about which little is known. This is not forecasting in the style of economic prediction, which is a kind of analysis based on previous information redirected forward for decision-making purposes. Foresight intuition can occur based on one's experience or imagination. French novelist and poet Jules Verne imagined radical futuristic concepts that later became reality, including submarines, space travel, videoconferencing, and helicopters. Envisioning such future creations probably inspired others to develop them. Can we sense the future? Can we access information which is non-local? Studies of precognition or the ability to foresee future events in advance are not well recognized in mainstream science. Such precognition may emerge through dreams or intuitive sensations.

Bradley (2006) used the concept of focused emotional attention on an object of interest (such as a potential future business opportunity) and examined how the alignment of psychophysiological systems works in this process. This is a form of intuition by the body, in which foreknowledge of a future event, or non-local intuition, can be sensed in the body, chiming with popular perceptions of intuition that it is not mediated by our five senses but is in some way an unmediated interaction between our minds and a nonlocal source of information: a kind of sixth sense. The brain and the heart are both involved in this process. Bradley uses quantum holography as an explanation of such perceptions of the future: Energy moves at the quantum level and is a field of information that exists separate from space and time. If we attune our psychophysiological systems to the quantum level of an object such as a future condition, then we can experience that information as an intuition. Such perceptions are experienced with a sense of absolute certainty and often quite strong emotions, either positive or negative. Focused emotional attention affects the whole psychophysiological system of the person, including, especially the heart.

There is some resonance here with the concept of emergence and nonlinear information studied within the field of complex adaptive systems. Focused emotional attention unleashes an outgoing wave of energy generated partly by the heart, which now changes its pattern of rhythmic activity. Research is at the early stages of this field, and we have not as yet identified the exact underlying physical and biological mechanisms (Radin, cited in Williams, 2019). A similar concept of indwelling (Dörfler and Bas, 2020) may allow enhanced perception and heightened awareness through sustained concentration (Hallo and Nguyen, 2021). The threefold categorization of intuition by Sinclair (2011) is about the processes that we use to interact with the world. The work by Peter and Reimer (2024) presenting the seven capabilities of AI in a stack, on the other hand, is a way of describing how AI is now operating in assisting us in decision-making.

Decision-making and the constraints of speed and data overload are one area in which intuition has been discussed: Another is creative problem-solving (Dörfler and Ackermann, 2012). Complex problem-solving may require an incubation period, as described in Sinclair's creative intuition style. Problem-solving is often combined with critical thinking in the literature. Kuhn (1999) proposed a developmental model of critical thinking and highlighted the importance of argumentative reasoning in this process. She also emphasized metacognitive awareness, which is the ability to reflect upon our own thinking processes. Tang *et al.* (2020) explored the development of critical thinking via complex problem-solving and asserted that learning to think critically is a very individual experience. Bezanilla *et al.* (2019) suggested six categories of activities supporting the development of critical thinking: analyzing/organizing, reasoning/arguing, questioning oneself, evaluating, taking a position/taking decisions, and acting/compromising. Critical thinking involves evaluating the evidence and using it to support claims. Other components of critical thinking, according to this author, include a questioning attitude and open-mindedness toward alternative perspectives. Critical thinking ability is positively related to problem-solving ability. Mascarenhas *et al.* (2024) discussed the real need for critical thinking in dealing with wicked global problems and listed descriptive critical thinking skills (for example, identifying hidden assumptions and biases), analytical thinking skills enhanced by proactive thinking, experiential critical thinking as entrained by questioning of one's own thinking values and beliefs, and sapiential critical thinking skills (associated with wisdom, values, virtue, and integrity) of divergent thinking, consensual thinking, morality thinking, and global sustainability thinking: These critical thinking skills they say should be inserted into MBA training. In our current time of information overload, critical thinking will be needed to examine the credibility and reliability of information and to see problems from various perspectives, as well as to evaluate solutions.

2.2. *AI: Its development and promise*

We can see AI everywhere in our daily life. This trend is growing quickly. People have become used to dealing with chatbots, even though they may be frustrated when the answers they are seeking are not addressed by the options offered (Hallo, Rowe and Duh, 2024). Many are unaware of the pervasiveness of AI in the systems with which we interact. We are becoming used to a world in which humans are not always available. Newell and Marabelli (2015) addressed the issue of long-term societal effects of "datafication," noting the lack of clarity about the implications for people and for wider society. Digitization of our everyday life is no small thing. Multi-disciplinary approaches are needed to properly examine cultural, economic, psychological, legal, and ethical consequences of this development for various groups in society. There needs to be a debate that goes beyond optimizing business value to encompass broader issues of equality and democracy.

In discussing AI, it is relevant to consider definitions of "artificial" and "human" and how they differ. Something artificial is defined as something made by people, often as a copy of something natural. The Cambridge Dictionary defines artificial as "made by people, often as a copy of something natural." In food, we see artificial flavors and sweeteners. We know about artificial selection in biology. There is a sensation of lack of naturalness and spontaneity. The definition of the adjective "human," on the other hand, refers to human qualities. The Cambridge Dictionary defines the adjective "human" as "having the qualities, faults, and feelings that people have, as opposed to gods, animals, or machines." As technology advances, the line between people and machines may become blurred (Mazis, 2007). However, as noted by De Cremer and Kasparov (2021), "Will smart machines really replace human workers? Probably not." The remainder of this paper presents a new look at this question through the lens of AI decision-making.

The integration of AI into decision-making processes has implications for organizations and society in general. AI can enhance management decision-making by the provision of recommendations and information.

As noted by Steyvers and Kumar (2024), collaboration between humans and AI still faces challenges, both in terms of AI accuracy and humans' understanding of AI capabilities and constraints. Human decision-makers need to understand how to use AI support for this collaboration to be fully functional. Humans bring unique values of critical thinking and ethical considerations into the decision process. Other concerns are about whether overdependence on AI will lead to a reduction in human decision-making skills (Ahmad *et al.*, 2023), as well as privacy and security concerns. Kerasidou (2020) also discussed the challenges in incorporating human values of empathy, compassion, and trust in an AI-focused health-care setting. The clear message is that AI does not provide these qualities in that setting. On the other hand, Srinivasan and González (2022), in discussing the relationship between empathy and accountability in general, wrote about empathetic AI systems and potential pathways here. It can be observed that the nature of empathy in this study is construed as providing convincing explanations of decisions and minimizing negative impacts, which seems like a somewhat limited application. An intriguing article by Zhiqiang *et al.* (2019) floats the term "artificial empathy," but notes that human-based empathy co-occurs with consciousness and therefore this could be a challenge for AI. Others have also written about artificial empathy: for instance, Liu-Thompkins *et al.* (2022), who noted that AI marketing agents often seem cold and uncaring but that increasing their perspective taking, empathetic concern, and emotional contagion can produce a type of empathy that chimes to some extent with some people. They conclude that artificial empathy can have a positive impact under certain circumstances but at times can be detrimental, and this will depend upon how the individual person responds to a chatbot displaying affect.

The term AI refers to machines performing cognitive functions that people used to undertake using their natural intelligence (Nyholm 2024). There are now systems that can learn, adapt, and act autonomously to a fair degree. Algorithms use data which has already been captured and prepared for processing. They are becoming more powerful and reliable over time, and they do perform better than humans in some tasks. AI now has a significant influence on many aspects of society, including in the legal domain, marketing, and politics, where algorithms are able to influence people's choices by providing customized communications (Hopcroft *et al.*, 1983; Shaffer *et al.*, 2017). Work by Epstein, for example, Epstein *et al.* (2024) have evoked interest in the ease with which people can be influenced by biased search engine results, and this influence extends to how they vote. While we are familiar with well-defined routine cognitive tasks being undertaken by learning algorithms, advances are moving the system toward dealing with tacit knowledge (or knowledge that is not explicitly stated); for example, accurate image recognition, formerly the domain of people based upon their experience, but now able to be undertaken by algorithms. Manyika (2017) proposed that jobs with a component of tacit knowledge could have 30% of tasks taken over by algorithms. As noted by Faraj *et al.* (2018), very large datasets enable AI machines now to generate responses and predictions rather similar to those of a knowledge worker in previous times.

It is very clear that AI can be of tremendous value in supporting (and in places replacing) humans in administrative work. Algorithms have been found to be less than optimal in other fields, especially when qualitative and complex matters are concerned. The interaction between people and machines in this context occurs on a spectrum between automation and augmentation. Automation occurs when the machine takes over the human task, and this development is expanding. Some tasks can be automated using robots, speech recognition, and conversational agents for customer interaction. More advanced automation based on algorithms was still fairly rare when McAfee and Brynjolfsson (2017) wrote their book: Nevertheless, there were then and still are plenty of debates about human jobs being taken over by machines. As noted by Hallo and Nguyen (2023), AI has limitations in situations of high complexity, and there will always be a role for the kinds of intuition at which people excel.

Within augmentation or hybrid intelligence, humans are included in the loop of artificial systems (Gómez-Carmona *et al.*, 2024), so that users can improve and personalize the automatic solutions provided by AI. The user interacts and provides input, guidance, and feedback as needed. This is a more active role of end-users in assisting the system to improve with time. The phrase "human in the loop" (HITL) implies that the human can override the AI output or that the AI may query the human if needing additional input (Grønsund and Aanestad, 2020). Agrawal *et al.* (2019) concluded in their paper that sometimes humans will delegate decisions to the machines even when there would have been a better result if they had kept agency for themselves. This is an interesting finding, indicating the kind of mystique that AI has accrued.

A recent paper by Apple researchers (Mirzadeh *et al.*, 2024) concluded that LLMs cannot actually reason. These authors noticed that LLMs are not reliable when answering variations of the same question. Their focus was mathematical reasoning, and their conclusion was that currently LLMs cannot undertake genuine logical reasoning: Rather they replicate the steps in their training data, representing a critical flaw in their ability to understand mathematical concepts. The researchers called the reasoning of such models "fragile." Further research will be needed to produce AI models that can reliably undertake formal reasoning beyond pattern recognition to solve problems in a more robust way. They note the following: "This remains a critical challenge for the field as we strive to create systems with humanlike cognitive abilities or general intelligence."

In a TEDx talk, Dörfler (2024) discussed which functions can be replaced by AI in the teaching arena, suggesting that shallow knowledge or unprocessed information is already provided by AI. However deep knowledge, the kind of knowledge that is possessed by people with a high level of mastery in their field, is still important. Dörfler refers to the Grandmaster-Apprentice relationship and asserts that the master cannot be replaced by a machine. The relationship with the Grandmaster is deep and personal because they know what the student needs, what they think, what they want, even before the student does. The student may want to copy the Grand Master, but they will only ever be a pale copy. The miracle occurs when the student emerges as a new Grandmaster standing on their personal ground. The quality of the Grandmaster-Apprentice relationship is not discernible when a person interacts with a machine. Even Mozart was apprenticed to JC Bach.

2.3. *Artificial intuition in the world of visual art*

"Artificial intuition" is a term that encapsulates the imbuing of humanlike qualities into AI. While an attractive term, it needs to be better understood and that is the focus of this paper. The paper now draws upon the field of visual art to better understand the role of intuition within human creative processes and to elaborate on the distinction between people and machines. The field of art can give us a grasp of what it could mean to have intuition beyond pattern matching imbued into AI. A famous quote by Tolstoy described art as follows: "A human activity consisting in this, that one man consciously, by means of certain external signs, hands on to others feelings he has lived through, and that others are affected by these feelings and also experience them" (Schanzer, 1951). This appreciation of art highlights the transmission of feelings and the nature and purpose of art in society. According to this definition, AI-created art is not art. Aristotle, writing in 4th century BCE Greece, commented on art as follows: "The aim of art is to represent not the outward appearance of things, but their inward significance." His understanding of art was very much about art as an imitation of nature (Cavarnos, 1978). Art can reveal core universal truths and deeper meanings. Art is a kind of therapy for Aristotle. AI-generated art is an interesting development to consider in this discussion.

We might naturally expect that the world of art would be more driven by intuitive processes than the world of management. There is quite a large literature about the role of intuition in creativity, with the focus being on the creation of novel concepts and solutions. While discussions of pattern recognition in the guise of expert intuition are present in this literature, there are also references to emotions and insights that arise spontaneously, the combination of unfamiliar concepts and unexpected associations, and the combination of intuition with analysis in the form of critical thinking as this applies to aspects such as public acceptance and saleability. Within the realm of visual art, intuition may guide the arrangement of different elements within a piece to create a pleasing appearance, including the selection of colors as these may affect mood (Warburton, 2018), experimenting with different mediums (Andrew, 2013), the selection of topics that resonate with the artist (Baumann, 2007), and a perception of balance (Locher 2020).

AI has permeated into the world of visual art. Work by Kim *et al.* (2024) described how models such as chatGPT have revolutionized the production of art in a promising but also challenging way. They note resistance to what is seen by some as an intrusion, but also that the addition of AI into a visual arts training course in Korea did result in an increase in students' creativity. Similarly, Zeilinger (2023) discussed AI-generated abstract art and audiences' perceptions of it. When images are ambiguous and difficult to interpret, viewers need to actively interpret within themselves to find their meaning. This can lead to a deeper connection with the piece of art. Viewers are prompted to find meaning in this art, just as they are with human created abstract art.

Recently we have seen the development of many AI art-generating tools such as DALL-E 2 and Midjourney, which create highly detailed images of a very high quality with interesting color combinations and forms (Reddy *et al.*, 2021). The response to artworks created with these tools appears to range between acceptance and dislike. Ranjan *et al.* (2024) explored the use of art generator AIs in this field and how they can produce novel features. Zhao (2024) compared traditional layout design methods in new media art with various AI layout design algorithms and reported promising and innovative results. A paper by Cetinic and She (2022) reviewed the use of AI for creative purposes to generate novel works and identified technological milestones including the arrival of DALL-E and CLIP in 2021. The creation of art from text is another major development. The sale in 2018 of an AI-developed artwork at the auction house Christie's entitled "Portrait of Edmund Bellamy" for US $432,500 provoked much discussion about the authorship and ethics of AI-produced art (Christie's, 2018). Much more recently, in November 2024, a portrait of the British mathematician Alan Turing created by a robot called Ai-Da sold for US$1.08M at Sotheby's digital art sale in New York (BBC, 2024).

There are now many online platforms that feature AI-generated art, as well as conferences and exhibitions dedicated to this form. It is quite common now for artists to use a range of AI tools in a sequence to produce their own unique outputs. This process may produce completely novel works that would not have been produced by humans alone, prompting us to think once again about what is really different between people and machines (Stephensen, 2019). Using AI for the generation of ideas is a different proposition from using AI to produce a work of art without human intervention (Sadler-Smith, 2022). If creativity itself is simply a recombination of existing elements, then art generated solely by AI is not problematic. If conscious intention and emotion are necessary features, can a machine produce an artwork which has an emotional quality?

3. Methodology

This initial exploratory chapter aims to guide future, more detailed research on the nature of artificial intuition within management decision-making. A variety of data collection approaches were employed for this purpose. The paper uses a mixed method approach combining literature review, conceptual analysis, and qualitative research. The primary focus is to develop a conceptual framework for understanding AI in management decision-making by synthesizing existing literature on decision-making, intuition, and AI.

Literature reviews were conducted on the topic of AI and intuition within the field of management decision-making. A separate search investigated the understanding of intuition in visual art created through AI. Rapid reviews were conducted given the current lack of literature on both these topics and the emerging nature of the field of artificial intuition. Such reviews can clarify key concepts and definitions as well as identify gaps in the literature (Dobbins, 2017). The literature review used three prominent academic databases: Google Scholar, Scopus, and Web of Science. These databases were chosen for their extensive coverage of multidisciplinary research and high-quality peer-reviewed papers. The search was conducted using the following key terms and Boolean operators: "artificial intuition," "management decision-making," "artificial intelligence," and "intuitive decision-making." The Google Scholar search produced 31 articles. Restricting the search to articles about management decision-making resulted in a final set of six articles, one of which was a PhD dissertation, and they are surveyed here. A similar search of the database Scopus searching within title, abstract and keywords produced no documents. A search on Web of Science produced four articles: three of the same as those produced in the Google Scholar search and one article which was unrelated to management decision-making. In addition, literature reviews were conducted in these three databases regarding the understanding of intuition in visual art created through AI. A Google Scholar search using the terms artificial intuition and visual art produced 10 results, only one of which was on the topic. The Scopus search again (searching within title, abstract, and keywords) produced no articles. The Web of Science search for artificial intuition and visual art also produced no results. Clearly, we are at the very early stage of producing literature here.

Qualitative research was also conducted via unstructured interviews with successful visual artists. Qualitative research is useful in exploring the perceptions of people and is frequently used in social science research, and interviews are very useful tools in this genre (Elhami and Khoshnevisan, 2022). Unstructured interviews allow for a spontaneous conversation and the possibility of follow-up questions to explore unexpected topics that arise (Marvasti and Tanner, 2020). Such data collection can provide rich and detailed data via probes and exploration. Marvasti and Tanner (2020) viewed the unstructured interview through the metaphor of the traveler who explores and wanders through the landscape. A convenience sample of four artists, all of whom have had commercial success and have held exhibitions, were interviewed on a range of topics including the following: What is art? What is the purpose and function of art? Does art involve emotion? Can AI produce artwork without human involvement? What is the difference between AI produced art and human produced art? Who is the main beneficiary of art: the artist or the viewer? The sample consisted of two males and two females, all with over 20 years of experience in the field. Visual art is a highly creative workspace and is therefore a suitable area in which to explore intuition and artificial intelligence. Visual artists who operate commercially need to make business decisions about the nature of their products, likely audiences, and commercial success (Berzins, 2012). As noted by Bosch (2009), economic drivers are important drivers of making art. The interviews were conducted by the author and thematic analysis was used to uncover key themes.

The primary purpose of the chapter is to develop a conceptual framework for understanding artificial intuition in management decision-making, building upon Sinclair's typology of intuition, which includes intuitive expertise, intuitive creation, and intuitive foresight. The aim of the paper is to broaden the discussion on whether machines can act intuitively.

4. Results and Discussion

4.1. *What is the definition of intuition within AI as conceptualized in management decision-making?*

Definitions of artificial intuition identified in the literature search rapid review are as follows:

Trovati *et al.* (2022) state that embedding artificial intuition within AI would provide novel ways to process information. In this article, they define artificial intuition as follows: "The ability of a system to assess the problem context and identify novel links among the corresponding knowledge components to facilitate the decision process in an automated manner. Further, intuition is dependent on past knowledge and experience …." These authors compared the output produced by embedding artificial intuition of this kind within data and using a computational approach showed that there were advantages as a result. This definition emphasizes dependence on past knowledge and experience.

Trovati *et al.* (2023) again discussed the embedding of artificial intuition in data science, defining it as follows: "The ability to evaluate a problem within a specific context and discover new connections to enable the automation of decision-making processes." They go on to say that intuition depends on prior knowledge and experiences. They differentiate this from artificial creativity focused on achieving artistic beauty, once again achieved by identifying data patterns. The focus is still on subconscious pattern recognition based on prior knowledge and experience. In such models, important components will include knowledge and experience acquired over time, as well as similarity recognition involving cues from the past. This definition differentiates artificial intuition from artificial creativity.

Diaz-Hernandez and Gonzalez-Villela (2017) defined artificial intuition as follows: "A limited representation of human intuition," commenting that this hybrid concept had to date been studied solely from the computational perspective. This paper, like others, limits discussion to the kind of intuition labeled above as intuitive expertise; that is, pattern matching enabling rapid recognition and action and deriving from practice and experience. Again, the focus is on intuitive expertise through pattern matching.

Another definition of artificial intuition by Johanssen and Wang (2021) in the related field of technology journalism is as follows: "The ability of a system to assess the problem context and use pattern recognition or properties from a dataset to choose a course of action or aid the decision process in an automatic manner." They described this as magical thinking, involving hyped-up and exaggerated claims, and term artificial intuition an industry buzzword. These authors are critical of inflated claims about intuition in AI.

Johnny (2020a) referred to two different concepts: artificial creativity and artificial intuition. The definition of artificial intuition in this thesis is as follows: "The ability of a system to assess a problem context and use pattern recognition or properties from a dataset to choose a course of action or aid the decision process in an automatic manner." The focus is on prior knowledge and experience of the problem at hand. It is the recognition of a pattern from the past that allows this kind of intuitive decision-making. In later work, Johnny *et al.* (2020b) referred to intuitive decision-making as being affected by the recognition of patterns rather than rational choices, seeing it as an automated process partly deriving from recollected pieces of human experiences. According to these authors, the requirements of their artificial intuition model consist of pattern recognition, multidimensionality capacity, or the ability to map patterns. They conclude the following: "Essentially, modelling of artificial intuition is accomplished through recognition of significant patterns and properties that are made available by prior knowledge and experience, given the context of the problem." Johnny's definition matches that of Johanssen and Wang (2021).

Three articles discovered by further reading throw light on this appreciation. Amoore (2020) referred to machine learning as looking for patterns and clusters in the data. Artificial intuition is therefore fundamentally experimental and generative; using advanced forms of pattern recognition, it discovers "associations and relations otherwise unknowable." Similarly Dong *et al*. (2020) wrote about collaborative AI in the marketing field, and how marketers, customers, and machines can work with AI, and the issue of customers' preferences to work with a human or a human-like agent. We can see again the assumption that unconscious pattern recognition is at work here. Another relevant paper is that of Pedwell (2023). Her discussion of the way intuition can be integrated with algorithms views intuition as a "trained thing"; that is, it is recursively trained through lived experience. Intuition is pattern recognition in the form of expert decision-making. AI is not really open to novelty and generating new insights. These supplementary perspectives reinforce the belief that intuition in this field of AI is limited to recursive training through experience and the capacity of AI for genuine novelty such as that produced by humans is not presently accepted. Table 1 summarizes the results of the rapid literature review, which reveals that artificial intuition is quite a truncated concept in the field of management decision-making. Pattern recognition is dominant in all definitions as is experience-based learning, with its emphasis on past knowledge. Automated processing focuses on systematic decision-making. It really is not sensible to assert that AI is becoming intuitive based solely on pattern matching. In fact, pattern matching seems almost anti-intuitive. There is no reference to the second and third categories of creative intuition and foresight intuition proposed by Marta Sinclair. This could be a reflection of the mindset of people within management, accustomed to rationalization and analysis. Can AI exhibit intuition beyond pattern matching? There is certainly an opportunity for exploration in the domains of creative and foresight intuition. As we see in the following section, there is relevant literature in the field of visual art and AI.

4.2. *How does literature view the role of intuition within the production of creative art by AI?*

The single paper identified by the second rapid review, the paper by Karimov *et al*. (2021) discusses robotic painting; that is, an artist creating

Table 1. Summary of the results of the literature review.

Author(s) and Year	Definition/Key Concept	Core Components	Key Findings/Perspective	Limitations/Critiques
Trovati *et al.* (2022)	"The ability of a system to assess problem context and identify novel links among knowledge components to facilitate automated decision process"	Problem context assessment/knowledge linking/past experience dependency	The advantages of embedding artificial intuition within data-processing	The focus is primarily on a computational approach
Trovati *et al.* (2023)	"The ability to evaluate a problem within specific context and discover new connections to enable automation of decision-making processes"	Context evaluation/discovery of connections/decision automation	Distinguishes artificial intuition from artificial creativity	This is still centered on pattern recognition
Diaz-Hernandez and Gonzalez-Villela (2017)	"A limited representation of human intuition"	Pattern matching/rapid recognition/experience-based action	Studied solely from a computational perspective	Approaches limited to an intuitive expertise understanding
Johanssen & Wang (2021)	"System's ability to assess context and use pattern recognition from dataset for automated decision-making"	Context assessment/pattern recognition/automated decisions	Critical of the concept of artificial intuition as an "industry buzzword"	Views the concept as overhyped
Johnny *et al.* (2020a)	Similar to Johanssen and Wang's definition with focus on intuitive thinking	Pattern recognition/multidimensionality/pattern mapping	Links to intuitive decision-making process	Limited to pattern-based decisions

(*Continued*)

Table 1. (*Continued*)

Author(s) and Year	Definition/Key Concept	Core Components	Key Findings/Perspective	Limitations/Critiques
Amoore (2020)	Machine learning as pattern/cluster recognition	Pattern discovery/ experimental nature/ generative capability	Views AI intuition as experimental and generative	Focus is on pattern recognition
Dong *et al.* (2020)	Collaborative AI perspective	Human AI interaction/ customer preferences/ pattern recognition	Explores human preference in AI interactions	Based on a marketing context
Pedwell (2023)	Intuition as a "trained thing"	Recursive training/lived experience/pattern recognition	Questions the capacity of AI for novelty	Skeptical of true AI intuition

a painting on canvas according to a map that had been produced by AI from a source image. These authors talk about the difference between artificial intuition and artificial creativity. They comment that machines may be technically more skilled than a human artist. The techniques outlined in this paper are unfolded to mimic human artistic styles, through interactive corrections by the artist to make the final output, similar to manually painted artwork. To this extent, intuition used will be of the creative kind.

4.3. *AI-generated art: Comments from artists*

Unstructured interviews were conducted with four artists who have been successful in selling their art and who have held exhibitions. Two respondents do not use AI in their art production and two do. The conversations were around what constitutes art, what the purpose of art is, what its impact on the artist and the viewer is, whether art is mainly about the artist or about the viewer, and their response to AI-generated art. A summary of their comments is as follows:

When asked "What is art?", several key responses emerged. Art is a means of personal expression of one's feelings and understanding of the world. It communicates the artist's perspective on reality. It's a form of visual communication that aims to generate some response in the viewer. The response from the viewer will vary and will be intuitive. Art evokes a wide range of emotions and can provide relief and immersion, an escape from everyday life. The meaning of art is not fixed, because viewers will interpret individually what they see in a piece. Some artists are not concerned about other people's reactions to their work. Art can be beautiful, but its primary purpose is not necessarily aesthetic. Its primary purpose is to trigger responses. Art can create a relationship between the artist, the viewer, and the world around them. It's a window into the artist's mind and a trigger of emotional engagement and reflection on the world. Three artists commented upon the broadness of the meaning of art now. One said, "Is fashion art? Is art in everyday activity? Can everyone be an artist?". Another respondent said, "My understanding of art is very broad. I would label as art a very beautiful meal created by a chef."

The role of emotion in visual art was strongly supported by all respondents. While art doesn't have to be beautiful: The point is to make the viewer feel something. "I want to generate a subjective intuitive response.

I want to trigger some subjective experience in the person. Everyone responds differently," said one respondent. Another commented as follows: "I think art is a place of relief from today's world, people can get immersed as a form of release. I see my art as an island, you can see what you like in it." Another respondent said, "Yes emotion is involved for both the viewer and the artist: I look for things to be responsive and reactive."

The occurrence of intuition within AI-generated art is limited, according to these artists. One stated that AI lacks consciousness and that intuition is based upon subjective human experience. One respondent, the self-identified AI artist, while using AI tools, still relies upon their own decision-making and completes the process via manual painting to create the final artwork. This person referenced the work of Hungarian painter Moholy-Nagy, who opined that artists should be free to use the materials of their time and AI is a material of our time. This opinion was repeated by another artist who suggested the following: "We can use AI like we can use any other technique: AI is just another method, and we need to learn how to use it."

Regarding the difference between AI-produced art and art produced by humans, one respondent said; "All art is a thought pattern of a person." Another comment was as follows: "If the computer does something I don't like, well then, I can change it. I can put things together in a way that the computer really cannot." This person also commented: "I do think people want to see the brushstrokes and little mistakes; they don't want to see straight lines and perfection. And they are not interested in prints produced by the thousand." Another respondent said, "If you generate something from DALL-E and then say that is the finished work, it contains elements of other people's work. They have already had this argument in music: it's a bit like DJs putting together other people's work." Such activity does contain a form of creativity.

In relation to foresight intuition, one respondent agreed that LLMs can alter the future. He said, "If you think about schoolkids writing essays using chatGPT, that is then forming student thoughts and ideas and that is then a bit deterministic." He also talked about the existence of a reinforcement loop: "AI platforms are self-learning. We change our behaviour as a result of something they do, and then that teaches the algorithms to recognize that we are changing our behaviour, so they then change what they are serving up to us. That could have a big effect on the future."

These interviews suggest several key differences between people and machines in the field of art creation. These respondents talked about consciousness and subjective experience, the ability to create new patterns, imperfections, and the human touch in the final product, aesthetic decisions can be combined with market analysis, and combining AI-generated elements with human creativity and physical techniques can produce an artwork that people will buy. It seems that, according to these artists, there is still quite a strong component of unique human elements that contribute to the creative process and to the final work, and the artist will generally be in charge. The main themes arising from these unstructured interviews highlight personal expression, the response of the viewer, and the broader context. The role of emotion was mentioned by all respondents, with its focus on wanting to create a subjective and immersive experience.

Regarding the integration of AI into art, respondents talked about the lack of consciousness of AI and its limited intuitive capability, asserting that AI does not have within it subjective human experience. As a tool, AI is material of our time and can be compared with other artistic techniques, but it requires human direction and completion. The artists distinguished human art in the following ways: Art creation contains human thought patterns, there are values within human imperfection, the artist needs to have control over the final product, and unique products are quite different from mass production. AI tools can be successfully combined with human creativity, but AI is viewed as a supplementary tool rather than a replacement for the human elements that are essential to the final artwork. Table 2 presents a summary of these unstructured interviews.

5. Conclusion

Artificial intuition is a new concept that warrants further research. Within management decision-making, understandings of the application of intuition to AI are very limited. Researchers and commentators in this field need to sharpen their understanding and expand their thinking to encompass a broader understanding of intuition. The paper has reviewed the three types of intuition posited by Sinclair of expert intuition through pattern matching, creative intuition through recognition of current but unacknowledged truths, and foresight intuition through an understanding of future conditions. Regarding expert intuition, it is alleged that AI is very good at pattern-matching, but in fact humans still need to be present as part of the process by inputting their questions and examining the outcome. It may be that we are not currently doing this very well. This may

Table 2. Summary of artist interviews on AI and visual art.

Theme	Key findings	Artists' quotes	Implications
Definition of art	Personal expression of feelings/ visual communication/generates viewer response/broad definition including everyday activities	"Is fashion art? Is art an everyday activity? Can everyone be an artist?"/"My understanding of art is very broad. I would label as art, a very beautiful meal created by a chef."	Art boundaries are expanding beyond traditional definitions
Emotional role	Create subjective responses/provides relief and immersion/individual responses will vary/art is not necessarily about aesthetics	"I want to generate a subjective intuitive response. I want to trigger some subjective experience in the person. Everyone responds differently"/"I think art is a place of relief from today's world, people can get immersed as a form of release."	Emotion and subjective experience are central to artistic value
AI integration	AI lacks consciousness/it has a limited intuitive capability/it can be used as a tool material/art requires human completion	"AI is just another method, and we need to learn how to use it"/"We can use AI like we can use any other technique"	AI is viewed as a complementary tool rather than a replacement
Human versus AI art	Human thought patterns are essential/there is value in human-made imperfections/the artist maintains control/people prefer uniqueness over mass production	"If the computer does something I don't like, well then, I can change it"/"I do think people want to see the brushstrokes and little mistakes; they don't want to see straight lines and perfection"	Human elements remain crucial to artistic value

AI generated content	There are questions about originality and concerns about its derivative nature/there is some similarity to music sampling debates as a unique creation	"If you generate something from DALL-E and then say that is the finished work, it contains elements of other people's work"/"They have already had this argument in music: it's a bit like DJs putting together other people's work"	Copyright and originality concerns need addressing
Future impact	Can AI influence our future thinking/ reinforcement loops between AI and human behavior/adaptive learning effects	"AI platforms are self-learning. We change our behaviour as a result of something they do, and then that teaches the algorithms"/"If you think about schoolkids writing essays using chatGPT, that is then forming student thoughts and ideas"	Potential long-term effects on creativity and artistic expression
Artist control	Artists maintain creative direction/ combination of AI with physical techniques/ the importance of marketing considerations	"All art is a thought pattern of a person"/"I can put things together in a way that the computer really cannot"	Human agency remains central to the artistic process

be because we are entranced by the mystique of AI and very trusting of it. It may also be that we are lazy. But critical thinking is vital and needed more than ever in framing the questions and examining the output of LLMs.

Regarding creative intuition, some have suggested that AI may be getting better at this and certainly it can produce novel ideas that people may not think of. We can see this in AI-generated art. Innovative ideas and patterns can be produced and this will greatly expand the possibilities. Creative intuition is certainly present within AI-generated art. Foresight intuition is a different kind of consideration. People do not really understand this concept and it is not widely accepted. Whenever something new arrives it is often treated as unscientific or wicked in some way (Dörfler and Bas, 2020). Bradley's later work (Bradley, 2024) discusses the role of the heart as well as the intellect in perceiving and shaping reality.

The aim of the chapter was to explore intuition within the context of AI and to establish whether AI can produce intuitive responses of the creative type. The objective was to investigate literature on this topic and relate this literature to the practical business area of commercial visual art. The paper concludes that artificial intuition proper has not yet arrived. AI is not yet fully intuitive. The aims and objectives of the study were achieved. Literature supports the hypothesis that AI as currently understood is limited to pattern matching and expert tuition. Interviews with commercially successful visual artists support the conclusion that AI without human oversight is not viable. "Human in the loop" is an essential part of the operation of AI, or at least it should be. Critical thinking by people is necessary for the optimal use of AI for good purposes. People still need to give the prompts, and they still need to look carefully and critically at the outcome. In the book "The Hitchhiker's Guide to the Galaxy" by Adams (1989), the supercomputer Deep Thought reveals the answer to the ultimate question of life, the universe, and everything. Deep Thought eventually announces; "42." When asked for an explanation, Deep Thought responds: "I think the problem, to be quite honest with you, is that you've never actually known what the question is." This is a cautionary note for us in dealing with AI. We really do have to be clear about what the question is that we want to be resolved. If we don't understand the question, then any answer will do. We really need to know what we want to achieve when we ask AI to help us. As we have seen in this paper, intuition is much more than just pattern matching; it also means creative intuition and foresight intuition. Therefore, as AI is restricted to pattern matching at this stage, we cannot assert that AI has artificial intuition. Imagining that AI has intuition may encourage people to think that they can trust machines without too much oversight, and this would be a mistake. What is needed is more control, not less. A human must be in the loop.

Practical implications of these findings for managers might include being conscious of retaining human-in-the-loop practices as well as developing formal processes for assessing the outputs of AI. Maintaining critical thinking for evaluating both the input and the output of AI is important. Regarding inputs, managers need to carefully formulate questions and prompts to feed into AI. This will also entail ensuring clarity about the desired outcomes from the outset. Iteratively refining questioning and prompting strategies based on results will be worthwhile. Users of AI need to be informed about the limitations of AI capabilities and maintain an awareness that AI can only do pattern matching. Users also need to be assisted in developing skills to critically evaluate the output of AI. Critical thinking skills will become more important with AI adoption, not less.

At the organizational level, AI systems should be viewed as tools for pattern matching rather than for holistic decision-making. Processes need to incorporate human insight alongside AI capabilities. Over relying upon AI can pose risks. The mystique which has developed around AI could lead organizations to fail to provide adequate oversight, and there will need to be safeguards around complacency in AI usage.

6. Limitations and Future Research

This is conceptual work in a field that is at an early stage. A more detailed systematic literature review is planned for future research. Future research could also test and validate the findings of that literature review with senior managers to obtain their opinions about the capabilities of AI and whether it could ever go beyond pattern matching and exhibit truly creative intuition, and what that would mean for us. The sample for interviews with artists should be expanded in future research to provide greater clarity about the use of AI in the visual arts field. Interviewees from other industries could also be included to compare their views on this matter. Further explanation of the nature of foresight intuition, its potential relationship with AI, and the light this throws on the relationship between people and machines would be valuable and prescient. Our relationship with AI needs to be investigated more thoroughly. Is this relationship just like our relationship with another person? Can we learn from AI just as we learn from other people? Can using AI bring about some cognitive extension and human enhancement? While some considerations of these issues have occurred at a philosophical level, practical research based on the real world is needed to tease out the implications. Future research regarding enhancing human–AI collaboration will be important.

Funding: This research received no external funding.
Institutional Review Board Statement: Not applicable.
Informed Consent Statement: All volunteer participants have signed a consent form.
Data Availability Statement: Data sharing is not applicable to this article.
Conflicts of Interest: There are no conflicts of interest to disclose.

References

Adams, Douglas. (1989). The Restaurant at the End of the Universe: Hitchhiker's Guide to the Galaxy Book 2. Vol. 2, *Tor UK.*

Agrawal, Ajay, Joshua S. Gans, and Avi, Goldfarb. (2019). Exploring the impact of artificial intelligence: Prediction versus judgment. *Information Economics and Policy*, Vol. 47, 1–6.

Ahmad, Sayad Fayaz, Heesup Han, Muhammad Alam, Mohd. Khairul Rehmat, Muhammad Irshad, Marcelo Arraño-Muñoz, and Antonio Ariza-Montes. (2023). Impact of artificial intelligence on human loss in decision making, laziness and safety in education. *Humanities and Social Sciences Communications*, Vol. 10(1), 1–14.

Akinci, C. and Sadler-Smith, E. (2023). The Intuitive Executive Revisited. In *Developing the Intuitive Executive* (pp. 1–16). Auerbach Publications.

Amoore, Louise. (2020). Cloud ethics: Algorithms and the attributes of ourselves and others. US: Duke University Press.

Andrew, Sonja. (2013). The medium carries the message? Perspectives on making and viewing textiles. *Journal of Visual Art Practice*, Vol. 12, 195–221.

Baldacchino, Leonie, Deniz Ucbasaran, Laure, Cabantous, and Andy, Lockett. (2015). Entrepreneurship research on intuition: A critical analysis and research agenda. *International Journal of Management Reviews*, Vol. 17, 212–231.

Bankins, Sarah, and Paul, Formosa. (2023). The ethical implications of artificial intelligence (AI) for meaningful work. *Journal of Business Ethics*, Vol. 185, 725–740.

Baumann, Shyon. (2007). A general theory of artistic legitimation: How art worlds are like social movements. *Poetics*, Vol. 35, 47–65.

BBC. Meet the AI Robot whose artwork sold for over $1m. https://www.bbc.com/news/videos/cn4vwq0v9v5o, accessed December 12, 2024

Berzins, Gundars. (2012). Strategic management in creative industry organizations: Specifics in strategic decision making. *Organizacijų vadyba: sisteminiai tyrimai*, Vol. 62, 7–23.

Bezanilla, María José, Donna, Fernández-Nogueira, Manuel, Poblete, and Hector, Galindo-Domínguez. (2019). Methodologies for teaching-learning critical thinking in higher education: The teacher's view. *Thinking Skills and Creativity*, Vol. 33, 100584.

Bosch, Johanna. (2009). The strategic studio: How to access and assess decision-making in visual art practice. *University of Northumbria at Newcastle (United Kingdom)*.

Bradley, Raymond. (2024). Harnessing the Force of All Creation: Part One. The Power of Love to Shape Reality 1. *World Futures*, 1–35.

Bradley, Raymond. (2006). The psychophysiology of entrepreneurial intuition: A quantum-holographic theory. *Proceedings of the Third AGSE International Entrepreneurship Research Exchange*, 8–10.

Buttazzo, Giorgio. (2023). Rise of artificial general intelligence: Risks and opportunities. *Frontiers in Artificial Intelligence*, Vol. 6, 1226990.

Cavarnos, Constantine. (1978). Art as a means of therapy according to Aristotle. *The Classical Outlook*, Vol. 56, 25–32.

Cetinic, Eva, and James, She. (2022). Understanding and creating art with AI: Review and outlook. *ACM Transactions on Multimedia Computing, Communications, and Applications (TOMM)*, Vol. 18, 1–22.

Christie's. (2018). Obvious and the interface between art and AI. Available online: https://www.christies.com/en/stories/a-collaboration-between-two-artists-one-human-one-a-machine-0cd01f4e232f4279a525a446d60d4cd1 (accessed on 20/10/2024).

De Cremer, David, and Garry, Kasparov. (2021). AI should augment human intelligence, not replace it. *Harvard Business Review*, Vol. 18, March 18.

Diaz-Hernandez, Octavio, and Victor, Javier Gonzalez-Villela. (2017). Analysis of human intuition towards artificial intuition synthesis for robotics. *Mechatronics and Applications: An International Journal (MECHATROJ)*, Vol. 1, 23–39.

Dobbins, Maureen. (2017). Rapid review guidebook. *Hamilton, ON: National Collaborating Centre for Methods and Tools*; 2017. Available at https://www.nccmt.ca/capacity-development/rapid-review-guidebook. Accessed October 1, 2024.

Dong, Yanyan, Jie, Hou, Ning, Zhang, and Maocong, Zhang. (2020). Research on how human intelligence, consciousness, and cognitive computing affect the development of artificial intelligence. *Complexity*, Vol. 2020, 1680845.

Dörfler, Viktor, and Fran, Ackermann. (2012). Understanding intuition: The case for two forms of intuition. *Management Learning*, Vol. 43, 545–564.

Dörfler, Viktor, and Alina, Bas. (2020). Intuition: Scientific, non-scientific or unscientific? In *Handbook of Intuition Research as Practice*. Edward Elgar Publishing.

Dörfler, Viktor. (2024). "Grandmasters and Apprentices in the Age of AI." *TED talks: TEDx John von Neumann University*.

Elhami, Ali, and Babak, Khoshnevisan. (2022). Conducting an Interview in Qualitative Research: The Modus Operandi. *Mextesol Journal*, Vol. 46, 1–7.

Epstein, Robert, Yunyi, Huang, Miles, Megerdoomian, and Vanessa R. Zankich. (2024). The "opinion matching effect" (OME): A subtle but powerful new form of influence that is apparently being used on the internet. *PLOS one*, Vol. 19, e0309897.

Epstein, Seymour, Rosemary, Pacini, Veronika, Denes-Raj, and Harriet, Heier. (1996). Individual differences in intuitive–experiential and analytical–rational thinking styles. *Journal of Personality and Social Psychology*, Vol. 71, 390–405.

Evans, Jonathan St BT. (2008). Dual-processing accounts of reasoning, judgment, and social cognition. *Annual Review of Psychology*, Vol. 59, 255–78.

Faraj, Samer, Stella, Pachidi, and Karla, Sayegh. (2018). Working and organizing in the age of the learning algorithm. *Information and Organization*, Vol. 28, 62–70.

Gigerenzer, Gerd, and Wolfgang, Gaissmaier. (2015). Decision making: Nonrational theories. In *International Encyclopedia of the Social and Behavioral Sciences*. Elsevier, pp. 911–16.

Gigerenzer, Gerd. (2020). Intelligence and decision making. In *The Cambridge Handbook of Intelligence*. UK: Cambridge University Press, pp. 580–601.

Gómez-Carmona, Oihane, Diego, Casado-Mansilla, Diego, López-de-Ipiña, and Javier, García-Zubia. (2024). Human-in-the-loop machine learning: Reconceptualizing the role of the user in interactive approaches. *Internet of Things*, Vol. 25, 101048.

Grønsund, Tor, and Margunn, Aanestad. (2020). Augmenting the algorithm: Emerging human-in-the-loop work configurations. *The Journal of Strategic Information Systems*, Vol. 29, 101614.

Hanzis, Anastasia, and Hallo, Leonie. (2024). The Experiences and Views of Employees on Hybrid Ways of Working. *Administrative Sciences*, Vol. 14(10), 263.

Hallo, Leonie, and Nguyen, Tiep. (2021). Holistic view of intuition and analysis in leadership decision-making and problem-solving. *Administrative Sciences*, Vol. 12(1), 4.

Hallo, Leonie, Rowe, Caroline, and Duh, Gergely. (2024). Metaverse versus Descartes: Free Will and Determinism All over Again. Paper presented at the

Advances in Intelligent Networking and Collaborative Systems (IISA), Crete, Greece.

Hallo, L. and Nguyen, T. (2023). Intuition and Analysis: Past, Present, and Future: And the Impact of Artificial Intelligence. In *Developing the Intuitive Executive* (pp. 39–62). Auerbach Publications.

Henden, Gisle. (2004). Intuition and its role in strategic thinking. *Oslo, Norway: Handelshøyskolen BI.*

Hopcroft, John E., Jeffrey D. Ullman, and Alfred, Vaino Aho. (1983). Data Structures and Algorithms. Vol. 175, *Addison-Wesley Boston, MA, USA*.

Jarrahi, Mohammad Hossein. (2018). Artificial intelligence and the future of work: Human-AI symbiosis in organizational decision making. *Business Horizons*, Vol. 61, 577–86.

Johanssen, Jacob, and Xin, Wang. (2021). Artificial intuition in tech journalism on AI: Imagining the human subject. *Human-Machine Communication*, Vol. 2, 173–90.

Johnny, Olayinka. (2020a). A Computational Model of "Artificial Intuition" in Decision Making, *Doctoral Dissertation, Edge Hill University, Ormskirk, UK*.

Johnny, Olayinka, Marcello, Trovati, and Jeffrey, Ray. (2020b). Towards a computational model of artificial intuition and decision making. Paper presented at the *Advances in Intelligent Networking and Collaborative Systems: The 11th International Conference on Intelligent Networking and Collaborative Systems (INCoS-2019)*.

Julmi, Christian. (2024). Analysis and intuition effectiveness in moral problems. *Journal of Business Ethics*, Vol. 191, 179–193.

Kaggwa, Simon, Tobechukwu, Francisa Eleogu, Franciscamary, Okonkwo, Oluwatoyin, Ajoke Farayola, Prisca, Ugomma Uwaoma, and Abiodun, Akinoso. (2024). AI in decision making: Transforming business strategies. *International Journal of Research and Scientific Innovation*, Vol. 10, 423–44.

Kanfer, Frederick and Jerome, Busemeyer. (1982). The use of problem solving and decision making in behavior therapy. *Clinical Psychology Review*, Vol. 2(2), 239–266.

Karimov, Artur, Ekaterina, Kopets, Georgii, Kolev, Sergey, Leonov, Lorenzo, Scalera, and Denis, Butusov. (2021). Image preprocessing for artistic robotic painting. *Inventions*, Vol. 6, 19.

Kerasidou, Angeliki. (2020). Artificial intelligence and the ongoing need for empathy, compassion and trust in healthcare. *Bulletin of the World Health Organization*, Vol. 98, 245.

Kim, Hyeonjin, Yeongjo, Kim, Donghyeon, Yun, and Hanjin, Lee. (2024). Empirical research on the interaction between visual art creation and artificial intelligence collaboration. *The Journal of the Convergence on Culture Technology*, Vol. 10, 517–24.

King, Scott, and Brittany, Mason. (2020). Myers-Briggs Type Indicator. in *Wiley-Blackwell Encyclopedia of Personality and Individual Differences*, Vol. II, eds B. J. Carducci, C. Nave, J. S. Mio, and R. E. Riggio (New York, NY: Wiley Blackwell).

Klein, Gary. (2011). Expert intuition and naturalistic decision making. *Handbook of Intuition Research USA*. Edward Elgar Publishing, 69–78.

Kuhn, Deanna. (1999). A developmental model of critical thinking. *Educational Researcher*, Vol. 28, 16–46.

La Pira, Frank. (2011). Entrepreneurial intuition, an empirical approach. *Journal of Management and Marketing Research*, Vol. 6, 1–22.

Liu-Thompkins, Yuping, Shintaro, Okazaki, and Hairong, Li. (2022). Artificial empathy in marketing interactions: Bridging the human-AI gap in affective and social customer experience. *Journal of the Academy of Marketing Science*, Vol. 50, 1198–218.

Locher, Paul. (2020). Experimental scrutiny of the role of balance in the visual arts. In *New Directions in Aesthetics, Creativity and the Arts*. Routledge, pp. 19–32.

Manyika, James. (2017). Jobs lost, jobs gained: Workforce transitions in a time of automation. *McKinsey Global Institute*, Vol. 150.

Marvasti, Amir, and Sam, Tanner. (2020). Interviews with individuals. In *Handbook of Qualitative Research in Education*. Edward Elgar Publishing, pp. 329–37.

Mascarenhas, Oswald, Munish, Thakur, and Payal, Kumar. (2024). Critical Thinking to Harness Global Social "Wicked" Problems: New Curriculum, Content, and Challenges in the Redesigned MBA Program. In *A Primer on Critical Thinking and Business Ethics*. Emerald Publishing Limited, pp. 147–88.

Mazis, Glen. (2007). Ecospirituality and the blurred boundaries of humans, animals, and machines. *Ecospirit: Religions and Philosophies for the Earth*, 125–55.

McAfee, Andrew, and Erik, Brynjolfsson. (2017). *Machine, Platform, Crowd: Harnessing Our Digital Future*. WW Norton & Company.

Meskó, Bertalan. (2023). Prompt engineering as an important emerging skill for medical professionals: Tutorial. *Journal of Medical Internet Research*, Vol. 225, e50638.

Meziani, Nora, and Laure, Cabantous. (2020). Acting intuition into sense: How film crews make sense with embodied ways of knowing. *Journal of Management Studies*, Vol. 557, 1384–419.

Mirzadeh, Iman, Keivan, Alizadeh, Hooman, Shahrokhi, Oncel, Tuzel, Samy, Bengio, and Mehrdad, Farajtabar. (2024). GSM-Symbolic: Understanding

the Limitations of Mathematical Reasoning in Large Language Models. *arXiv preprint arXiv:2410.05229*.
Newell, Sue, and Marco, Marabelli. (2015). Strategic opportunities (and challenges) of algorithmic decision-making: A call for action on the long-term societal effects of 'datification'. *The Journal of Strategic Information Systems*, Vol. 24, 3–14.
Nyholm, Sven. (2024). Artificial intelligence and human enhancement: Can AI technologies make us more (artificially) intelligent? *Cambridge Quarterly of Healthcare Ethics*, Vol. 33, 76–88.
Okoli, J., and Watt, J. (2018). Crisis decision-making: The overlap between intuitive and analytical strategies. *Management Decision*, Vol. 56, 1122–1134. 10.1108/MD-04-2017-0333.
Paydas Turan, Ceyda and Eugene, Sadler-Smith. (2023). A dual-process model of hybrid intelligence for improved decision-making in the digital age. In *Academy of Management Proceedings* (Vol. 2023, No. 1, p. 12866). Briarcliff Manor, NY 10510: Academy of Management.
Pedwell, Carolyn. (2023). Intuition as a "trained thing": Sensing, thinking, and speculating in computational cultures. *Subjectivity*, Vol. 30, 348–72.
Peter, Sandra and Kai, Reimer. (2024). "Wondering what AI actually is? Here are the 7 things you can do for you." In *The Conversation*, Australia.
Ranjan, Rajneesh, Anjana, Mishra, Smruti Pratisruti Maharana, and Sweety Kumari. (2024). AI in Visual Arts: Exploring Generative Algorithm. In *The Pioneering Applications of Generative AI*. IGI Global, pp. 41–60.
Reddy, Murahari, Masthan, Basha, Chinnaiahgari, Hari, and Narasapuram, Penchalaiah. (2021). Dall-e: Creating images from text. *UGC Care Group I Journal*, Vol. 8, 71–75.
Sadler-Smith, Eugene and Vita, Akstinaite. (2022). Identification of linguistic markers of insight and intuition using computer-assisted text analysis. *The Journal of Creative Behavior*, Vol. 56(2), 296–303.
Sadler-Smith, E. (2022). Intuition in business. *Oxford University Press*.
Schanzer, George. (1951). Rodó's Notes on Tolstoy's What is Art? Paper presented at the *Symposium: A Quarterly Journal in Modern Literatures*, Vol. 2, 248–255.
Shaffer, Kris, CE Carey, and Ben, Starling. (2017). Democracy hacked: A massive, pro-Le Pen disinformation campaign hits Twitter, 4chan, and the mainstream media. *Data for Democracy*.
Shen, Wangbing, Yuan, Yuan, Chang, Liu, and Jing, Luo. (2016). In search of the 'Aha!'experience: Elucidating the emotionality of insight problem-solving. *British Journal of Psychology*, Vol. 107, 281–98.
Simon, Herbert. (1991). Bounded rationality and organizational learning. *Organization Science*, Vol. 2, 125–34.
Sinclair, Marta, Eugene Sadler-Smith, and Gerard Hodgkinson. (2009). The role of intuition in strategic decision making. In L. A. Costanzo & R. B. McKay

(Eds), *The Handbook of Research on Strategy and Foresight* (pp. 393–417). Cheltenham: Edward Elgar.

Sinclair, Marta. (2011). An integrated framework of intuition. In Sinclair, M. (ed.), *Handbook of Intuition Research*. Edward Elgar, Cheltenham.

Sinclair, Marta. (2020). An introduction to intuition theory and practice: A summary and a research agenda. In M. Sinclair (Ed.), *Handbook of Intuition Research as Practice* (pp. xix–xxii). Edward Elgar Publishing.

Slade, Patrick, Christopher, Atkeson, Maxwell, Donelan, Han, Houdijk, Kimberly, Ingraham, Myunghee, Kim, Kyoungchul, Kong, Katherine, Poggensee, Robert, Riener, and Martin, Steinert. (2024). On human-in-the-loop optimization of human–robot interaction. *Nature*, Vol. 633, 779–788.

Sobkow, Agata, Jakub, Traczyk, Scott, Barry Kaufman, and Czeslaw, Nosal. (2018). The structure of intuitive abilities and their relationships with intelligence and openness to experience. *Intelligence*, Vol. 67, 1–10.

Srinivasan, Ramya, and Beatriz, San Miguel González. (2022). The role of empathy for artificial intelligence accountability. *Journal of Responsible Technology*, Vol. 9, 100021.

Stephensen, Jan. (2019). Towards a Philosophy of Post-creative Practices?–Reading Obvious' "Portrait of Edmond de Belamy". Paper presented at the *Politics of the Machine*. Beirut, Lebanon.

Sterman, John. (1989). Modeling managerial behavior: Misperceptions of feedback in a dynamic decision making experiment. *Management Science*, Vol. 35, 321–339.

Steyvers, Mark and Aakriti, Kumar. (2024). Three challenges for AI-assisted decision-making. *Perspectives on Psychological Science*, Vol. 19(5), 722–734. https://doi.org/10.1177/17456916231181102

Sukhov, Alexandre, Antti, Sihvonen, Johan, Netz, Peter, Magnusson, and Lars, Olsson. (2021). How experts screen ideas: The complex interplay of intuition, analysis and sensemaking. *Journal of Product Innovation Management*, Vol. 38, 248–270.

Tabesh, Pooya, and Dusya, Vera. (2020). Top managers' improvisational decision-making in crisis: A paradox perspective. *Management Decision*, Vol. 58, 2235–2256.

Tang, Tang, Valentina, Vezzani, and Vikki, Eriksson. (2020). Developing critical thinking, collective creativity skills and problem solving through playful design jams. *Thinking Skills and Creativity*, Vol. 37, 100696.

Trovati, Marcello, Olayinka, Johnny, Xiaolong, Xu, and Nikolaos, Polatidis. (2022). A New Model for Artificial Intuition. Paper presented at the *International Conference on Artificial Neural Networks*. Bristol UK.

Trovati, Marcello, Khalid, Teli, Nikolaos, Polatidis, Ufuk, Cullen, and Simon, Bolton. (2023). Artificial intuition for automated decision-making. *Applied Artificial Intelligence*, Vol. 37, 2230749.

Walsh, Christian, Jamie, Collins, and Paul, Knott. (2022). The four types of intuition managers need to know. *Business Horizons*, Vol. 65, 697–708.
Wang, Zhen-Dong, Yi-Meng, Wang, Kang, Li, Juan, Shi, and Feng-Yan, Wang. (2021). The comparison of the wisdom view in Chinese and Western cultures. *Current Psychology*, 1–12.
Warburton, David. (2018). Thinking colours. *Colour Turn*, Vol. 1, 1–16.
Westcott, Malcolm. (1968). Toward a contemporary psychology of intuition: A historical, theoretical, and empirical inquiry. *US: Holt, Rinehart and Winston.*
Williams, Bryan. (2019). Real magic: Ancient wisdom, modern science, and a guide to the secret power of the universe by Dean Radin. *Journal of Scientific Exploration*, Vol. 33, 1–13.
Zeilinger, Martin. (2023). The politics of visual Indeterminacy in Abstract AI Art. *Leonardo*, Vol. 56, 76–80.
Zhao, Yan. (2024). The synergistic effect of artificial intelligence technology in the evolution of visual communication of new media art. *Heliyon*, Vol. 10.
Zhiqiang, Yan, Jin-Long, Su, and Pan-Cha, Su. (2019). From human empathy to artificial empathy. *Journal of Psychological Science*, Vol. 299.

https://doi.org/10.1142/9789819816347_0010

Chapter 10

Innovative AI Applications in Business: Cases and Insights

Yang Song* **and Wenkai Zhou†**

Techlent Inc., USA

†*Roy E. Crummer Graduate School of Business, Rollins College, Winter Park, Florida, USA*

1. Introduction

Artificial intelligence (AI) has garnered significant attention in recent years, driven by the rise of large language models such as OpenAI's ChatGPT and Anthropic's Claude. While many perceive AI as a once-futuristic concept that has suddenly become a reality, the truth is that AI has been a transformative force for decades (Boden, 1998; Liebowitz, 2001), steadily advancing various aspects of society, including the business world (Dirican, 2015).

AI was first conceptualized as a branch of computer science dedicated to designing systems capable of performing tasks that typically require human intelligence, such as visual perception, speech recognition, decision-making, and language translation (McCarthy *et al.*, 1955). Building on this foundational definition, the understanding of AI has evolved significantly over time. A widely accepted modern definition comes from the Organization for Economic Co-operation and Development (OECD), which describes AI as a machine-based system designed to achieve human-defined objectives by making predictions, recommendations, or decisions that impact real or virtual environments (Yeung, 2020).

The European Commission defines AI as systems capable of analyzing their environment and autonomously taking actions to achieve specific goals (European Commission, 2018). Similarly, UNESCO offers a more detailed perspective, describing AI as human-designed systems that operate in physical or digital environments to achieve complex objectives. These systems perceive their surroundings through data acquisition, reason based on knowledge, and determine the best course of action to accomplish their goals (UNESCO, 2021). Comparing these modern definitions to the foundational ones, a key shift is evident: The focus has moved from AI's identity as an academic discipline within computer science to its practical objectives and applications. After decades of development, AI has become a robust and versatile toolkit for solving real-world challenges across various domains.

Business innovation is crucial in today's rapidly evolving marketplace, as it enables companies to remain competitive, respond effectively to shifting consumer demands, and foster sustainable long-term growth (Ahlstrom, 2010). AI plays a transformative role in this process by automating repetitive tasks, analyzing extensive datasets to uncover actionable insights, and enabling predictive decision-making capabilities. For instance, Enholm *et al.* (2022) examined how AI technologies contribute to business value by increasing revenue, reducing costs, and enhancing overall efficiency. Similarly, Echeberria (2022) analyzed AI's influence on business models, market deployment, and anticipated shifts in economic structures. In another paper, Giuggioli and Pellegrini (2023) identified how AI supports innovation, operational efficiency, and competitive advantage for startups and small businesses, especially through the integration of Industry 4.0 technologies. Meanwhile, Åström *et al.* (2022) proposed that AI can significantly improve cost efficiency and revenue generation by creating new value propositions, and they introduce a three-phase framework to guide businesses in innovating their models through AI.

While researchers work tirelessly to develop theories and frameworks to facilitate the integration of AI into business innovations, many AI applications are already thriving across organizations of various scales. From customer risk assessment and inventory optimization to business document revisions and automated chatbots, the boundaries of AI's potential in the business world appear to be limited only by human imagination.

In this chapter, we present several real-world AI projects drawn from our professional experiences, highlighting how they created value and contributed to business growth. By sharing these successful AI use cases, we aim to spark ideas and inspire our readers to embrace the transformative possibilities of AI in their own organizations.

Our focus remains on the strategic and practical implications of these cases, avoiding overly technical details and exploring only those necessary for understanding the context. This high-level approach ensures that readers can grasp the key insights and actionable strategies to guide their businesses into the AI-driven future.

2. AI Use Cases Driving Business Innovation

After the release of ChatGPT (short for Chat Generative Pre-trained Transformer) as the first widely accessible generative large language model (Zhou *et al*., 2023), two primary types of AI have emerged for business applications: traditional machine learning (ML) models and generative large language models (LLMs).

Traditional ML models excel at tasks such as predicting specific variable values and classifying (or labeling) data records. For instance, they can predict the optimal weekly inventory levels for a grocery store to minimize shortages or overstock or estimate a customized risk score to assess the claim risk of insurance customers. On the classification side, ML models can segment customers based on purchase behavior, enabling tailored marketing campaigns, or identify customers at risk of churn, allowing businesses to intervene proactively.

In contrast, LLMs represent a cutting-edge approach, leveraging deep learning technologies to generate content, such as text, images, and even videos. For example, when interacting with a chatbot on a website or speaking with an automated service agent on the phone, the responses are often powered by LLMs. These models enhance customer interactions while significantly reducing costs associated with call centers.

In this section, we explore two business cases for each type of AI, examining how these technologies address real-world business challenges and deliver measurable value to organizations.

2.1. *Optimizing car warranty monthly premiums with smart pricing*

Monthly premiums play a pivotal role in customer acquisition, retention, and the financial performance of warranty vendors. Setting premiums too high can deter potential customers and reduce retention rates due to affordability concerns. On the other hand, setting premiums too low may attract more customers but risks undermining revenue streams and profitability.

Traditionally, premium pricing has relied on experience and rule-based strategies. For example, determining the monthly premium for a new customer typically involves answering a series of questions such as the following: "Is this a new customer?" "Is the car new or used?" "How old is the car being covered?" "Has the customer filed any warranty claims in recent years?" These questions are designed to assess a customer's risk for claims, enabling the salesperson to assign the customer to a risk group (e.g., high, medium, or low). Based on this classification, an empirical premium is applied to the customer, drawn from the salesperson's experience and predefined group rates.

While this rule-based, qualitative approach was practical—and perhaps the only feasible method—before the era of data-driven innovation, it has limitations in accuracy and scalability. With proper data collection and analysis, this approach can now be significantly enhanced through ML models. These models predict claim risks with greater precision, enabling more dynamic, tailored, and data-driven pricing strategies that balance customer needs with organizational profitability.

A warranty vendor's goal is to predict the likelihood and value of claims for a new customer in the upcoming year using historical data collected from existing customers, such as the dataset illustrated in Table 1. This prediction allows the vendor to set an appropriate monthly premium tailored to the new customer by leveraging the power of ML models for more accurate and data-driven pricing. Among the various ML models available for this purpose, the linear regression model is a fundamental and widely used approach, providing a solid foundation for building predictive insights.

Table 1. Sample data for existing customers.

Customer Id	Age	Income ($)	Make	Model	Mileage (miles)	…	Claim($)
001	35	53k	Honda	Civic	34k	…	450
002	25	82k	Ford	Mustang	4.5k	…	2300
003	67	125k	Volvo	XC90	12k	…	934
…	…	…	…	…	…	…	…

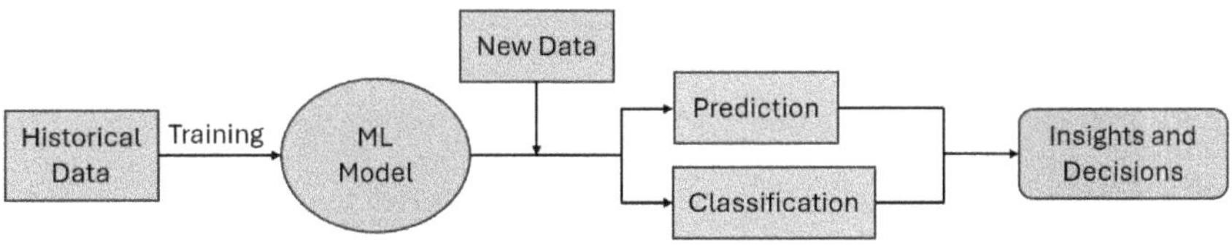

Figure 1. A generic pipeline for ML model-based AI projects.

In a linear regression model, the target variable (also known as the dependent variable) Y is assumed to have a linear relationship with a set of features (also called independent variables) X. This relationship is represented through coefficients ($\beta_1, \beta_2, \beta_3, \ldots, \beta_n$) that quantify the impact of each feature on Y.

In our example, the claim amount serves as the target variable Y, while the features ($x_1, x_2, x_3, \ldots, x_n$) include variables such as age, income, car make, model, mileage, and other factors that are assumed to be linearly correlated with the claim amount. The linear relationship is captured by the following formula:

$$Y = \beta_0 + \beta_1 x_1 + \beta_2 x_2 + \beta_3 x_3 + \cdots + \beta_n x_n \tag{1}$$

where Y represents the claim amount, $x_1, x_2, x_3, \ldots, x_n$ are the features used to predict Y, β_0 is the intercept (a constant), and $\beta_1, \beta_2, \beta_3, \ldots, \beta_n$ are coefficients derived from historical data. These coefficients quantify the strength and direction of the linear relationship between the features and the target variable. Using Equation (1), a linear regression model can be trained on historical data to predict the claim amount for new customers. A generic pipeline for an AI project based on ML models is illustrated in Figure 1. While this case focuses on regression models for prediction, Figure 1 also highlights other types of ML models, such as those used for classification or labeling tasks. We explore these classification models in the next case.

Although linear regression is the only model discussed here, in a real-world project, multiple predictive models should be trained and evaluated to identify the one that delivers the best performance. By leveraging ML models to estimate potential claim amounts for customers, warranty vendors can achieve significant benefits: reducing costs by accurately identifying high-risk customers and increasing revenue by offering more transparent and tailored warranty products. This data-driven approach not only enhances operational efficiency but also fosters greater trust and satisfaction among customers.

2.3. *Advanced techniques for credit card fraud detection*

Credit card fraud involves the unauthorized use of credit cards or card information for purchases, fund withdrawals, or other financial transactions without the cardholder's consent. Common examples of credit card fraud include the following:

- *Lost or stolen cards*: Using a lost or stolen credit card for unauthorized purchases.
- *Card-not-present fraud*: Exploiting credit card information to conduct fraudulent online transactions without the physical card.
- *Card skimming*: Illegally copying credit card information from the magnetic stripe of the card.
- *Account takeover*: Gaining unauthorized access to cardholders' accounts to perform fraudulent activities.

Credit card fraud has a profound impact on financial institutions. When fraudulent transactions occur, card issuers must allocate resources to investigate and resolve cases, increasing operational expenses. Cardholders are often reimbursed for losses, resulting in significant monetary costs for the institutions. Beyond these direct financial losses, institutions also face reputational damage, which can erode customer trust and lead to customer attrition. To make matters worse, frequent failures to prevent fraud can expose financial institutions to regulatory penalties from government authorities at various levels, compounding the overall impact.

Traditionally, credit card fraud is detected using rule-based systems. These systems rely on predefined, static rules to flag transactions that align with known fraudulent patterns. Examples of such rules include transactions exceeding a certain monetary threshold, those occurring in a geographic area the cardholder has never visited, or multiple transactions executed in quick succession from different locations. Once flagged, these transactions are manually reviewed by the fraud department, which decides whether to halt the suspicious activity.

While widely used, rule-based systems have significant limitations. First, because the rules are static, they must be updated frequently to keep pace with evolving fraud tactics. Failure to do so can result in a rapid increase in losses as fraudsters exploit outdated systems. Second, these systems often produce high false-positive rates, flagging legitimate transactions as fraudulent. This frustrates customers, undermines their confidence in the card issuer, and can damage customer relationships. Finally, many rule-based systems are reactive rather than proactive—they detect fraud only after it has occurred, meaning the damage is already done before intervention is possible.

Rule-based methods established the groundwork for credit card fraud prevention, but they have largely been replaced by modern approaches powered by ML technologies, offering more proactive and efficient fraud detection. Among these advanced methods are classification models, a specific type of ML model tailored for tasks involving categorization.

Unlike predictive models, which estimate numerical values, classification models aim to assign labels to each data record based on a specific topic. Common applications include customer segmentation (e.g., high-value, medium-value, or low-value customers), sentiment analysis (e.g., positive, neutral, or negative sentiment), or predicting customer churn (e.g., likely to churn or loyal).

In the context of credit card fraud detection, classification models are used to label each transaction as either "Yes" (fraudulent) or "No" (not fraudulent), making this a binary classification problem. These models enable financial institutions to analyze vast amounts of transactional data in real time, identifying suspicious patterns and potential fraud with greater accuracy and speed than traditional rule-based systems.

Logistic regression is a simple yet effective algorithm for solving binary classification problems, where the goal is to categorize each record—such as a transaction or a customer—into one of two possible outcomes (e.g., yes/no, spam/not spam, churn/not churn). Despite its name, logistic regression is not a predictive model in the sense of estimating numerical values; instead, it focuses on assigning probabilities to each possible outcome and labeling the data accordingly. The foundation of logistic regression lies in the following formula:

$$P(y=1\mid x)=\frac{1}{1+e^{-(\beta_0+\beta_1x_1+\beta_2x_2+\cdots+\beta_nx_n)}} \tag{2}$$

where P represents the probability that a data record belongs to the positive class—in this case, the probability that a transaction is fraudulent, or labeled as 'yes'. The variables $x_1, x_2, x_3, \ldots, x_n$ are features deemed relevant for identifying fraudulent transactions, while $\beta_1, \beta_2, \beta_3, \ldots, \beta_n$ coefficients learned from the training data.

It's important to note that logistic regression produces a probability rather than a direct label (e.g., 'yes' or 'no'). To convert this probability into a binary label, a threshold is required. By default, this threshold is set at 0.5, meaning that transactions with a probability equal to or greater than 0.5 are labeled as 'yes' (fraudulent), while those below 0.5 are labeled as 'no' (non-fraudulent). However, this threshold can be adjusted to suit specific scenarios, optimizing the model's performance for particular use cases. Exploring threshold optimization is a more advanced topic beyond the scope of this chapter.

To apply logistic regression, as defined by Equation (2), a training dataset is required to estimate the coefficients $\beta_1, \beta_2, \beta_3, \ldots, \beta_n$. Table 2 provides an example of such a dataset. In this case, the "fraud label" serves as the target variable for the logistic regression model, while features such as transaction amount, merchant risk score, and same-country transactions are inputs used to train the model. There are no universal standards for the number or type of features to include, as the selection of features significantly impacts the performance of ML models. Consequently, data scientists must combine expertise in ML theory with domain knowledge and practical experience to perform effective feature engineering, ultimately improving the quality and accuracy of the models.

Table 2. Sample data for credit card transactions.

Transaction Id	Amount	Merchant Risk Score	Same-Country Transaction	...	Fraud
1	46.54	0.26	1	...	No
2	544.30	0.87	0	...	Yes
3	1382.00	0.33	1	...	No
...	...	...	...	...	...

Compared to traditional methods, ML models bring substantial improvements to credit card fraud detection. First, they enable proactive detection, analyzing transactions in real time and flagging suspicious activities before they occur, which helps prevent potential losses. Second, ML models are highly adaptable to evolving fraud tactics. Unlike static rule-based systems, they dynamically adjust to emerging trends, continuously learning and adapting as fraudsters evolve their methods. Lastly, ML models offer lower false positive rates and strong scalability. With high-quality data and proper fine-tuning, ML models significantly reduce false positives, enhancing the customer experience by minimizing disruptions to legitimate transactions. Additionally, they scale effortlessly, handling vast volumes of transactions across millions of customers automatically, making them ideal for high-frequency transaction environments.

2.4. *Refining academic papers with LLMs and prompt engineering*

English is the most widely accepted language for academic writing, serving as the primary medium for publishing in prestigious academic journals. However, meeting the high writing standards required for publication poses a significant challenge, particularly for researchers whose first language is not English. Even those conducting groundbreaking research may find it difficult to publish their work due to language barriers. In this sense, English can become an obstacle that limits the dissemination of valuable scientific contributions.

To address this issue, academic paper revision services have emerged as a valuable resource. These companies offer comprehensive support to enhance the quality of academic manuscripts through language editing, structural improvements, formatting, and submission guidance. By bridging the gap between rigorous research and polished presentation, these services help researchers effectively communicate their findings and overcome language-related barriers to publication.

Academic paper revision is a complex and labor-intensive process. When a manuscript is received from a customer for revision, a copyeditor begins by thoroughly polishing the document. This includes correcting grammar and syntax errors, improving clarity and readability, and reorganizing paragraphs to enhance logical flow. After this initial editing, the manuscript is often assigned to a specific research field (e.g., computer engineering, biotechnology, and chemistry) and sent to a domain expert for a second round of revision. These domain experts are crucial as they are familiar with field-specific standards, understand technical terminology, and can anticipate the expectations of journal reviewers.

Once the domain expert completes their review, the manuscript is returned to the editorial staff, who ensures that the formatting adheres to the exact guidelines of the target journal. A final round of proofreading is conducted before the revised manuscript is delivered back to the customer for submission. This meticulous process can take weeks to complete.

AI has the potential to streamline and enhance this workflow. Unlike tasks that involve predicting target variable values or classifying data records into predefined categories, academic paper revision may require content generation—a capability central to generative models, as represented by the "G" in GPT. By leveraging AI, parts of this time-consuming process can be accelerated without compromising quality.

GPT, which stands for Generative Pre-trained Transformer, has fundamentally transformed the landscape of AI research and applications. A transformer is a type of deep learning model designed for natural language processing (NLP) (Vaswani *et al.*, 2017). Using advanced self-attention mechanisms, transformers efficiently capture long-range dependencies in sequences, enabling them to process, understand, and generate lengthy texts with remarkable speed and accuracy. The introduction of transformers marked a pivotal moment in NLP, showcasing the immense potential of self-attention mechanisms.

Today, the majority of LLMs, including GPT, BERT, and T5, are built upon the transformer architecture. These models excel in natural language tasks by leveraging their vast training on diverse datasets. When using LLMs such as ChatGPT, Claude, or Gemini, prompts serve as the primary medium for communication between the human user and the AI. Simple prompts might include questions such as the following: "Who wrote the book A Tale of Two Cities?" or "When was the United States of America established?" LLMs can answer these questions because they are trained on extensive datasets, effectively functioning as interactive encyclopedias.

However, the true power of LLMs lies in their versatility. By carefully crafting prompts—a process known as prompt engineering—users can optimize the outputs of LLMs for a wide range of applications. In the following, we outline some simple yet impactful use cases enabled by effective prompt engineering:

- A job interview assistant: *You are an expert data science job interview assistant with in-depth knowledge of data science concepts, tools, and real-world applications. Your role is to simulate an interviewer for a data scientist position, asking a mix of technical, behavioral, and scenario-based questions. You should adapt your questions based on the specific skills and experience outlined and provide constructive feedback after each response.*
- A business analyst assistant: *You are my business assistant, specializing in analyzing and summarizing complex business reports, financial data, and market research. Your role is to process the business report I provide, extract key insights, summarize critical information, and generate actionable business recommendations based on the analysis. Additionally, you should tailor your insights to align with specific business objectives or challenges.*
- A short story creator: *You are a creative short story writer who crafts engaging stories based on keywords or parameters I provide. These keywords will specify elements such as genre, themes, characters, tone, and length. For each set of keywords, generate two distinct story drafts, allowing for comparison and refinement based on preferences or additional feedback.*

With initial prompts crafted by the user, they can be further refined through iterative communication with LLMs. For example, suppose you ask ChatGPT to write a science fiction story about a robot surviving in a post-apocalyptic world using the short story writer prompt and it generates two candidates. After reviewing both, you find the second story more engaging than the first. To ensure future stories align with the writing style of the second candidate, you can use a follow-up prompt like this:

"I prefer the second story you generated. Please refine the initial prompt so that future stories match the same writing style."

Through several iterations, ChatGPT will refine the original prompt into a more detailed and specific version that captures all your preferences. This iterative process enables you to develop a comprehensive prompt, ensuring the AI consistently delivers short stories that meet your exact requirements and stylistic expectations.

Let's return to the academic paper polishing task discussed earlier. At the outset, the prompt provided to an LLM could look something like this:

* "You are a writing assistant tasked with refining the English language in research papers. The user will provide you with paragraphs from research papers. You should follow these rules:

1. *Maintain the same number of paragraphs as the original input.*
2. *Use formal, scholarly language. Avoid slang, contractions, first-person pronouns, and emotional expressions. Use precise, unambiguous terms that convey meaning clearly.*
3. *Pay close attention to grammar, spelling, punctuation, clarity, and precision. Proofread thoroughly and ensure there are no errors.*" *

With this initial prompt, the LLM can generate a basic revision of the raw manuscript, initiating an interactive process between the user and the AI. Through iterative refinements, a detailed and well-structured prompt incorporating specific rules and examples can be developed. This optimized prompt ensures the LLM performs more nuanced revisions, facilitating batch processing of manuscripts with high-quality results. For instance, a more advanced version of the prompt might look like this:

* *"You are a writing assistant tasked with refining the English language in research papers. The user will provide you with paragraphs from research papers. Please follow these rules:*

1. *Maintain Structure:*
   - *Preserve the same number of paragraphs as in the input text.*
   - *Ensure the length of the rewritten text is similar to the original, altering less than 40% of the total words.*
2. *Titles and Headlines:*
   - *Identify and analyze titles, section headings, or subtitles.*
   - *Retain the existing capitalization format in titles and headings.*
3. *Use Scholarly Language:*
   - *Write in formal, academic English. Avoid slang, contractions, first-person pronouns, or emotional language.*
   - *Use precise, unambiguous terms to communicate ideas clearly.*

Examples:
   - *Before: "You won't believe how fast AI is changing things."*
   - *After: "The rapid advancements in artificial intelligence are transforming technological innovation."*

- *Before: "Research shows kids these days are totally hooked on their phones."*
- *After: "Contemporary research indicates a marked increase in smartphone dependency among adolescents."*

4. *Proofreading and Accuracy:*
   - *Ensure all grammar, spelling, punctuation, and phrasing are correct.*
   - *Proofread thoroughly to eliminate errors, ensuring clarity and precision.*

Examples:

- *Before: "Its a known fact that exercise helps with stress."*
- *After: "It is well-established that regular physical activity alleviates stress."*
- *Before: "Their findings was inconclusive."*
- *After: "Their findings were inconclusive."* *

With effective prompt engineering, LLMs can produce revisions of manuscripts with significantly improved writing quality. While final proofreading by an editor and a domain expert remains necessary, this AI-driven automation can drastically reduce the time and cost involved. What once took two to three weeks for manual polishing can now be streamlined to two or three days, offering a highly efficient solution for academic paper revision.

2.5 *Enhancing insurance services through a retrieval-augmented generation (RAG) chatbot*

A call center is a centralized hub where businesses manage customer interactions, primarily over the phone. In the insurance sector, call centers play a critical role as the primary point of contact between insurers and customers. Their key responsibilities include the following:

- Insurance sales and renewals: Call centers assist customers with policy inquiries, explain insurance products, and facilitate the purchase or renewal of policies.
- Customer service and support: Call centers provide comprehensive product information, including policy details, premiums, and coverage

options. They also simplify the claims process by guiding customers through necessary paperwork and procedures. Many insurance call centers operate 24/7, ensuring support during emergencies such as accidents or health crises.

- Customer retention and relationship management: Call centers proactively address customer concerns to reduce churn, follow up after claims or sales to ensure satisfaction, and strengthen customer relationships.

Despite their importance, maintaining call centers can be costly due to expenses associated with staffing, infrastructure, technology, and regulatory compliance. With the emergence of LLMs, the idea of replacing human agents in call centers with LLM-based chatbots has gained traction. These chatbots can simulate human-like conversations, potentially offering a cost-effective alternative to traditional call center operations.

However, in the insurance industry, a chatbot must act as a professional with robust domain knowledge, delivering accurate and up-to-date information to customers. Generic LLMs, while powerful, cannot meet these stringent requirements without augmentation. To address this gap, insurance chatbots must be enhanced with specialized knowledge and retrieval capabilities, ensuring they provide reliable, industry-specific support while maintaining the professionalism expected in customer interactions.

This requirement cannot be fulfilled by generic LLMs without augmentation. As discussed in the previous case, LLMs are pre-trained models developed using vast amounts of publicly available data from the internet. While this approach equips LLMs with broad knowledge, it does not make them "all-knowing AIs" due to two significant limitations:

- Lack of up-to-date knowledge: LLMs rely on static datasets compiled at the time of training. Consequently, their knowledge is limited to the information available during the data collection period. For instance, an LLM trained in 2015 would inaccurately state that Barack Obama is the current president of the United States. Updating an LLM to incorporate new information requires retraining with fresh data—a process that is resource-intensive and feasible only for organizations with substantial resources, such as OpenAI or Meta.

- Limitations of training data: The datasets used to train LLMs may be incomplete or contain conflicting information. As a result, LLMs often guess or interpolate when faced with gaps or inconsistencies. For example, if asked how many candies are in your pocket, an LLM can only make an uninformed guess. Similarly, if queried about the detailed recipe for Coca-Cola, it might generate an answer based on similar drink recipes in its training data. However, such a response would be inaccurate since Coca-Cola's recipe is a closely guarded trade secret.

Incorrect answers generated by LLMs due to outdated knowledge or limitations in their training data are commonly referred to as hallucinations. These hallucinations are particularly intriguing because, while factually incorrect, nonsensical, or entirely fabricated, they are often delivered with an air of confidence and coherence, making them appear credible to the user.

If an LLM is used directly to replace human agents in a call center without any augmentation, it is bound to fail. This is because the training data of a generic LLM does not include specific information about the products, policies, or customers of a particular insurance company. As a result, the LLM would be unable to provide accurate or reliable answers tailored to the unique needs of the business and its clients. This limitation highlights the necessity of enhancing LLMs with company-specific data and domain expertise to ensure their effectiveness in specialized applications.

A solution to equip LLMs with domain expertise and up-to-date information is retrieval-augmented generation (RAG). This approach is intuitive: it enhances pre-trained LLMs by integrating a retriever system that accesses relevant, factual data from a predefined knowledge base.

In a basic RAG system, the process begins by creating a vector database that stores domain-specific knowledge (Figure 2). When a user submits a query, the system converts it into an embedding, which is then compared with the data in the vector database. This comparison extracts context directly related to the user's query. Unlike a standalone LLM, which relies solely on the information learned during training, an RAG system enables the LLM to leverage both its training and the additional context retrieved from the vector database. This dual approach results in answers that are more accurate, reliable, and domain-specific.

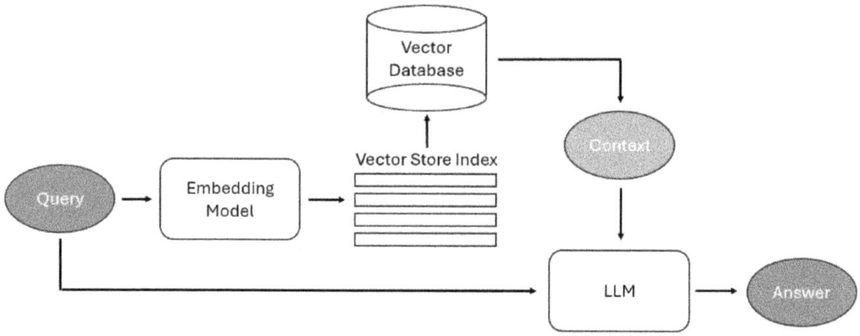

Figure 2. A simple RAG system.

The quality and content of the vector database are critical to the effectiveness of the RAG system. The database determines the scope of domain knowledge the LLM can access and directly influences the accuracy and relevance of the generated responses. A well-constructed vector database ensures that the LLM is equipped with precise, up-to-date information tailored to the needs of a specific domain or application.

When leveraging RAG to develop a chatbot for replacing an insurance call center, it is crucial to populate the vector database with relevant, structured, and well-organized information. This database serves as the chatbot's knowledge backbone, enabling it to retrieve accurate and contextually relevant responses to customer inquiries.

While there are no strict rules governing what information should be included in the vector database, the guiding principle is to comprehensively cover the domain of interest and ensure all data is accurate and up to date. The effectiveness of the chatbot heavily depends on the quality and breadth of the information stored in the database. Following are key categories of information that may be used to build a robust vector database for an insurance chatbot:

- Insurance policy documents: such as various policy types (auto, health, home, and business), coverage terms and conditions, premium rates, exclusions, and limitations.
- FAQs and common queries from real call center cases. Here are some examples:
  - General questions: "How does a claim affect premium rates?" "What is a deductible?" "What does exclusion mean?" "How can I choose the best policy based on my needs?"

  - Policy-specific questions: "What does my auto insurance policy cover?" "How can I get a group discount if I work for a local university?" "What payment options are available for premiums?"

- Claim processing information: Required documents and submission methods, typical claim timelines, and procedures for checking claim status.
- Customer support knowledge base: Contact details for customers and support teams, procedures for escalating unresolved cases, operating hours, and locations for in-person assistance.
- Regulatory and compliance information: Local insurance regulations and legal requirements, privacy policies related to customer and company data, anti-fraud measures, and related guidelines.

When populating a vector database, it's important to include as much relevant detail as possible, but perfection isn't necessary on the first attempt. The database can be polished and updated iteratively as missing elements are identified or as existing information needs revisions. After several rounds of refinement, creating a chatbot that meets the basic requirements of a virtual insurance agent becomes a practical and achievable goal.

Replacing call centers with AI-powered chatbots offers significant business value. First, it boosts cost efficiency. AI chatbots can handle a high volume of customer inquiries without the need for salaries, benefits, or physical infrastructure. They operate 24/7, eliminating the need for extra staffing to cover night shifts, weekends, or holidays. Second, chatbots provide strong scalability for businesses. Unlike human agents, who handle one customer at a time, chatbots can manage thousands of conversations simultaneously. This capability allows them to easily handle seasonal spikes, such as natural disasters, policy renewal deadlines, or holiday seasons, without adding overhead. Third, they enhance the customer experience by providing quick and accurate answers to routine queries with no waiting time. Chatbots can use customer data to deliver tailored recommendations, policy details, or claim updates. With AI-based translation, they can offer services in multiple languages, improving accessibility for a diverse customer base. Lastly, chatbots are ideal for generating data-driven business insights. Unlike conversations between human agents and customers, every interaction with a chatbot is easily logged and analyzed, offering valuable insights into customer behavior, preferences, and pain points. Additionally, chatbots learn from these interactions, becoming more effective over time.

3. Conclusion

AI has become a powerful driver of transformation in the business world. By harnessing its capabilities, businesses are reimagining operations, enhancing customer experiences, and uncovering new opportunities for growth and innovation. The examples explored in this chapter highlight the diverse applications of AI, ranging from optimizing pricing strategies and detecting fraud to refining academic writing and revolutionizing customer support.

AI empowers businesses in several key ways: providing predictive insights, automating routine processes, and personalizing customer interactions. For example, traditional ML models excel at data-driven tasks such as assessing customer risks or designing tailored premium pricing strategies. Generative models such as ChatGPT, meanwhile, open doors to creating high-quality content, improving customer engagement, and reducing operational costs. RAG systems, particularly in industries such as insurance, showcase how domain-specific AI solutions can boost accuracy and scalability, enabling businesses to deliver highly relevant and timely support.

These innovations go beyond mere technological upgrades—they are reshaping competitive landscapes. AI allows businesses to anticipate market trends, respond rapidly to changing consumer needs, and streamline workflows, fostering adaptability and resilience. Moreover, its ability to scale operations with precision provides a critical edge in industries that demand swift decision-making and actionable insights. AI's impact is not just about efficiency—it's about enabling businesses to thrive in a dynamic, data-driven future.

The adoption of AI brings tremendous potential, but it is not without its challenges. First, data quality and accessibility are critical. AI systems rely on vast amounts of accurate, relevant, and well-structured data to produce meaningful outcomes. Unfortunately, many organizations struggle with poor-quality or fragmented data, which can significantly undermine model performance. Second, talent and expertise are essential but often scarce. Successfully implementing AI requires not only skilled data scientists but also domain experts who can guide feature engineering, model selection, and the interpretation of results in alignment with specific business goals. Achieving this balance between technical expertise and business insight can be a significant hurdle. Lastly, ethical considerations and compliance present growing challenges. As AI becomes more integrated into business operations, organizations must navigate complex issues such as data privacy, security, and fairness. The regulatory environment for AI is evolving rapidly, requiring companies to stay ahead of emerging legal and ethical standards to maintain trust and avoid reputational risks.

In summary, AI is not just a tool but a transformative force enabling businesses to thrive in an increasingly digital and competitive world. The cases discussed in this chapter highlight AI's vast potential to drive innovation, improve efficiency, and create value. For organizations ready to embrace this transformation, AI offers solutions to today's challenges and a roadmap to seize tomorrow's opportunities.

References

Ahlstrom, D. (2010). Innovation and growth: How business contributes to society. *Academy of Management Perspectives*, Vol. 24(3), 11–24.

Åström, J., Reim, W., & Parida, V. (2022). Value creation and value capture for AI business model innovation: a three-phase process framework. *Review of Managerial Science*, Vol. 16(7), 2111–2133.

Boden, M. A. (1998). Creativity and artificial intelligence. *Artificial Intelligence*, Vol. 103(1-2), 347–356.

Dirican, C. (2015). The impacts of robotics, artificial intelligence on business and economics. *Procedia-Social and Behavioral Sciences*, Vol. 195, 564–573.

Echeberria, A. L. (2022). The impact of AI on business, economics and innovation. In *Artificial Intelligence for Business: Innovation, Tools and Practices* (pp. 67–96). Cham: Springer International Publishing.

Enholm, I. M., Papagiannidis, E., Mikalef, P., & Krogstie, J. (2022). Artificial intelligence and business value: A literature review. *Information Systems Frontiers*, Vol. 24(5), 1709–1734.

European Commission. (2018, December 7). Coordinated plan on artificial intelligence (Communication COM(2018) 795 final). *Shaping Europe's Digital Future*. Retrieved December 10, 2024, from https://digital-strategy.ec.europa.eu/en/library/coordinated-plan-artificial-intelligence

Giuggioli, G., & Pellegrini, M. M. (2023). Artificial intelligence as an enabler for entrepreneurs: a systematic literature review and an agenda for future research. *International Journal of Entrepreneurial Behavior & Research*, Vol. 29(4), 816–837.

Liebowitz, J. (2001). Knowledge management and its link to artificial intelligence. *Expert Systems with Applications*, Vol. 20(1), 1–6.

McCarthy, J., Minsky, M. L., Rochester, N., & Shannon, C. E. (2006). A proposal for the Dartmouth summer research project on artificial intelligence, august 31, 1955. *AI Magazine*, Vol. 27(4), 12–12.

UNESCO, D. (2021). Preliminary report on the first draft of the recommendation on the ethics of artificial intelligence. *United Nations Educational, Scientific and Cultural Organization.*

Vaswani, A. (2017). Attention is all you need. *Advances in Neural Information Processing Systems.*

Yeung, K. (2020). Recommendation of the council on artificial intelligence (OECD). *International Legal Materials*, Vol. 59(1), 27–34.

Zhou, W., Zhang, C., Wu, L., & Shashidhar, M. (2023). ChatGPT and marketing: Analyzing public discourse in early Twitter posts. *Journal of Marketing Analytics*, Vol. 11(4), 693–706.

https://doi.org/10.1142/9789819816347_0011

Chapter 11

Threat Avoidance or Opportunity Chasing? The Three Levels of AI Adoption and the Implications for Business Performance

Marigo Raftopoulos

Tampere University, Finland

1. Introduction

Artificial intelligence is widely claimed to be driving the advancement of next-generation information systems (IS) that will facilitate business performance improvement and innovation (Duan *et al.*, 2019; Dwivedi *et al.*, 2021; Berente *et al.*, 2021). Yet, we have a limited understanding of how organizations can translate AI potential into creating business value, with recent studies suggesting that organizations are falling short of realizing performance expectations from AI (Shollo & Müller, 2022; Pumplun *et al.*, 2019) and at best it was found to have shown inconsistent or mixed results (Langer & Landers, 2021; Cubric, 2020).

The Technology Acceptance Model and the Unified Theory of Acceptance and Use of Technology (UTAUT) (Venkatesh *et al.*, 2003) are extensively employed in existing IS literature however these theories have limitations in explaining and predicting the behavioral intentions of users to adopt AI (Gansser & Reich, 2021). Given the complexities of AI technologies, acceptance issues go beyond the utility of the technology into complex psycho-social factors that affect human–machine performance such as fear (Cabrera-Sánchez *et al.*, 2021), AI Anxiety (Oh *et al.*, 2017), algorithm aversion (Dietvorst 2015), bias and mistrust (Ishowo-Oloko *et al.*, 2019), and wilful lack of co-operation.

Upon deeper investigation of the extant literature on AI adoption at the individual level, we propose it's become necessary to extend our understanding of technology adoption by presenting a novel three-level hierarchy of AI adoption that distinguishes between passive utilitarian acceptance of AI (Langer & Landers, 2021) to active collaboration (Seeber *et al.*, 2020) and technology co-creation (Waardenburg *et al.*, 2022). This hierarchy or progression has largely evolved out of the increasing maturity and availability of cognitive AI technologies in business applications (Ienca, 2019). Given the unique attributes of each of these types of AI technologies and how they are perceived differently by system users, we theorize that it is important to investigate them separately and comparatively rather than view AI adoption as a monolithic or homogenous construct.

We use the lens of Technology Threat Avoidance Theory (TTAT) which purports that human adoption and avoidance behavior are qualitatively different (Liang & Xue, 2009). Where individuals perceive a technology threat, as is becoming more and more prominent in AI IS literature, they are engaged in either actively or passively avoiding the perceived threat. We also draw on the Coping Model of User Adoption (CMUA) developed by Beaudry and Pinsonneault (2005) which explains the cognitive, emotional, and behavioral responses of individuals in coping with significant technology events in their work environment.

Our work is guided by the following research questions: (1) What individual factors explain the likelihood of AI acceptance, AI collaboration, and AI co-creation? (2) What unique factors shape a positive attitude toward the adoption of more sophisticated technologies such as AI collaboration and co-creation? The purpose of this research is twofold: The first is to build a deeper understanding of the adoption of AI technology at the individual level to enable organizations and developers to design human-centric AI systems, particularly in more complex areas of human–machine collaboration and AI technology co-design. Second, this work can inform individuals to gain a deeper understanding of their personal frames and mindsets that can shape their approach to improving personal learning and workplace self-efficacy strategies in the adoption and management of AI technologies.

2. Theoretical Background

There are three primary conceptual dimensions of AI adoption prevalent in extant literature being acceptance, collaboration, and co-creation, each representing increasing levels of complexity in terms of human engagement and interaction with artificial intelligence. We theorize that each dimension requires unique human attributes, mindsets, and cognitive frames to successfully participate in productive human–machine relationships in the workplace. Furthermore, an understanding of these unique human attributes may enable us to (a) accurately predict human behaviors (Kosinski *et al.*, 2013; Sohn *et al.*, 2020) and (b) design socio-technical systems that effectively enable such relationships (Fügener *et al.*, 2021; Seeber *et al.*, 2020). We offer the following definitions of the three conceptual dimensions of AI adoption that are prevalent in the literature:

AI Acceptance: This refers to the passive use of AI solutions or technologies to improve existing processes or outcomes where users may not have a direct role in shaping the AI's functionality and only use it as a tool or resource in their job function. Until recently, acceptance has been the primary focus of AI research in the information systems domain as it has largely risen out of the early AI implementations that were focused on simpler AI automation technologies (Kaber & Endsley, 2004; Jarrahi, 2018; Dellermann *et al.*, 2019).

AI Collaboration: AI collaboration involves an interactive relationship between humans and AI, where humans proactively work alongside AI systems in partnership to achieve specific goals. Humans provide input, guidance, and feedback to AI, and AI, in turn, assists and augments human decision-making and tasks (Carroll *et al.*, 2019; Stowers *et al.*, 2021). Collaboration is characterized by interactive communication and cooperation between networked actors that rely on a common vision, strategy, common identity, and joint obligations (Camarinha-Matos *et al.*, 2008; Smorodinskaya *et al.*, 2017). This represents the next level of AI acceptance that requires human acknowledgment of AI as a team member and collaborator that entails a higher skills and capability base for individuals. This is often seen as a requirement of human–machine working relationships in complex and ambiguous operating environments (Hyland-Wood *et al*., 2019; Fügener *et al*., 2021).

AI Co-creation: AI co-creation takes collaboration a step further, where stakeholders actively participate in designing, developing, or evolving AI systems (Waardenburg & Huysman, 2022; Wagner, 2020). This can involve interdisciplinary teams working together to build AI models, customize algorithms, or shape AI solutions according to specific needs. It's a deeper and more involved form of partnership. The concept of co-creation has been around for some time in strategy literature (Ranjan & Read, 2016; Prahalad & Ramaswamy, 2000) and is now an emergent field in AI development. It's been proposed as a solution to overcome limitations in the transparency and explainability of AI algorithms, interfaces, interactions, and recommendations, and to account for the increased blurring of the boundaries between AI use and its development (Waardenburg & Huysman, 2022; Wagner, 2020). The proposition is that if stakeholders were more involved in the design and development process, then current limitations in AI development and performance would be overcome.

There are several different approaches and definitions for co-creation. This study focuses on co-creation as a specific form of collaboration, adapted from Pulkkinen & Hautamaki (2019), and Liwång (2022), where activities and resources of organizations are systematically integrated to produce results that would not have been possible without a joint approach. The view of co-creation in this chapter is that cooperation between stakeholders creates a shared responsibility for system development, promotes fruitful dialog on central capability aspects and challenges, and promotes the exchange of results from research. For example, consider a case study by Andersson (2018) on the development of two military concept development projects, a combat vehicle and a naval vessel, with close co-operation between demonstrators, research, government agencies, and industry organizations.

2.1. *Technology threat avoidance theory*

The central tenet of the Technology Threat Avoidance Theory (TTAT) is that human adoption and avoidance behavior are qualitatively different (Liang & Xue, 2009). Where users perceive a technology threat, they either engage in (a) actively avoiding the threat by engaging in *safeguarding measures* or (b) passively avoiding the threat by taking *emotion-focused coping behaviors*. According to Liang and Xue (2009), human perceptions of whether a technology is what they call 'malicious' or 'virtuous' are based on the designer's intention or the perception of the user. A *malicious technology* is defined by Liang & Xue (2009) as a system perceived by users to be 'repulsive' and to cause negative outcomes for them, whereas a *virtuous technology* is perceived by users to be attractive as it creates positive outcomes through its use. Key challenges arise when a technology has been designed to be virtuous but is perceived to be malicious in some way by users' context or situation or through conflicts of interest and will therefore engage in threat avoidance.

According to Liang and Xue (2009), technology acceptance theories such as TAM and UTAUT cannot fully explain people's technology threat avoidance behavior which limits the explanatory power of those theories in the context of technology threat avoidance. The idea that an individual's perception of technology threat influences the person's adoption behavior is well regarded in extant literature examining AI technologies such as Cao *et al.* (2021), Duan *et al.* (2019), Dwivedi *et al.* (2021), and Ransbotham *et al.* (2018).

We selected TTAT as the most appropriate theoretical lens for this research given the widely reported phenomenon of fear and concern about the impact of AI technologies on job losses and loss of autonomy and opportunity at work (Mirbabaie *et al.*, 2021; Gansser & Reich, 2021). Based on our literature review, we theorized that the incidence of technology threat avoidance behavior will accelerate as AI technologies become more sophisticated, as depicted in our model of the three levels of adoption: acceptance, collaboration, and co-creation. TTAT proposes that users' threat perceptions are determined by the perceived probability of the threat's occurrence and the perceived severity of the threat's negative consequences (Cao *et al.*, 2021). This is also supported by other theoretical perspectives such as social identity theory (SIT) (Hogg, 2016) which identifies that human perception of self is significantly derived from work roles, and a potential destabilization of that may affect human behaviors toward AI technology.

This phenomenon is well articulated in the Coping Model of User Adaption (CMUA) developed by Beaudry and Pinsonneault (2005) which purports that users adapt to a major technology event by employing a wide range of responses to restore emotional stability, modify tasks, adapt the technology or even resist it. A key tenet of CMUA, which is expanded upon later in our discussion, is that how people cope with a significant technological event in their workplace is largely determined by the resources that are available to them, and this includes financial, material, physical, psychological, cognitive, and social. All these factors play a significant role in workplace acceptance of AI technologies which has implications for business outcomes.

In the following sections of this chapter, our results show decreasing support for increasing levels of sophistication of AI technologies. Our survey respondents report increasing perceptions of threat and vulnerability, and intentions to engage in increasing threat avoidance behavior at higher levels of AI technology sophistication.

3. Method

In this study, we undertook a survey of 305 professionals in Europe and recruited participants from the *prolific.com* platform, screened for professionals residing in Europe with full-time employment and who use a high amount of technology at work. This was a purposive sample (Etikan *et al.*, 2016) selecting candidates that would most likely be open to technology collaboration and co-creation so we could investigate the upper limits of perceptions toward the adoption of sophisticated AI technologies. Participants were rewarded a small monetary fee as recommended by the platform. We received 332 surveys however after screening for attention checks and incomplete surveys, we collated the data from 305 participants which were transferred into *SPSS* for the statistical analysis, and into *Atlas.ti* for the qualitative analysis.

3.1. *Behavioral intention to adopt AI*

The measures of the behavioral intentions on the willingness to adopt AI technology at increasing levels of sophistication were based on the work of Araujo *et al.* (2020) and Adell (2010). We theorized that the most effective way to measure these variables is to present different scenarios to survey participants on AI adoption, collaboration, and co-creation with each depicting increasing levels of complexity with human interaction with AI. For example, Adell (2010) presented scenario-based questions by asking respondents to imagine a stated situation in the adoption of intelligent transport systems, and Araujo *et al.*, (2020) on perceptions on algorithmic management. We based our scenarios on a brief outline and allowed respondents to derive meaning from each statement. Given the AI domain is constantly changing and is dominated by fragmented definitions, interpretations, and siloed technologies, we didn't pursue the need to determine respondents' understanding of the technical meanings of each level due to the lack of common industry agreement and standards (Cubric 2020; Collins *et al.*, 2021). Furthermore, our rationale was that this survey was not a test of technical knowledge, but one of identifying the psycho-social and threat and opportunity responses of respondents to the rise of AI technology capability. We came to this position by forming and consulting with a panel of five academic and AI practitioner experts that we established to check for the adequacy of our definitions and refine the questions. After several reviews and iterations, we agreed that this approach would meet our stated research objectives. We also ran a pilot survey with 50 respondents, and we were satisfied with how respondents interpreted and answered the survey. The three scenario-based questions used in the final survey are as follows:

AI Acceptance scenario (AIA): "Imagine your organization is introducing a basic AI technology that would make some of your work tasks easier and more effective."

AI Collaboration scenario (AIC): "Imagine your organization is introducing a sophisticated AI technology that performs half of your work tasks and you would need to team or collaborate with it to do your work effectively."

AI Co-creation scenario (AICC): "Imagine your organization is planning to develop a highly sophisticated AI technology in your area of expertise and they have asked you to allocate dedicated time over the next 6–12 months to work with the developers on its design, training, and implementation."

For each scenario, two questions with a 5-point Likert scale were asked: (1) Whether they would be happy to work with the AI and (2) an open-ended question asking for an explanation of their reasoning for their answers to each scenario.

3.2. *Statistical analysis*

The demographic profile of our respondents, as outlined in Table 1, shows that 64.6% of our respondents were female, the majority were in the 26–32-year-old age range followed by 33–45s. The majority were university-educated with undergraduate and postgraduate qualifications. As mentioned above, we filtered potential respondents by full-time employment and working with a high level of technology at work.

We ran comparative tests to examine the mean difference of the latent constructs which included independent sample T-test for gender and one-way ANOVA tests for variables of age and qualification. The results of the independent sample T-test indicated that there are no significant statistical differences in the mean values of the constructs between males and females. The results of the one-way ANOVA indicated that that there are no significant statistical differences in the mean values of the constructs between groups of age, and levels of education qualifications.

A broad range of AI technologies and use cases were reported by respondents. The majority of the core functional areas where AI technologies were implemented were located in Information Technology (16% of

Table 1. Frequencies and percentages of the demographic variables.

Profile (n = 305)	**F**	**%**
Gender		
Male	108	35.4
Female	197	64.6
Age group		
18–25	66	21.6
26–32	110	36.1
33–45	103	33.8
46–59	24	7.9
60+	2	0.7
Education level attained		
High school certificate	35	11.5
Diploma, college, or trade	38	12.5
University undergraduate	114	37.4
University postgraduate	118	38.7

total respondents), Information Systems (13%), Marketing and Sales (18%), Human Resources (9%) and Finance (9%). In terms of the key functional roles performed by AI technologies, they concentrated in the areas of customer service (21%), business analytics (18%), forecasting and prediction (17%), and optimization and automation (16%). The AI technology stack included a range of different technologies for each application, for example combining machine learning, computer vision, and virtual assistants. In answering the technology stack question, over half of the respondents mentioned (without prompting) the use of the top tier AI technology providers in the development of their AI applications such as Oracle, SAP, IBM, Accenture, and AWS, as well as other smaller solutions providers. Less than 10% of respondents mentioned the use of popular generative AI technologies or tools in their work. This may be because we had screened for professionals working with high levels of technology in large organizations; therefore, these respondents may be focused on more significant enterprise-level AI technology investments such as machine learning, data analytics, optimization, forecasting, prediction, and automation.

3.3. *Results*: *The three levels of adoption*

Our analysis of the responses to our survey on the behavioral intention to accept, collaborate, or co-create artificial intelligence found declining support for AI adoption at increased levels of technological sophistication. Positive adoption of AI (those who selected Strongly Agree or Agree) started at 86% for scenario 1 (acceptance of basic AI), then dropped to 63% for scenario 2 (collaborative AI), and down to 59% for scenario 3 (co-creating AI). See Figure 1.

The qualitative responses were uploaded into specialized qualitative software *Atlas.ti* and were coded in detail using a codebook we developed for the study. We also ran a comparative analysis utilizing *Atlas.ti's* AI-generated code feature (which is currently still in beta). However, even though the software's AI codes were significant in number and generated at speed, we did not find that it provided any material differences or additions to our insights from the data compared to us running the software without their AI coding.

We segmented the qualitative data into three clusters according to how the respondents answered their likelihood of adopting the AI technology for each scenario: (1) Positive: These were those who answered

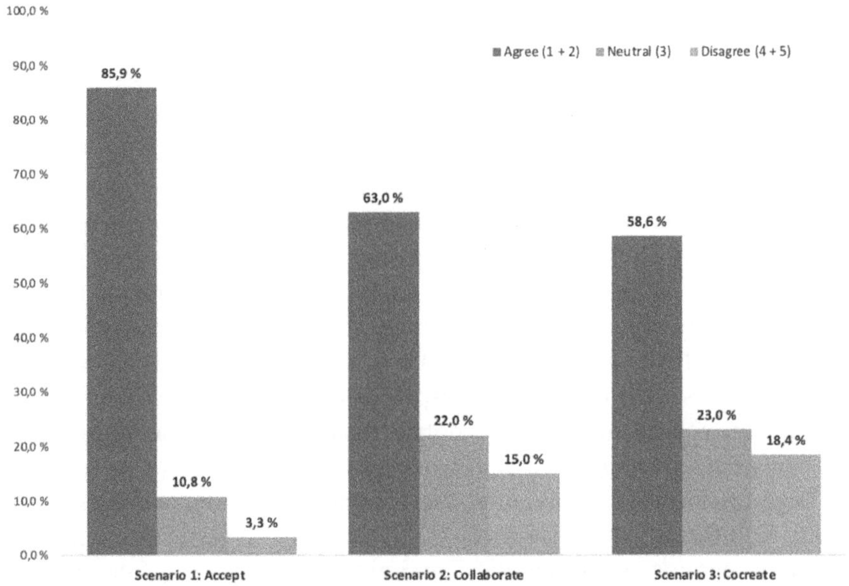

Figure 1. Levels of agreement to adopt AI.

Strongly Agree or Agree to the three scenario questions, (2) Neutral: these were those who answered Neutral, or (3) Negative: these were those who answered Disagree or Strongly Disagree. In this chapter, we present the findings of the responses to **Scenario 3: Co-Creation** as this represents the most challenging category of AI adoption. Using a grounded approach, our thematic analysis found the following: **Positive cluster:** Five categories were derived from 109 codes as outlined in Table 2. It should be noted that respondents who answered Strongly Agree or Agree to the scenario questions only wrote positive responses in the open-ended questions. Interestingly, no negative or downside qualifiers were mentioned in their responses.

Neutral cluster: Seven categories were derived from 65 codes as outlined in Table 2. Note that those who answered neutral mentioned many of the positive themes already recorded in the positive cluster, but in addition to these, neutral respondents added a negative statement or qualifier in their responses.

Negative cluster: Seven categories were derived from 49 codes as outlined in Table 2. Those who answered Disagree or Strongly Disagree in the scenario questions tended to only write negative or downside statements in

Table 2. Thematic categories and clusters.

Thematic categories and clusters		**Codes**	
Positive Cluster: 5 categories		**%**	**n**
1	Making a contribution and future thinking	26.0	28
2	Desire for influence, control	22.6	25
3	Excitement, desire, and challenge	18.5	20
4	Workplace and org benefits	17.1	19
5	Professional development, growth, and job security	15.8	17
	Total:	**100**	**109**
Negative Cluster: 7 categories		**%**	**n**
1	Concern for job loss	21.6	11
2	Not interested	17.1	8
3	Not my job	17.0	8
4	Resistance	15.9	8
5	Lack of confidence	11.4	6
6	Emotion, fear, scared	9.0	4
7	Skepticism, AI not ready	8.0	4
	Total:	**100**	**49**
Neutral Cluster: 7 categories		**%**	**n**
1	Implementation issues	25.8	17
2	Concern for job loss	20.7	13
3	Human touch needed	13.8	9
4	AI not ready	12.1	8
5	Disruption to business	12.1	8
6	Guarantee or reward expectation	8.6	6
7	Don't know/unsure/confused	6.9	4
	Total:	**100**	**65**
	Total number of thematic codes:		**223**

their open-ended responses. While there was some overlap with the negative or qualifier statements made by the neutral cluster (for example, job losses) the responses tended to be unique to this cluster. For example, many neutral respondents focused on implementation challenges whereas negative respondents did not. Many negative respondents mentioned a lack of confidence, emotion, or outright resistance, whereas the neutral cluster did not.

The thematic clusters derived from our research suggest that there are very distinct positions that indicate implications for AI technology threat avoidance and coping adaptation unique at each level of AI adoption. First an examination of each cluster:

Positive: The positive cluster exhibited unique characteristics in terms of their motivations and cognitive frames. As can be seen in Table 2, it is notable that motivations are centered on higher-order, personal benefits from adopting increasingly sophisticated AI. For example, 58% of reasons centered on notions of making a personal contribution, desire to be more influential in the organization, and excitement and challenge. A smaller percentage is focused on the economics of more tangible benefits such as economic benefits and job security in working with sophisticated AI. Notable as well is that no mention was made of implementation challenges for the organization (which was dominant in the neutral cluster) or for fear of job losses which dominated in the negative cluster.

Quotes by respondents in their own words to illustrate the depth of their convictions are as follows: "I currently work on the development of new AI technologies, and it is what I intend to do the rest of my work life. Therefore, dedicating my time to developing AI technology is the way I want to live."

"Collaborating with a team on the development and implementation of AI technologies could prove extremely valuable for my professional development."

"This scenario, while being demanding, would have a very high return, both in terms of productivity and business health, but also in terms of the fact that if I helped design this AI, this would enhance my resume and my know-how and people would identify me and the AI and even at work it. It would improve my network and the consideration others have of me."

Implications of these findings are that organizations will need to manage the expectations from this group of employees, otherwise, the positivity may start to wane. These challenges are amplified given that, industry hype aside, it is unclear if AI technologies will provide this level of opportunity. In all likelihood, this group of individuals may be from professions that currently do not feel vulnerable as AI advances. Thought needs to be made as to how this group is managed when new AI technologies emerge which may challenge their personal situations and professions.

Neutral: The perceptions of the neutral cluster also exhibited unique characteristics in terms of respondent motivations and cognitive frames.

While respondents also expressed many of the positive perceptions mentioned in the positive cluster, they also reported parallel negative statements or drawbacks. As can be seen in Table 2, it is notable that this cluster expressed major concerns with implementation challenges that included the need for the human touch in technical systems, AI not being ready to perform more challenging work, and overall disruptions to business that need to be addressed; these implementation challenges took up 51.7% of responses. This was followed by 20.7% being concerned about job losses and 8.6% about expectations about some form of guarantee about their position or reward expectation if they were to work with developers in the co-creation of more sophisticated AI in their field. Interestingly, while the positive cluster was overwhelmingly eager to adopt AI, they did not express concerns about the business challenges of AI implementation as per the neutral cluster.

Quotes by neutral respondents in their own words: "I would find it interesting to design, train, and implement the AI technology, so I will be an expert about it. But I am still concerned about how this AI technology will affect the business and the employees in the future."

"AI is not yet at a level of confidence or capability to be helpful or trustworthy enough in our business."

"I find AI fascinating so I would love to work on implementing one in a real use-case, but I'd be scared that the AI could replace me one day."

"Highly sophisticated AI technology could be disruptive and could take too much control of the company business, making us too dependent on the AI technology. This technology could be harmful both for employees and for the employer."

The implications of these findings are that the unique expectations and concerns of the neutral group will need to be actively managed by organizations, to avoid a loss of positivity from this group that may even recede into more negativity if the concerns are not adequately addressed. In addition to the positive expectations covered above, managing the negative perceptions of loss of autonomy and job losses—new social contracts will need to be developed commensurate with the altering of the nature of work, and employment brought about by increasingly sophisticated AI. Organizations need to question what more can be done to ease the impact on employees, and how can they differentiate themselves to attract the best talent. Most importantly, consideration needs to be made of the implementation challenges raised by this group. These concerns are consistent with the issues raised in extant literature (Fügener, *et al.*, 2021;

Newlands, 2021) and in our other work (Raftopoulos & Hamari, 2023; Raftopoulos & Hamari, 2024) where both solutions providers and employees have identified how these technical and implementation challenges have been ignored and have resulted in sub-optimal AI performance.

Negative: The perceptions of the negative cluster were unique compared to the other two. Concerns over job losses were highly rated in this cluster, however, there was a sizeable proportion of disinterest in adopting AI that ranged from no interest to feelings that 'it's not my job' to active and passive resistance. There was some emotion also mentioned in terms of a lack of personal and professional confidence for the job of working with increasingly sophisticated AI, to feelings of fear and being scared. A small percentage also expressed skepticism that AI was not ready to take on more advanced work compared to what humans can do.

Quotes of respondents in their own words: "It's not my job." "I'm not interested in this." "I don't feel competent, educated and qualified for this." "I will sabotage."

"I will cooperate with my colleagues to develop this technology, but I would have great concerns about my future since AI may replace me. So, I probably would contribute the development of this technology unwillingly."

"The difference here is I'm working on the AI tool that will be so sophisticated it's outside of the 'co-worker' range and everyone knows it. Either you work for me or you blow us all away, I don't want AI to be similar to Fred from the next desk, that feels off."

Organizations will need to manage the perceptions and concerns of this group of employees as they engage in threat avoidance behavior. Otherwise, organizations may see a continued decline in staff motivation and morale exacerbated by AI. In addition to the discussion presented in the positive and neutral clusters above, organizations need to be cognizant of the reality of AI-induced loss of autonomy and job losses, and how this affects the entire organization. Perhaps, more work needs to be done for this cluster of employees that is beyond the scope of an organization—it may require industry effort or at the policy level which are prevalent notions in extant literature (Tschang & Almirall, 2021).

This group of 'negative' individuals may already feel vulnerable to job insecurity as AI advances, compared to those in the positive cluster. This is what CMUA describes as an emotional response to perceived threats brought on by technology through avoidance and resistance, usually by individuals who have little or no personal power and resources to cope (Beaudry & Pinsonneault, 2005). As our research shows, such deep fears or even misconceptions may lead to behavior that will passively or actively resist AI adoption in the workplace or compromise its effectiveness. For example, in their work on AI identity threat, Mirbabaie *et al.*, (2021) identified loss of status position, changes to work, and AI identity as significant predictors influencing AI identity threat to employees with AI experience in the workplace. Overall, organizations looking to implement increasingly sophisticated AI technologies will be challenged with (a) meeting or managing the ambitious expectations of 58% of its workforce which has positive and enthusiastic attitudes, (b) managing the implementation and technical challenges raised by concerned 'neutral' employees which are around 23%, and (c) managing the negative attitudes of a critical and distrusting 18% of the workforce. The challenge for all organizations and developers is to identify the veracity and potential consequences of employee cognitive frames, attitudes, perceptions, and possible behaviors (whether they are real, probable, or misinformed) and develop corrective or supportive strategies accordingly.

4. Discussion

Extant literature on human adoption of AI technology is still emergent and is often absent and inconclusive on the complex psycho-social drivers affecting adoption. Our model of the three levels of AI technology adoption is supported given the levels of definitive rating in (a) their mean average scores on their likelihood to adopt and (b) the distinct and nuanced explanations given by our survey respondents on why they would or would not adopt increasingly sophisticated AI technologies.

The attitudes toward adopting increasingly sophisticated AI technologies appear to be universal. The results of the comparative tests indicated that there are no significant differences in the mean values of the constructs between males and females, between age groups, and education qualifications. Similar results can be seen in the work of Araujo *et al.* (2020) where they found inconclusive or mixed results when it comes to demographic characteristics as predictors of user perceptions and adoption of AI technologies. This suggests that there are deeper socio-cognitive-emotive factors at play that cannot be simply reduced to gender, education, and age-related factors. For example, AI technologies in the workplace have implications for meaningful work and human flourishing

(Bankins & Formosa, 2023; Bailey *et al*., 2019) that are still underserved in technology adoption literature.

While the positive cluster appears to be enthusiastic and supportive of adopting increasingly sophisticated AI, it is coming from a place of personal gain, and not necessarily mindful of full impacts on the business; it can be seen that this group may potentially have more power and influence in the workplace, and will seek more of it with AI. Conversely, the negative clusters are predominately focused on concern and fear and even expressed both passive and active resistance to AI adoption. Assumptions can be made that this group may perceive themselves to currently have limited power and influence in their roles, and stand to lose more with increasingly sophisticated AI. The neutral group can be seen in the middle—they see both the positives and the negatives from a personal level but tend to be predominately concerned with the impact on the business. This supports assertions that AI may invertedly reinforce existing power structures and mental models (Birhane *et al*., 2021) which becomes an obstacle for future focused business innovation if algorithms are anchored in past assumptions and practices.

In Figure 2, we have adapted the Coping Model of User Adaption to indicate how the clusters, positive, neutral, and negative are positioned in terms of (a) initial primary appraisal of threat or opportunity from the introduction of AI, (b) secondary appraisal of the adaption response based on an assessment of personal power and control over the situation, and (c) the outcomes of the chosen adaption strategy based on maximizing benefit and personal efficiency and effectiveness (the positive cluster from our research) to the self-preservation mode of the negative group which focuses on restoring emotional stability or exit.

The differences in the views and perceptions of each cluster also represent different challenges for AI developers and investors in AI technologies. The current business model of AI technology development is modular, fragmented, and difficult for developers to trace responsibility and accountability (Widder & Nafus, 2023). Raisch & Krakowski (2021) claimed that technical solutions to building business systems seldom consider the complexity of socio-technical interactions between stakeholders, yet these interactions have considerable impacts on organizations and society. Consideration needs to be made of the adequacy of the AI development models moving forward, however, researchers believe that the current system of AI software development is unlikely to change any time soon (Widder & Nafus, 2023).

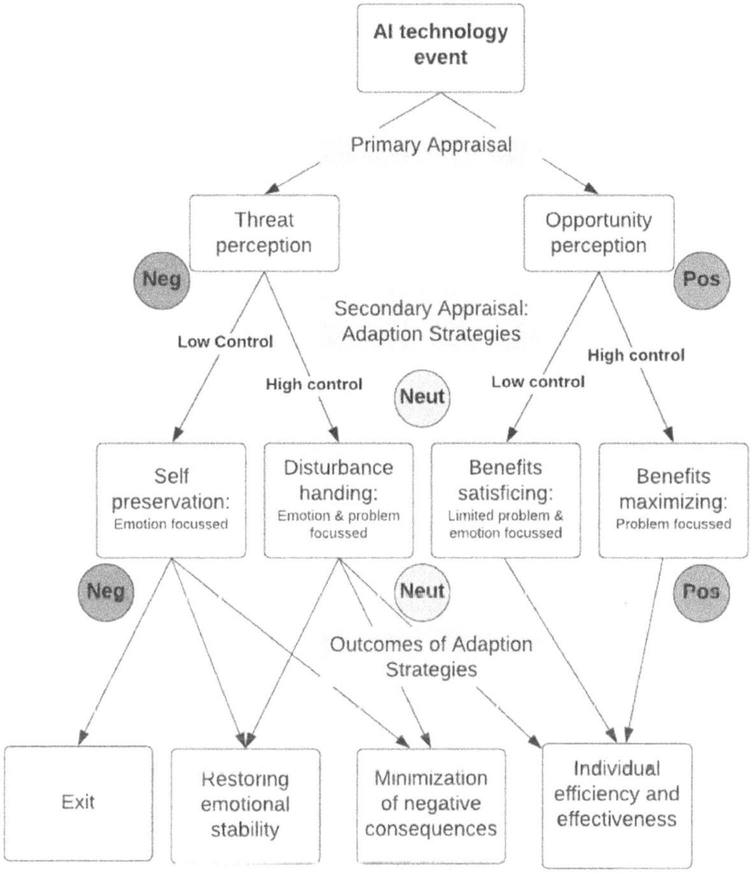

Figure 2. Adaption of CMUA showing three clusters.

Our concluding remarks are that the adoption of increasingly sophisticated AI is challenged on several fronts—user threat avoidance and opportunity chasing, organizational strategic capability to manage expectations and threat avoidance, and AI developers' capability to engage users in meaningful co-creation of socio-technical systems.

5. Theoretical Implications

Our research identifies three key categories of employees in terms of how they respond to working with increasingly sophisticated AI. The positive cluster believes AI offers opportunities, the neutral group that is positive but has reservations, and the negative group focuses on the downside. Our work supports TTAT as we found that individuals clearly distinguish between *malicious* and *virtuous* AI. According to TTAT a virtuous technology is perceived by users to be attractive as it creates positive outcomes through its use (Liang & Xue, 2009), and this is a key finding in our study concerning the characteristics of our 'positive cluster' who engaged in opportunity chasing. The 18% of respondents in our 'negative cluster' is consistent with what Liang and Xue call threat avoidance behavior. However, our key contribution is to show that there is a middle ground not directly addressed by TTAT or CMUA prevalent in our neutral cluster. TTAT is defined by dichotomies: *either* virtuous *or* malicious. Users are *either* actively, *or* passively avoiding threats. A clearer articulation of the mid-points in these theories is worthy of further investigation in the complex age of AI.

Our final and most critical theoretical contribution arising from our work is highlighting that there is an implied or indirect assumption in both TTAT and CMUA on technological functionality that is fit for purpose. As these theories were originally based on mature technology architectures, we propose that they did not account for the level of immaturity of emergent AI technologies that have perhaps gone to market much earlier than technologies in the past. The current generation of AI technologies is still young and underdeveloped, and the industry is rife with hype and overselling of capabilities and the promise of returns on investment (Birhane *et al.*, 2021; Newlands, 2021; Bender *et al.*, 2021). Furthermore, AI technologies are introducing systemic challenges of market concentration, inequities, and ethical problems compared to previous waves of automation and robotization (Ernst *et al.*, 2019). These are conditions that can trigger emotions of perceived AI technology 'maliciousness' to a level that may not have been accounted for in TTAT in the past. TTAT arose on the premise that IT acceptance theories could not fully explain peoples' IT threat avoidance behavior and developed a new theory to explain threat avoidance behavior (Liang & Xue, 2009; Cao *et al*, 2021). We believe the opportunity has now presented itself to further adapt TTAT to consider a third phenomenon, where individuals engage in threat avoidance behavior when the maturity of the technology is compromised due to its technical limitations and its ability to cause unintended harm to organizations, workplaces, and society in general.

6. Implications for Practice

Our implications for practice cover both organizations investing and implementing AI technologies, and solutions providers that are developing and assisting clients in AI implementations. Organizations will need to be mindful of the attitudes, perceptions, and potential behaviors unique to each of the three key categories of employees when looking to invest in increasingly sophisticated AI technologies. It is widely accepted that the successful adoption of an information system depends to a great extent on users' perceptions of the information system as we have identified in our research. We have identified that individual cognitive frames are key factors in managing the adoption of information systems consistent with the findings of Lin & Silva (2005) where the three different types of adoption trigger different responses in individuals. The additional challenge here is that individual cognitive frames are dynamic and highly situational (Orlikowski & Gash, 1994). This leaves an open question of how organizations continually adapt their workplace and managerial practices in tandem with the constant changes in AI progression and advancement.

AI technologies require a more sophisticated approach to organizational design and digital transformation than have been offered by the conventional frameworks of the past (Hanelt *et al.*, 2021). The adoption of AI depends not only on the intrinsic qualities of the information system but also on the changing contexts in which the information system is evaluated. Lin & Silva (2005) argued that the management of information systems adoption is a social and political process in which stakeholders constantly frame and reframe their perceptions of that system. This implies that organizations may need to develop more ongoing dynamic and consultative practices with their employees and stakeholders with AI development and enablement. Transformational leadership is needed to avert technophobia (Khasawneh, 2020; McClure, 2018) and technostress (Tarafdar *et al.*, 2007) emerging from workplace concerns over job losses, underemployment, anxiety burnout, and surveillance that are fueled for many by artificial intelligence. The importance of this cannot be underestimated as creating business value from AI technologies still requires that humans and machines work together collaboratively at this early stage of AI technology development.

7. Limitations and Further Research

Respondents were sourced from Europe which may limit the generalizability of this work beyond this jurisdiction. Survey respondents came from a variety of different industries in which they were employed (and hence had limited exposure to their industry-specific AI technologies) which means our results offer a generalization across all sectors. As cognitive frames are influenced by situational aspects and are temporal in nature, future opportunities lay in running our model and survey on industry, organization, or even regional-specific audiences. Furthermore, we only surveyed professionals already working with high levels of digital technologies in large organizations and who are theoretically already comfortable working with technology. We suggest that survey opportunities for further research in extending this work to focus on respondents with limited use of technology in the workplace which may or may not potentially see differences in intended adoption rates and differences in the profile of reasons behind their intended threat avoidance or opportunity chasing behavior.

8. Conclusions

The findings of our research show declining support for AI adoption at increased levels of technological sophistication. We identified a complex heterogeneity of issues reported by our respondents regarding the adoption of increasingly sophisticated AI which raises issues for practice for organizations investing in AI as well as for AI developers. Technology threat avoidance theory can partially explain user reticence to adopt more sophisticated technologies, as it's unclear whether AI threat avoidance may in part be attributed to genuine concern with the limitations inherent in the AI technology, the veracity of organizational workplace implementations, or its ability to provide for secure or meaningful work. The implications of our research are that if current industry challenges regarding limited returns on investment from AI technologies are prevalent today, then this may be exacerbated with the introduction of more sophisticated AI technologies in the future. Individual cognitive and behavioral responses such as threat avoidance and opportunity chasing are shaped by a perception of personal power and resources. An understanding of these drivers will enable organizations and developers to recalibrate their processes to produce improved and effective socio-technical systems and practices, and better outcomes for society as a whole.

9. Acknowledgments

The author wishes to thank Professor Juho Hamari for his feedback on this research. This project has received funding from the European Union's Horizon 2020 research and innovation programme under the Marie Sklodowska-Curie grant agreement No 101023024 for Augmented-Humans.

References

Adell, E. (2010), Acceptance of driver support systems. *Proceedings of the European Conference on Human Centred Design for Intelligent Transport Systems*.

Andersson, K. E. (2018). Key requirements in the procurement of future low observable combat vehicles: A European perspective. *Systems Engineering*, Vol. 21(1), 3–15.

Araujo, T., Helberger, N., Kruikemeier, S., & De Vreese, C. H. (2020). In AI we trust? Perceptions about automated decision-making by artificial intelligence. *AI & Society*, Vol. 35, 611–623.

Bailey, C., Yeoman, R., Madden, A., Thompson, M., & Kerridge, G. (2019). A review of the empirical literature on meaningful work: Progress and research agenda. *Human Resource Development Review*, Vol. 18(1), 83–113.

Bankins, S., & Formosa, P. (2023). The ethical implications of artificial intelligence (AI) for meaningful work. *Journal of Business Ethics*, Vol. 185(4), 725–740.

Beaudry, A., & Pinsonneault, A. (2005). Understanding user responses to information technology: A coping model of user adaptation. *MIS Quarterly*, Vol. 493–524.

Bender, E. M., Gebru, T., McMillan-Major, A., & Shmitchell, S. (2021). On the Dangers of Stochastic Parrots: Can Language Models Be Too Big? In *Proceedings of the 2021 ACM Conference on Fairness, Accountability, and Transparency* (pp. 610–623).

Berente, N., Gu, B., Recker, J., & Santhanam, R. (2021). Managing Artificial Intelligence. *MIS Quarterly*, Vol. 45(3), 1433–1450.

Birhane, A., Kalluri, P., Card, D., Agnew, W., Dotan, R., & Bao, M. (2021). The Values Encoded in Machine Learning Research. http://arxiv.org/abs/2106.15590

Cabrera-Sánchez, J. P., Villarejo-Ramos, Á. F., Liébana-Cabanillas, F., & Shaikh, A. A. (2021). Identifying relevant segments of AI applications adopters — Expanding the UTAUT2's variables. *Telematics and Informatics*, Vol. 58, 101529.

Camarinha-Matos, L.M. & H. Afsarmanesh. (2008). "Concept of Collaboration", in *Encyclopedia of Networked and Virtual Organizations*, G.D. Putnik and M.M. Cruz-Cunha. (eds.) IGI Global.

Cao, G., Duan, Y., Edwards, J. S., & Dwivedi, Y. K. (2021). Understanding managers' attitudes and behavioral intentions towards using artificial intelligence for organizational decision-making. *Technovation*, Vol. 106, 102312.

Carroll, M., Shah, R., Ho, M. K., Griffiths, T. L., Seshia, S. A., Abbeel, P., & Dragan, A. (2019). On the Utility of Learning about Humans for Human-AI Coordination. http://arxiv.org/abs/1910.05789

Collins, C., Dennehy, D., Conboy, K., & Mikalef, P. (2021). Artificial intelligence in information systems research: A systematic literature review and research agenda. *International Journal of Information Management*, Vol. 60, 102383.

Cubric, M. (2020). Drivers, barriers and social considerations for AI adoption in business and management: A tertiary study. *Technology in Society*, Vol. 62, 101257.

Dellermann, D., Calma, A., & Lipusch, N. (2019). The Future of Human-AI Collaboration: A Taxonomy of Design Knowledge for Hybrid Intelligence Systems.

Dietvorst, B. J., Simmons, J. P., & Massey, C. (2015). Algorithm aversion: People erroneously avoid algorithms after seeing them err. *Journal of Experimental Psychology: General*, Vol. 144(1), 114.

Duan, Y., Edwards, J. S., & Dwivedi, Y. K. (2019). Artificial intelligence for decision making in the era of Big Data – evolution, challenges and research agenda. *International Journal of Information Management*, Vol. 48, 63–71.

Dwivedi, Y. K., Hughes, L., Ismagilova, E.,… Williams, M. D. (2021). Artificial Intelligence (AI): Multidisciplinary perspectives on emerging challenges, opportunities, and agenda for research, practice and policy. *International Journal of Information Management*, Vol. 57.

Ernst, E., Merola, R., & Samaan, D. (2019). Economics of artificial intelligence: Implications for the future of work. *IZA Journal of Labor Policy*, Vol. 9(1).

Etikan, I., Musa, S. A., & Alkassim, R. S. (2016). Comparison of convenience sampling and purposive sampling. *American Journal of Theoretical and Applied Statistics*, Vol. 5(1), 1–4.

Fügener, A., Grahl, J., Gupta, A., & Ketter, W. (2021). Will humans-in-the-loop become borgs? merits and pitfalls of working with AI. *MIS Quarterly: Management Information Systems*, Vol. 45(3), 1527–1556.

Gansser, O. A., & Reich, C. S. (2021). A new acceptance model for artificial intelligence with extensions to UTAUT2: An empirical study in three segments of application. *Technology in Society*, Vol. 65, 101535.

Hanelt, A., Bohnsack, R., Marz, D., & Antunes Marante, C. (2021). A systematic review of the literature on digital transformation: Insights and implications for strategy and organizational change. *Journal of Management Studies*, Vol. 58(5), 1159–1197.

Hogg, M. A. (2016). Social identity theory (pp. 3–17). Springer International Publishing.

Hyland-Wood, D., Harrison, A., & Kolera, B. (2019). Righting writing's wrongs: Toward effective writing partnerships between humans and AI. *Universal Journal of Educational Research*, Vol. 7(5), 1306–1318.

Ienca, M. (2019). Democratizing cognitive technology: A proactive approach. *Ethics and Information Technology*, Vol. 21(4), 267–280.

Ishowo-Oloko, F., Bonnefon, J.-F., Soroye, Z., Crandall, J., Rahwan, I., & Rahwan, T. (2019). Behavioural evidence for a transparency–efficiency tradeoff in human–machine cooperation. *Nature Machine Intelligence*, Vol. 1(11), 517–521.

Jarrahi, M. H. (2018). Artificial intelligence and the future of work: Human-AI symbiosis in organizational decision making. *Business Horizons*, Vol. 61(4), 577–586.

Kaber, D. B., & Endsley, M. R. (2004). The effects of level of automation and adaptive automation on human performance, situation awareness and workload in a dynamic control task. *Theoretical Issues in Ergonomics Science*, Vol. 5(2), 113–153.

Khasawneh, O. Y. (2020). Transformational leaders help their employees overcome their technophobia. *International Journal of Technology and Human Interaction (IJTHI)*, Vol. 16(3), 70–85.

Kosinski, M., Stillwell, D., & Graepel, T. (2013). Private traits and attributes are predictable from digital records of human behavior. *Proceedings of the National Academy of Sciences*, Vol. 110(15), 5802–5805.

Langer, M., & Landers, R. N. (2021). The future of artificial intelligence at work: A review on effects of decision automation and augmentation on workers targeted by algorithms and third-party observers. *Computers in Human Behavior*, Vol. 123.

Liang, H., & Xue, Y. (2009). Avoidance of information technology threats: A theoretical perspective. *MIS Quarterly*, Vol. 71–90.

Lin, A., & Silva, L. (2005). The social and political construction of technological frames. *European Journal of Information Systems*, Vol. 14, 49–59.

Liwång, H. (2022). Defense development: The role of co-creation in filling the gap between policy-makers and technology development. *Technology in Society*, Vol. 68, 101913.

McClure, P. K. (2018). "You're fired," says the robot: The rise of automation in the workplace, technophobes, and fears of unemployment. *Social Science Computer Review*, Vol. 36(2), 139–156.

Mirbabaie, M., Stieglitz, S., Brünker, F., Hofeditz, L., Ross, B., & Frick, N. R. (2021). Understanding collaboration with virtual assistants–the role of social identity and the extended self. *Business & Information Systems Engineering*, Vol. 63, 21–37.

Newlands, G. (2021). Lifting the curtain: Strategic visibility of human labour in AI-as-a-Service. *Big Data and Society*, Vol. 8(1).

Oh, C., Lee, T., Kim, Y., Park, S. H., Kwon, S., & Suh, B. (2017). Us vs. Them: Understanding artificial intelligence technophobia over the Google DeepMind Challenge Match. *Conference on Human Factors in Computing Systems - Proceedings*, Vol. 2017-May, 2523–2534.

Orlikowski, W. J., & Gash, D. C. (1994). Technological frames: Making sense of information technology in organizations. *ACM Transactions on Information Systems (TOIS)*, Vol. 12(2), 174–207.

Prahalad, C. K., & Ramaswamy, V. (2000). Co-opting customer competence. *Harvard Business Review*, Vol. 78(1).

Pulkkinen, K., & Hautamäki, A. (2019). Co-creation with Companies: A Means to Enhance Societal Impact of University Researchers? *The Responsible University: Exploring the Nordic Context and Beyond*, 145–172.

Pumplun, L., Tauchert, C., & Heidt, M. (2019). A New Organizational Chassis for Artificial Intelligence - Exploring Organizational Readiness Factors. *European Conference on Information Systems*.

Raftopoulos, M., & Hamari, J., (2024). Organizational Challenges in Adoption and Implementation of Artificial Intelligence. *Hawaii International Conference on System Sciences (HICSS) 2024*, Waikiki, Hawaii, USA.

Raftopoulos, M., & Hamari, J., (2023). Artificial Intelligence in the Workplace: Implementation Challenges and Opportunities. *The Americas' Conference on Information Systems (AMCIS) 2023*, Panama City, Panama.

Raisch, S., & Krakowski, S. (2021). Artificial intelligence and management: The automation–augmentation paradox. *Academy of Management Review*, Vol. 46(1), 192–210.

Ranjan, K.R. & S. Read. (2016). Value Co-creation: Concept and Measurement, *Journal of the Academy of Marketing Science*, Vol. 44(3), 290–315.

Seeber, I., Bittner, E., Briggs, R. O., de Vreede, T., de Vreede, G. J., Elkins, A., Maier, R., Merz, A. B., Oeste-Reiß, S., Randrup, N., Schwabe, G., & Söllner, M. (2020). Machines as teammates: A research agenda on AI in team collaboration. *Information and Management*, Vol. 57(2).

Shollo, A., Hopf, K., Thiess, T., & Müller, O. (2022). Shifting ML value creation mechanisms: A process model of ML value creation. *The Journal of Strategic Information Systems*, Vol. 31(3), 101734.

Smorodinskaya, N., Russell, M. G., Katukov, D., & Still, K. (2017). Innovation Ecosystems vs. Innovation Systems in Terms of Collaboration and Co-creation of Value.

Sohn, K., & Kwon, O. (2020). Technology acceptance theories and factors influencing artificial Intelligence-based intelligent products. *Telematics and Informatics*, Vol. 47.

Stowers, K., Brady, L. L., MacLellan, C., Wohleber, R., & Salas, E. (2021). Improving Teamwork Competencies in Human-Machine Teams: Perspectives from Team Science. *Frontiers in Psychology*, Vol. 12.

Tarafdar, M., Tu, Q., Ragu-Nathan, B. S., & Ragu-Nathan, T. S. (2007). The impact of technostress on role stress and productivity. *Journal of Management Information Systems*, Vol. 24(1), 301–328.

Tschang, F. T., & Almirall, E. (2021). Artificial intelligence as augmenting automation: Implications for employment. *Academy of Management Perspectives*, Vol. 35(4), 642–659.

Venkatesh, V., Morris, M. G., Davis, G. B., & Davis, F. D. (2003). User acceptance of information technology: Toward a unified view. *MIS Quarterly*, Vol. 425–478.

Waardenburg, L., & Huysman, M. (2022). From coexistence to co-creation: Blurring boundaries in the age of AI. *Information and Organization*, Vol. 32(4), 100432.

Wagner, D. N. (2020). The nature of the Artificially Intelligent Firm-An economic investigation into changes that AI brings to the firm. *Telecommunications Policy*, Vol. 44(6).

Widder, D. G., & Nafus, D. (2023). Dislocated accountabilities in the "AI supply chain": Modularity and developers' notions of responsibility. *Big Data & Society*, Vol. 10(1), 205395172311776.

https://doi.org/10.1142/9789819816347_0012

Chapter 12

Human–AI Symbiosis: Opportunities for Business Innovations and Worker Upskilling

Kuanchin Chen

Department of Computer Information Systems and Center for Business Analytics, Western Michigan University, Kalamazoo, MI, USA

1. Human–AI Symbiosis (HAS)

The computing literature is rich with studies exploring the collaboration and interaction between humans and technology. While many of these studies highlight the positive aspects of human-computer interaction, they often overlook the potential threats posed by these interactions. Negative effects such as technostress, internet or gaming addiction, and user disorientation are well-documented consequences of technology use. Moreover, human–computer interaction research often adopts a human-centric perspective, focusing solely on the human side of the relationship. However, this limited view risks neglecting the broader dynamics at play. For instance, interactions with generative AI—through user prompts and corrections—can serve as training data to refine future versions of AI models, ultimately resulting in more accurate and effective AI systems (Sundar, 2020). Shifting from a human-only perspective to one that examines the symbiotic relationships between all entities involved could provide valuable insights into human–AI interactions and their broader implications.

Interaction alone does not guarantee a symbiotic relationship. In biological terms, symbiosis is defined as “an intimate interaction between different organisms, where at least one of the parties is obligatorily dependent on the association as a part of its life history” (Leung & Poulin, 2008, p. 107). While obligatory dependency involves entities entirely relying on each other for survival, facultative dependency describes situations where entities engage in a non-obligatory relationship (Douglas, 2010).

Fairclough (2015) argued that human–AI symbiosis represents an obligatory relationship, as technology has become deeply ingrained in the human experience, making it unlikely for humans to sever their dependency on it. However, the nature of symbiotic relationships with AI is highly individual. What proves essential for one person or profession may not even be relevant for another. A recent Pew Research Center report revealed that 19% of workers are highly exposed to AI in their jobs, experiencing impacts such as task or job replacement, productivity enhancement, and the creation of entirely new roles. Certain occupations, such as machine repair and personal care, are less vulnerable to full job replacement but may experience task-level replacement or augmentation. Notably, while AI can assist in these professions, its use is not always necessary. This suggests that facultative dependency, characterized by non-essential yet beneficial interactions, may be more common—particularly at the task level.

Both forms of dependency require interaction between the entities involved. When such dependency produces positive outcomes, it fosters future symbiotic interests. This dependency is commonly categorized into three forms: (1) **mutualism**, where both parties benefit from the relationship; (2) **commensalism**, where one party benefits without affecting the other; and (3) **parasitism**, where one party benefits at the expense of the other. The prevailing perspective on human–AI symbiosis, or human–computer symbiosis, largely aligns with a mutualism viewpoint or simply focuses on the interaction itself, paying little attention to other forms of symbiotic relationships or how these forms might evolve over time. For instance, researchers have explored symbiosis as a collaboration between two parties (Grigsby, 2018; Zakershahrak, 2021), as a relationship that empowers both parties (Jarrahi, 2018), and as a form of co-existence (Karnouskos, 2022). Collaborative symbiotic activities have the potential to enhance team trust, promote knowledge sharing, and foster co-creation, which, in turn, can drive business innovation. This chapter aims to closely examine the nature of symbiotic relationships between AI and humans and their broader implications for fostering business innovation.

2. Definition of Human–AI Symbiosis (HAS)

2.1. *Human–AI symbiosis as a collaborative relationship*

Human–AI Symbiosis (HAS) is defined in various ways, often emphasizing the collaborative relationship between humans and AI. Fairclough (2015) described HAS as "… the relationship between machine and person that occurs within a shared space or task" and as "… a computer that is capable of both monitoring and affecting the cognitions, emotions, and behaviors of the user" (p. 59). Similarly, Lyu (2022) defined man-computer symbiosis as "… the human and the machine offer different yet complementary capabilities" (p. 2). Gamberini *et al.* (2015) further described a symbiotic system as a dyad of user and technology "… which is capable of adjusting rapidly (possibly in real time) to the user's characteristics, in order to improve the quality and efficiency of the interaction." This relationship manifests in two primary forms: machines serving as human assistants to achicvc goals of automation, information, or augmentation, and humans acting as assistants to machines to achieve machine-oriented goals (Döppner *et al.*, 2016). These definitions collectively highlight not only the collaborative nature of human–AI interactions but also the prerequisites for building such symbiotic relationships.

2.2. *Human–AI symbiosis as a way for enhanced capability*

Gamberini *et al.* (2015) defined a symbiotic system as "… a dyad composed of the user and a given technology, which is capable of adjusting rapidly (possibly in real-time) to the user's characteristics, in order to improve the quality and efficiency of the interaction" (p. 69). Jarrahi (2018) emphasized the mutual benefits of symbiosis, noting that both humans and AI become smarter over time through their interaction. Similarly, Lu *et al.* (2021) identified key elements of Human–AI Symbiosis (HAS), including human centrality, social wellness, and adaptability to learn from the environment and adjust behavior accordingly. While Lu *et al.*'s perspective is human-centered, there is a broad consensus that HAS benefits both parties. For instance, interactions with General

AI tools may appear to primarily benefit humans, but the feedback and corrections generated during these interactions also serve as training data to enhance the AI model's accuracy and tailor its responses. These dynamics illustrate that HAS transcends mere collaboration. It represents a partnership where each party complements the other to tackle tasks that were previously challenging or unattainable, fostering a relationship that empowers both humans and AI.

Although long-term collaboration and interaction are often considered prerequisites for symbiosis (Vidalis & Andreatos, 2022), collaboration alone does not guarantee that the resulting benefits will continue to empower both entities. This becomes particularly evident when advancements in AI capabilities disrupt the balance of contributions, potentially replacing tasks traditionally performed by humans. Inga *et al.* (2023) echoed this concern, defining human–AI collaboration along a continuum called "Symbiosis as a multivariate concept." They proposed four stages of human–AI interaction: coexistence, cooperation, collaboration, and symbiosis. Symbiosis, as they explained, involves interactions characterized by shared leadership, role flexibility, and mutual understanding, all aimed at achieving synergistic outcomes through coordination.

Ren *et al.* (2019) expanded on this idea with the concept of Human-Engaged Computing (HEC), an evolution of Human–Computer Interaction (HCI) that emphasizes synergistic and symbiotic relationships between humans and machines to achieve enhanced outcomes. The cornerstone of HEC is balance, which they described as follows:

> "Balance is not an equal amount of time, expense, investment, significance and importance given to both sides of a symbiotic relationship of unlike participants; balance is considered to be the independent consideration and equal proportional treatment of both participants (H & C) according to their kind" (p. 54).

As Ren *et al.* highlighted, achieving such balance requires designing computer systems that not only address current human needs but also actively enhance human capacities and capabilities, unlocking new potentials.

2.3. *A new look at the HAS definition*

Whether viewed through the lens of relationship-based or capability-based perspectives, current definitions of Human–AI Symbiosis (HAS) predominantly focus on the present status quo. However, technology evolves at an unprecedented pace, and today's symbiotic relationships may look entirely different tomorrow as AI continues to advance. This characteristic sets HAS apart from biological symbiosis, where evolutionary and adaptive processes occur at a much slower rate.

As illustrated in Figure 1, the telephone took 75 years (900 months) to reach 100 million users, while mobile phones achieved the same milestone in just 16 years (192 months). TikTok reached 100 million users in a mere 9 months, and ChatGPT accomplished this in only 2 months. Not only is technological advancement accelerating, but also the time required to achieve mass adoption is shrinking dramatically. This rapid evolution underscores the need for humans to upskill or reskill their abilities to sustain their contributions in this evolving dynamic. Consequently, the current definition of HAS may require reconsideration. Adding this to the relationship-based and capability-based definitions, several critical elements emerge as foundational to technology-based symbiosis:

(1) **Awareness of capabilities**: At least one entity must be aware of the other's capabilities (including cognition, emotions, and behaviors of humans) and their potential contributions to the relationship.

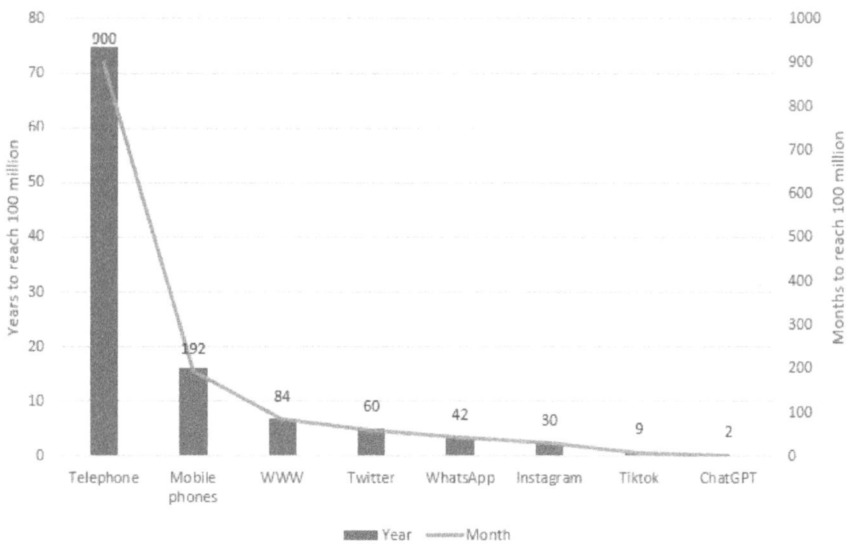

Figure 1. Years/Months took for IT to reach 100 million users.

Source: https://www.linkedin.com/pulse/evolution-technology-adoption-from-telephone-chatgpt-peeyush-sharma/.

(2) **Complementary contributions**: Each entity should contribute in ways that complement the other, resulting in an enhanced and synergistic outcome.
(3) **Adaptability to changes**: Both entities must possess the ability to adjust rapidly to changes in the environment, use contexts, each other's capabilities, and the desired goals of collaboration.

These elements highlight the evolving and dynamic nature of HAS, necessitating a forward-looking approach to its definition and practice.

3. The Hidden Costs of HAS

Numerous examples of biological symbiosis illustrate physical benefits (e.g., protection from predators) and associated costs. One well-known example is the mutualistic relationship between clownfish and sea anemones. Clownfish gain physical protection by hiding in the anemone, while the anemone benefits from nutrients provided by the clownfish's leftovers. In contrast, human–AI symbiosis or human–technology symbiosis rarely results in physical or pathological harm to the human "host." However, these relationships can produce benefits and harms in other forms, such as psychological damage, shifts in ownership, or security threats.

Leung and Poulin (2008) highlighted three examples of hidden costs in biological symbiosis that extend beyond immediate physiological effects: (1) cymothoid isopod parasites feeding on cardinal fish's blood and tissues reduce the fish's ability to evade predators, (2) parasites infecting deep-snouted pipefish impair the fish's ability to discern parasitized mates, thereby decreasing reproductive success, and (3) microsporidian infections harm the overall fitness of two-spotted gobies despite causing little to no direct negative effects.

These examples suggest that the benefits and costs of symbiotic relationships, whether biological or technological, can be far-reaching and multifaceted, often extending beyond the surface-level dynamics of the interaction.

3.1. *Vendor lock-in*

Similar dynamics can be observed in the computing world. For instance, adopting an AI application can lead to vendor lock-in, where the investment required to adapt to a specific vendor's ecosystem becomes a sunk cost, and transitioning to a different vendor entails significant switching costs. This issue becomes particularly pronounced when comparable products are limited or nonexistent, akin to the parasitic relationship in cardinal fish mentioned earlier.

As companies deepen their reliance on a vendor's solutions, the unintended costs of vendor lock-in tend to escalate. Conversely, the switching costs decrease when alternative options of comparable quality are readily available. In the case of generative AI products, the cost of transitioning from one solution to another is generally lower—at least until the reliance extends to features or functionalities that are uniquely offered by a specific vendor. This highlights the delicate balance organizations must navigate between adoption and flexibility in a rapidly evolving technological landscape.

3.2. *The downside of inability to distinguish AI quality*

The inability of pipefish to discriminate between parasitized and healthy mates finds a parallel in human–AI interactions. For instance, when considering word processing software, users often expect similar functionality across products from different vendors. However, AI is not a single, monolithic technology. Apple's Siri, Amazon's Alexa, and Google's Digital Assistant, for example, are all products within the voice recognition and processing branch of AI. Similarly, tasks such as investment selection, product bundling, and forecasting fall under the machine learning branch, while image tagging and content extraction belong to the image processing branch of AI. Even everyday tools such as email spam filters rely on expert systems and machine learning.

Without a solid understanding of these AI branches and their underlying mechanisms, it becomes difficult to distinguish the true capabilities and potential of AI products offered by various vendors. This leads to a tendency to treat AI products as "black boxes," evaluating their quality solely on advertised features and limited product trials rather than on a comprehensive assessment of their actual performance, and even their potential.

For example, evaluating a vendor's AI product based solely on its advertised predictive capabilities provides little insight into whether it can adapt effectively to a company's ecosystem, deliver predictions with the expected level of accuracy, or handle anomalies without requiring extensive model retraining. This lack of transparency and deeper understanding creates challenges in distinguishing AI quality to make informed adoption decisions, ultimately increasing the risk of investing in tools that may not meet long-term needs.

3.3. *Reduction in overall contribution to the relationship*

As outlined earlier, a defining characteristic of Human–AI Symbiosis (HAS) is the relationship in which both parties offer unique, complementary skills that enable them to become "smarter over time" (Jarrahi, 2018). This mutual enhancement leads to upskilling, particularly for humans, as they leverage new tools, algorithms, and techniques to address emerging challenges. Indeed, the evolution of technology has created entirely new job positions; Autor *et al.* (2024) reported that approximately 60% of job titles today did not exist in 1940, with this figure rising to 74% in occupations that have added the most workers.

However, HAS does not automatically translate into lasting skill development or meaningful contributions. First, a relationship characterized primarily by consumptive use—with minimal input or engagement from humans—diminishes the likelihood of sustaining a significant human contribution. Examples include commanding Siri to play music, passively accepting Netflix's video recommendations, or relying on AI-generated outcomes without critical evaluation. While such usage provides immediate benefits, it does little to empower humans or enhance their skill sets, ultimately limiting their ability to sustain meaningful contributions to the symbiotic relationship.

Furthermore, the entry barrier for many consumptive uses of AI is relatively low. Most individuals, with minimal training or even basic trial-and-error, can achieve the same level of proficiency in using these tools. This ease of access quickly erodes any competitive edge, as others adopt similar AI usage patterns. Without efforts to move beyond passive consumption and toward skill-building and active engagement, the potential of HAS to foster sustained human growth and meaningful collaboration remains unrealized.

3.4. *The assumption of no change to the status quo*

In biological symbiosis, relationships between two species develop gradually through adaptation, trial and error, and environmental influences. These relationships are relatively stable, with minimal disruptions. For example, the mutualistic relationship between a clownfish and a sea anemone persists because neither species evolves rapidly enough to negate the need for the other's contributions, such as shelter or nutrients. This does not mean that such a relationship will never change. Evolution in the biological world is a slow process, taking significant time for one entity to acquire capabilities that render the symbiotic relationship obsolete.

However, this assumption of stability does not apply well to Human–AI Symbiosis (HAS). While human skills may be enhanced through such relationships, humans do not evolve quickly enough to match the accelerated pace of AI advancements. Figure 2 illustrates how AI has evolved dramatically in just a few years since Google's publication of the seminal paper "Attention is All You Need" (Vaswani *et al.*, 2017), which fueled the rapid development of GPT (Generative Pre-trained Transformer) models that we see in ChatGPT and other generative AI today. For instance, after OpenAI released ChatGPT-1 in 2018, the platform garnered over 100 million user accounts by 2023. Self-driving cars, pilot-tested in 2018, are expected to reach mass production with the release of Tesla's CyberCab and CyberTruck. Similarly, Microsoft's integration of CoPilot into its product ecosystem has significantly shortened the time required to achieve a critical mass of users.

This rapid progression underscores that all major branches of AI—machine learning, natural language processing, image processing, video processing, and robotics—have experienced substantial advancements in recent years, with no signs of slowing down. As AI capabilities continue to grow at an accelerated rate, the original balance of contributions within a human–AI symbiotic relationship is likely to shift. AI's ability to adapt, improve, and take on increasingly complex tasks will redefine the status quo, potentially resulting in task or job replacement through intelligent

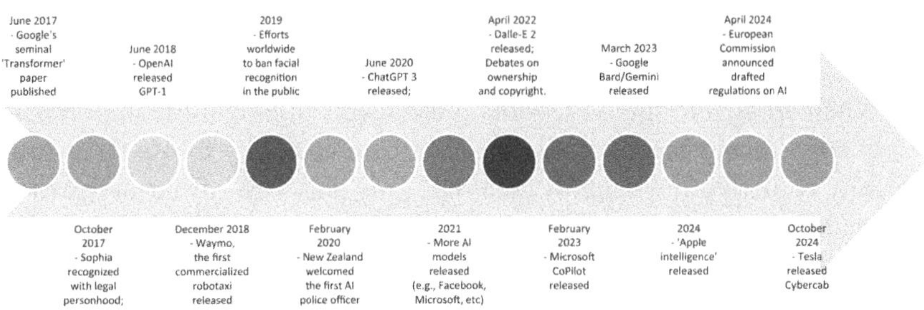

Figure 2. Examples of AI milestones since 2017.

automation. Humans, in contrast, may struggle to keep pace with this rapid evolution, raising questions about their sustained role and contribution in such relationships. This is where HAS to foster worker reskilling and upskilling become more important than ever.

3.5. *AI-divide is not a hard cut-off*

The term Digital Divide and its related concepts—such as information inequality, the information gap, and the knowledge gap—describe disparities in access to and use of technology (Van Dijk, 2006). Van Dijk identifies four levels of technology access that contribute to these disparities: motivational access, material access, skills access, and usage access. These levels provide a useful framework for understanding the emerging AI Divide:

(1) **Motivational Access**: This refers to an individual's willingness or motivation to engage with technology. Without the desire to use AI, the other levels become irrelevant.
(2) **Material Access**: Once motivated, an individual must have access to the necessary hardware and software required to leverage AI technology effectively.
(3) **Skills Access**: Material access alone is insufficient without the necessary skills to utilize the technology. Van Dijk categorizes these skills into:
    (a) **Information skills**: The ability to search for, select, and process information effectively.
    (b) **Strategic skills**: The ability to use technology to achieve specific goals, including those that enhance one's position in society.
(4) **Usage Access**: Finally, this refers to the actual and sustained use of the technology for its intended purpose.

When applied to the AI Divide, these levels highlight the importance of not only having access to AI tools but also the ability to use them strategically to derive meaningful benefits. This pathway—from motivation to actual usage—defines whether an individual can effectively bridge the AI Divide.

However, as previously noted, the assumption of a stable status quo in the relationship between humans and AI is flawed. AI technology is advancing at an unprecedented pace, frequently redefining the landscape of skills, tools, and applications needed to maintain access. While humans may adapt their environments or behaviors to accommodate these changes, few actively engage in continuous learning to track new AI developments or assess how they may impact their social status, jobs, or identity.

Van Dijk emphasizes this dynamic nature of technology access gaps, stating: "*A final wrong connotation might be the suggestion that the divide is a static condition while in fact the gaps observed are continually shifting*" (Van Dijk, p. 222). This underscores the ongoing challenge: as AI capabilities evolve, so too must human capacities to navigate, adopt, and utilize these advancements effectively. Bridging the AI Divide requires not just addressing current disparities but also anticipating and adapting to the shifting technological landscape.

3.6. *Antibiosis in business competition*

Antibiosis, or amensalism, refers to a biological interaction in which the presence of one organism—or the substances it produces—negatively impacts another organism by inhibiting its growth or survival (Vidalis & Andreatos, 2022). In the business world, innovations with AI can similarly exhibit antibiosis effects by disrupting competitors and reshaping markets.

For example, Netflix's video recommendation system, powered by the recommendation system branch of AI, not only improved user engagement but also increased the likelihood of vendor lock-in within its streaming platform. This innovation revolutionized the entertainment industry, creating a new business model that ultimately led to the demise of traditional video rental stores. Similarly, the evolution of cloud computing services illustrates another form of business antibiosis. Initially offering cloud-based storage, major providers such as Google, Amazon, and Microsoft, have expanded their services to include advanced features such as cloud-based data analysis, databases, and proprietary tools designed exclusively for data stored within their ecosystems.

Microsoft has taken this model further by embedding Generative AI tools, such as CoPilot, into both their cloud and non-cloud product offerings. As consumers deepen their investment in these ecosystems, the cost of switching to a competitor—whether due to financial, technical, or learning curve reasons—can become prohibitively high.

In this form of business antibiosis, the negative effects for consumers often manifest as high switching costs, steep learning curves, and increased adoption expenses if they decide to transition to a competitor's product. However, the impact of these innovations extends beyond consumers. They reshape the competitive landscape, disadvantaging smaller or less-resourced vendors who struggle to compete against the comprehensive ecosystems and dominant market positions of larger providers.

By creating significant barriers to entry and limiting consumer choice, such antibiosis effects highlight the complex dynamics of Human–AI Symbiosis (HAS) in business innovation—where technological advancements can empower consumers while simultaneously entrenching competitive imbalances.

3.7. *Loss of contribution*

The antibiosis effects discussed in the previous section may not always directly impact the immediate task or application in use (Ren *et al.*, 2019). However, their broader consequences can still undermine the overall human–AI collaboration. Ren *et al.* illustrated this with an example of a child losing their intrinsic motivation to complete tasks unless incentivized. Similarly, in human–AI symbiosis, a loss of meaningful human contribution can occur when cognitive effort is no longer required to perform the tasks by humans. This decline in engagement can result from several factors. Becks and Weis (2022) identified key reasons for this phenomenon, including scenarios where AI merely asks users to confirm its decisions, the habitual reliance on AI for answers, insufficient communication between humans and AI, and AI's ability to handle everyday tasks autonomously.

These patterns of interaction can foster over-reliance on AI, diminishing humans' active role in decision-making and problem-solving. Over time, this erosion of cognitive engagement not only weakens the collaborative dynamic between humans and AI but also risks undermining the adaptability and critical thinking skills that are essential for humans to thrive in increasingly automated environments.

4. How Human–AI Symbiosis Inspires Business Innovations

While human–AI collaborations may sometimes lead to task or job displacement, they also hold significant potential to augment human capabilities. Through symbiotic partnerships, human skills can be "upgraded" in tandem with AI, fostering innovation and efficiency. The literature has identified several forms of symbiotic opportunities that can drive business innovation.

Organizational research distinguishes between two primary forms of decision-making: intuitive and analytical (Jarrahi, 2018). These approaches are not mutually exclusive; instead, they often complement each other to address diverse decision-making needs. This interplay between intuition and analysis offers fertile ground for symbiotic opportunities, where humans contribute intuition, and AI handles analytical tasks.

Jarrahi further categorizes decision-making challenges into three key areas—uncertainty, complexity, and equivocality—where human–AI symbiosis can play a transformative role:

- **Uncertainty**: In situations where decision alternatives and their consequences are unclear, humans can rely on their intuition to make quick decisions. AI complements this by providing access to real-time information and identifying emerging patterns, ensuring decisions are informed by the latest data.
- **Complexity**: Complex scenarios involve numerous variables and vast datasets that exceed human cognitive capacity. In such cases, humans decide on the information to seek, while AI excels in collecting, processing, and analyzing large volumes of data, empowering humans with actionable insights.
- **Equivocality**: Equivocal situations arise when there are multiple, conflicting alternatives, often due to different stakeholder interests. Here, humans take the lead in negotiation, consensus-building, and managing relationships, while AI supports by analyzing stakeholder sentiments and presenting diverse interpretations or solution pathways.

By addressing these challenges collaboratively, human–AI symbiosis enhances the decision-making process, enabling organizations to tackle uncertainties, manage complexities, and resolve conflicts more effectively. This synergy not only improves decision quality but also fosters innovation by leveraging the unique strengths of both humans and AI.

5. Scholarly Examples of Human–AI Symbiosis

Scholarly disciplines illustrate how Human–AI Symbiosis (HAS) can foster business innovations by addressing the three decision-making challenges identified by Jarrahi (2018)—complexity, uncertainty, and equivocality. Following are a few examples showcasing how AI enhances decision-making and reduces challenges in these areas.

5.1. *Addressing complexity: Enhancing strategic planning with AI*

SWOT (Strengths, Weaknesses, Opportunities, and Threats) analysis is a widely used strategic planning tool. However, it often suffers from high subjectivity, limited empirical validation, slow adaptation to a changing environment, and a lack of actionable steps (Cheng *et al.*, 2021). Cheng *et al.* demonstrated how change mining for association rules on product reviews and comments can address these shortcomings. By analyzing user-generated product reviews, top management gains empirical validation for high-level SWOT elements and uncover variables not initially included in the analysis.

This process exemplifies Jarrahi's "complexity" challenge by addressing issues such as objectivity, timeliness, and empirical validity, which traditionally hinder the viability of SWOT outcomes. AI, through change mining (a subfield of machine learning), reduces complexity by extracting actionable insights from timely, customer-level data. This augmentation empowers decision-makers to base their strategies on validated and nuanced insights rather than subjective assumptions.

5.2. *Tackling uncertainty: Optimizing consumer marketing with AI*

Uncertainty often arises from insufficient information about internal and external factors, disruptive technologies, or the emergence of new markets and competitors (Jarrahi, 2018). In consumer marketing, message priming—a technique that triggers a network of associated words in consumers' minds—helps reinforce brand recall. However, priming effectiveness diminishes when similar products are added to a consumer's shopping cart, as the selected products often share comparable attributes (e.g., style, quality, or price).

To overcome this, vendors may resort to price competition, which erodes profit margins, or use subsequent priming to stand out. Cheng and Chen (2022) employed deep learning models to identify the optimal product recommendation strategy by analyzing consumer behavior over time. By tracking patterns in repeated visits to product reviews, their approach identified keywords that resonated with each consumer. These keywords represented what the consumer found meaningful and became the basis for subsequent priming efforts, helping vendors differentiate their products without first resorting to sacrificing their profit margins.

This example illustrates Jarrahi's "uncertainty" challenge by addressing unknown variables, such as the primed messages that would effectively engage individual consumers. AI, through deep learning, reveals these insights by analyzing and interpreting consumer behavior, reducing uncertainty and enabling vendors to refine their strategies with precision.

6. Conclusion

Human–AI symbiosis holds significant potential for driving business innovation by enhancing decision-making and worker reskilling/upskilling. As illustrated in the examples provided, AI can augment human capabilities, transforming traditional decision-making processes into more efficient, data-driven practices. In strategic planning, AI can address the decision complexities by providing real-time, customer-driven insights that validate or challenge traditional assumptions. Similarly, in consumer marketing, AI helps reduce uncertainty by uncovering patterns in consumer behavior, optimizing marketing strategies, and enhancing brand engagement.

By leveraging AI in these symbiotic relationships, businesses can move beyond basic automation and tap into the potential for more informed, dynamic, and innovative decision-making. However, the continuous evolution of AI technology also means that the boundaries of human–AI collaboration are constantly shifting, presenting both opportunities and challenges. As AI continues to advance, organizations that harness the power of AI in tandem with human intuition and expertise will be well positioned to navigate the increasingly complex and uncertain business landscape, ultimately achieving greater competitiveness and resilience in their industries.

References

Autor, D., Chin, C., Salomons, A., & Seegmiller, B. (2024). New Frontiers: The Origins and Content of New Work, 1940–2018. *The Quarterly Journal of Economics*, Vol. 139(3), 1399–1465. https://doi.org/10.1093/qje/qjae008

Becks, E., & Weis, T. (2022). Nudging to Improve Human-AI Symbiosis. *2022 IEEE International Conference on Pervasive Computing and Communications Workshops and Other Affiliated Events, PerCom Workshops 2022*, 132–133. https://doi.org/10.1109/PerComWorkshops53856.2022.9767539

Cheng, L. C., & Chen, K. (2022). Mining longitudinal user sessions with deep learning to extend the boundary of consumer priming. *Decision Support Systems*, Vol. 162. https://doi.org/10.1016/j.dss.2022.113864

Cheng, L. C., Chen, K., Lee, M. C., & Li, K. M. (2021). User-Defined SWOT analysis—A change mining perspective on user-generated content. *Information Processing and Management*, Vol. 58(5). https://doi.org/10.1016/j.ipm.2021.102613

Douglas, A.E. (2010). The Symbiotic Habit. *Princeton University Press*, New Jersey.

Döppner, D. A., Gregory, R. W., & Schoder, D. (2016). Exploring Design Principles for Human-Machine Symbiosis: Insights from Constructing an Air Transportation Logistics Artifact. 1–21. https://www.researchgate.net/publication/308611625

Fairclough, S. (2015). A Closed-Loop Perspective on Symbiotic Human-Computer Interaction. In B. Blankertz, G. Jacucci, L. Gamberini, A. Spagnolli, & J. Freeman (Eds.), *Symbiotic Interaction* (Vol. 9359, pp. 57–67). Springer International Publishing. https://doi.org/10.1007/978-3-319-24917-9_6

Gamberini, L., Spagnolli, A., Blankertz, B., Kaski, S., Freeman, J., Acqualagna, L., Barral, O., Bellio, M., Chech, L., Eugster, M., Ferrari, E., Negri, P., Orso, V., Pluchino, P., Minelle, F., Serim, B., Wenzel, M., & Jacucci, G. (2015). Developing a Symbiotic System for Scientific Information Seeking: The MindSee Project. In B. Blankertz, G. Jacucci, L. Gamberini, A. Spagnolli, & J. Freeman (Eds.), *Symbiotic Interaction* (Vol. 9359, pp. 68–80). Springer International Publishing. https://doi.org/10.1007/978-3-319-24917-9_7

Grigsby, S. S. (2018). Artificial Intelligence for Advanced Human-Machine Symbiosis. In D. D. Schmorrow & C. M. Fidopiastis (Eds.), *Augmented Cognition: Intelligent Technologies* (pp. 255–266). Springer International Publishing. https://doi.org/10.1007/978-3-319-91470-1_22

Inga, J., Ruess, M., Robens, J. H., Nelius, T., Rothfuß, S., Kille, S., Dahlinger, P., Lindenmann, A., Thomaschke, R., Neumann, G., Matthiesen, S., Hohmann, S., & Kiesel, A. (2023). Human-machine symbiosis: A multivariate perspective for physically coupled human-machine systems. *International Journal of Human Computer Studies*, Vol. 170. https://doi.org/10.1016/j.ijhcs.2022.102926

Jarrahi, M. H. (2018). Artificial intelligence and the future of work: Human-AI symbiosis in organizational decision making. *Business Horizons*, Vol. 61(4), 577–586. https://doi.org/10.1016/j.bushor.2018.03.007

Karnouskos, S. (2022). Symbiosis with artificial intelligence via the prism of law, robots, and society. *Artificial Intelligence and Law*, Vol. 30(1), 93–115. https://doi.org/10.1007/s10506-021-09289-1

Leung, T. L. F., & Poulin, R. (2008). Parasitism, commensalism, and mutualism: Exploring the many shades of symbioses. *Vie et Milieu - Life and Environment*, Vol. 58(2), 207–225.

Lu, Y., Adrados, J. S., Chand, S. S., & Wang, L. (2021). Humans Are Not Machines—Anthropocentric Human–Machine Symbiosis for Ultra-Flexible Smart Manufacturing. *Engineering*, Vol. 7(6), 734–737. https://doi.org/10.1016/j.eng.2020.09.018

Lyu, D. (2022). Towards Trustworthy Decision-Making in Human-Machine Symbiosis [Doctoral dissertation]. *Auburn University*.

Ren, X., Silpasuwanchai, C., & Cahill, J. (2019). Human-Engaged Computing: The future of Human–Computer Interaction. *CCF Transactions on Pervasive Computing and Interaction*, Vol. 1(1), 47–68. https://doi.org/10.1007/s42486-019-00007-0

Sundar, S. S. (2020). Rise of machine agency: A framework for studying the psychology of Human–AI Interaction (HAII). *Journal of Computer-Mediated Communication*, Vol. 25(1), 74–88. https://doi.org/10.1093/jcmc/zmz026

Van Dijk, J. A. G. M. (2006). Digital divide research, achievements and shortcomings. *Poetics*, Vol. 34(4–5), 221–235. https://doi.org/10.1016/j.poetic.2006.05.004

Vaswani, A., Shazeer, N., Parmar, N., Uszkoreit, J., Jones, L., Gomez, A. N., Kaiser, Ł., & Polosukhin, I. (2017). Attention is All you Need. *Proceedings of Advances in Neural Information Processing Systems*. https://arxiv.org/pdf/1706.03762.pdf

Vidalis, M. A., & Andreatos, A. S. (2022). Humankind and Ubiquitous Autonomous AI: A Symbiotic or Dystopian Interaction? A Socio-Philosophical Inquiry. *Journal of Engineering Research and Sciences*, Vol. 1(5), 109–118. https://doi.org/10.55708/js0105012

Zakershahrak, M. (2021). Towards Human-Machine Symbiosis: Design for Effective AI Facilitation. *Arizona State University*.

https://doi.org/10.1142/9789819816347_0013

Chapter 13

Navigating Industry 5.0: Integrating Artificial Intelligence with Innovation and Management Competencies for the Future of Business

Zafer Adiguzel

Sakarya University of Applied Sciences, Turkey

Koc University Turkey

1. Introduction

As advances are being made toward a new era of technological innovation, the integration of Artificial Intelligence (AI) into industry practices is significantly reshaping the way companies operate. Artificial Intelligence (AI) stands out as one of the most transformative technologies that is reshaping industries and redefining the scope of innovation (Gruetzemacher & Whittlestone, 2022). The fourth industrial revolution, referred to as Industry 4.0, has ushered in a wave of digitalization, but the advent of Industry 5.0 pushes the boundaries even further, enhancing human-AI collaboration. In this new paradigm, AI serves not only as a tool to automate repetitive tasks, but also as a catalyst to drive business innovation, competitiveness, and sustainable growth (Haldorai *et al.*, 2024). The rapid evolution of technology has radically transformed industries and spurred a shift toward smarter, more interconnected, and more sustainable production systems. Industry 5.0 represents the latest stage of this transformation, characterized by the combination of human creativity with advanced technological systems such as AI, robotics, and the Internet of Things (IoT) (Chander *et al.*, 2022). While Industry 4.0 focused on automation, smart factories, and digitalization, Industry 5.0 emphasizes human-centered innovation and integrates AI to increase collaboration between humans and machines to drive sustainable development.

Today, businesses are grappling with the challenges of driving this technological change while addressing sustainability concerns. The adoption of AI and other Industry 5.0 technologies has great potential to increase operational efficiency, improve decision-making, and drive innovation (Bécue *et al.*, 2024). However, realizing these benefits requires more than technological investment; it requires rethinking management capabilities and a strategic focus on sustainability.

AI enables businesses to leverage large amounts of data, make informed decisions, and optimize operations (Bharadiya, 2023). As companies worldwide integrate AI into their processes, there is a growing need for leaders to develop management competencies to fully leverage the potential of AI. The importance of AI for business innovation is particularly rooted in the context of Industry 5.0, which focuses on the synergy between humans and machines.

Characterized by collaboration between humans and machines, Industry 5.0 marks the next evolution in this industrial transformation, emphasizing both technological innovation and human-centric applications. The integration of AI into management systems and business innovation is driving unprecedented growth, leading to improved productivity, decision-making, and overall company performance.

AI has emerged as a key enabler for optimizing business processes, predicting market trends, and driving product innovation. It plays a critical role in enhancing business competitiveness by streamlining operations, reducing costs, and enabling more agile responses to changing market conditions. Beyond operational efficiency, the role of AI in innovation is important for companies in creating new business models, products, and services that meet evolving consumer demands.

This chapter discusses how AI can be used to drive innovation and sustainability, the role of Industry 5.0 in shaping future business models, and the critical management competencies businesses need to succeed in this new era. It examines how AI-driven technologies are transforming industries, the competencies management needs to use these tools, and the role of innovation in driving competitive advantage. It provides an in-depth examination of the benefits and challenges facing businesses navigating the rapidly evolving Industry 5.0 landscape. It also examines the management competencies needed to successfully navigate the integration of AI into business operations, highlighting the key ways companies can not only keep pace with technological advancements but also leverage them to stay ahead of the competition.

2. Literature Review

2.1. *Technology and artificial intelligence in Industry 5.0*

The transition from Industry 4.0 to Industry 5.0 represents a shift from machine-driven automation to human-machine collaboration. While Industry 4.0 introduces the concept of smart factories powered by the IoT, big data, and artificial intelligence, Industry 5.0 emphasizes the relationships between advanced technologies and human creativity, especially in the areas of decision-making, design, and problem-solving (Nahavandi, 2019). Therefore, the concept of Industry 5.0 has emerged as the next stage of industrial evolution, where human intelligence and creativity work together with smart technologies such as artificial intelligence, the IoT, and advanced robotics. Unlike Industry 4.0, which primarily focuses on automation and cyber-physical systems, Industry 5.0 emphasizes human-machine collaboration, personalization, and sustainability (Aheleroff *et al.*, 2022).

The human-centered approach focuses on leveraging artificial intelligence to enhance human potential, not to replace human roles, and creates a balance between automation and human expertise. In Industry 5.0, technology becomes a collaborative partner that enables personalized production, greater customization, and the ability to meet specific consumer needs more effectively.

The shift to Industry 5.0 reflects a growing recognition that technology should enhance human capabilities rather than replace them. In this context, AI plays a key role by complementing human decision-making processes and providing faster and more accurate results. Industry 5.0 also emphasizes the importance of sustainability, with AI being used to optimize resource use and reduce waste (Rame *et al.*, 2024).

In manufacturing, Industry 5.0 aims to create more flexible and responsive production systems, where AI-enabled systems work in harmony with employees to meet customer demands for personalized products (Nahavandi, 2019). This shift toward mass customization represents a significant departure from the mass production models of previous industrial revolutions. The ability of AI to process large data sets and produce real-time insights allows companies to tailor their offerings to individual preferences, increasing customer satisfaction and loyalty (Kusiak, 2017).

2.2. *The role of AI in Industry 5.0*

AI is at the forefront of Industry 5.0, driving innovation and transformation across industries. From predictive analytics to autonomous systems, AI provides businesses with the tools to operate efficiently while also offering customized solutions. Machine learning (ML) and deep learning algorithms allow companies to predict market trends, optimize supply chains, and improve customer experiences (Acemoglu & Restrepo, 2018). Furthermore, AI's ability to process large amounts of data in real time has revolutionized decision-making processes. Companies can now make data-driven decisions with unprecedented speed and accuracy, positively impacting improved operational efficiency and innovation capabilities. Additionally, AI-enabled systems contribute to product design and development, enabling the creation of innovative solutions that meet increasingly complex consumer demands.

2.3. *Innovation in the age of AI*

Traditionally seen as the introduction of new products or processes, innovation has taken on a new meaning in the context of AI and Industry 5.0. While innovation was defined as the success of a new product/service in the marketplace, it now encompasses the ability to integrate AI technologies into existing business models to create value in new ways. This can be seen in areas such as smart manufacturing, where AI-powered robots collaborate with humans to produce highly customized products, or service industries, where AI-powered tools provide personalized customer support (Brynjolfsson & McAfee, 2014). In today's competitive business environment, innovation is not just about adopting the latest technology.

It also involves rethinking organizational structures, processes, and cultures to enable continuous adaptation and improvement. AI facilitates this by providing insights that allow companies to innovate more effectively, whether through enhanced customer engagement, supply chain optimization, or data-driven product development.

3. The Role of AI in Industry 5.0: Key Innovations

AI serves as a critical enabler of Industry 5.0 by facilitating innovation in several key areas:

Human-Machine Collaboration: AI systems are designed to take over repetitive and time-consuming tasks, freeing workers to focus on the more creative and complex aspects of their jobs. Collaborative robots (cobots) powered by AI are increasingly being used in factories to increase productivity and reduce the risk of injury to workers (Borboni *et al.*, 2023).

Mass Customization: One of the defining characteristics of Industry 5.0 is its focus on personalization. AI enables businesses to collect and analyze customer data at scale, providing valuable insights into individual preferences and behaviors. This allows companies to offer customized products and services, improving the customer experience (Ameen *et al.*, 2021).

Sustainability and Efficiency: AI is also driving innovation in sustainability, helping companies optimize resource use, reduce waste, and reduce energy consumption. In industries such as energy and agriculture, AI is being used to monitor environmental conditions, forecast demand, and optimize supply chains (Hosseini *et al.*, 2024). These applications not only improve efficiency but also contribute to a broader goal such as sustainability.

Autonomous Systems and Robotics: AI-enabled robots and autonomous systems play a central role in the realization of Industry 5.0. In manufacturing, AI-enabled robots can perform tasks that were once too dangerous or complex for humans, while AI algorithms help optimize production lines to reduce errors and increase efficiency (Ghobakhloo, 2020). Similarly, AI is enabling the development of autonomous vehicles and drones that are transforming industries such as logistics and transportation (Nwankwo & Etukudoh, 2023).

3.1. *The impact of AI on business model innovation*

Artificial intelligence plays a significant role in business model innovation, particularly by enabling companies to transition from traditional linear models to more dynamic data-driven approaches. Companies such as Uber and Airbnb have demonstrated how AI can be used to disrupt entire industries by creating platforms in innovative ways (Lee *et al.*, 2019).

Business model innovation through AI also includes improving value propositions. AI enables companies to better understand customer needs, personalize products and services, and streamline operations. For example, AI-powered recommendation systems on e-commerce platforms improve customer experience by offering personalized product recommendations, while increasing customer loyalty (Agrawal *et al.*, 2019).

Artificial intelligence has been seen as one of the most important drivers of innovation in recent years. Businesses that successfully implement AI technologies not only streamline operations but also provide new revenue streams through the development of innovative products and services (Shrestha *et al.*, 2019). AI is advancing innovation in a variety of ways: by improving decision-making processes, automating routine tasks, and enabling businesses to analyze and act on large amounts of data in real time. As AI becomes more accessible, industries ranging from healthcare to finance and manufacturing have discovered its potential for innovation (Brock & von Wangenheim, 2019). In the manufacturing sector, AI insights are providing convenience, reducing downtime, and increasing efficiency (Lee *et al.*, 2020). In retail, AI-powered recommendation systems and chatbots are improving customer service and personalized marketing (Bhuiyan, 2024). Similarly, in finance, AI is being used for risk management and fraud detection, increasing the ability of firms to effectively manage and mitigate risks (Rehan *et al.*, 2024).

However, the successful application of AI for business innovation requires more than just technological prowess. Companies need to develop a strategic vision for AI integration and invest in the right talent and infrastructure (Brynjolfsson & McAfee, 2017). Companies that approach AI as a strategic innovation enabler are more likely to see tangible results than those that view AI as a cost-cutting tool (Wilson & Daugherty, 2018).

AI has emerged as one of the most transformative technologies in business, driving innovation across a variety of industries. AI technologies, such as machine learning and natural language processing, are used in industries ranging from healthcare and finance to manufacturing and retail, allowing businesses to analyze large amounts of data, automate routine tasks, and gain valuable insights into consumer behavior (Brynjolfsson & McAfee, 2014; Davenport & Ronanki, 2018).

A study by Dwivedi *et al.* (2021) highlights the role of AI in driving product and service innovation. AI enables businesses to develop personalized offerings, predict market trends, and innovate faster than ever before. The use of AI-powered algorithms allows companies to analyze consumer preferences and predict market needs, which leads to the creation of new products and services tailored to customer demands.

AI also supports process innovation by increasing operational efficiency and reducing costs. For example, AI-powered automation systems can optimize supply chain management, reduce waste in manufacturing processes, and increase the accuracy of demand forecasting (Huang & Rust, 2018). In the financial sector, AI is being used to develop automated trading systems, fraud detection tools, and chatbots in customer service, all of which contribute to more efficient business operations.

However, while AI has tremendous potential for innovation, its successful implementation requires strong alignment between AI capabilities and organizational strategy. The literature emphasizes the importance of developing a clear AI strategy that outlines how AI will be used to achieve specific business goals (Castrounis, 2019). Without such alignment, businesses may struggle to fully leverage the potential of AI, resulting in missed opportunities for innovation.

3.2. *Fostering a culture of innovation through AI*

An important aspect of using AI for innovation is developing a culture that supports continuous learning, creativity, and experimentation. Companies that encourage their employees to adopt AI-driven tools and analytics can create an environment where innovative ideas can flourish (Bughin *et al.*, 2018). Leadership plays a critical role in this transformation, as leaders must not only advocate for AI adoption but also encourage employees and create an atmosphere where failures are seen as learning opportunities. Furthermore, fostering an innovative culture in an AI-driven world requires a focus on developing employees' skills. AI can complement human creativity, but employees also need to have the right skills to collaborate effectively with AI systems. This means training employees in areas such as data analytics, machine learning, and digital literacy to fully realize the potential of AI-driven innovation.

3.3. *Industry 5.0: The human-centric revolution*

Industry 5.0 represents the next step in industrial evolution, building on the technological advances of Industry 4.0 and placing greater emphasis on human-machine collaboration. Characterized by automation and smart technologies, Industry 4.0 is transforming manufacturing by integrating artificial intelligence, IoT, and cyber-physical systems. Industry 5.0 takes this a step further by promoting human-machine collaboration, where artificial intelligence augments human capabilities rather than replacing them (Zafar *et al.*, 2024). According to Nahavandi (2019), Industry 5.0 emphasizes the need for personalized manufacturing, where humans and machines work together to deliver products that meet individual customer preferences.

One of the key features of Industry 5.0 is its focus on sustainability. Researchers argue that Industry 5.0 aims to address the environmental and social challenges posed by previous industrial revolutions by integrating sustainability into production processes (Sharma, 2024). Artificial intelligence plays a critical role in achieving this goal by enabling more efficient use of resources, reducing waste, and optimizing energy consumption.

4. Management Competencies for Leveraging AI and Industry 5.0

As AI and Industry 5.0 technologies become an integral part of business operations, the competencies expected from leaders are also increasing. The literature identifies several core competencies that managers need to develop to successfully lead organizations in the new era of technological transformation and sustainability.

Technological literacy is a core competency for managers in the AI and Industry 5.0 era. Leaders must have a strong understanding of AI technologies and their potential applications in their organizations. This includes knowledge of AI tools, data analytics, and automation systems and the ability to assess the impact of these technologies on business operations (Schwab, 2017).

Strategic foresight is another critical competency. Managers must be able to anticipate future trends and adapt their strategies accordingly. AI technologies can provide managers with the information they need to make informed decisions about the future direction of the business by providing insights into market trends, consumer behavior, and competitive dynamics (Schoemaker *et al.*, 2018). However, taking advantage of these insights requires managers to develop a long-term vision for their companies and the ability to integrate AI into their strategic planning processes.

Agility and adaptability are also key competencies in a rapidly changing business environment. The literature emphasizes that managers need to be flexible and responsive to new challenges and opportunities (Engelbrecht *et al.*, 2024). AI technologies can provide businesses with the agility they need to respond to changing market conditions, but managers must be able to quickly adapt their strategies and operations to take advantage of these opportunities.

In the context of AI and Industry 5.0, leadership also requires a focus on sustainability. Leaders must be able to integrate sustainability into decision-making processes and ensure that their companies contribute to environmental and social goals. These include developing sustainable business models, reducing the environmental impact of operations, and promoting corporate social responsibility (CSR) initiatives (Pisano, 2019).

4.1. *Key competencies for managing AI-driven organizations*

As AI becomes increasingly integrated into business operations, the competencies required of managers are also evolving. In the context of Industry 5.0, management competencies go beyond traditional skills to include the ability to navigate and manage complex AI systems. Managers must develop competencies in areas such as data analysis, AI ethics, and the strategic application of AI technologies (Colbert *et al.*, 2016).

In addition, managers need to be agile, able to quickly adapt to new technological developments, and understand how AI can be used to create competitive advantages. This requires not only technical competencies but also strong leadership skills to inspire and lead teams in a rapidly changing business environment. Emotional intelligence, critical thinking, and the ability to foster collaboration between human and AI-driven systems are also essential management competencies in the AI era (Chui *et al.*, 2018).

As businesses transition to Industry 5.0, the role of management is also evolving. Traditional leadership competencies are no longer sufficient to navigate the complexities of AI-driven innovation. Instead, managers must develop new skills and adopt a more flexible, strategic approach to decision-making (Jarrahi, 2018).

Data-Driven Decision-Making: One of the most critical competencies for managers in the AI era is the ability to make data-driven decisions. AI generates vast amounts of data, but the real value lies in the ability to interpret that data and use it to inform strategic decisions. To use data effectively, managers need to develop strong analytical skills and a deep understanding of AI technologies (Brynjolfsson & McElheran, 2016).

Collaboration and Communication: AI-driven innovation requires high levels of collaboration across teams with diverse skill sets. Managers must create a culture of collaboration by ensuring that data scientists, engineers, and business leaders work together to achieve common goals (Adamson, 2021). Effective communication is also crucial, as managers need to be able to explain the benefits and limitations of AI to stakeholders at all levels of the organization.

Agility and Adaptability: The rapid pace of technological change means that managers need to be agile and adaptable, constantly learning to stay on top of the latest developments. This requires a growth mindset as well as the ability to manage risk and uncertainty in an environment where technological disruption is the norm (Ahlstrom *et al.*, 2020).

Ethical Leadership: As AI becomes more integrated into business processes, ethical considerations are becoming increasingly important. Executives must ensure that AI is used responsibly, focusing on fairness, transparency, and accountability. This can support addressing issues such as bias in AI algorithms and ensuring that AI-driven decisions align with the organization's values (Floridi *et al.*, 2021).

4.2. *The role of AI in enhancing managerial decision-making*

AI supports managerial decision-making by providing tools that enable more informed and accurate decisions. Machine learning algorithms can analyze large amounts of data, identifying patterns and trends that humans may miss. This allows managers to make decisions based on data-driven insights rather than relying solely on intuition (Liebowitz, 2024) or past experience (Davenport and Ronanki, 2018). AI-powered decision support systems can also perform predictive analysis, allowing managers to anticipate future challenges and opportunities. For example, AI can predict market shifts, customer behavior, and supply chain disruptions, helping managers proactively investigate these issues. However, while AI improves decision-making, managers must also be equipped to interpret and act on the insights provided by AI systems.

4.3. *Challenges and ethical considerations in the AI era*

Despite its many benefits, the adoption of AI in business raises several ethical concerns. One major issue is the potential for bias in AI algorithms, which can lead to discriminatory outcomes in areas such as hiring, lending, or customer service. Ensuring that AI systems are transparent, fair, and accountable is a significant challenge for businesses operating in the AI era (Binns, 2018). Another ethical concern is the potential for job loss due to automation. As AI takes over more tasks traditionally performed by humans, businesses must consider the impact of automation on employment. This includes not only retraining employees but also considering the broader societal impacts of widespread AI adoption (Autor, 2015).

4.4. *Managing the risks associated with AI implementation*

AI applications carry inherent risks, such as data security, privacy concerns, and the potential for system failures. As businesses become increasingly reliant on AI, they need to develop robust risk management strategies to mitigate these risks. This includes ensuring data protection, maintaining system integrity, and developing contingency plans in the event of AI system failures (Rahwan *et al.*, 2019). Additionally, businesses should ensure that their AI systems align with their ethical values and corporate social responsibility goals. This includes establishing clear guidelines for the use of AI and regularly auditing AI systems to ensure they are operating consistently with corporate policies.

4.5. *Emerging trends in AI and business*

AI is likely to be shaped by several emerging trends. One important trend is the development of explainable AI, which aims to make AI decision-making processes more transparent and understandable to humans. This is particularly important for building trust in AI systems in industries where decisions have significant impact, such as finance, healthcare, and legal services (Gunning & Aha, 2019). Another trend is the increasing use of AI for sustainability and environmental management. AI-driven technologies can also be used to optimize energy consumption, reduce waste, and increase the efficiency of resource management. This is also in line with the broader goals of Industry 5.0, which emphasizes sustainability and human-centered innovation.

4.6. *Strategic recommendations for businesses*

To fully leverage AI for business innovation, companies need to take a strategic approach to AI integration. This includes not only investing in AI technologies but also encouraging a culture of continuous learning and innovation. Businesses should prioritize developing employee skills, encouraging collaboration between AI systems, and investing in ethical AI applications. Additionally, businesses must be able to adapt to emerging trends in AI by constantly monitoring technological advancements and exploring new applications of AI in their industries. This proactive approach will enable businesses to remain competitive and responsive to the changing needs of the market.

5. Discussion

The role of AI in innovation shows that several key themes are important regarding the emergence of Industry 5.0 and the competencies required for management. The most important criterion is the profound impact that AI has on innovation, allowing companies to streamline processes, develop new products and services, and optimize their operations (Wamba-Taguimdje *et al.*, 2020). The transition from Industry 4.0 to Industry 5.0 represents a development toward more human-centric approaches where AI augments human capabilities.

One of the most important trends is the increasing interest in sustainability and mass customization. Industry 5.0 is characterized by a focus on personalized products and services, as well as the need for businesses to adopt more sustainable practices (Ghobakhloo *et al.*, 2023). AI plays an important role in both of these areas, enabling companies to collect and analyze data to offer customized solutions and optimize resource utilization.

The adoption of AI and Industry 5.0 technologies presents both opportunities and challenges for businesses. These technologies also offer significant potential for innovation, efficiency, and sustainability. AI can optimize business processes, improve decision-making, and enable the development of innovative products and services that meet evolving consumer demands (Sjödin *et al.*, 2021). Industry 5.0 further enhances these benefits by promoting human-machine collaboration and personalized production and is developing more sustainable and resilient industrial systems.

Furthermore, the successful implementation of AI and Industry 5.0 technologies requires significant changes in management practices and competencies. Leaders must have the knowledge and skills to effectively leverage AI technologies, drive innovation, and integrate sustainability into their strategies. This requires not only technological literacy, but also strategic foresight, agility, and a strong commitment to sustainability.

By aligning AI capabilities with their strategic goals, creating a culture of innovation, and prioritizing sustainability, businesses can leverage the full potential of these transformative technologies. However, the adoption of AI and Industry 5.0 is not without its challenges. One of the key challenges is the need for organizational change. Businesses must be willing to adapt their structures, processes, and cultures to fully leverage the potential of AI and Industry 5.0 technologies (Maddikunta *et al.*, 2022). This includes fostering a culture of continuous learning where employees are encouraged to develop new skills and adopt new technologies. It also requires businesses to invest in the infrastructure and tools needed to support AI and Industry 5.0 initiatives.

Another challenge is the ethical and social impacts of AI. As AI becomes more integrated into business operations, there are concerns about its impact on employment, privacy, and decision-making. Leaders should address these concerns by developing ethical guidelines for the use of AI and ensuring that AI technologies are used in ways that benefit both the business and society.

Another important insight is the evolving role of management in the age of AI. As AI becomes more integrated into business processes, managers must develop new competencies to successfully navigate this complex environment. Data-driven decision-making, collaboration, agility, and ethical leadership are critical skills for managers in this new era. These competencies are important not only for managing AI-driven innovation but also for ensuring that businesses can adapt to the rapid pace of technological change.

6. Conclusion

The integration of AI into Industry 5.0 represents a fundamental shift in the way businesses operate and innovate. By leveraging AI, companies can improve decision-making, optimize operations, and create a culture of innovation. However, successful adoption of AI requires not only technological investment, but also the development of new management competencies, ethical frameworks, and risk management strategies.

As businesses embrace AI-driven thinking, they must also consider the opportunities and challenges presented by Industry 5.0. By doing so, companies can position themselves for long-term success in an increasingly competitive and dynamic global marketplace.

AI is proving to be a transformative force in the world of innovation. Its ability to process large amounts of data, make real-time decisions, and optimize operations is reshaping industries and providing new opportunities for growth. As businesses transition to the Industry 5.0 era, the role of AI is becoming even more critical, encouraging human-machine collaboration.

However, successfully integrating AI into business processes requires more than just technological prowess. Companies need to develop a strategic vision for AI, invest in the right talent, and foster a culture of collaboration and innovation. Executives need to develop the skills needed to use AI effectively, including data-driven decision-making, collaboration, agility, and ethical leadership.

The transition to Industry 5.0 also raises important questions about the future of work and the role of humans in an AI-driven world. While AI has the potential to automate many tasks, the human element remains important for creativity, innovation, and ethical decision-making. Therefore, the future of business model innovation is not in replacing humans with machines, but in creating a harmonious partnership where AI augments human capabilities.

As AI continues to evolve, businesses that embrace its potential and develop the necessary management competencies will be best positioned to thrive in the Industry 5.0 era. Future research will be important to explore the long-term impact of AI on business models, workforces, and society. By understanding the challenges and opportunities presented by AI, businesses can develop strategies that leverage its power for innovation while ensuring its benefits are shared equitably across all stakeholders.

As a result, AI and Industry 5.0 present significant opportunities for businesses to drive innovation, increase efficiency, and achieve sustainability goals. These technologies provide businesses with the tools to optimize operations, develop innovative products and services, and create more sustainable and resilient business models. However, realizing these benefits requires significant changes in management practices and capabilities. Leaders must develop a strong understanding of AI technologies, create a culture of innovation, and prioritize sustainability in decision-making. By doing so, businesses can position themselves for success in the age of AI and Industry 5.0. The future of business innovation lies at the intersection of AI, Industry 5.0, and sustainability. As businesses continue to adopt these technologies, the role of management in driving innovation and sustainability will become increasingly important. Businesses that can effectively leverage AI and Industry 5.0 technologies while also considering the ethical and social impacts of these technologies will be better positioned for the future.

References

Acemoglu, D., and Restrepo, P. (2018). Artificial intelligence, automation, and work. In *The Economics of Artificial Intelligence: An Agenda* (pp. 197–236). University of Chicago Press.

Adamson, J. (2021). Minding the machines: Building and leading data science and analytics teams. John Wiley & Sons.

Agrawal, A., Gans, J., and Goldfarb, A. (Eds.). (2019). The economics of artificial intelligence: An agenda. University of Chicago Press, Chicago, USA.

Aheleroff, S., Huang, H., Xu, X., and Zhong, R. Y. (2022). Toward sustainability and resilience with Industry 4.0 and Industry 5.0. *Frontiers in Manufacturing Technology*, Vol. 2, 1–20.

Ahlstrom, D., Arregle, J. L., Hitt, M. A., Qian, G., Ma, X., and Faems, D. (2020). Managing technological, sociopolitical, and institutional change in the new normal. *Journal of Management Studies*, Vol. 57(3), 411–437.

Ameen, N., Tarhini, A., Reppel, A., and Anand, A. (2021). Customer experiences in the age of artificial intelligence. *Computers in Human Behavior*, Vol. 114, 1–14.

Autor, D. H. (2015). Why are there still so many jobs? The history and future of workplace automation. *Journal of Economic Perspectives*, Vol. 29(3), 3–30.

Bécue, A., Gama, J., and Brito, P. Q. (2024). AI's effect on innovation capacity in the context of industry 5.0: A scoping review. *Artificial Intelligence Review*, Vol. 57(8), 1–29.

Bharadiya, J. P. (2023). Machine learning and AI in business intelligence: Trends and opportunities. *International Journal of Computer (IJC)*, Vol. 48(1), 123–134.

Bhuiyan, M.S. (2024). The role of AI-Enhanced personalization in customer experiences. *Journal of Computer Science and Technology Studies*, Vol. 6(1), 162–169.

Binns, R. (2018). Fairness in machine learning: Lessons from political philosophy. In *Conference on Fairness, Accountability and Transparency* (pp. 1–11), January. Proceedings of Machine Learning Research.

Borboni, A., Reddy, K. V. V., Elamvazuthi, I., AL-Quraishi, M. S., Natarajan, E., and Azhar Ali, S. S. (2023). The expanding role of artificial intelligence in collaborative robots for industrial applications: A systematic review of recent works. *Machines*, Vol. 11(1), 1–28.

Brock, J. K. U., and Von Wangenheim, F. (2019). Demystifying AI: What digital transformation leaders can teach you about realistic artificial intelligence. *California Management Review*, Vol. 61(4), 110–134.

Brynjolfsson, E., and McAfee, A. (2014). The second machine age: Work, progress, and prosperity in a time of brilliant technologies. *WW Norton & Company*. New York, USA.

Brynjolfsson, E., and Mcafee, A. (2017). Artificial intelligence, for real. *Harvard Business Review*, Vol. 1, 1–31.

Brynjolfsson, E., and McElheran, K. (2016). Data in action: Data-driven decision making in US manufacturing. *University of Toronto-Rotman School of Management*. Working Papers 16-06, Center for Economic Studies, U.S. Census Bureau. 1–55.

Bughin, J., Seong, J., Manyika, J., Chui, M., and Joshi, R. (2018). Notes from the AI frontier: Modeling the impact of AI on the world economy. *McKinsey Global Institute*.

Castrounis, A. (2019). AI for people and business: A framework for better human experiences and business success. *O'Reilly Media*. Sebastopol, California, USA.

Chander, B., Pal, S., De, D., and Buyya, R. (2022). Artificial intelligence-based internet of things for industry 5.0. *Artificial Intelligence-Based Internet of Things Systems*, 3–45. Springer, Cham.

Chui, M., Manyika, J., and Miremadi, M. (2018). What AI can and can't do (yet) for your business. *McKinsey Quarterly*, 1–11.

Colbert, A., Yee, N., and George, G. (2016). The digital workforce and the workplace of the future. *Academy of Management Journal*, Vol. 59(3), 731–739.

Davenport, T. H., and Ronanki, R. (2018). Artificial intelligence for the real world. *Harvard Business Review*, Vol. 96(1), 108–116.

Dwivedi, Y. K., Hughes, L., Ismagilova, E., Aarts, G., Coombs, C., Crick, T., ... and Williams, M. D. (2021). Artificial Intelligence (AI): Multidisciplinary perspectives on emerging challenges, opportunities, and agenda for research, practice and policy. *International Journal of Information Management*, Vol. 57, 1–47.

Engelbrecht, A., Yitmen, I., and Almusaed, A. (2024). Industry 4.0 Transformation Towards Industry 5.0 Paradigm-Challenges, Opportunities and Practices: Challenges, Opportunities and Practices. IntechOpen, London, UK.

Floridi, L., Cowls, J., King, T. C., and Taddeo, M. (2021). How to design AI for social good: Seven essential factors. *Ethics, Governance, and Policies in Artificial Intelligence*, 125–151.

Ghobakhloo, M. (2020). Industry 4.0, digitization, and opportunities for sustainability. *Journal of Cleaner Production*, Vol. 252, 1–21.

Ghobakhloo, M., Iranmanesh, M., Tseng, M. L., Grybauskas, A., Stefanini, A., and Amran, A. (2023). Behind the definition of Industry 5.0: A systematic review of technologies, principles, components, and values. *Journal of Industrial and Production Engineering*, Vol. 40(6), 432–447.

Gruetzemacher, R., and Whittlestone, J. (2022). The transformative potential of artificial intelligence. *Futures*, Vol. 135, 1–11.

Gunning, D., and Aha, D. (2019). DARPA's explainable artificial intelligence (XAI) program. *AI Magazine*, Vol. 40(2), 44–58.

Haldorai, A., Murugan, S., and Balakrishnan, M. (2024). Harnessing Intelligent AI to Elevate Business Modeling: A Perspective. In *Artificial Intelligence for Sustainable Development* (pp. 429–440). Cham: Springer Nature Switzerland.

Hosseini, A., Rahmani, S., Khedri, M. A., and Goli, A. (2024). Agricultural supply chain planning considering the role of Industry 4.0: Technology assessment approach. In *Supply Chain Management* (pp. 140–169). CRC Press.

Huang, M. H., and Rust, R. T. (2018). Artificial intelligence in service. *Journal of Service Research*, Vol. 21(2), 155–172.

Jarrahi, M. H. (2018). Artificial intelligence and the future of work: Human-AI symbiosis in organizational decision making. *Business Horizons*, Vol. 61(4), 577–586.

Kusiak, A. (2017). Smart manufacturing must embrace big data. *Nature*, Vol. 544(7648), 23–25.

Lee, J., Singh, J., Azamfar, M., and Pandhare, V. (2020). Industrial AI and predictive analytics for smart manufacturing systems. In *Smart Manufacturing* (pp. 213–244). Elsevier.

Lee, J., Suh, T., Roy, D., and Baucus, M. (2019). Emerging technology and business model innovation: The case of artificial intelligence. *Journal of Open Innovation: Technology, Market, and Complexity*, Vol. 5(3), 1–13.

Liebowitz, J. (ed.) (2024). Developing the Intuitive Executive: Using Analytics and Intuition for Success. Taylor & Francis.

Maddikunta, P. K. R., Pham, Q. V., Prabadevi, B., Deepa, N., Dev, K., Gadekallu, T. R., ... and Liyanage, M. (2022). Industry 5.0: A survey on enabling technologies and potential applications. *Journal of Industrial Information Integration*, Vol. 26, 1–19.

Nahavandi, S. (2019). Industry 5.0—A human-centric solution. *Sustainability*, Vol. 11(16), 1–13.

Nwankwo, C. O., and Etukudoh, E. A. (2023). The Future of Autonomous Vehicles in Logistics and Supply Chain Management. *International Journal Advanced Multidisciplinary Research and Studies*, Vol. 4(3), 244–248.

Pisano, G. P. (2019). The hard truth about innovative. *Harvard Business Review*, Vol. 97(1), 62–71.

Rahwan, I., Cebrian, M., Obradovich, N., Bongard, J., Bonnefon, J. F., Breazeal, C., ... and Wellman, M. (2019). Machine behaviour. *Nature*, Vol. 568(7753), 477–486.

Rame, R., Purwanto, P., and Sudarno, S. (2024). Industry 5.0 and sustainability: An overview of emerging trends and challenges for a green future. *Innovation and Green Development*, Vol. 3(4), 1–20.

Rehan, R., Sa'ad, A. A., and Haron, R. (2024). Artificial Intelligence and Financial Risk Mitigation. *Artificial Intelligence for Risk Mitigation in the Financial Industry*, 53–79.

Schoemaker, P. J., Heaton, S., and Teece, D. (2018). Innovation, dynamic capabilities, and leadership. *California Management Review*, Vol. 61(1), 15–42.

Schwab, K. (2017). The fourth industrial revolution. *Crown Business*. New York, USA.

Sharma, R. (2024). Analysis of Industry 5.0 contributions to sustainable development: From Welfare to Wellbeing. In *Modern Technologies and Tools Supporting the Development of Industry 5.0* (pp. 259–300). CRC Press.

Shrestha, Y. R., Ben-Menahem, S. M., and Von Krogh, G. (2019). Organizational decision-making structures in the age of artificial intelligence. *California Management Review*, Vol. 61(4), 66–83.

Sjödin, D., Parida, V., Palmié, M., and Wincent, J. (2021). How AI capabilities enable business model innovation: Scaling AI through co-evolutionary processes and feedback loops. *Journal of Business Research*, Vol. 134, 574–587.

Wamba-Taguimdje, S. L., Wamba, S. F., Kamdjoug, J. R. K., and Wanko, C. E. T. (2020). Influence of artificial intelligence (AI) on firm performance: The business value of AI-based transformation projects. *Business Process Management Journal*, Vol. 26(7), 1893–1924.

Wilson, H. J., and Daugherty, P. R. (2018). Collaborative intelligence: Humans and AI are joining forces. *Harvard Business Review*, Vol. 96(4), 114–123.

Zafar, M. H., Langås, E. F., and Sanfilippo, F. (2024). Exploring the synergies between collaborative robotics, digital twins, augmentation, and industry 5.0 for smart manufacturing: A state-of-the-art review. *Robotics and Computer-Integrated Manufacturing*, Vol. 89, 1–29.

https://doi.org/10.1142/9789819816347_0014

Chapter 14

Intersection of Generative Artificial Intelligence with Intellectual Property Rights

Terry M. Sanks

Beusse Sanks, PLLC, Orlando, Florida, USA

1. Intersection of Generative Artificial Intelligence with Intellectual Property Rights

Though generative artificial intelligence is becoming a leading tool used to create intangible assets, protecting such assets with government-granted intellectual property protection vehicles may not be possible. For example, with respect to patents and copyrights, United States (U.S.) laws only allow for granting patent rights and copyright registration rights if the creation is made by a natural person. Even in view of this impediment, there are still avenues to utilize generative artificial intelligence to provide a business with a competitive advantage where the creation has some form of intellectual property protection.

2. The Rise of Intangible Assets

The world is in the midst of transitioning from the Fourth Industrial Revolution to the Fifth Industrial Revolution (Nosta, 2023). With each Industrial Revolution, the world has experienced technological, socioeconomic, and cultural advances (Editors of Encyclopedia Britannica, 2024). The First Industrial Revolution used water and steam power to mechanize production (Schwab, 2016). During this Revolution, known as the Age of Mechanical Production, the U.S. began the transition away from being primarily an agriculturally based society to an industrial-based society. There was a transition from hand production methods to machines, new chemical manufacturing, use of iron production processes, and increased use of steam and waterpower. Factories then became the center of community life. Industrialization created a middle class of skilled workers. Overall, economic growth grew as cities and industries grew.

The Second Industrial Revolution used electric power to create mass production (Schwab, 2016). This Revolution is known as the Technological Revolution or the Age of Science and Mass Production. There was an expansion of rail, telegraph lines, and the use of assembly lines in factories. The introduction of electrical power and telephones occurred during this time as well. The Second Industrial Revolution also ushered in the modern world as a new wave of globalization also occurred.

The Third Industrial Revolution, known as the Digital Revolution, used electronics and information technology to automate production. There also was a shift from mechanical and analog electronic technology to digital technology. The beginning of the Information Age occurred during this Industrial Revolution when the Internet, computers, handheld computing devices, space research, and biotechnology started to develop.

The Fourth Industrial Revolution, or 4IR, was built on the Third Industrial Revolution by the fusion of technologies that blur the lines between the physical, digital, and biological spheres (Schwab, 2016). One of the emerging technological breakthroughs of the Fourth Industrial Revolution that is leading the transition into the Fifth Industrial Revolution is the field of artificial intelligence ("AI"). For the most part, the world is still in the Fourth Industrial Revolution.

The Fifth Industrial Revolution, known as 5IR, is expected to be cognitive in nature by further enriching human experience with sensory dimensions that are being realized with generative artificial intelligence (Nosta, 2023). The Fifth Industrial Revolution encompasses the notion of harmonious human–machine collaborations (Noble, Martin, Grewal, & Parasuraman, 2022). There will be a specific focus on the well-being of the multiple stakeholders, such as society, companies, employees, and customers. Society is already seeing a rethinking and leveraging of human–machine collaborations for greater societal well-being. With the rapid advances in artificial intelligence, specifically generative artificial intelligence, the dawn of the Fifth Industrial Revolution may already be here.

3. The Increasing Value of Intangible Assets

Though not directly tied to the advancements realized with each Industrial Revolution, the market value of companies in the United States is transitioning from physical assets, such as brick-and-mortar buildings and equipment, to intangible assets, namely intellectual property (Ocean Tomo, A Part of JS Held, 2020). Generally, "intellectual property" is defined to include patents, trademarks, copyrights, and trade secrets. Trade secrets may include data or information that a company typically maintains. As an example, data collected by companies such as Amazon, Google, and Facebook on its consumers is generally maintained by these companies as trade secrets.

As shown in Figure 1, over the last quarter century, the value of intangible assets has increased from 17% to 90% of the market value of U.S. companies. Hence, the market value of most U.S. companies is now based on the intangible assets owned by companies. In addition to the industrial revolutions, other economic factors and conditions have also contributed to the increased value of intangible assets.

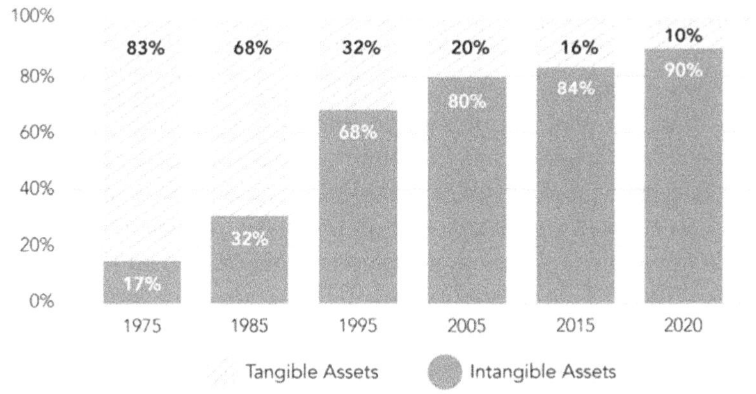

Figure 1. Components of S&P 500 market value.

For example, in 2020, the acceleration in intangible assets as controlling market value is attributed to the novel coronavirus where, in the U.S., the COVID-19 lockdowns were a key factor (Ocean Tomo, A Part of JS Held, 2020). When compared to the Republic of Korea ("South Korea"), for example, the same acceleration in intangible assets value did not occur. South Korea was commended for being more successful in controlling the outbreak within its borders while never fully locking down (Ocean Tomo, A Part of JS Held, 2020).

With the continued technological advances that have resulted in the growth of companies such as Amazon, Google, Facebook, etc., where their market value has always primarily been in their intangible assets, the trend of the value of intangible assets outpacing the value of tangible assets is expected to continue. The market value of companies that are utilizing their data with generative artificial intelligence is likely to continue to grow the value of intellectual property as the driving factor in a company's market value.

4. Generative AI and Use Cases for Business

Generative AI ("GenAI") is a type of AI that can create new content such as texts, images, audio, videos, or software codes, in response to a user's prompt or request (Stryker & Scapicchio, 2024). As GenAI advances, users may not be natural people but could also be AI entities. GenAI models are trained using large amounts of data. The data is then used to create new or original content by predicting what comes next in a pattern.

GenAI utilizes machine learning models, sometimes called deep learning models which are algorithms that simulate the learning and decision-making processes of a human brain (Stryker & Scapicchio, 2024). The models identify and encode patterns and relationships in huge amounts of data and then use that information to understand the users' natural language requests or questions and respond with relevant new content.

Approximately one-third of organizations are already using GenAI regularly in at least one business function. The increase in the use of GenAI is not slowing. There is a prediction that more than 80% of organizations will use GenAI applications or generative AI application programming interfaces (APIs) by 2026 (Stryker & Scapicchio, 2024).

GenAI is not being developed by simply building a model and letting it operate. Instead, there is ongoing training, tuning, and continual improvement required. Specifically, a foundation model is developed that serves as a basis for the AI application. Though large language models are used to create text-generation applications, as discussed herein, models exist for image generation, video generation, sound generation, music generation, and software code generation. The learning model is trained using huge volumes, terabytes, of data. The data is usually raw, unstructured, unlabeled data that is taken from the Internet or some other huge data source. The algorithm performs and evaluates millions of "fill in the blank" exercises, trying to predict the next element or sequence (Stryker & Scapicchio, 2024).

The foundation model is tuned or tailored for a specific application. Specifically, fine-tuning includes feeding the model labeled data specific to the content generation application. As an example, questions or prompts are provided to the application and corresponding correct answers in the desired format are produced. Tuning and then fine-tuning is labor intensive. Human feedback is also utilized to assist with creating greater accuracy or relevance of responses generated (Stryker & Scapicchio, 2024).

Continual improvement may involve tuning the model as often as once a week. Retrieval augmented generation ("RAG") may also be used. RAG may extend the data by supplementing and refining parameters or presentations in the original model with relevant sources outside of the original or previously used training data. By applying RAG, the GenAI model has access to the most current information (Stryker & Scapicchio, 2024).

Businesses and organizations are already using GenAI to streamline various tasks. In general, GenAI is also being used to reduce the cost of production. More specifically, depending on the task, GenAI is replacing natural workers who used to perform such or similar tasks.

Exemplary areas of use of GenAI include, but are not limited to, content creation, drafting legal documents, data analytics, new product development, coding, customer service, handling human resource processes, enhanced sales, and fraud detection. Several representative GenAI models available today include the following: (1) DALL-E: image generation tool that creates original images based on prompts; (2) ChatGPT: text-to-text generative AI chatbot that can answer questions and write text in different styles; (3) Roll: AI-powered payroll application that can run payroll in under a minute; (4) Bard: generative AI that creates music based on user input; (5) OpenAI GPT-4: AI model that helps generate code; and (6) TensorFlow: open-source machine learning library to produce images, language text and synthesize audio data for various applications. In general, because of the varied purposes of the AI systems/tools identified above, the term GenAI has been described as "a catch-all name for a massive ecosystem of loosely related technologies, including conversational text chatbots such as ChatGPT, image generators such as Midjourney and DALL·E, coding assistants such as GitHub Copilot, and systems that compose music and create videos" (Lee, Cooper, & Grimmelmann, 2024).

Though most of these models are shown to have a singular function, GenAI foundation models and APIs are widely employed to create and refine new generative AI models and products. Many enterprises have developed customer service and chatbot solutions based on OpenAI foundation models, showcasing the versatility and potential of generative AI in product development and management.

Though GenAI has been broadly identified as a tool to improve work efficiency, that explanation may be limited as to the scope GenAI is capable of. Specifically, the improved work efficiency of GenAI may also include being able to create and invent. For example, though not GenAI, Google has utilized AI to accelerate materials discovery. In November 2023, Google announced that it had discovered "2.2 million new crystals–equivalent to nearly 800 years' worth of knowledge" (Merchant & Cubuk, 2023). Three hundred eighty thousand (380,000) of the new crystals are stable enough to be candidates to power future technologies. As identified with the identification of GenAI models/tools, even GenAI is capable of inventing and creating. However, as explained in the following, even if inventing and creating is possible, obtaining U.S. statutory protection may not be possible.

5. Copyrights and Generative AI

A case[1] that has resulted in the legal position that AI systems cannot be copyright creators involved a monkey. A macaque (the monkey) took multiple photographs of itself using a photographer's camera. After the photographer published the photos and credited the monkey with taking the photos, others began publishing the monkey's photos as well. The photographer sued those other entities.

The photographer's case was dismissed since the monkey took the photos and as such could not be the author of the photographic works.

[1]Naruto v. Slater, 2016 U.S. Dist. LEXIS 11041 (N.D. Cal. 2016).

The court noted that the Copyright Act[2] did not "plainly" extend the concept of authorship or statutory standing to animals. There is actually no mention of animals anywhere in the Copyright Act. However, the Copyright Act does refer to an author's "children," "widow," "grandchildren," and "widower." Furthermore, since the U.S. Supreme Court has repeatedly referred to "persons" or "human beings" when analyzing authorship under the Copyright Act, the monkey could not be the author.

As for the photographer, the court concluded he was not the author. The photographer did not, at a minimum, exercise control over the taking of the photographs, such as putting the person (or in this case the monkey) in position and arranging the place where the monkey was to be. Relating back to the Copyright Act, the photographer did not actually translate an idea in a fixed, tangible expression since the photographer did not take the photographs.

In 2023, the Copyright Office issued a policy statement to clarify its practices for examining and registering works that contain material generated by the use of artificial intelligence technology (Copyright Office, Library of Congress, 2023). The Copyright Office's statement provides that "[i]f a work's traditional elements of authorship were produced by a machine, the work lacks human authorship and the Office will not register it." "[W]hen an AI technology receives solely a prompt from a human and produces complex written, visual, or musical works in response, the 'traditional elements of authorship' are determined and executed by the technology—not the human user." Users of generative AI "do not exercise ultimate creative control over how such systems interpret prompts and generate material. Instead, these prompts function more like instructions to a commissioned artist."

In compliance with this policy statement, in a case decided in August 2023, the U.S. District Court for the District of Columbia ruled that a work generated entirely by artificial intelligence without any human involvement is not eligible for copyright protection.[3] In this case, the plaintiff claimed ownership of a computer system called the "Creativity Machine" which was used to autonomously generate visual artwork titled "A Recent Entrance to Paradise." The plaintiff listed the Creativity Machine as the author when seeking to register the work for copyright with the U.S. Copyright Office. The Copyright Office denied the

---

[2] 17 U.S.C. 101 *et al.*

[3] Thaler v. Perlmutter, 687 F. Supp. 3d 140 (D.D.C. 2023).

application on the grounds that the work lacked human authorship. The court reiterated similar reasons as discussed above regarding the *Naruto* case.

When human creativity is mixed with AI production, the Copyright Office has actually distinguished between what is able to be registered and what is not. The Copyright Office granted limited copyright protection to a graphic novel titled "Zarya of the Dawn" (Analla, 2023). Originally, full copyright protection was granted to the text, arrangement of images, and the images. Upon learning that the text and arrangement of images were done by a human but that the individual images were created with MidJourney, a form of GenAI, the Copyright Office removed copyright rights from the images.

Though work created by AI is not eligible for copyright protection, the prompt itself might qualify for protection, if sufficiently original. Furthermore, compilation of AI-generated material, as compiled by a human, may have sufficient human authorship to constitute a copyright claim, provided that the resulting work as a whole constitutes an original work of authorship, at least as the Copyright Act defines "compilation." Such a result has been suggested in the "Zarya of the Dawn" copyright where the arrangement of images, by a human, was afforded copyright protection.

It is no secret that various AI systems with their large language models are being trained to utilize copyright-registered material. As a result of how copyrighted content is being used to train AI systems, numerous copyright infringement lawsuits have been filed since 2023. For example, in general, copyright owners have asserted that the use of copyrighted images to train generative AI without a license violates U.S. copyright laws. There have also been allegations that AI platforms themselves could have secondary liability for any infringements.

An example of several ongoing lawsuits since December 23, 2024, include the following: (1) A legal research company alleges that a now-defunct legal research company violated plaintiff's copyright by reproducing headnotes from one of its programs with the intention of training a legal AI tool[4]; (2) class action lawsuit brought by GitHub contributors

[4]Thomson Reuters Enter Ctr. GmbH v. Ross Intel. Inc. No. 1:20-cv-613-SB (D. Del. filed May 2020).

who object to Microsoft's Copilot and Codex tools were trained[5]; (3) class action lawsuit brought by visual artists against AI companies alleging firms trained image generators on plaintiffs' work without consent[6]; (4) plaintiff alleges defendant infringed its copyrights by taking more than 12 million of plaintiff's photographs, along with corresponding captions and metadata, to train defendant's AI image generator[7]; high profile authors, including Sarah Silverman and Ta-Nehesi Coates, allege that defendant used their writing not only to train its large language model without permission but to use with another model[8]; another case involving high profile authors, including Silverman and Coates, alleging that defendant's AI system unlawfully trained several of its large language models on their work (originally three cases now combined into one)[9]; plaintiffs, led by journalist Jill Leovy, whose case was recently consolidated with a case brought by visual artist, allege that defendant pulled data from the Internet to train its language models whereas the other now consolidated case alleged that defendant trained its text-to-image generation tools on images of their work without permission[10]; three cases consolidated into one, including one brought by The Authors Guild, alleging that defendant infringed on the copyright of many high-profile authors, including George R.R. Martin and Jia Tolentino, by using their works to train defendant's AI models without permission[11]; and Former Arkansas governor Mike Huckabee and a group of Christian writers allege that defendant (Bloomberg) violated their copyright by training its large language model on books without permission[12]; and music publishers allege that an AI

---

[5]Doe v. Github, Inc., No. 4:2022cv06823 (N.D. Cal. filed Nov. 3, 2022).

[6]Andersen v. Stability AI Ltd., No. 3:2023cv00201 (N.D. Cal. filed Jan. 13, 2023).

[7]Getty Images v. Stability AI, Inc., No. 1:23-cv-00135-UNA (D. Del. filed Feb. 3, 2023).

[8]Kadrey v. Meta Platforms, Inc., No. 3:2023cv03417 (N.D. Cal. filed July 7, 2023).

[9]In re OpenAI ChatGPT Litigation, No. 23-cv-03223-AMO (N.D. Cal. filed June 28, 2023).

[10]In re Google Generative AI Copyright Litigation, No. 5:23-cv-03440 (N.D. Cal. filed July 11, 2023).

[11]Authors Guild v. OpenAI Inc., No. 1:23-cv-08292 (S.D.N.Y. filed Sep. 19, 2023).

[12]Huckabee v. Meta Platforms, Inc., No. 3:2023cv06663 (N.D. Cal. filed Oct. 17, 2023) (though Meta is no longer in the case).

company's text generators were trained on plaintiff's copyrighted lyrics—the case only involves the lyrics and not musical scores[13] (Knibbs, 2024). On January 3, 2025, Anthropic settled a part of its lawsuit by agreeing to utilize "guardrails" to keep its chatbot from generating copyrighted song lyrics (Brittain, 2025).

How these lawsuits will be resolved is still unknown. Many of these cases likely will settle, but some may not be resolved until either a court rules on a motion or the case goes to trial. In many of these cases, the defendants likely will raise a fair use defense if produced AI material cannot be shown to be substantially similar to the original works alleged to have been infringed.

However, Matthew Sag, Professor of Law in Artificial Intelligence, Machine Learning, and Data Science at Emory University School of Law, testified before the U.S. Senate and stated that if a large language model is working as intended, it does not (or rarely) copy the training data at all. Copyright takes place before when the training corpus is assembled and preprocessed. If the AI system is trained properly and operates with appropriate safeguards, its output will not resemble the input in a way that would trigger copyright liability. Furthermore, the things AI learns from data are generally fairly abstract, and if so, uncopyrightable (Sag, 2023).

Professor Sag believes that whether GenAI produces new content or simply conjures up an infringing work in the training data depends on how it is trained. He further testified before the U.S. Senate that text-to-image models may be prone to produce potentially infringing works when the same text descriptions are paired with duplicates of images, or relatively simple images that vary only slightly. Hence, this makes such AI systems more likely to generate images that would infringe on copyrightable characters such as, but not limited to, Snoopy and Baby Yoda, which appear often enough in the training data that the AI system learns the consistent traits and attributes that are associated with these images (Sag, A response to Lee and Grimmelmann, 2024).

---

[13] Concord Music Group, Inc. v. Anthropic PBC, No. 5:2024cv03811 (N.D. Cal. filed Oct. 18, 2023).

6. Patents and Generative AI

GenAI cannot be a named inventor on a U.S. patent. Specifically, in *Thaler v. Vidal,*[14] the Federal Court of Appeal ruled that the Patent Statute[15] defined "inventor" as a natural person. As a result, an AI system may not be listed as the inventor on a patent. In *Thaler*, the plaintiff, Stephen Thaler ("Thaler") claimed that an AI system autonomously conceived two inventions without human assistance. Upon filing the patent applications, he only listed the AI system as the inventor. The United States Patent and Trademark Office ("USPTO") determined that the patent applications were incomplete since no human inventor was listed (Hickey & Zirpoli, 2024).

After losing at the U.S. District Court for the Eastern District of Virginia, Thaler appealed his case. The U.S. Court of Appeals for the Federal Circuit agreed with the USPTO and the lower court. Here, the court concluded that an inventor must be a natural person since the term "individual" normally refers to a human being. An appeal to the U.S. Supreme Court was turned down by the U.S. Supreme Court.

Thaler had filed his patents in other countries as well. For most of these other countries, the same reason was given for rejecting his patent applications. However, one country, South Africa, granted his patents, apparently only because South African laws do not define "inventor" and do not require substantive examination of patent applications (Congressional Research Service, 2024).

To provide clarity on the patentability of AI-assisted inventions, the USPTO published an inventorship guidance and examples for AI-assisted invention on February 13, 2024 (United States Patent and Trademark Office, 2024). This publication was then updated with an effective date of July 17, 2024 (Federal Register, 2024). The February 13th publication of two detailed examples of when to assist in determining and when to file for a patent application with AI are utilized.

A hypothetical example pertained to a transaxle for a remote-controlled car where AI is used to develop the invention (United States Patent and Trademark Office, 2024). In this example, a natural person uses AI to develop transaxles for a remote control (RC) car where an initial AI

[14] Thaler v. Vidal, 43 F.4th 1207 (Fed. Cir. 2022).

[15] 35 U.S.C. 100(f) ("inventor means the individual or, if a joint invention, the individuals collectively who invented or discovered the subject matter of the invention)."

prompt states "creates an original design for a transaxle for a model car, including a schematic and description." Based on the AI-generated schematic and description, the company the natural person works for prepares a patent application. In this scenario, whether the natural inventor or the AI model is listed as an inventor, a patent should not be issued. Though the natural person provides the prompt, to make a significant contribution, the natural person must have contributed in some significant manner to the conception of the invention and made a contribution to the claimed invention that is not insignificant in quality, when the contribution is measured against the dimension of the full invention, and did more than merely explain the well-known concepts and/or the current state of the art.

In general, a natural person only presenting a problem to an AI system should not be considered an inventor of the output of the AI system. However, if the natural person could demonstrate a significant contribution to how the prompt was constructed in view of a specific problem to elicit a particular solution from the AI system, it may be sufficient for the natural person to be a named inventor.

Next, suppose that while building the transaxle, the natural person discovers improved ways to build the transaxle, which is different than the AI system's description and schematics. Typically, reducing an invention to practice alone is not a significant contribution that rises to the level of inventorship. However, here, since the natural person developed improvements beyond what the AI system provided, the natural person may be a named inventor in a patent application. Thus, a natural person's use of an AI system in creating an AI-assisted invention does not nullify the natural person's independent contribution as an inventor. In drafting the patent claims, the independent claims should include the natural person's invention.

Continuing development of the transaxle, after completing the transaxle model, the natural person uses the AI system to provide additional manufacturing suggestions. One of the AI model's suggestions is to mill the casing out of aluminum using a Computer Numerical Control (CNC) machine routing machine. If this manufacturing suggestion were included as a dependent claim (meaning you would have to read the independent claim invented by the natural person in combination with this dependent claim), patenting would still be possible. This is because the natural inventor's contribution is significant when measured against the full scope of these dependent claims, therefore the AI's contribution does not negate that of the natural person.

The creation and training of the AI system is performed by a secondary individual. Even though this secondary individual had "intellectual domination" over the AI system, creating, training, or maintaining an AI system does not make this secondary individual an inventor. To be a named inventor, the secondary individual must have provided a significant contribution to the invention. Simply owning or overseeing the AI system used in the creation of the invention is not enough.

As is evident by the scenarios above, a determination must be made when or whether an invention is eligible to be patented. This responsibility falls on the natural person(s) claiming ownership and, if the patent is prepared with a patent attorney or agent, the natural person(s)' representative at the USPTO. Usually, USPTO patent examples do not inquire about inventorship as the presumption is that the named inventor(s) in the application are the actual inventor(s) to be named on the patent.

With the use of AI systems, a heightened standard of inventorship has not been created. Prior to filing patent applications, the preparer already was expected to determine the correct inventorship. Now, with the advent of AI systems, the current inventorship analysis still requires considering human contribution to the conception of the invention where questions about the use of AI to assist in the creation of the invention should be raised when interviewing the natural person(s).

Currently, there is no additional duty to disclose information beyond what is already required regarding inventorship. Specifically, there is no need for an applicant of a patent application to disclose whether an AI system was used in the creation of the invention. The USPTO will continue to presume the named inventor(s) are the actual inventor(s) where the responsibility for meeting the existing inventorship duties will remain solely with the applicant(s) and individual(s) associated with the filing or prosecution of the patent application.

Thus, AI systems may be used during the inventing phase, namely the conception phase. However, the eventual claims filed must have a natural person listed as the inventor where the natural person made a significant contribution to the invention. Since dependent claims require the associated independent claim for completeness, if the natural person provided significant contribution to the independent claim, a dependent claim may be completely AI-conceived.

7. Application of Trade Secrets with Generative AI

In 2016, the Defend Trade Secrets Act ("DTSA") was signed into law and became effective May 11, 2016. One of the intents of the DTSA was to provide a common trade secret law, especially with respect to the theft of trade secrets at the federal level, and not rely on differing results at the state level. Before May 11, 2016, the American Bar Association had proposed the Uniform Trade Secrets Act ("UTSA") in 1979 and then approved enactment by the states in 1985.[16] Variation of the UTSA had been adopted by many of the states as a common law tort to address perceived gaps with U.S. patent laws. Since each state had its own law, undue uncertainty of trade secret parameters and various remedies existed from state to state.

One of the intents of the UTSA, which also carries over with the enactment of DTSA, is to provide a form of legal protection if businesses elect to protect commercially valuable information without relying on U.S. patent laws (if the information to be protected is even patentable).[17] This form of protection does not require a governmental agency to review and approve, such as by granting a legal right. Instead, it is up to the entity that is claiming trade secret rights to properly protect the trade secret.

Under the UTSA, "trade secret" means "[i]nformation, including a formula, pattern, compilation, program, device, method, technique, or process that: (a) [d]erives independent economic value, actual or potential, from not being generally known to, and not being readily ascertainable by proper means by, other persons who can obtain economic value from its disclosure or use; and (b) is the subject of efforts that are reasonable under the circumstances to maintain its secrecy.[18]" The definition of trade secret in the DTSA is slightly different but is not expected to result in different scopes of protection. The essential difference is that the UTSA recites that the trade secret is not generally known to more than one person; whereas, the DTSA is narrowed to not being known to only one other person.

Since there are no time limits on how long a trade secret can be maintained, for some companies this is the most common form of intellectual property. Examples of trade secrets include, but are not limited to the following: (1) customer and/or vendor lists (not if the list can be readily compiled by third parties) when it is the subject of time, effort, and expense applies primarily to an active client list and not necessarily to a prospective client list; (2) marketing strategies, plans, and information;

---

[16] Florida enacted the Florida UTSA in 1988.

[17] Uniform Trade Secrets Act, Prefatory Note, February 11, 1986.

[18] *trade secret*, Legal Information Institute, https://www.law.cornell.edu/wex/trade_secret.

(3) pricing information; (4) chemical formulas; (5) recipes (such as Kentucky Fried Chicken recipe or the formula for Coca Cola); (6) new inventions for which a patent application has not been filed (if qualified to obtain a patent); (7) manufacturing techniques; (8) survey methods used by professional pollsters; (9) computer algorithms (such as Google's search algorithm); (10) knowledge of what does not work; and (11) data collected (such as the data collected by Amazon, Facebook, and Google on customers).

While patent law and copyright law limit the creation of these forms of intellectual property to natural individuals or persons, the same is not true with trade secrets. Entities that have used GenAI to create a competitive advantage may seek to protect their advantage as a trade secret, which by design reduces public disclosure of corresponding inventions and, as such, still will inhibit AI innovation.

If GenAI is used to create a trade secret, there are several questions to ask to determine whether protecting it as a trade secret is optimum. First, is the concept or invention discoverable when used or provided in the marketplace? For example, can it be reverse-engineered? Can another independently derive the concept or invention once the general concept is known? Are there other lawful or unlawful means to acquire or determine the trade secret? Remember, once a trade secret is known by third parties, it loses legal protection as a trade secret.

If a trade secret is created using GenAI, other considerations must be considered. Namely, if litigation ever arises over the GenAI-created trade secret, identifying the trade secret within an AI system may be difficult. For example, though not specific to trade secrets maintained in an AI system, in September 2023, in *T2 Modus LLC v. Williams-Arowolo*,[19] the U.S. District Court for the Eastern District of Texas rejected that the plaintiff had sufficiently identified the alleged trade secrets at issue. The court concluded that it was not enough to "merely describe the end results of or functions performed by the claimed trade secrets," or "merely describe the claimed trade secret in conclusory terms such as 'artificial intelligence,' 'machine learning,' or 'proprietary software' without including additional specific information."

Courts will likely require plaintiffs to describe their alleged secrets with sufficient specificity to reveal actual trade secrets, not just categories of information that could be trade secrets. This standard may be difficult

[19] T2 Modus, LLC v. Williams-Arowolo, 2023 U.S. Dist. LEXIS 170656 (E.D. Tex. 2023).

with GenAI because an employer may not know the specific inputs used without computer log information. Furthermore, unless detailed records are maintained, training data may be difficult to define, and the algorithm at issue could require the submission of extremely sensitive source code. Also, AI systems will continue to learn such that training data and outputs will continue to change over time. With AI, the situation that may be reached is that owners of AI tools may not know how or why a certain output is generated.

Other considerations may include whether the trade secret portion is available involves how the AI system is utilized. If a company is using overlapping training sets and open-source code, it is possible the company may end up mistakenly believing that it owns unique and valuable information that is in fact widely known among other companies that used similar code or training sets. Training data may be widely available to use and/or purchase, and there are many open-source AI tools. This could arise because to be a trade secret, the information must "derive independent economic value, actual or potential, from not being generally known to, and not being readily ascertainable through proper means" by those who can obtain economic value from its use. Trade secret laws do not offer protection against discovery by fair and honest means, such as by independent invention, accidental disclosure, or so-called reverse engineering.

Furthermore, the "not generally known" and "not readily ascertainable" requirements raise questions as to what aspects of AI are valuable by being kept secret. For example, publicly disclosing outputs may prevent trade secret protection from being applicable to the outputs themselves.

8. How to Protect AI Advancements Internal to an Entity

Given that use of AI is rapidly evolving and becoming more commonplace, generic practices adopted by a company for its use of AI may be insufficient to protect as a trade secret.

For example, generic agreements may not provide clear and reasonable guidance regarding what aspects of AI a company believes are confidential and assigned to the company by virtue of employment. As the use of AI continues to evolve, companies may need to reevaluate what aspects of their AI use the company considers confidential and ensure that employees are informed through agreements, such as employee handbooks, and training. A sophisticated company developing its own internal AI platform(s) may need to take different and additional measures. Examples of these additional measures may include, but are not limited to, restricting access, and specific agreements directed to AI innovations. Documenting the data or aspects of the AI system the entity considers a trade secret is also recommended only if a former employee ever departs and takes valuable content to another company.

9. Conclusion

The rapid advancements in the development and uses of artificial intelligence are likely to revolutionize entire industries. With such a realization, there are areas to pay attention to, such as intellectual property, as AI begins being used more regularly to design, create, and invent. U.S. laws and policies have been established regarding the role of AI systems with regard to patents and copyrights. However, though an available approach to protecting AI system creations is to maintain creations in confidence, namely via trade secret laws, sufficient documentation will likely be needed in order to explain the trade secrets with sufficient specificity if there is ever theft of the trade secret. As one example, the trade secret owner may be required to know specific content used by the AI system while continuing to train (where new data may be data determined by the AI system and autonomously entered). Having proper protection in place is designed to protect the AI system's trade secrets to minimize employees being able to cease employment and take trade secrets to another company.

References

Analla, T. (2023, March 6). Zarya of the Dawn: How AI is Changing the Landscape of Copyright Protection. *Jolt Digest*. https://jolt.law.harvard.edu/digest/zarya-of-the-dawn-how-ai-is-changing-the-landscape-of-copyright-protection

Brittain, B. (2025, January 3). Anthropic Reaches Deal on AI 'Guardrails" in Lawsuit Over Music Lyrics. *Reuters*. https://www.reuters.com/legal/litigation/anthropic-reaches-deal-ai-guardrails-lawsuit-over-music-lyrics-2025-01-03/

Congressional Research Service. (2024, July 17). 2024 Guidance Update on Patent Subject Matter Eligibility, Including on Artificial Intelligence.

Federal Register. https://www.federalregister.gov/documents/2024/07/17/2024-15377/2024-guidance-update-on-patent-subject-matter-eligibility-including-on-artificial-intelligence

Copyright Office, Library of Congress. (2023, March 17). Copyright Registration Guidance: Works Containing Material Generated by Artificial Intelligence. *Federal Register*. https://www.federalregister.gov/documents/2023/03/16/2023-05321/copyright-registration-guidance-works-containing-material-generated-by-artificial-intelligence

Editors of Encyclopedia Britannica. (2024). Industrial Revolution. *Britannica*. https://britannica.com/event/industrial-Revolution

Hickey, K. & Zirpoli C. T. (2024). Artificial Intelligence and Patent Law. *Congressional Research Service Legal Sidebar*. https://crsreports.congress.gov/product/pdf/LSB/LSB11251

Knibbs, K. (2024, December 19). Every AI Copyright Lawsuit in the US, Visualized. *Wired*. https://www.wired.com/story/ai-copyright-case-tracker/

Lee K., Cooper, A. F. & Grimmelmann J. (2024, March 4). Talkin' 'Bout AI Generation: Copyright and the Generative-AI Supply Chain. *SSRN Cornell University Law School*. https://papers.ssrn.com/sol3/papers.cfm?abstract_id=4523551

Lee, K., Cooper, A. F., & Grimmelmann, J. (2024, March 4). Talkin' 'Bout AI Generation: Copyright and the Generative-AI Supply Chain. *Journal of the Copyright Society 2024*. https://papers.ssrn.com/sol3/papers.cfm?abstract_id=4523551

Merchant, A. & Cubuk, E.D. (2023). Millions of New Materials Discovered with Deep Learning. *DeepMind*. https://deepmind.google/discover/blog/millions-of-new-materials-discovered-with-deep-learning/

Noble, S. M., Martin, M., Grewal, D., & Parasuraman, A. (2022). The Fifth Industrial Revolution: How Harmonious Human-Machine Collaboration is Triggering a Retail and Service [R]evolution. *Journal of Retailing*, 199–208. https://www.sciencedirect.com/science/article/pii/S0022435922000288

Nosta, J. (2023). The 5th Industrial Revolution: The Dawn of the Cognitive Age. *Psychology Today*. https://www.psychologytoday.com/us/blog/the-digital-self/202310/the-5th-industrial-revolution-the-dawn-of-the-cognitive-age

Ocean Toma, A Part of JS Held. (2020). Intangible Asset Market Value Study. https://oceantomo.com/intangible-asset-market-value-study/

Sag. M. (2023, July 12). Hearing on "Artificial Intelligence and Intellectual Property–Part II: Copyright and Artificial Intelligence. *Testimony before the U.S. Senate Committee on the Judiciary Subcommittee on Intellectual Property*. https://rightofpublicityroadmap.com/2023-07-12_pm_-_testimony_mattsag

Sag, M. (2024, February 21). A Response to Lee and Grimmelmann. *Matthew Sag Blog*. https://matthewsag.com/a-response-to-lee-and-grimmelmann/

Schwab, K. (2016, January 14). The Fourth Industrial Revolution: what it means and how to respond. *World Economic Forum*. https://www.weforum.org/stories/2016/01/the-fourth-industrial-revolution-what-it-means-and-how-to-respond/

Stryker C. & Scapicchio M. (2024, March 22). What is Generative AI. *IBM*. https://www.ibm.com/think/topics/generative-ai

United States Patent and Trademark Office. (2024, February 13). Example 1: Transaxle for Remote Control Car. *USPTO AI Inventorship Guidance*. https://www.uspto.gov/sites/default/files/documents/ai-inventorship-guidance-mechanical.pdf

https://doi.org/10.1142/9789819816347_0015

Chapter 15

Multimodal Generative and Agentic AI for Business Process Improvement in High-Consequence Training and Decision-Making

David Metcalf*, Devon Veller*, Michael Eakins*, Angela Hamilton*, and Max Hooper†

**Institute for Simulation and Training, University of Central Florida, Orlando, USA*

†Global Blockchain Ventures, Orlando, USA

The world of business process innovation and improvement is rapidly changing in the face of artificial intelligence (AI). Creating multimodal data types such as audio, text, video, and images with assistance from AI serves as a force multiplier—augmenting and accelerating existing development capabilities and business processes. Such advances point to future research building upon the current work in producing better, faster, and cheaper solutions that use advanced AI capabilities for business efficiency.

Within the University of Central Florida (UCF), the Institute for Simulation and Training's Mixed Emerging Technology Integration Lab (IST METIL) has been exploring practical applications of AI to improve the production of advanced simulations for leadership, decision-making, and training applications within government, health, and industry. In addition to conducting extensive analysis for partners such as the Navy and Department of Energy to advise on the tools and processes that hold the most promise for integrating AI into their training enterprise processes, we have also used our own R&D project portfolio as a testbed for ongoing evaluation of AI tools to enhance production workflows.

IST METIL has recently employed AI to enhance the production of applications and scenario authoring capabilities for next-generation training for quantum preparedness cybersecurity, digital twins for surgical pre-planning, mission rehearsals for military operations and disaster recovery scenarios on a holo-AI 3D holographic table, and AI-automated 3D object generation among others.

Within this chapter, we provide an overview of the potential benefits of AI-enhanced workflows for production pipelines as well as selected case studies elaborating on use cases and applications, workflows, lessons learned, and tangible outcomes.

1. The AI Value Proposition for Production Pipelines

A typical production pipeline for simulation and training applications involves agile and iterative spirals for requirements analysis, instructional design, content development, technical development and integration, and testing. AI-assisted workflows offer potential for significant reductions in time, effort, and required expertise for a variety of tasks within the entire production pipeline. A wide range of available tools offer distinct capabilities in areas such as AI-assisted generation of storyboards and animatics, 3D development, audio effects generation, and programming—leveraging natural language processing (NLP) for collaboration between a human developer and AI.

1.1. *Specific tools and functions*

Some of our early analysis and experimentation with generative AI including tools and use cases are detailed in Table 1.

The more recent rise of agentic AI—autonomous AI agents that perform tasks with minimal human input—brings additional opportunities for simulation and training development beyond AI-assisted content creation and problem-solving. Agentic AI has the potential to orchestrate adaptive learning environments, analyze performance to provide feedback and insights, and deliver personalized learning pathways.

Table 1. Generative AI tools for production.

Tools	Function/Use Case
ChatGPT	Gain general knowledge of nearly any domain up to intermediate and sometimes a high level of expertise.
MidJourney	Generation of images and iconography. Ideal to generate some initial concepts for imagery, pairs well with DALL-E. Favors fantastical compositions.
Claude 2	Co-programmer assistant that is high performing to generate classes of code and functions of code. Less expertise in overall programming structures.
DALL-E 3	General Image generation favors realism.
CoPilot	Pair-programmer, used in line with vs code, provides auto complete.
Stable Diffusion	Model for image generation, basic outcomes.
Leonardo AI	Focused on generating with creative variation, strengths in generating imagery for an artist to react to.
Audio Gen	Text-to-audio generation. Allows for generation of simple sound bites from text.
Stable Audio	Text-to-audio generation. Generates commercially viable music based on a description ranging various genres, tempo, instruments, and themes.
Local LLM	Cloud workstation for hosting large language models locally.

Exploration of both generative and agentic AI tools has led to several case studies with valuable lessons learned on the optimal use cases, development processes, and prompt engineering for a range of applications.

2. Case Study: AI for Performance Analysis and After-Action Review in Navy Training Exercises

Beyond the production pipeline for simulation and training applications, AI may also be leveraged after training has been deployed to automate the analysis of human performance in live and virtual training environments. In 2023, the Naval Air Warfare Center's Training Systems Division (NAWCTSD) and the Central Florida Tech Grove sought to explore current and emerging AI solutions capable of processing video and audio to identify key events such as a two-second gunshot from hours of footage. To that end, IST METIL conducted a market survey and technical analysis to identify and assess AI tools capable of analyzing real-time or recorded audio and visual data streams.

3. Case Study: Human–AI Collaboration for Solution Discovery—AI as a Responsive Knowledge Base in Augmented Reality Development

The development of a multi-platform virtual environment and augmented reality tabletop exercise for alarm response training for the Department of Energy (see Figure 1)—with the need to create a custom,

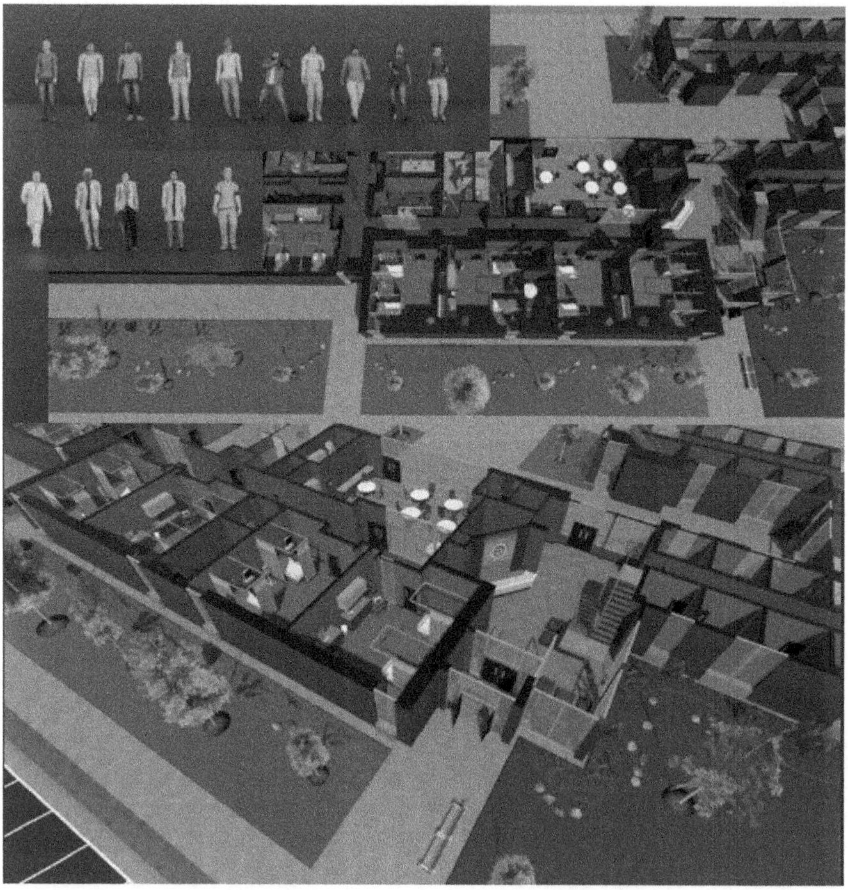

Figure 1. Department of Energy virtual exercise for alarm response training.

high-performance pathfinding system—highlighted the transformative potential of integrating human expertise with AI. The project, spearheaded by a single intermediate developer, achieved extraordinary results—reducing pathfinding delays (the amount of time it takes for the application to calculate an avatar's navigational path from Point A to Point B in the virtual environment) from up to 10 s to as low as 1.5 ms while performing a high quantity of requests. This case study explores the interplay between human ingenuity and AI-driven discovery in creating a scalable and efficient solution.

3.1. *Identifying the challenge: Unity's framework limitations*

The project's pathfinding requirements exceeded the capabilities and resolution of Unity Engine's default framework (see Figure 2). Specifically, the limitations in Nav Mesh resolution led to improperly generated barriers in the AR environment. Characters would erroneously navigate through thin walls and small doorways, resulting in an unacceptable user experience. Recognizing these limitations, the developer evaluated Unity's framework and determined that only a custom solution could meet the performance and accuracy demands of the project.

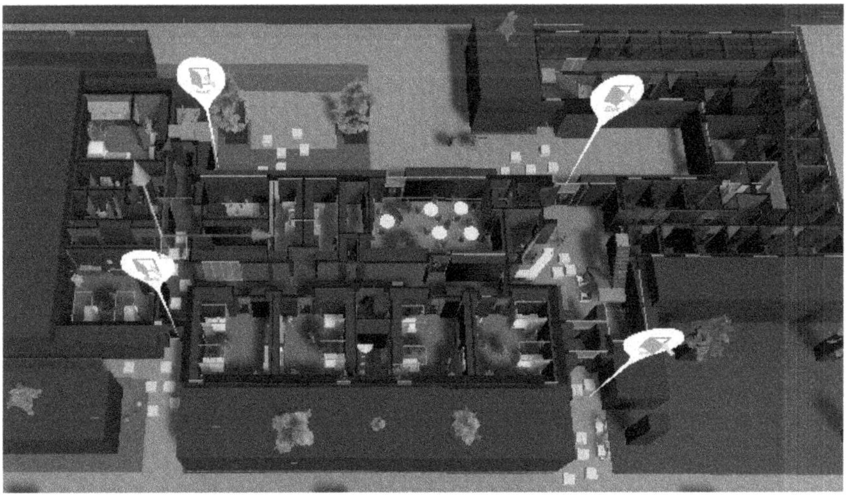

Figure 2. Pathfinding in unity.

3.2. *Leveraging AI to bridge knowledge gaps*

Without prior experience in developing custom pathfinding solutions, the developer turned to AI—initially GPT-3.5 and later GPT-4. Following a structured outline, the developer used AI to uncover insights, explore potential solutions, and iteratively refine their understanding; the following is a simplified outline of the iterative step-by-step approach the developer took to solve challenges, including the custom pathfinding:

1. **Overview:** Gaining a clear understanding of the topic's domain.
2. **Industry Insights:** Exploring practices beyond the developer's immediate experience.
3. **Solution Identification:** Discovering frameworks and existing solutions, including hierarchical pathfinding.
4. **Development Guides:** Creating actionable plans and outlines to implement solutions.

The AI served as a knowledge base, enabling the developer to expand beyond their existing expertise and adopt a discovery-driven approach. Each iteration brought deeper understanding, often leading to new questions and solutions that reshaped the development process.

3.3. *Discovering hierarchical pathfinding*

A key breakthrough came with the discovery of hierarchical pathfinding (see Figure 3). While the developer had experience with grid-based systems, this higher-performance approach to pathfinding was discovered by the developer through AI, allowing for a more efficient pathfinding solution, particularly in large-scale AR environments, by dividing the navigation space into regions and simplifying path calculations.

Integrating this framework required significant restructuring of the existing codebase. AI assisted not only in conceptualizing and discovering the new architecture but also in refactoring the existing implementation. Despite the complexity, once the requirements were clearly defined, the new system took only 20 min to implement—a testament to the effectiveness of preparation and iterative learning.

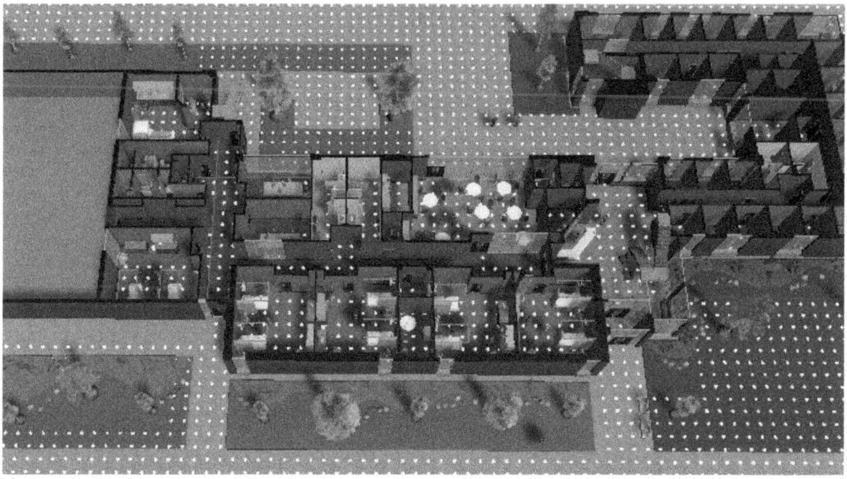

Figure 3. Hierarchical pathfinding in unity.

3.4. *Performance gains and user experience transformation*

Figures 4 and 5 provide the performance statistics before and after the shift to hierarchical pathfinding, which yielded remarkable improvements:

- **Minimal Demand:** Delays reduced from 30 ms to 1.2 ms—a performance gain of 25x.
- **Heavy Demand:** Delays reduced from 10 s to 1.5 ms—a staggering 6,666x improvement.

These gains eliminated the stutter experienced in AR interactions, ensuring a smooth and immersive user experience. The trade-offs were minimal: While restructuring the framework demanded additional effort, the results far outweighed the costs.

3.5. *Lasting impact on development philosophy*

With over 13 years of experience transitioning from a 3D artist to a seasoned developer, this individual has always thrived as a "jack of all trades," tackling challenges across multiple domains. AI has become a

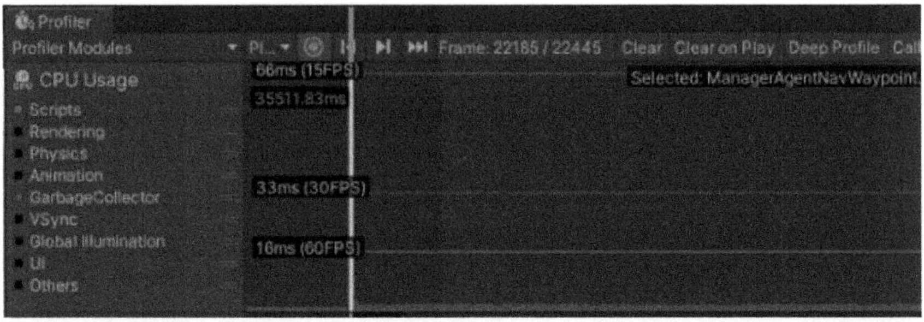

Figure 4. Unity performance profiler before improvements were made.

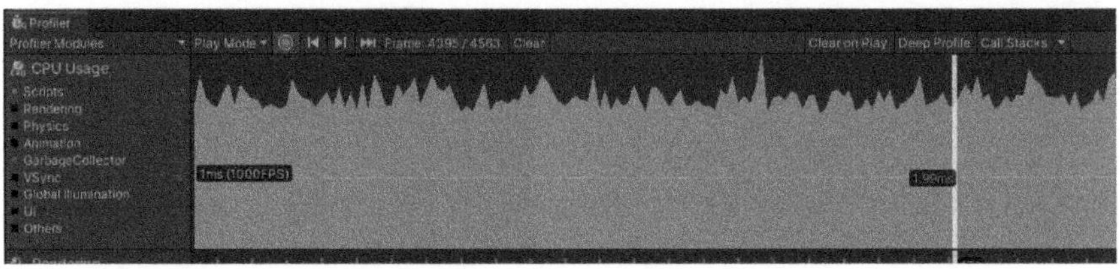

Figure 5. Unity performance profiler after improvements were made.

powerful enabler in this journey, filling knowledge gaps quickly and providing tools to deepen expertise across diverse fields. By acting as a responsive knowledge base, AI has streamlined the process of learning and problem-solving, allowing the developer to master new disciplines with efficiency.

As the developer noted, "AI enables the 'jack of all trades' to become a master of many." While the developer's ability ultimately drives deliverables to completion, AI remains integral to solution discovery. AI not only supported technical execution but also reinforced a development philosophy rooted in adaptability, exploration, and continuous growth.

The alarm response training project (see Figure 6) exemplifies how AI can augment human expertise to solve technical challenges at an accelerated pace. Through iterative learning, discovery, and implementation, the developer achieved a solution that was not only functional but also scalable and high-performing. The insights gained from this collaborative process provide a blueprint for leveraging AI in tackling complex development problems, offering inspiration for professionals across industries.

Figure 6. Virtual exercise with hierarchical pathfinding implemented.

4. Case Study: AI-Enabled Speech-to-Text Generation of 3D Models

During the analysis and design phases of a simulation project, an assessment is made to determine whether 3D can add sufficient value to justify the higher development costs and longer timelines that 3D production typically entails compared to traditional 2D media. 3D assets for training and performance support are especially beneficial in domains or scenarios in which enhanced understanding of spatial relationships and depth are critically important. For example, studies in clinical medicine and aviation have found up to 30% improvement in cognitive performance outcomes in 3D compared to 2D (Rautenhaus *et al.*, 2013; Getty, 2008).

Traditional 3D production for simulation can vary from days to months depending on the scale and complexity of the assets, their application, and many other factors. This typically requires digital media artists to produce 3D models, textures, animations, etc. based on design guidelines for the final simulation. The introduction of AI to the 3D production pipeline, as with other areas of content creation, has provided new ways to expedite this process. While still early, numerous tools have emerged to speed up components of the pipeline, such as animation and texture/image generation and we are now even seeing tools that can create a *finished* asset (i.e., geometry, texture, and rigging for animation). The output quality of these tools varies but is improving rapidly. The speed at which these assets are generated creates a strong use case for scale and ease of implementation into real-time applications as seamlessly as using your voice to generate the asset through a simple description similar to using other AI-generated image tools.

Within METIL, voice-to-3D integration began with the simple use of Siri to enable a text-to-3D model generator. We initially focused our evaluation on three candidate AI tools, but several of the students on our team found and evaluated additional tools that proved more useful in terms of the number of formats in which the models could be exported. Another distinction was certain tools' ability to create 3D models capable of integration with the Unity and Unreal engines as well as the 3D holographic table customized software depicted in Figure 7.

An early example included speaking into a voice AI agent and populating the text of the words "3D image of an F-35." In 55 seconds, the application built a working 3D model of an F-35 military fighter jet from the voice/text prompt integration. The rendered output (see Figure 8) was then put into a specific listening directory for a human operator to take and manually populate into a 3D holographic scene on the Holo-AI built upon the NOVAC table from Avalon Holographics.

Over the next few months, the future-state plan is to speed up the model generation process to seconds rather than closer to a minute and

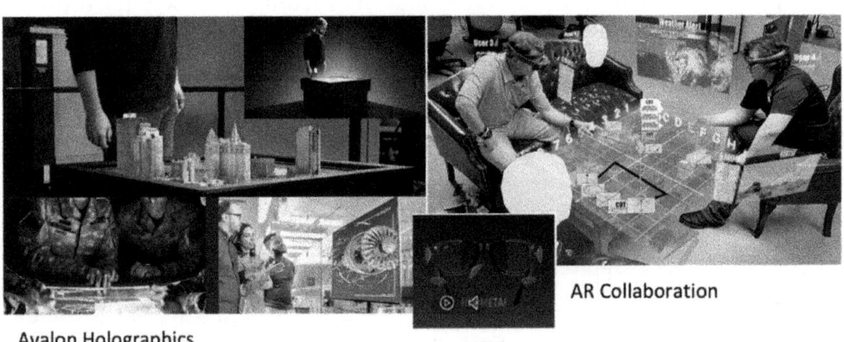

Figure 7. Integration of holographic table, AI agent, and augmented reality exercises.

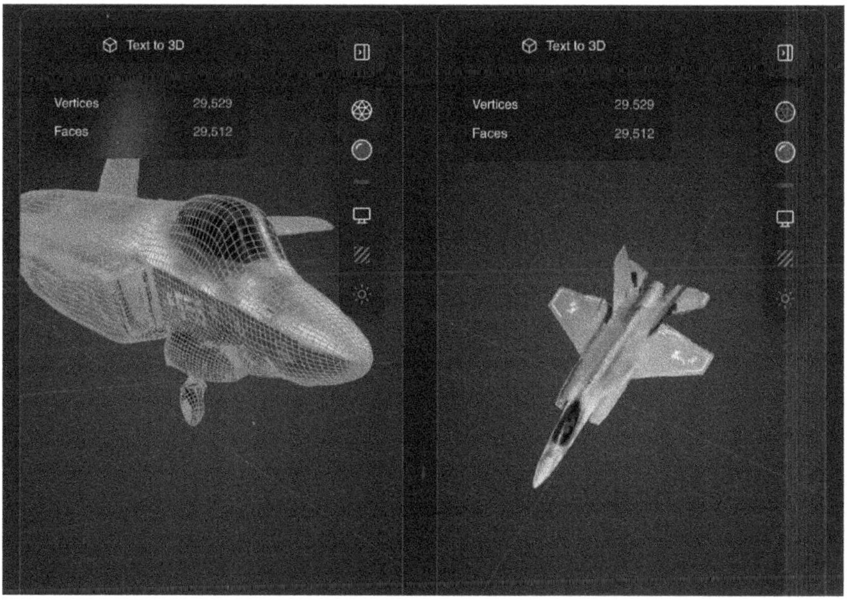

Figure 8. Example of voice-prompted AI generation of a 3D holographic image.

also build an automation feature that would auto-populate the voice-generated 3D models onto the table. This will enable commanders' intent and easier operation of scenarios and scenes for complex military, disaster recovery, and surgical pre-planning for mission-critical collaborative decisions. This promise of near-real-time flexibility and multiple scenario "what-ifs" for mission-critical operations stands to be a game-changer for advanced scenario planning and business modeling.

5. Conclusion: Future AI Use Cases and Macro-Economic Trends

AI will generate massive needs for training, rethinking of business processes, and decision-making. Predictions for 2025 about new AI use cases are wide ranging, including DeFAI—AI-driven DeFi (decentralized finance)—projects that aim to simplify finance with real-time insights, trading, and personalized strategies. Although DeFAI needs to mature to overcome hurdles in transparency and security, the merging of DeFi and AI has opportunities to change the way one thinks about finance, accessibility, automation, and more personalized tools for crypto applications (Wright, 2025).

Another area that will generate needs for training and business process expertise is tokenization. Tokenization of all types of Real-World Assets (RWA) will be one of the emerging trends that will change global business processes. Franklin Templeton states that Agentic AI—agents that act autonomously with minimal human input—will "revolutionize" social media and could send tokens soaring in value. This global investment manager's report states AI agents could lift tokens by 30–90%. The convergence of AI and blockchain is the real driver of these tokens' value that "enables these tokens to represent real technological capabilities. The excitement stems from the realization that AI agents can operate autonomously, creating value in ways that are tangible and scalable" (Jakobson, 2025).

These findings and case study examples point to larger-scale macroeconomic trends that will affect a wide variety of industry vertical markets and serve as integration points between major technological trends in our "ABC model"—AI, Blockchain, and Cybersecurity in the Post Quantum Era. Understanding how tokens underlie a measure of a unit of value to show time savings, cost efficiency, and quality improvement will drive the next-generation economy and connect the underlying capabilities of AI, blockchain, and quantum-resistant computing for decades to come.

References

Getty, D. J. (2008). An evaluation of stereoscopic digital mammography for earlier detection of breast cancer and reduced rate of recall. BBN Technologies, Cambridge MA.

Jakobson, L. (2025). Franklin Templeton says AI agents will 'revolutionize' social media, sending tokens soaring. Retrieved from: https://thedefiant.io/news/markets/franklin-templeton-says-ai-agents-will-revolutionize-social-media-sending-tokens-soaring.

Rautenhaus, M., Grams, C. M., Schäfler, A., and Westermann, R. (2013, April). Interactive 3D visualisation of ECMWF ensemble weather forecasts. In *EGU General Assembly Conference Abstracts*, Vol. 15, p. 8441.

Wright, L. (2025). What is DeFAI? The AI-enabled DeFi narrative looking to take 2025 by storm. Retrieved from: https://cryptoslate.com/what-is-defai-the-ai-enabled-defi-narrative-looking-to-take-2025-by-storm/.

https://doi.org/10.1142/9789819816347_bmatter

Index

www.ingramcontent.com/pod-product-compliance
Ingram Content Group UK Ltd.
Pitfield, Milton Keynes, MK11 3LW, UK
UKHW020400150926
8624IPUK00004B/265

9 789819 816330